BOMBAY
Metaphor for Modern India

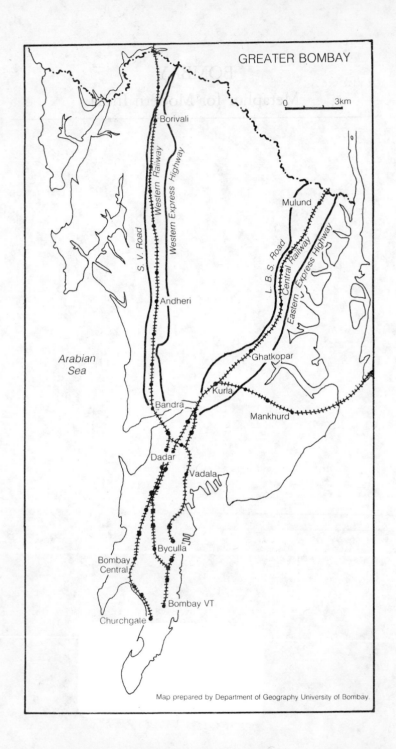

GREATER BOMBAY

0   3km

Borivali

Mulund

S. V. Road

Western Railway

Western Express Highway

L.B.S. Road

Central Railway

Eastern Express Highway

Andheri

Arabian
Sea

Ghatkopar

Kurla

Bandra

Mankhurd

Dadar

Vadala

Byculla

Bombay
Central

Bombay VT

Churchgate

Map prepared by Department of Geography University of Bombay.

BOMBAY
Metaphor for Modern India

Edited by

SUJATA PATEL and ALICE THORNER

Bombay
Oxford University Press
Delhi Calcutta Madras
1996

Oxford University Press, Walton Street, Oxford OX2 6DP

Oxford New York
Athens Auckland Bangkok Bombay
Calcutta Cape Town Dar es Salaam Delhi
Florence Hong Kong Istanbul Karachi
Kuala Lumpur Madras Madrid Melbourne
Mexico City Nairobi Paris Singapore
Taipei Tokyo Toronto

and associates in

Berlin Ibadan

ISBN 0 19 564086 1

Typeset by Alliance Phototypesetters, Pondicherry 605 013
Printed at Pauls Press, New Delhi 110020
and published by Manzar Khan, Oxford University Press
YMCA Library Building, Jai Singh Road, New Delhi 110001

Contents

POLITICS, POPULISM AND VIOLENCE

Preface to the Paperback Edition

Reading the reviews—for the most part very generous—which have appeared in the Indian press during the last few months, we realize that we should have made clearer in our original preface the relations between the two books and the two editors. Although Alice has written the introduction to *Bombay: Mosaic of Modern Culture* and Sujata the introduction to *Bombay: Metaphor for Modern India*, the volumes were conceived and edited jointly. We shared equally in the organization of the workshop, the selection of the papers to be included and the lengthy process of revising them in close consultation with the authors. It was decided to publish the books simultaneously but separately; neither is volume one or volume two. For purely practical considerations, each of us undertook the job of drafting one of the opening essays; we susequently read and revised the essays together line by line before finalizing the versions which were published. Both of us take full responsibility for any errors or omissions as well as any positive features of both books.

Sujata Patel, Alice Thorner
Bombay, Paris, April 1996

Preface

This is one of two books arising from a workshop held in Bombay from 16 to 19 December 1992, under the auspices of the SNDT Women's University and the Maison des Sciences de l'Homme, Paris. Just ten days before our meeting was scheduled to begin, the destruction by organized Hindu fundamentalists of a sixteenth-century mosque in the north Indian town of Ayodhya had triggered a wave of violent confrontations in many parts of India. In Bombay an outbreak of destruction of government property by enraged Muslims was met with police shootings and attacks on Muslim homes and business places located in Hindu-majority areas. The death toll of over 200 was greater than in any other city. As a modicum of calm returned, we were able to inform the workshop participants by telephone and fax that the sessions would go ahead as planned. Practically all of them managed to attend; only a couple of papers had to be read in absentia.

What we did not foresee was that our colloquium was to take place during a lull preceding a second and greater bout of violence, which set dozens of localities all over the Bombay metropolitan area literally on fire. Large-scale destruction of property took place in an atmosphere tense with mistrust and fear. Far more murderous than the December riots, the January killings (over 500 victims) amounted to a virtual pogrom against Muslims, large numbers of whom fled the city. Yet a third jolt was to come in March with the nearly simultaneous explosion of powerful bombs at the Stock Exchange, the Air India building, the Century Bazaar crossroads and other key spots symbolic of Bombay's economic prominence.

The successive waves of brutality shocked not only the city's residents but also the whole of India since Bombay had enjoyed a reputation of cosmopolitanism, tolerance and effective local government. To what extent was this reputation warranted? In the period of intensive self-questioning brought on by these devastating outbursts, the topics addressed by our workshop—centred on the evolution of Bombay's cultural identity over the last two centuries—gained added pertinence. English, Marathi and Gujarati newpapers printed feature stories with photographs for a number of days. Bombay's intellectuals of all communities took part in relief activities, carried out enquiries into what had actually occurred, and came together in informal discussion groups to continue the process of reflection on the causes of the cataclysm.

The idea of organizing the meeting had arisen two years earlier in Delhi in the course of conversations between Alice Thorner and Jim Masselos; later in Bombay Alice discussed the possibility with several other friends. Actual preparations began in early 1992 when Dr Suma Chitnis, the Vice-Chancellor of the SNDT Women's University, encouraged Alice and Sujata Patel, who had joined SNDT as Professor of Sociology, to go ahead with the project. Professor D.N. Dhanagare, then Member-Secretary of the Indian Council of Social Science Research (ICSSR), gave valuable advice at all stages of the planning process. Maurice Aymard, the Administrateur of the Maison des Sciences de l'Homme (MSH), supplied seed money and indispensable institutional support. In addition to the MSH and the ICSSR, we received financial aid from UNESCO and from the Indian Council of Historical Research. The Vice-Chancellor, faculty and staff of the SNDT University, and in particular the members of the Sociology Department and the Library personnel, gave generously of their time and talents. Mariam Dossal of the Bombay University was an ever-willing source of good counsel.

We set up a programme of morning and afternoon sessions, each accommodating three or four speakers, a number of invited discussants, and time for general debate. The selected topics were 'The Making of Urban Identity: Personal, Cultural and Institutional', 'Political Economy of Bombay', 'Land Use, Planning, Slums and Health', 'Workers, Strikes, Popular Consciousness', 'Politics, Identity, Protest and Violence', and 'Literature and Theatre'. To focus attention on the context in which the workshop was proceeding, we invited a local journalist to give us a review of what had actually taken place.

There were also three evening sessions devoted respectively to a reading by Bombay poets of their works, a presentation by activists on the Bombay housing problem, and a round-table of film makers and critics. These meetings were followed by dinners typical of three different styles of Bombay cuisine: Gujarati vegetarian, Parsi, and Malwani (from the coastal area of Maharashtra State south of the metropolis). A visit to colonial and modern neighbourhoods of Bombay was organized for the final afternoon.

Each of the ten sessions brought together from 70 to 100 academics, journalists, administrators, activists, creative writers and critics. Participants were drawn mainly from Bombay itself. Pune, Delhi, Calcutta, Paris, The Hague, London, Cambridge (UK), Berkeley (California), Binghamton (New York), Kingston (Canada), and Sydney (Australia) were also represented.

The papers prepared for the colloquium are presented in two books, *Bombay: Metaphor for Modern India* and *Bombay: Mosaic of Modern Culture*. Two additional contributors were invited. We should like to express our appreciation to all of the authors. It has been a great pleasure for us to take part with them in the sessions of the colloquium, to become acquainted with those who were not already good friends, and to work with them on their manuscripts.

We should like to thank collectively every one of the friends, colleagues and others who have helped us in this enterprise. We must mention the names of a few persons without whom we could not have held the workshop and prepared the two books. We have had help from many individuals in the SNDT Women's University, beginning with Dr Chitnis, the Vice-Chancellor. We are particularly grateful to Leena Patwardhan for assistance from the very first stages to the present day, and also to our faithful typist, Mr N. Krishnan Kutty. We thank Jyotiben Vora, Vasudha Thakur, Sharayu Anantram, and Anila Barot in the Sociology Department; Mr Shirish Barodia, Mr Amirali A. Burwani, and Mr Bakul V. Rawal in the administration; Mr M. K. R. Naidu and Harsha Parekh of the Library, who supervised the preparation of a bibliography; Kunjulatha Shah and Mitra Parikh who organized the city tour; Usha Thakkar who advised us on administrative issues, Subhadra Patwa who registered the participants; Hemant Shanker Dabre, our messenger; and the students of the Department of Home Science who volunteered to help with the daily luncheons. Kamala Ganesh obtained contributions toward the cost of the dinners from the ITC Ltd. and the Indian Hotels Company Ltd. Kamala, Mariam Dossal, Veena Devasthali, Aruna Pendse, Mitra Parikh, Mridula Ramanna and Smita Gandhi each prepared a detailed report of a session. Mariam, Narendra Panjwani, Indira Munshi and Denzil Saldanha had earlier assisted Alice in drawing up tentative plans for the workshop.

In Paris, we are grateful to Clemens Heller, Maurice Aymard and

Rosette de Monfalcone of the Maison des Sciences de l'Homme. We should like to thank Mme Francine Fournier and Mme Maria Louisa Nitti of UNESCO for kindness above and beyond their official responsibilities. On three different occasions the MSH, the ICSSR and the Institute of Development Research of the University of Amsterdam respectively made it possible for Sujata Patel to come to Paris to prepare the workshop and the two books together with Alice Thorner. We have been fortunate to enjoy an efficient, yet always gracious, collaboration on the part of the staff of the Bombay branch of the Oxford University Press.

Alice would like to record her appreciation of the exceptional hospitality offered by Jyotiben Trivedi and Sita Setalvad. Sujata wishes to thank Sonalben and Sitaben for their encouragement and her parents, Leelaben and Vajubhai Patel, for their staunch support.

Both of us feel privileged to have been able to work together in producing these books as a tribute to Bombay, the city to which we remain devoted.

Sujata Patel   Alice Thorner
Paris, August 1994

Bombay's Urban Predicament

SUJATA PATEL

In both popular and academic literature Bombay is typically characterized as India's most modern city. In view of its range of manufacturing,
finance and service activities, Bombay has been described as the first
Indian town to experience the economic, technological and social
changes associated with the growth of capitalism. To a number of
writers, the city serves as a paradigm for the achievements of post-
independence India. As in other parts of the world, economic changes
have entailed changes in life-styles. With the growth of trade, industry
and modern tertiary occupations, Bombay has developed relatively
efficient transport and communication systems. Basic civic amenities
such as water and electric supply, sanitation and public health measures
have made possible a degree of urban sophistication.

But what is the actual content of Bombay's 'modernity'? More than
half of the city's population of ten million inhabitants[1] live in slums or
are altogether homeless. They must perforce struggle to find and then to
retain unoccupied spaces under bridges, along railway tracks, on
pavements or even on rooftops. They are crowded together in tight
clusters of one-room huts. With a land area restricted to 600-odd square
kilometres, Greater Bombay supports a density of 16,500 persons per
square kilometre. Very many Bombayites do not have access to clean
water or to waste disposal systems. Only a minority of the city's
inhabitants enjoy incomes adequate to ensure a comfortable existence.
A number of surveys indicate that half or less than half of Bombay's
slum dwellers fall below the generally accepted 'poverty line'.[2] It is also
the case that most of the victims of urban crime and collective violence,

such as the communal outbursts of December–January 1992–93 are precisely the people who are poor and disadvantaged.

The blatant contrasts in housing and all other forms of consumption, the difficulty of maintaining services with an infrastructure that has become altogether inadequate, and the sordid nature of the city's civic politics add up to a situation of acute urban crisis. This background, together with the explosion set off by the demolition of the Babri Masjid, was the setting in which the workshop on Bombay's identity was held in December 1992. Participants sought to specify and examine current trends in the city, and also to reconsider critically certain propositions regarding Bombay's 'modernity', taken for granted by earlier commentators. They raised questions about Bombay's reputation for cosmopolitanism, about the primacy of technology as an engine of development, about the shifting relations between the organized and informalized processes in manufacture, about the way contemporary globalization would affect the city's inhabitants, about the capacity of its local institutions to cope with ethnic and religious conflicts, about the possibility of Bombay, and by extension India, attaining prosperity for the whole of its population.

It was clear that there were flaws in the received image that projected Bombay as representative of India's aspirations for the future. Ironically, the predicament in which Bombay now finds itself may well provide an augury of the direction in which the entire country is heading. Bombay can serve as a metaphor for the nature of the changes taking place in contemporary Indian society. It is our hope that the contributors to this volume and to its companion *Bombay: Mosaic of Modern Culture*, may help in understanding the processes of modernization in Bombay and in India as a whole.

Defining the Contexts of Bombay's Modernity

Bombay is quintessentially a colonial city fashioned to a large degree by external inputs and demands. Foreign conquest set the stage for the establishment of the city. Imperial rule defined the parameters within which it grew. Bombay served as an open gateway for the exploitation of its hinterland and, indeed, the country as a whole. Through the city of Bombay resources were transferred from the colony to the centre of the empire.

From its inception, Bombay has been closely linked with the world market. In its early years, the requirements of British commerce and

British industry dictated the choice of Bombay as the principal point of entry on India's western coast. These interests determined the selective recruitment to the city of merchants, artisans and labourers, as well as the education of a class of clerks and petty officials. The same considerations affected the spatial implantation of port, factories, market-places, railway lines, public buildings and residential quarters. Evolving forms of municipal government responded to similar exigencies.

After India obtained political independence in 1947, local industrialists, traders and bankers who had risen to prosperity during the colonial period came to dominate Bombay's economy and its urban choices. In the most recent years, however, increasing globalization of commerce and industry has had the effect of integrating the city, and through the city the country, in the international orbit.

Most of the papers presented in this book are concerned with the nature and consequences of the urban process initiated in the 1920s and 1930s.[3] At this time, the textile industry, originally created to export yarn and, later, cloth to China and Japan, found a domestic market. In terms of both profit and employment, this industry reached its peak during and after the First World War. The period that followed the Second World War is notable for the growth of capital-intensive manufacturing industries, light and medium engineering, pharmaceuticals and petrochemicals. These innovations served to firmly intermesh Bombay's manufacturing capacity with the Indian national economy, thereby weakening the hold on the city of the world market. Whereas in the early nineteenth century the city attracted capital from outside, in the mid-twentieth century Bombay's profits began to be invested in the rest of India. As a consequence, its business and industrial elite assumed national roles. Without losing its links with the exterior, Bombay turned towards its own extended national hinterland, to become the symbol of India's modern national development.

The burgeoning economic activities of the city attracted migrants from nearby rural districts and eventually from the whole country. Nineteenth century newcomers hailed principally from the areas today included in Maharashtra and Gujarat. Workers from the coastal Konkan strip and the Western Ghats manned the docks and cotton textile mills. Most of business and trading groups came from Gujarat.[4] In the twentieth century, and particularly after independence, new waves of migrants arrived from both north and south India.

Except for the plague years at the end of the nineteenth century, the city witnessed a steady but modest increase in population. In sharp contrast, the mid-twentieth century was a time of phenomenal expansion. In the 30-year period between 1901 and 1931, the population had increased by about 40 per cent. With the wartime economic boom followed by the influx of refugees from districts allotted to Pakistan, the decade from 1941 to 1951 chalked up a rise in population of 76 per cent. Comparable figures for the next three decades were respectively 40, 44 and 38 per cent. Between 1941 and 1971, two-thirds of Bombay's inhabitants had been born outside of the city.[5]

The pace of growth appears to have slowed down during the most recent decade. The population of Greater Bombay recorded by the 1991 census was 9.9 million, an increase of a mere 8 per cent over 1981. The 1991 count for the whole of the Bombay Metropolitan Region rose to 12.5 million. The substantial gain by the surrounding areas reflects the scarcity and consequent astronomical prices of housing in the city itself.

This book explores the ways in which the city has coped with its expanding population in a context of a shifting economic structure; an extremely skewed distribution of incomes, housing and services; and the dramatic growth of a chauvinist party, the Shiv Sena, openly espousing ethnic and religious divisiveness. At the time this has been written, the Shiv Sena has just taken over the reins of government in the state of Maharashtra in coalition with the Bharatiya Janata Party.

The thirteen chapters of this volume are grouped in three sections: 'Labour and Enterprise'; 'Claims on Land, Housing and Health'; 'Politics, Populism and Violence'. The first examines social and economic aspects of the city's development into India's premier manufacturing and financial centre. It explores various facets of the city's economy, notably the toil and struggle of labour, and the accomplishments of enterprise. The second brings together papers dealing with land use and land distribution; the history of city planning; efforts at slum amelioration; and the interrelations of space and health. The last attempts to identify the underlying political forces and to describe the day-to-day functioning of municipal institutions. Two papers are devoted to the Shiv Sena. An analysis of the communal outburst of 1992–93 ends the volume. The content of these three sections may be approached as responses to three sets of questions.

First: Which historical processes made possible the emergence of the city from the shackles of colonialism and its leading role in the development of an independent Indian economy? How competitive are Bombay's old cotton mills and the capital-intensive industries established in the 1940s? Can the recent wave of liberalization and globalization offer new perspectives to Bombay? How will the relative decline of manufacturing and the increasing importance of the services in the city today affect the city and the various strata of entrepreneurs, managers and labour? To what extent have the workers whose toil and sweat have created the city been able to construct an identity of their own? How was Bombay in the 1980s able to sustain the world's longest textile strike? What can we learn from an analysis of the strike about the links between Bombay and the rural areas from which the millhands came?

Second: How has the city handled the needs of its growing population for land, housing and services? By what processes are decisions regarding housing reached? What plans and programmes are proposed for the solution of the acute shortage of shelter and urban amenities? Which sectors of the population are covered by these initiatives? How far has implementation progressed?

Third: In delineating the play of politics in the city, how do we account for the emergence of the Shiv Sena? How is it structured? What are the links between its changing ideological focus and the changing political economy of the state of Maharashtra? From what constituency does the Shiv Sena draw its adherents? Wherein lies its appeal? What programmes and policies have other parties put forward in contesting municipal elections? Once in power, how have the mayors and the members of the municipal council governed the metropolis? Why was the outbreak of violence after the destruction of the Babri Masjid, more than a thousand kilometres away, more ferocious in Bombay than anywhere else in India?

Labour and Enterprise[6]

Both Bombay's modernity and its contemporary urban predicament stem to a large extent from the nineteenth century implantation of the textile industry and the subsequent diversification into more techno-logically advanced manufacture such as light and medium engineering, pharmaceuticals, food products and petrochemicals. Despite the overall dominance of British capital, particularly in banking and finance, local business groups managed to initiate and sustain a substantial number of profitable enterprises. On the one hand, Bombay was locked into the world market as the pivot of British colonial exploitation of western India. On the other, Bombay proved capable of establishing a national industry based on the domestic market. Claude Markovits in his paper,

'Bombay as a Business Centre in the Colonial Period: A Comparison with Calcutta', explores this paradox.

Until the mid-nineteenth century, Markovits writes, Calcutta retained an unquestioned primacy. Only after the defeat of the Peshwas and the imposition of British political control on western India could Bombay embark upon its upward growth curve. At this stage the most important economic activity was the trade in cotton and opium. Railways built from 1857 onwards reinforced Bombay's links with its hinterland, facilitating the expansion of commercial networks.

Experienced hindu and jain banias, parsi merchants and members of the muslim trading communities had been drawn to the city from Gujarat. The early Indian entrepreneurs who invested in cotton spinning and weaving mills came from these mercantile groups. By the late nineteenth century, the textile industry had taken precedence over trade.

The era of dual dominance of Bombay and Calcutta, each exploiting the resources of its own region, lasted until the First World War. Markovits argues that initially Calcutta had a definite advantage, yet by the 1920s Bombay forged ahead. Why? Markovits combines economic explanations with political and cultural considerations. He suggests that both British and Indian entrepreneurs in Bombay reacted more rapidly to changing trade conditions. In part, their adaptability reflected the equilibrium maintained between the two groups. Bombay businessmen faced less racial discrimination. Acceptance in Bombay of ethnic and community groups contrasted sharply with Calcutta's oligopolistic and polarized economic and social structure.[7]

While Markovits analyses the processes that allowed Bombay to emerge as a leader in the integration of the domestic market as a national project, Nigel Harris in 'Bombay in the Global Economy', focuses on the opening of new opportunities by developments in the international sphere. Harris contends that today's globalization has been preceded by, and is a consequence of, certain significant changes in the city's economy. The first is the decline in the organized textile industry, a decline that was inaugurated in the sixties, with employment falling by almost 50 per cent. Over the same period, there has been a growth of unregistered units. A substantial part of the textile production has moved into the decentralized and the so-called 'informalized' processes of manufacturing. Meanwhile modern capital-intensive industry has been created outside of the city's boundaries. Within the city, the shift out of factory production has been accompanied by an increasing importance of the services, and particularly financial services. These trends, according to Harris, show that the pace of globalization of Bombay is already rapid.

The city, he argues, is ready for the challenges of competition in the world market because it is an important centre of transport networks— rail, sea and air—as well as of banking, insurance and stock trading. For instance, Bombay banks control 12 per cent of national deposits and a quarter of the nation's credits.[8] It has developed a pool of highly qualified personnel in such fields as consumer research and computer software. In addition, Bombay is the home of India's premier image industry: the production of Hindi films.[9] As of today, Bombay possesses the skills, educational facilities and aptitudes that can enable it to play a major role in the global process.[10]

If there are problems that impinge on Bombay's full-scale development as a global city, these relate to the incapacity of its public authorities to tap existing resources for the provision of essential (urban) services. Harris maintains that the political choices of the central government of India act as a major restraint on Bombay's attainment of global status. In his opinion, Delhi's aim is to remove the bottlenecks which impede the integration of the city in the national economy. These restrictive policies have curtailed the full play of the market, particularly with regard to hiring and firing labour, and have refused to local authorities the powers which would enable the city to take advantage of new international developments.

The pace of decline and the subsequent restructuralization of the textile industry which Harris has highlighted was hastened by a strike which continued for more than eighteen months before petering out. The failure of this longest textile strike in world history has generated a heated debate about its causes and its conduct.[11] Starting on a bonus issue,[12] the movement rapidly turned into a massive expression of a whole series of long-standing grievances, the most critical of which was refusal of legitimacy to the trade union recognized by government as the sole accredited representative of textile labour in industrial negotiations in the city.[13] Hub van Wersch in his paper, 'Flying a Kite and Losing the String: Communication during the Textile Strike', takes up a particular dimension of the strike, the relation between the workers and Dr Datta Samant, the controversial leader in whose hands they had entrusted the direction of their movement.

Van Wersch explains that the rural origins of the workers made it possible for them to hold out; nearly 40 per cent of them left the city for their village homes. But the leadership underestimated the importance of maintaining contact with these workers. On the few occasions when the leaders actually toured the rural areas, they failed to give advance notice of their programmes. Even workers who had remained in the city were often unaware of fund raising campaigns and of distribution of money and food. In the absence of clear signals from the leadership, strikers fell prey to disinformation circulated by spokesmen for the millowners which disheartened them and helped to break their resolve. By highlighting this aspect of communication, van Wersch illustrates the arbitrary and chaotic organization of the strike. He puts the blame squarely on Dr Datta Samant for the final disintegration of the strike and the hardships this entailed on the workers.[14]

The textile industry, already in the process of restructuring, took full advantage of the collapse of the strike definitively to shut down a considerable number of mills.[15] With little possibility of finding other factory jobs, for survival, the retrenched textile workers found themselves forced to resort to jobs in informalized modes of manufacturing and service occupations. It is estimated that the non-organized processes of manufacture and services account for a quarter to half of the total workforce in the city.[16] Whether in manufacturing or in services, the employment is unregulated in respect of wages, working conditions, security of tenure or rights to health care and retirement pay.[17]

Sandeep Pendse's paper, 'Toil, Sweat and the City', is concerned with this category of workers. He presents his thesis at a moment in the city's history when the voices of labour have largely faded into silence. In the past, a vigorous left-wing trade union movement played a central role in the life of the city as, for example, by their participation in Gandhi's civil disobedience campaigns or the support they offered to the naval mutineers in 1946. Hard-fought strikes in textiles, transport and other fields succeeded in obtaining substantial gains for the organized workers.

The growing class of insecure and unprotected workers exists at the margins, both literally and figuratively.[18] Pendse explores three aspects of the individual and collective lives of the toilers: organization of space; importance, relevance and precision of time; and reordering of the rhythms of existence. Pressures impinging on the toilers in these three aspects of their lives lead to a sense of cultural deprivation. Paradoxically, this deprivation forms the basis upon which they can build a new identity in terms of solidarity with others in the same position. This collective identity, Pendse argues, makes possible an assertion of strength and fearlessness.

We start this volume with Pendse's paper, in order to emphasize that, while the city would not have become a premier manufacturing and financial centre without the enterprise of its business communities, this could not have been achieved without the sweat of the toilers.

Claims on Land, Housing and Health

In the last few decades, urban historians, economists and sociologists have paid increasing attention to the study of patterns of land use and control. The purposes to which city tracts can be put vary widely; these include public and private housing, government and institutional structures; temples, churches, mosques; roads, railways, airports; gardens, beaches, recreational facilities; industrial and commercial establishments. Access to these different categories of land use is typically unequal. Concentration of ownership of urban property makes for fictitious scarcity, speculation and capital accumulation through rent. Intervention by the state at three levels—local, regional and national—may have results contrary to expressed aims. For example, in India the announced purpose of the Urban Land (Ceiling and Regulation) Act, 1976, was to enlarge the area on which lower and middle class housing could be built. In practice, this law has been misused to build upper-middle-class housing and retain control of land and housing in the hands of the few.[19] Provision of services has generally gone hand-in-hand with class determinants; thus adequate to better services are made available to residents of housing colonies and apartment blocks. Spatial concentration of commercial areas and upper-class residential areas has led to the concentration of transport networks, leading to the rich being subsidized by the poor even in this matter.

The papers in the second part of this book investigate primarily the intended and unintended results of the implementation of government urban policies. The ideology of modern India has been set in the Nehruvian mould of concern for the good of the masses. Post-audit by contemporary critics, including social scientists, journalists and political activists has documented the subversion of this policy in the domain of agricultural land reforms. Much less is known about the fate of similar programmes in the cities, where the state has attempted to control the land market through town planning. Conflicting urban interests have operated over the years to retard or impede the implementation of successive city plans.

We begin this part with a paper by Mariam Dossal entitled 'Signatures

in Space: Land Use in Colonial Bombay'. She points out that, while a
substantial body of literature exists on trading activities in nineteenth
century Bombay, there is very little information or analysis with regard
to land rights and land use. Dossal traces the mechanisms through
which the colonial state attempted to obtain control of the land in the
city, till then in the hands of the indigenous population. By the end of
the eighteenth century, when the East India Company's power over the
city had been made secure, the colonial authorities staked vast claims to
ownership of the soil and branded occupation by the indigenous
population as encroachment. In order to ensure a clear title to the land
so as to obtain rent which would fill the coffers of the Company, the
local government commissioned two surveys, the first conducted by
Thomas Dickinson between 1811 and 1827 and the second by Lieut.
Col. G. A. Laughton between 1865 and 1872. The authorities were
subsequently able to distribute land rights to favoured merchants, most
of whom were themselves British.

   Swapna Banerjee Guha in her paper, 'Urban Development Process in
Bombay: Planning for Whom?' explores the same theme a century later.
She contends that urban planning in Bombay has consistently served
the interests of the dominant elite to the exclusion of the majority of the
city's inhabitants. Her study focuses on three urban development
schemes: the Backbay scheme, the New Bombay project and the
speculative Vasai-Virar developments. Through an analysis of these
three projects, Banerjee-Guha is able to trace the changing nature of the
role of the state in the planning process and identify the interest groups
that have intervened to impede planning and orient it to their needs.

   The demand for dredging up earth from the sea bed to extend the
already built-up central business district in Bombay came not only from
financial capital which wanted additional space but also from the
growing upper middle class which hoped for conveniently located
apartment accommodation. A series of committees set up by the
planning authorities during the decades from 1922 to 1930 and once
again from 1958 to 1970 recommended that the Backbay scheme should
be abandoned as an intensive commercial land use pattern would lead
to congestion as well as pressure on transport and other services. It
would also, the successive reports judged, monopolize available resources to the detriment of improvement programmes sorely needed in
other parts of the city. The financial interests were able to subvert the
recommendations of these committees and to implement the Backbay
scheme to suit their needs. In fits and starts the reclamation work was

largely completed by the 1970s. It has resulted, as had been visualized earlier, in overcrowding and congestion of services and an abnormal increase in real estate values, simultaneously having a snowballing effect in distorting the city's land and housing market.

In the case of New Bombay, the role of the state has been more ambiguous. New Bombay was to be a planned town for middle-class settlements. As originally proposed, the resettlement on the mainland shore of the Thane creek was intended to integrate lower and middle class housing with local commerce and industry laid out along specially designed railway lines. Place was to be reserved for the local people displaced. But, as Banerjee-Guha tells us, this harmoniously conceived town never materialized. Employment was not created; schools, hospitals and parks were not provided; neither the internal railway nor the promised rail link with the metropolis was built; most of the displaced original inhabitants remained without jobs or urban housing. Middle-income homes financed by the development authority stood empty or were eventually offered on the market at greatly reduced prices. Eventually, as housing within Bombay city limits grew scarcer and dearer and rapid transport to New Bombay was at last assured, the new town became yet another commuters' satellite. Private enterprise moved in to throw up unplanned but profitable blocks of flats for high-income families, leading, paradoxically, to an increase in real estate and housing prices. Commercial establishments crowding a couple of favoured locations in New Bombay further increased unequal access to services within the region.

Banerjee-Guha uses the case of the Vasai-Virar area north-west of Bombay city as an example of complete abandonment by the state of its responsibility for controlling land markets and providing affordable housing for lower-income groups. The government had passed the Urban Land Ceiling Act to prevent concentration of land in the hands of the few and to bring about an equitable distribution of land. The purpose of this Act was frustrated and its provisions misused in the Vasai-Virar township development through a series of manoeuvres in which, initially, private developers, politicians and administrators colluded to exclude a parcel of the land from the Urban Land Ceiling and Regulation Act under the pretext that low-income housing was being created. Once the exemption had been obtained, residential blocks rapidly grew, to be followed almost immediately by additional unauthorized housing which was subsequently legalized. No services were provided or even planned by the builders; no electricity, no drainage.

Once a settlement started taking shape, the government was pressurized to invest in order to create a minimum of infrastructure. In effect, private developers did not allow the planning process to be implemented. In this case, it was systematically hijacked by the developers.

Only 12,000 of 43,000 hectares of the city is occupied by private residential housing. What kind of role has the state played in the case of those who have no legal title to land? Their number has been increasing. For instance, in 1971, it was estimated that the slum population was about one and a quarter million. Today, the slum and pavement dwellers number five million, more than 50 per cent of Bombay's population. For several decades, in many cities of the world, municipal bodies have tried to solve the slum problems by demolition of unauthorized (and hence illegal) structures such as huts which had sprung up on unoccupied private or public property. The procedure of tearing down these colonies has aroused an outcry from civic and democratic organizations. They argue that there is enough land in the city for distribution. Data collected in 1985 show that slum dwellers occupied only 2000 of 43,000 hectares of land area of the city. Today, a decade later, only 8 per cent of the land in Bombay is occupied by slums. The 1985 data indicate that there was at that time 10,000 hectares of vacant land, most of which was owned by government bodies, chiefly the Bombay Port Trust. Of the vacant land in possession of private builders, about 90 landlords owned 55 per cent of land.[20]

Even more to the point, the task of relocating squatter families, usually against their will, becomes daunting. New wisdom has therefore called for on the spot upgrading of existing unsatisfactory conditions by improving both the hovels and their environment and providing essential services. Pratima Panwalkar, in her paper, 'Upgradation of Slums, A World Bank Programme', examines the administrative problems involved in a programme of this kind. It is admittedly limited since it covers only slums which have come up on *state* government land. In 1984, 50 per cent of the slums were located on private land and only 16 per cent on state government land; the rest were on land owned by different government bodies, including the central government. The distinctive and major positive aspect of the programme is the security of tenure that it offers to cooperative societies of slum dwellers.

Panwalkar describes in detail the lengthy process of drafting and institutionalizing such a scheme; organizing the series of steps required for its execution; identifying the beneficiaries; mediating among state and municipal officers, community workers, politicians and the slum dwellers themselves. She brings out vividly the bureaucratic lethargy that the slum dwellers have to face and the bureaucratic language they have to learn and use in order to obtain the benefits held out to them by this scheme, the only one that caters to the slum dwellers of the city, which indicates the nature of priorities of the state towards those who have no housing and enjoy no services.

Dossal in her paper regarding land use patterns in the colonial period dealt with the stratification inherent in the early settlement patterns of the city: the British and the Indian merchants with whom they maintained close relations occupied respectively the south and north sectors of the Fort; while the rest of the 'natives' lived outside the walls. As the city expanded, distinctions of race, class and caste governed the moves of particular groups to new areas within the island city or in the city suburbs.

'Spatial Patterns of Health and Mortality' by Radhika Ramasubban and Nigel Crook explores differentials of disease and mortality in the population of the different wards of the city. The paper traces the long-term decline of the death rate and its relationship with changing patterns of location over the last century and a half. The authors divide this period into five phases: the phase of industrialization in the late nineteenth century; the plague years; the economic depression of the 1920s; the years of growth in the 1930s and '40s; and finally, the period after India's independence.

They find close correlations between population increases, density, extent of in-migration, availability of services and death rates. Changes in settlement patterns resulting from decisions by members of the upper class to seek airier and less crowded locations and from possibilities remaining open to other classes are related to differentials in morbidity and mortality. Even today, the authors insist, appalling conditions in the slums affect the health status of all the city's inhabitants.

Ramasubban and Crook relate the steady decline in the death rate, at least in part, to interventions by the municipal administration such as improvements in sanitation and water supply. Areawise high differentials continue, particularly in the case of infant mortality. The overall decrease in mortality is attributed by the authors to the greater availability of curative drugs rather than to a better state of health of the lower sections of society.

Upgradation of slums as described in an earlier paper by Panwalkar, may result in better living conditions and eventually better health. But this is not possible for all the slum dwellers, since many of the locations which they occupy can never be serviced with sanitation and water supply. However, absolute paucity of space in the city in relation to pressure of population has led in some areas to heterogeneity in terms of proximity of settlements of the rich and the poor. Ramasubban and Crook hope that this development may help to narrow differentials in the provision of basic services. They conclude, however, that the state has contributed and continues to contribute to the persistence of social-spatial inequality, so that class and unequal access to space remain the prime determinants of health.

Panwalkar's paper highlighted the significance of recent, new political initiatives such as offering security of tenure and the raising of the FSI (Floor Space Index, that is the extent of floor area construction permitted as a multiple of the plot area), for those who do not have housing or have no legal title to the land they occupy but who form cooperative societies. Banerjee-Guha discussed the changing concerns of the state in her account of the role of the state in the Vasai-Virar scheme. A paper by a practising architect, P. K. Das, entitled 'Manifesto of a Housing Activist', traces the evolution, over the last decade, in rules and regulations affecting the land market. The state, he charges, has abandoned its responsibility to provide public housing. Rather, it has turned over this task to the private sector, to which it provides substantial subsidies, thereby diverting institutional funds to private profiteering. The state has equally failed to implement the Urban Land Ceiling and Regulation Act. The recently announced increase of Floor Space Index from 1 to 2.5, Das contends, plays into the hands of developers who can proceed to construct and sell off a larger number of flats without regard for the existing infrastructure or considerations of urban amenity.[21] The new regulations will further exacerbate the existing inequalities of land and services distribution in the city.

Politics, Populism and Violence

We end the book with a set of papers that examine contemporary trends in the city's politics. In her paper, Usha Thakkar takes up the embodiment of struggles for power in the conflict between successive city municipal commissioners and the elected Municipal Council. The three other authors focus on recent outbursts of violence in the city and the crucial role played by the Shiv Sena in the city's politics.

The two papers on the Shiv Sena in this book, Jayant Lele's 'Saffronization of the Shiv Sena: The Political Economy of City, State and Nation', and Gérard Heuzé's 'Cultural Populism: The Appeal of the

Shiv Sena', trace the growth of the Sena from its early years and evaluate its present political stance, on the eve of its rise to governmental status in the state. Lele situates the Sena's origins and its present face as a defender of *Hindutva* (militant Hinduism) in the context of the changing economic and political history of the country, the state of Maharashtra and the city. Heuzé emphasizes the cultural aspects of the Sena's appeal. He relates the ambiguity and vacuousness of the Sena's shifting agenda to the instability in the lives of the popular classes in the city.

Since its founding in 1966, the Sena has been largely labelled as an ethnic, nativist or a religiously chauvinist movement or organization. Some commentators have suggested it fits into all three categories. There is a general agreement that the Shiv Sena propagates an ideology of violence and instigates violent encounters. It has taken a major part in the riots that engulfed Bombay earlier and again in 1992–93. Both Jayant Lele and Gérard Heuzé characterize the Shiv Sena as populist. Its strength surges and recedes according to its success at a particular moment in mobilizing its followers for direct, seemingly spontaneous action. In the Sena's early phase, action took the form of a campaign for the sons of the soil, that is Maharashtrians, as against South Indians, blamed for monopolizing clerical jobs and petty commerce in the city. A subsequent programme in favour of a clean and green Bombay targeted slums and slum-dwellers. In the violent aftermath of the demolition of the Babri Masjid, the Sena organized physical attacks on the homes and work premises of Bombay's muslim community. The Sena called upon the hindus to attend *maha aartis* (mass public prayer sessions occupying city roads) as a response to the overflow into adjoining streets from mosques of congregations offering their Friday *namaz*.

Throughout its ups and downs of popularity, the Sena has retained its appeal to a sizeable constituency and has in fact become a significant political force in the city. Today it numbers 40,000 hard-core activists plus about two lakh sympathizers organized in and around a couple of hundred *shakhas* (branches). In addition, a thousand or so units of mass organizations like youth clubs, women's circles, trade union fronts, and a thousand or more cultural mandals function to assure the Shiv Sena leaders of up-to-date assessments of the changing moods of the populace, as also to provide a pool for recruitment into the *shakhas*. Lele and Heuzé both point out that the Sena draws its support from a hetero-geneous and seemingly contrary combination of groups: middle-class salaried, Marathi-speaking white-collared workers; sections of the organized working class; and unemployed and underemployed youth.

The Sena emerged in Bombay at a time of local and national movements protesting against food shortages, rising prices and growing income disparities. As a pole of economic growth and opportunities for employment, Bombay had attracted a mass of in-migrants. By 1971, two-thirds of the city's population had arrived during the previous 30 years. In Lele's words, the Shiv Sena reflected a 'populist eruption' of the desperate and diffused discontent of the Marathi-speaking inhabitants. At this stage the Sena raised the slogan, 'Bombay for Maharashtrians'.

Lele emphasizes that the Sena's ethnic chauvinism was coloured by its equally strong anti-communist character. This thrust made it acceptable as a political ally to many parties on the right and the centre-left or anyone who wanted to make a dent on the influence of the communist unions in the city. The common aim of the whole array, from the Swatantra to the Socialists, and including the Congress, was to wrest from the communists the allegiance of the working classes. With the support of the discontented populace, as well as the ruling parties, the Sena was able to exploit the underside of the capitalist development in the city. It organized protection and extortion rackets, dabbled in illegal land deals, and participated in the drug and contraband markets. Although its popularity decreased in the seventies, the Sena ensured its survival through these economic activities.

Lele attributes the Shiv Sena's contemporary *avataar*, as a proponent of *Hindutva*, to the economic and political developments in the 1980s in India as a whole. He points to the growth of a substantial upper layer of 'rich and middle-income urban and rural households' with an effective demand for luxury consumer goods. In Lele's view, this socio-economic category has come to dominate governmental policies. This process, he continues, has been accompanied by a breakdown, as a result of penetration of capital into agriculture, of the 'patriarchal-patrimonial' system, which had till then maintained the hegemony of the upper castes and classes in the countryside. In this setting of a hegemonic crisis, parties needed an 'enemy' to focus the minds of the populace. They found it by creating an image of the distinctiveness of the 'Muslim' identity. The political arena of the eighties was dominated by issues such as the claim for maintenance by Shah Banu, a divorced muslim wife; the demand for subjecting muslims to a common personal law; and the fundamentalist Hindu campaign for building a temple to Rama on the site of the Babri Masjid at Ayodhya. The build-up in communal attitudes erupted into communal riots which further fed the flames of communal hatred. The process reached its denouement with the demolition of the mosque, followed by an outbreak of rioting all over the country, but most notably and most intensively in Bombay.

Lele's argument that the breakdown of the patriarchal-patrimonial hegemony has cleared the path for the rise of the *Hindutva* ideology is echoed by Heuzé. The latter suggests that the Sena intervenes in precisely this space, taking advantage of received paternalist authority patterns. In this manner the Sena is able to evoke symbols of masculinity, of *dadagiri* (literally, allegiance to an older sibling), 'of brotherhood constituted into action', which endow the organization with an aura of a substitute family.

Heuzé's paper explores the economic, demographic and social factors that have fashioned the urban culture of Bombay within which the Sena has created its own brand of cultural populism.[22] The Sena adopts, interprets, mediates, transforms and negotiates the symbols which arouse responses in a city largely populated by immigrants from the villages, packed densely in degraded areas and slums and subjected to feelings of a cultural angst. The Sena, Heuzé suggests, succeeds in integrating the city's poor on the level of culture rather than on the basis of social and economic concerns. It recognizes the need to promote the dreams, fantasies and aspirations of the youth. Their restlessness and their instability are thereby captured and manipulated to burst out in spontaneous action. Like the geography of the city, the Sena's agenda shifts over time. It links its followers emotionally with one another rather than propounding a coherent ideology. Yet, the Sena presents itself as a modern organization. Its programmes have incorporated calls for the development of industry, for city planning and beautification.

One traditional feature of Bombay life which the Sena has appropriated to legitimize its appeal is the celebration of festivals. To a considerable degree, mass sport, cinema and television have taken over as a substitute for games, *bhajan* singing and play acting. By the same token, people who formerly created their own entertainment have been metamorphosed into spectators. The Sena thrives by creating spectacles. It celebrates festivals of all communities except the muslims. It organizes these celebrations on a colossal scale, involving all its members and sympathizers in the collection of donations as well as in the elaborate preparations. These *pujas* (rituals) not only fulfil the function of mobilizing followers and gaining support from the people of the neighbourhood but also serve to extend networks of protection rackets and prepare the ground for popular participation in aggressive and violent behaviour, including rioting, as well.

The Sena has been active in Bombay for nearly three decades. Its definition of politics and its brand of political culture has had a strong impact on the city's political institutions and political life. Usha Thakkar, in her paper, 'The Commissioner and the Corporators: Power Politics at Municipal Level', highlights the recurring conflicts between the executive and the legislative sides of the Corporation. She provides example after example of the crude confrontations that have become embedded in the municipal politics of the city. Although Thakkar does not blame only the Sena for the ills besetting the Municipality, she points to the late sixties as a watershed in the deterioration of civic values. This date parallels Jayant Lele's specification of the seventies and the eighties as a period of sharp changes in the political scene at both national and local levels. From Thakkar's appendix table showing the strength of the different parties at successive elections, it becomes clear that the city has not had a stable government since the inception in 1948 of adult franchise.

We may well ask how Bombay, the birthplace of the Indian National Congress and the site of heroic working-class struggles, a city which has rarely experienced communal tensions over religious issues, fell under the sway of a narrowly nativist and blatantly communal movement that believes that, if its demands are not accepted, it has a right to mobilize the populace to commit violence. The Shiv Sena's popularity as the representative of the oppressed of the city has grown at the expense of the influence of the communist unions in the city. Of specific importance is the question of how this organization was able to influence and mobilize the organized working-class which, in spite of its limited strength in numbers, has had a significant political impact on the production and maintenance of a democratic political culture in the city.

The slow loss in legitimacy of the communist unions may have taken place because of their failure to recognize the need to extend their influence to workers in the informalized sections of manufacturing. As Sandeep Pendse has noted in his paper, it is increasingly becoming difficult to distinguish between the place of work and home. The rhythm of existence has got intermeshed with the organization of space. The Shiv Sena substituted the communist unions at the place of residence, in the slums, organizing access to space and to some measure of services and then protecting the populace from evictions. There may also be a more critical failure on the part of the left: a failure to recognize the psychological impact of unregulated and insecure work conditions, together with discontinuous and impermanent access to shelter. Pendse asserts that the toilers' sense of cultural deprivation is very acute. And this deprivation becomes, paradoxically, the basis for the reformulation of cultural identity via the Sena.

The left-wing unions were faced with a formidable alliance which sponsored the Sena when it emerged in the city. The Sena was initially supported by the textile millowners. Obviously the city's economic and political elite wanted it to be given a free hand in channelling popular discontent away from class issues. Since then it has received support from other sections of the upper classes in the city, including those involved in the construction business and the film industry. Certainly, as Jayant Lele suggests, the Sena would not have emerged and legitimized its influence without the emergence in the city and the country of a form of 'predatory' capitalism. Another factor that needs to be noted is the fallout of the successful movement of the late 1950s for a separate state of Maharashtra and the subsequent integration of the city, as the capital, in the new linguistic state. With this event there was a shuffling of the role that the city's elite had taken in the politics of the undivided state and their substitution by elements from outside the city.

Kalpana Sharma in her paper, 'Chronicle of a Riot Foretold', provides an account of the violent outbreaks of December 1992 and January 1993. She documents the complete collapse of the city's law and order machinery, with particular attention to the acts of commission and omission on the part of police as well as the administrative paralysis resulting from factional conflicts within the ruling party. Identifying more fundamental causes, Sharma reviews long-term conflicts of interest with regard to land and housing, competition for scarce services, utilization by politicians of the organized crime networks and, of course, the rise of the openly provocative Shiv Sena and the experience it had gained in similar earlier battles. The Shiv Sena founder and supreme leader, Bal Thackeray, had claimed that the riots were the work of his followers. Sharma catalogues the Shiv Sena's role in rumour-spreading, house-breaking, arson, looting and killing in practically every locality of the city.

Once again, as in the case of other riots in other towns and cities, sober analysis has revealed the bias of the state apparatus in favour of communal forces. What does this augur for the political future of Bombay? If governmental institutions prove ineffective in preventing or at least supressing communal outbursts, can we hope that this task will be taken over by alternative agencies? We may recall that in the early seventies, a spontaneous mobilization of women against price rise and for access to water and other services took place in Bombay. Earlier, during Indira Gandhi's repressive 'emergency' regime, focal points of opposition arose in the city. Bombay also figures as a staging platform for a dynamic modern women's movement which has spread throughout India. From the late seventies a number of non-government organizations have made an entry into the city's political landscape. While Panwalkar mentions sympathetically their intervention in the slum improvement programme, P. K. Das sharply criticizes the role they play in housing conflicts. During and after the violence of 1992–93, several spontaneously formed groups with no party affiliations provided timely relief to riot victims, confronted the Sena's propaganda on public platforms, in the press, and met together in informal discussion groups to work at an alternative agenda. Their disinterested concern suggests that, while the city's administrative and representative institutions have virtually abandoned all political space to the Shiv Sena, at least some of Bombay's inhabitants are ready to step into it.

Whither Bombay?

The papers in this volume attempt to capture a critical moment in the history of Bombay. Over the last 150 years, the city led the rest of India in fostering enterprises which helped to break the shackles of colonialism. Its current urban crisis reflects the contradictions inherent in the choices of the earlier economic and political elites as well as the challenge of new power brokers. Bombay evolved from a small British settlement into a metropolis; its expansion materialized the hopes and ambitions of the multitude of migrants it had attracted. Today, the city's elites are convinced that by restructuring and streamlining industrial and commercial activities they can assure their own future dominance and prosperity by linking Bombay more closely with the global powers that be. The papers in this book indicate that this transition may be traumatic for the city's poor, who survive at the edges of economic space, live in dense slums, and are subject to incitations to communal hatred by a populist party. Can Bombay's desperate population be persuaded to unite in order to redefine the city's agenda? Can it break the bonds of populist preoccupations and redirect the metropolis into a different trajectory? The answers to these questions will determine the history of twenty-first century Bombay, and to a considerable extent of India.

NOTES

[1] The 1991 census suggests that Greater Bombay's population is 9.9 million, which constitutes one per cent of India's population. The population of the Bombay Metropolitan Region is 12.5 million.

[2] A discussion on the surveys done to estimate the poor in the city is available in Madhura Swaminathan, 'Aspects of Urban Poverty in Bombay', *Environment and Urbanisation,* April 1995.

[3] The only exception to this is Mariam Dossal's paper in this volume.

[4] With the flourishing of trading communities there was an effervescence in Gujarati language and literature. The city became a locale for new developments in Gujarati culture. See Françoise Mallison, 'Bombay as the Intellectual Capital of the Gujaratis', and for subsequent developments, see Sonal Shukla, 'Gujarati Cultural Revivalism' in Sujata Patel and Alice Thorner (eds.) *Bombay: Mosaic of Modern Culture*, Bombay, Oxford University Press, 1995.

[5] Data drawn from a table in Malini Karkal: 'Population Growth in Greater Bombay: Some Emerging Trends', *Economic and Political Weekly*, Vol. 18, No. 4, 1982.

[6] I would like to thank Veena Devasthali for help in collecting information for this section.

[7] This ethnic diversity among the trading groups made possible a cosmopolitan outlook among Bombay's elite. This cosmopolitanism was flavoured with westernized attitudes. The cosmopolitan elite of Bombay, led by the parsi community, at home with the English language, kept their windows open to cultural trends in Britain, in Europe and later, North America. Their embrace of nationalism in the early part of the century did not lead itself to a cultural critique of western culture or of the English language. As a result, English remained a lingua franca of the elite of the city for over a century, nurturing thereby Indian English literature. For details on Indian English literature and Bombay city see, Roshan Shahani, 'Polyphonous Voices in the City: Bombay's Indian-English Fiction', in Patel and Thorner, ibid.

[8] Bombay accounts for 61 per cent of jobs in the oil sector, 41 per cent of domestic traffic, 25 per cent of income tax revenues and 60 per cent of customs revenues collected nationally.

[9] On the film industry, and its economics, see Amrit Gangar, 'Films from the City of Dreams', in Sujata Patel and Alice Thorner (eds.), op. cit. and on the relationship between the film industry and the Shiv Sena see, Heuzé, in this volume.

[10] For a contrary view on privatization and its effect on the land and housing market in the city, see P. K. Das, in this book. And on the way the global mass culture of TV and films is used by the Shiv Sena, see Heuzé in this volume, p. 242.

[11] These discussions range over wide areas. They include an assessment of the maverick leader, Datta Samant, who assumed the leadership of the strike, as well as an evaluation of the nature and form of workers' mobilization during the strike, the mode of its organization, and the millowners' and the government's responses. A detailed exegesis on the strike is available in H. van Wersch, *Bombay Textile Strike 1982–83*, Bombay, Oxford University Press, 1992.

[12] Since the 1960s the textile industry in Bombay has been going through a major restructuralization. Consequent to modernization, there has developed a differentiation between the units in the city. On the one hand there is a modern, automated and efficient sector; on the other, a backward sector. This has led to retrenchment of labour,

combination of jobs and double jobs and also abolition of jobs. Despite increasing work-load and productivity, wages have not increased. On the other hand, in other capital-intensive industries wages have been high. The reason for continued low wages seems to be the operation of the Bombay Industrial Relations Act. See note 13 below.

[13] Industrial relations of textile workers in Bombay city are governed by the Bombay Industrial Relations Act of 1948. This act allows the workers to have only one represen-tative union to negotiate their demands and bargain on their behalf. Since 1950, the ruling party has managed to get and maintain this status for its union, the Rashtriya Mill Mazdoor Sangh. The textile workers of Bombay have tried to dislodge the union through various strikes, the latest being in 1982–83. However, they have remained unsuccessful. A short history on the workers and their relationship with the Act is available in Bagaram Tulpule, 'Bombay Textile Worker's Strike. A Different View', *Economic and Political Weekly*, Vol. 17 Nos. 17 & 18, 1982.

[14] Bombay's textile workers were initially organized by the communists. Their trade union, the Girni Kamgar Sangh, led the workers through massive strikes in 1928–29. The role and significance of the Communist Party trade union in the textile industry decreased in the post-independence period after the passage of the Bombay Industrial Relations Act. The communist trade unions then unionized workers in the new manufacturing industries. Here too, they were marginalized by the philosophy of legalism that influenced trade unions in the sixties, with the entry into the labour movement of R. J. Mehta, who believed in raising wages through conciliation and arbitration. The mid-seventies saw the growth of personality-based trade unionism, that of Datta Samant. Like R. J. Mehta, his demands were confined to wage increases, but his strategy was action-oriented. He would call for strikes and continue them until the management yielded. Sandeep Pendse suggests that the economistic demands and result-oriented strategy attracted the workers to Datta Samant. Paradoxically, this support also undermined the organizational and ideological basis of a left trade union movement in the city. The slow decline in influence of the left led to an increase in the influence of the Shiv Sena. (Sandeep Pendse, 'The Datta Samant Phenomena', *Economic and Political Weekly*, Vol. 16 Nos. 17 and 18, 1981.)

[15] It is not a coincidence that the Shiv Sena became more popular among the workers after the collapse of the textile strike. See Lele and Heuzé in this book.

[16] Calculated on the basis of nature or size of employment from figures given in the census, Sudha and Lalit Deshpande have suggested that, in 1981, the informal sector or non-wage employment would not have exceeded more than a quarter of the workforce. They also make a second estimate using data culled from the Establishment Census. The proportion employed in the informal sector now increases to 27 per cent in 1970 and 33 per cent in 1980. If self-employed without premises is added the percentage further increases to 35 per cent. On the basis of a third estimate, calculated from the Employment Market Information Programme, they assert that those employed in the informal sector constituted 44 per cent in 1971 and 55 per cent in 1981. See Sudha Deshpande and Lalit Deshpande, 'Problems of Urbanisation and Growth of Large Cities in Developing Countries. A Case Study of Bombay', Population and Labour Studies Programme, Working Paper No. 17, World Development Programme Research, 1991.

[17] The data collected by Lakdawala et al. on the basis of a survey done in 1955–56 suggests that, while the number of workers in processing and manufacturing continued to increase during the first half of the century, the number in the service sector, other than commerce, remained steady at about one-third of the total work-force. If employment in commerce is taken into account, almost 56 per cent of the city's population was employed

in the service sector compared to 35 per cent in manufacturing and processing. It is unfortunate that economic historians have not emphasized the fact that the city has always had about 50 per cent of its population in services, even in the heyday of the manufacturing phase of the city. This has led many commentators to down-play the significance of those employed in non-manufacturing industries in the city. See D. T. Lakdawala, J. C. Sandesara, V. N. Kothari and P. A. Nair, *Work, Wages and Well-being in an Indian Metropolis. Economic Survey of Bombay City.* Bombay, University of Bombay, Series in Economics, No. 11, 1963.

[18] Narayan Surve's poem, 'Bombay', depicts the struggle, the tension and the anguish of living in slums. Also see Vidyut Bhagwat, 'Bombay in Dalit Literature'. Both these are available in Sujata Patel and Alice Thorner (eds.), op. cit.

[19] See for instance, Colin Gonsalves, 'Requiem for the Urban Ceiling Act' in *Janata*, 10 October 1982.

[20] Statistics regarding land use patterns in the city drawn from A. R. Desai, 'Rulers' Options for Squatters—Perish or Revolt', in A. R. Desai, *Trends of Urban Development in India and Proliferation of Slums and Squatting*, C. G. Shah Memorial Trust Publication, No. 11, Bombay 1985.

[21] Liberalization has led to the entry of global financial and real estate corporations into the city. Land and housing prices have escalated, making these comparable (at least in certain localities) with New York housing prices. The entry of global corporations into the housing industry has occurred soon after the entry of big business houses, like Godrej and the Tatas, into the housing sector.

[22] See the poems of Narayan Surve and Namdeo Dhasal, in Patel and Thorner, op cit. Certain films such as 'Dharavi' or 'Chakra' have also potrayed visually the culture that the city creates. See Amrit Gangar in ibid.

LABOUR AND ENTERPRISE

1
Toil, Sweat and the City

SANDEEP PENDSE

Technical details (mainly geographical, statistical and administrative information) apart, the reality of Bombay remains elusively beyond comprehension. The large volume of literature, academic and non-academic, furnishes only partial pictures. Representations in various media, be they factual-documentary, reflective-analytical or evocative-creative, provide illuminating, at times brilliant, insights which nevertheless remain limited if not fragmentary. The available material is more silent on some aspects than on others. Certain sections of the city's population and certain facets of the city's life are effectively hidden from view and difficult to grasp. The city as such, therefore, remains an enigma. The main reason, perhaps, lies in its complexity. It encompasses many different realities which seem distinct from and even opposed to each other, yet are all intricately interwoven in a many-layered mesh of interdependent relationships. Some of these realities are easily accessible to observation, investigation and representation. Others find no one to chronicle them adequately. Further, these realities are not fixed. They change over time. The change is, on occasion, rapid. In other periods it is practically imperceptible. In times of relatively rapid change, it becomes even more difficult to understand the city as a whole, since different sections of the population and different aspects of life in the city evolve at different paces. If the aim of inquiry is not purely academic but rather an activist intervention of one variety or another, the problem becomes all the more acute, immediate and urgent. This paper attempts at an exploration, obviously partial, into some aspects of the life of certain sections of the people in the city of Bombay, in a period of rapid change.

The City and Its Images

The very mention of the name of a city (in our case, Bombay) evokes certain powerful images. Many of these today are creations of the culture industry and therefore deliberate, even artificial, constructs. This is not, however, the whole story. Bombay (like many other cities in India and elsewhere) called forth characteristic images long before the modern means of communication came into existence and mass media came to shape public perceptions. Some aspects of these evoked images need to be noted. Rather than a single, universal image of Bombay, there are multiple images. A succession of images may be evoked in the mind of the same person, group or community. The evoked image depends not only on the reality of the city but also on the situation of the viewer— whether individual, group or community (always socially and historically definite entities). The image is thus not so much objective as symbolic. It is a social construction that signifies perceptions about the city from specific contexts. The image, therefore, is not permanent and fixed but changes over time in accordance with changing situations in and outside of Bombay. The images may lack factual accuracy but they do relate to realities of the city. They reflect the relationship of life within the city and life outside the city. Some of the images may be crude, gross and vulgar but such images are not accidental. Even if distorted, they are nonetheless symbolic representations. The images themselves may be complex. They may be visual, verbal, tactile, olfactory or a combination of any or all of these. The images may take the form of evocative symbols or descriptive-analytical statements. Some of the images have been known and variously recorded while others remain unknown except to specific groups. They may be formal or informal, articulate or nebulous. Often they are caste and class specific. The most prevalent ones represent the self-perception of the city's elite. They do not represent the realities and perceptions of the majority of the population of the city. The most populous classes in the city, the toilers, remain unrepresented, largely unknown and mostly ignored.

This is, of course, not surprising. The toilers in any society form the hidden, silent underbelly. At best they appear as lifeless statistics or as problems to be tackled. Information about the toilers is, therefore, 'naturally', scanty. Toilers appear in the available information as factors of production, as consumers or as sources of pressure upon the civic facilities. Details about numbers, work patterns, wages, housing etc. become from time to time obtainable. In the case of Bombay even this information is scanty and inaccurate. Multiplicity of laws, authorities, methods of registration and of record, for example, make it nearly impossible to determine the exact number of manufacturing units in the city of Bombay. The petty self-employed and the casually employed remain outside the pale of all records and registers; their numbers, hence, can never be accurately determined. Information about struggles (causes, numbers involved, duration, progress and outcome), can also be extracted in many cases from official and journalistic sources. Very little, however, is known about the toilers as human-beings. The non-economic and non-electoral aspects of their lives remain largely obscure. The quality of their life, their mentality, their leisure time activities, their aspirations, their thoughts, their family relationships etc., remain effectively hidden from view. The culture of the toilers in the city does not find adequate articulation and is not chronicled. A large number of questions then arise. What is the cultural impact of a city, particularly on the toilers? In what way do they acquire an urban culture? What is the nature and specificity of this urban culture? How do the toilers relate to the city and to their places of origin? Do these factors affect their social and political behaviour? The purpose of this paper is to seek answers to some of these questions. Although quantified, rigorous, theoretically impeccable answers to these questions are not available, indications can definitely be obtained from a number of sources. Dalit literature (writings, for the most part poetry, by militant members of scheduled castes who have chosen to call themselves 'dalit', meaning oppressed) in Marathi is one important source. The city of Bombay has found as much reflection in it as has the village. Some non-Dalit literary writings also depict the toiling strata of the urban society and describe their realities. A number of research studies and journalistic investigations also yield a fair amount of indicative material. Writings and reflections by social and political activists provide another rich source. It is possible on the basis of these sources to form some idea about the culture and cultural identities of the toilers in the city of Bombay. One unfortunate limitation of the literary sources is that they represent almost exclusively the Marathi-speaking sections amongst the toilers. Unfortunately other linguistic groups have not been depicted in literature about toilers in Bombay; or at least, such literature is not easily available in translation.

The exploration undertaken by this paper is shaped by a particular context. The social life of the city has been increasingly communalized over the past decade or so. The process culminated in the bloody communal violence that rocked the city in December 1992 and January

1993. These violent outbreaks also indicated that the culture and the cultural identities of the toilers have been heavily communalized. The key question before the paper, then, is why and how has this communalization occurred?

Toilers in the City

It is essential to state at this stage what is meant by toilers (or toiling classes) in the context of this paper. A certain confusion may exist about this category. Firstly, this stratum (or sections within it) have been variously described by different writers in different terms, most of which are non-specific and non-precise e.g.: workers, labouring masses, the poor, the underprivileged, urban subalterns, slum dwellers, popular classes. The ideological and analytical connotations of these terms are not necessarily shared by this paper. Secondly, flux, contradictions and ambiguities in the lives and realities of members of this stratum make delimitation of precise boundaries difficult. The flux, contradictions and ambiguities are crucial in shaping the cultural identities of the toilers; they need to be recognized and understood, not dismissed as impurities or obstacles in analysis. Further, the flux is not the product of an innate characteristic of the toilers but rather a function of the changing situation—economic, political and social—of the city. Bombay has undergone many transitions in terms of the dominant economic activity, the organization of activities, the structure of economic relationships, the spatial arrangements within the city and the relationship of the city with the rest of the country and the world. A Portuguese outpost in the 17th century, Bombay soon became a British foothold in the region, then successively, a port, a bustling hub of international trade, an important factory town, a megapolis functioning as the industrial and commercial capital of India, and in the current phase, a centre of speculative accumulation, globalized concentration and control in which commercial and financial activities dominate over manufacturing. These changes may be attributed to the changing nature of capital and capitalism in India. In such a situation it will clearly not be possible to define the toilers. It will be adequate, for the purposes of this paper, to describe them and to investigate some of their characteristics.

Toilers constitute the vast multitudes who perform all sorts of menial and physical tasks in the city. The mental labour they may be called upon to perform is minimal and incidental to the manual labour they are forced to undertake in order to survive. Taken as a whole, the group is diverse and comprises many sections, strata and fractions. Certain characteristics, however, are common and can be seen to determine the life situations of the toilers. They practice various occupations. Some have an opportunity of more or less stable participation in particular occupations so that skills and expertise are developed. In other cases occupations are constantly shifting, so that there is no opportunity for specialization. For some, the availability of gainful occupations is more or less assured, and leads to a certain stability. Other workers in the industrial and service sectors, both formal and informal, are unsure of any access to livelihood opportunities on a stable basis. The terms and conditions of employment are quite varied. These variations are produced by the diversity of capital in Indian business and industry. There are, hence, numerous fractions among the toilers, which often coincide with socio-cultural strata and thereby tend to become rigid. Many toilers are workers-in-waiting, aspiring to find employment as wage workers. Others are ex-workers, or workers who have now been thrown out of employment. Though socially identical to the regularly employed workers, economically they form detached elements engaged in quite different kinds of occupations and thus occupying different class positions. The foregoing could very easily be taken as the description of a working class in formation, if the industrial jobs dominated and if industry and industrial employment were expanding. In today's situation the split is not merely a difference between the standing and the reserve army of labour or between workers in the formal and informal sectors. There is a certain permanence to the separation, the proportions, and the stagnation. This situation may be ascribed to economic conditions which produce pauperization without proletarianization and urbanization without industrialization, creating destitute persons rather than workers.

The toilers, then, are sellers of labour power. Some sell their labour-power in the classical, direct manner. In the case of others, this sale is indirect and concealed. They may appear to sell their labour in the form of products but are in reality proletarians. Then there are petty commodity producers such as sandal makers, whose products and skills have not yet been industrialized or rendered totally obsolete by modern industrial products. There are also the petty self-employed who render various services which have not yet been organized in a capitalist manner. They provide services mainly to other toilers who have not yet been uniformly captured by the organized, formal capitalist markets, but also to other sections of the society in certain critical areas. Added to these are

the individuals who engage in all sorts of fringe and illegal, if not criminal, occupations.

One section of the working class which needs to be excluded from
this mass of toilers for the purpose of this paper, is that of the skilled,
specially trained or well-educated workers employed in modern, techno-
logically advanced, organized, stable industries, who draw comparatively high wages and have aspirations akin to those of the middle classes.
They are often drawn from the upper castes and have more or less real-
istic dreams of upward mobility, at least in generational terms.

Aside from this superior echelon the toiling masses are generally
characterized by a lack of control over most aspects of their lives. They
have no say over their process of production or over the disposal of the
products of their labour. The occupations they follow are rarely the
result of their own choice, usually imposed by force of circumstances.
Occupational mobility as well as choice occurs not through an exercise
of free will but as a result of the very absence of alternatives. The work
that they perform, the way in which they perform it, and the remuneration they obtain for it, are all decided by others, the rulers of the city.
Except a few, meagre, personal possessions, the toilers have no assets,
and count neither on security nor advancement. They have little or no
access to economic opportunities, credit or political power. Apart from
the vote, the apparatus, machinery and institutions of the state and
society are beyond their reach. There are exceedingly few avenues for
redressal of their grievances.

The life of these toilers is characterized by instability and insecurity.
There is no guarantee of livelihood. There is no assurance of adequate
remuneration. The employment situation is precarious. Jobs are held
under a constant threat of being made redundant. Legal machinery and
structures are typically loaded against the petty commodity producers
and the self-employed. Existence itself is constantly threatened. Even
many of the dwellings and residential areas in which they live are 'unauthorized' and thus constantly in danger of demolition. Impermanence marks the very existence of the toilers.

A large number of the toilers are first generation immigrants. They
may have been forced out of their original areas by natural disasters,
man-made calamities or development projects. Some have faced displacement more than once in their lives. Several have been lured to the
city by hopes of advancement. Migration produces the reality and the
realization of displacement—physical, spatial, social, and cultural.
Toilers acquire a sense of impermanence, instability, and insecurity.

With variations in degree, all toilers are victims of deprivation, both relative and absolute. There is a tremendous and obvious disparity between the lives of toilers and those of elites or even between toilers and the middle classes. Lives of many toilers are further characterized by an absolute lack of essentials for decent human survival. The precarious livelihood situation has already been discussed. Social welfare and security networks usually do not extend to cover all the toilers. Currently they have a tendency to shrink. Housing is often make-shift, unauthorized, unplanned, unhygienic. Very little urban space is available to toilers. Density of population in workers' quarters is extremely high and accompanied by a lack of open public areas. Civic amenities, like water, toilets, garbage disposal and lighting are scanty, if at all available. Health and educational facilities are at best inadequate. Cultural deprivation arises from the absence of innovative public effort to provide creative opportunities, but also from the sheer lack of space and facilities for leisure-time activities. The traditional, natural access to certain facilities which exists in the rural areas is not available in the city. At the limit, the urban existence forced upon the masses of toilers may be characterized as subhuman.

Toilers are relegated to the periphery of existence in the city, both literally and figuratively; actually and ideologically. Areas occupied by toilers may be located on the periphery of the city. They may be found near the municipal boundaries of the city or in the extended suburbs. Toilers typically occupy the least developed and the least desirable land in the city. Slums, which have come to be the characteristic residential areas of toilers since the specially built *chawls* can hold only a fraction of the working class, originally occupied the newly reclaimed, low lying areas which joined the islands which today are united to form the city of Bombay. These landfills are prone to waterlogging and flooding. Later slums were located on undeveloped outlying patches of land or vacant spots within the city. When unpaid labour develops these areas and makes the localities habitable, increasing their market value, urban development plans are invoked to 'relocate' the slum-dwellers to new, undeveloped areas. Spatial planning of the city has also a socio-political aspect. The effort, not always successful, is to shift slums to outlying sectors, at a distance from the nerve centres, and the arterial routes, and, if possible, from each other. Rational space utilization, efficient urban planning, smoother civic operations, uninterrupted traffic flows and even aesthetic considerations are advanced as goals. All these may be genuinely considered valid by the formulators of the plans. It is at the

same time true that this locational policy facilitates the political control
of the slum dwellers and makes for easier maintenance of law and order.
Possible upsurges of the toilers against 'public order' can be thereby
isolated in discrete pockets and any disruption of the smooth running
of the city prevented. The lives, activities and aspirations of a large
proportion of the toilers are thus kept effectively away from the lives
and realities of the middle classes. The city, in the sense of its elite and
middle classes, considers the toilers to be unnecessary invaders of the
city, burdens that endanger the city, creators of problems that need to
be controlled and managed. In point of fact, without the services provided and tasks performed by the toilers, the life of the city would
grind to a halt. Paradoxically, relegation to the periphery has had the
effect of persuading a sizeable section of the toilers to consider their
own existence in the city a burden upon it, and to develop the feeling
of being outsiders, of not belonging.

Far from being an amorphous, uniform or homogeneous mass, the
toilers are variously divided. Some of the divisions are traditional—based
on area of origin, religion, language, ethnicity and caste. Others are non-
traditional, specific to the existence in the city, based on nature of
occupation and employment, income, area and type of residence, length
of stay in the city, education, skills, inclusion in formal or informal
organizations as well as the social strength of these organizations. Most
of the divisions are hierarchical, and lead to a stratification of the toilers,
an absence of a commonality or unity amongst them. This to a large
extent renders them not only unorganized but also unorganizable.

The Other Face of Reality

The toilers, perhaps because of the very deprivation and relegation to
the periphery which they experience, develop certain survival and defence mechanisms. They have created informal networks and organizations which perform for themselves a number of functions that the
modern institutions do not provide. These may include access to living
space, credit, welfare, protection, nursing care etc. as well as preserva-
tion of identities. The networks may be based on caste, area (village,
district or subdistrict) of origin, urban neighbourhood, employment
or occupation. This process generally leads to the formation of narrow
but strong solidarities exerting conformist or disciplinarian pressures
in terms of attitudes and behaviour.

The multiple divisions and varied characteristics existing among the toilers raise the question as to whether it is at all legitimate to categorize the stratified, disunited mass as a common entity? Can any generalizations be made about it? As has been argued above, despite the differences, there are certain basic similarities. It is, thus, possible to consider the common factors which influence the formation of the cultural identities of the toilers in an urban setting. The identities are multiple and yet there is a commonality in the processes which crystallize them.

A cursory look at the population figures of Bombay in recent decades shows that its growth is not only a result of natural increase through births. Migration is necessarily a major factor. Although this in-migration cuts across classes, the greatest absolute growth is that of the work force and of slum-dwellers. As a matter of fact, the majority of the migrants join the ranks of the toilers. Some among them have migrated to the city in a more or less planned manner, in search of higher earnings and other urban advantages. This number, at least relatively, is likely to have declined in the recent past since such migration is dependent upon industrial expansion and increase in employment opportunities. A substantial proportion of the migrants are refugees of one kind or another. Some come into the city after calamities like floods, famines or earthquakes render them destitute; others come to escape caste or communal atrocities. Some are thrown out of gainful occupation by the march of development—loss of land, or traditional occupations being rendered obsolete. Yet others are victims of specific development projects—through submergence or forcible acquisition of their land holdings. There is thus a desperation in their move to the city. Few plan to spend only their working lives in Bombay and then return to the villages. Most are permanent migrants who have no longer any 'native place' to return to.

The meaning of the city to the toilers, however, is not solely negative. It has strong positive elements of hope and freedom. It represents in the first instance survival, an escape from starvation and destitution. It represents gainful employment which will provide enough to live on and perhaps for acquisition of some petty assets. It also represents an escape from drudgery, unfree labour, monotony, stagnation. However taxing the work in the city may be, it is formalized and governed by contract. The payments are not dependent on the will of the employer but fixed. Not only the amount of remuneration but also the modality and schedule of payment are fixed and known, therefore predictable and dependable. The discipline of urban work also means that there is a known regularity of the amount of labour the toiler can be called upon to perform as well as the time that s/he is expected to or can be made to spend at work. Contractual formalities provide certain justiciable norms and thus reliefs for a large section of toilers accustomed to virtual forced labour, whatever its outward appearance, in backward rural settings. The city also holds out the promise of liberation from traditional oppression—caste, class or ethnic. It holds out hope of freedom at an individual level—an escape from traditional bonds of community, caste and family, from ritualistic, unchanging and (in the villages) inescapable duties and obligations; freedom to become an individuated person and escape into a world of personal accomplishments and strivings. It provides the possibility of an entry into the civil society, whatever the reality.

Migration to the city also furnishes an opportunity for a move from joint to nuclear families in which personal relationships may come to play a significant role. The status of the woman also changes. The forms of gender equations change, bringing in their wake new expectations, aspirations and consciousness. The woman, at least at the level of aspirations, may for the first time become an individual rather than a mere element in a family enterprise. The very anonymity of city life can provide a breath of fresh air, arousing hopes or mirages of a good, easy, more fulfilling existence. It is necessary to remember these positive enticements that a city holds out. It is necessary to remember that every toiler does not cherish an ambition to return to his village; in fact, very few do. A permanent and desired linkage to the city is one factor that shapes urban cultural identities.

Impacts of the City

The cultural identities that exist in Bombay are not merely traditional rural identities transplanted into the city by means of spatial relocation. These are new identities which are essentially and irrevocably urban. Needless to say they do not come into existence overnight; they are not stamped onto a person the minute s/he enters the city. The development of an urban cultural identity is a process which involves the biography of an individual, group and/or community, particularly the phase of life history in the city. The specificities are dependent on numerous factors, some traditional and some modern. There are, however, certain common and general processes which are the products of urban existence that decisively shape these identities by almost dramatically and traumatically altering the lives of new city dwellers. These are not confined to the toilers, although it is they who feel the impacts with greater force and acuity because of the nature of their migration, the absence of mitigating defensive mechanisms and the lack of experiential or ideological preparation. They experience a culture shock in the very real sense of the term. The non-availability of formal, universalized, accepted, celebrated, articulate ideological and cultural institutions makes the impact of the traumatic changes indelible and profound.

The city exerts a radical impact on three aspects or facets of individual and collective life. These are (1) construction, organization and utilization of space; (2) importance, relevance and precision of time; and (3) restructuring of rhythms of existence. These factors have a decisive effect on the work-patterns, leisure times, family and collective lives of the toilers.

Space

A connurbation differs from a rural village dramatically in its relationship to space. The city occupies vast extents of physical and geographical space. Its sheer size is often daunting. The occupied space does not form a gentle and negotiable territory under leisurely control of its inhabitants. It cannot be easily traversed. It is, as a whole, beyond the intimate knowledge and comprehension of any of its inhabitants.

The extent of territory is not, however, the only characteristic of urban space. The utilization of space is far more intense than in non-urban areas. Even small areas of space are filled up. No place is left blank or unutilized.

Space in the city extends not only horizontally but also vertically. Man-made heights rather than natural elevations characterize the city. The urban landscape is marked not so much by exceptional two-storeyed mansions built as much for glory as for utility, but by the generalization of multi-storeyed, high-rise edifices.

In spite of this abundance through multiplication, space is also scarce in the city. This is particularly so in Bombay where peninsular geography sets limits to expansion. An urban area, necessarily, by the very process of urbanization itself destroys the natural resources available in its area. An urbanized tract does not produce food. The minerals under its land are not accessible for tapping. The availability of water—particularly potable water is crucial. These essentials have to be drawn by a city from the surrounding rural area—the hinterland. The physical limitations to expansion and the demands of growing economic (or, rarely, administrative) activity create a persistent shortage of space—industrial,

commercial and residential, private as well as public. The situation results in ever-greater intensification of use as well as an unequal and ini-
quitous distribution of space.

Space in a city is neither uniform nor homogeneous. As a direct result
of the above-discussed factors, a city is divided into many enclaves,
which differ from each other in many respects. These are not mere administrative divisions but artefacts of the social organization of the
city; they have economic and political as well as cultural dimensions.
These enclaves are distinguished by inclusive and exclusive aspects
which define them quite sharply. Differences are based on economic
activity, reciprocal impacts on other areas, and the status and power of
the inhabitants.

The Meaning of Space

The effects of these spatial characteristics of the city for the lives (activities, quality, standards and styles) of the toilers are tremendous. One
may reside in the city for years, may even be born and brought up in it,
and yet acquire familiarity only with definite localities and areas. Knowledge of large parts of the city may remain sketchy. Some of them one
may never visit in the course of a lifetime. There are always areas in the
city in which one feels an outsider and even experiences an alien's sen-
sations of insecurity and apprehension. The city as a total entity, in its
entirety, is only a notion, an abstraction, not something really known or
grasped.

Movement in the city, except in the almost immediate neighbourhood, similarly, involves an effort. It is almost never casual. It involves
the use of specialized modes of transport. Distances are often vast between residences and work places. The localities in between are often
unfamiliar. Particularly for toilers, commuting entails effort, dependence on facilities and modes outside one's control, expenditure of money,
energy and time. Movement in the city, further, is not all linear. It involves a vertical motion. Climbing into buildings by means of staircases
or elevators is an unfamiliar, acquired and relatively recent form of
movement. Residence or work high above the ground involves a different relationship with the surroundings. The relationship with nature
itself is altered in such perches. The artificial enclosure of space in the
city is so widespread and intense that almost everyone suffers from a
degree of claustrophobia. There is a constant, though at most times well
hidden and perhaps even unrealized fear that the 'closed-up' space may
conceal a danger or a death trap.

The boxed-in feeling is, in a different manner, intensified by crowding, which has two dimensions. Firstly, the density of the population itself creates absolute masses. One is surrounded in the residential area (sometimes inside the house/dwelling-place itself), in the streets, inside public transport vehicles and in the work-place with a large number of other human beings, often by people who are unfamiliar and, hence, vaguely threatening. Secondly, there is a constant contact with others, which makes an assault on sight, hearing, smell and touch. The sense organs are bombarded with a surfeit of unwanted, perhaps disagreeable stimuli. There results an exhaustion of the senses, an incapacity to deal with the data. As a defence, there may ensue a deadening of the senses, a numbing of sensibilities, an anaesthesia of perceptions.

Certain spaces in the city are denied to the toilers. They have practically no access to large areas which make them feel unwelcome. Even many public spaces and facilities can and do seem out of bounds. Little public space is readily available for their leisure and relaxation requirements. Liquor joints, neighbourhood tea shops, street corners, broken patches of open ground, a few tiny 'gardens' must perforce serve as collective space even for small groups. At home the toiler enjoys hardly any personalized space. Residences are crowded, often heavily shared, and at times impermanent. There is practically no privacy. Ordinary conversations become difficult. Other forms of expression are virtually ruled out. There is no possibility of personalizing any chunk of space, for purposes of isolation or contemplation. Space at work is also anonymous and always shared. Not even token personal effects can be kept in it. It cannot be 'humanized' in an individual, emotional and cultural sense. It is always both alien and dominating.

Among the toilers the woman suffers even more intensely from the lack of space. Urban space is primarily a male domain. The man can have at least an occasional recourse to the use of public space, however limited this may be. He also generally has greater chances of contact with the larger space of the city, outside of his own neighbourhood or locality. Once in a while he can take advantage of the anonymity provided by the crowds to avail of a (distorted) modicum of privacy. The woman, generally, has not even these limited possibilities at her disposal.

Space As A Cultural Determinant
The overall effects of this situation are quite significant. Practices, both individual and collective, relationships, sensibilities and thinking patterns

are influenced by the urban organization of space. Cultural identities are shaped by the space of (and in) the city. In addition to the direct impacts of the particular urban (industrial, large-scale commercial) utilization of space there are also individual and collective responses to the impacts. More often than not these are defence mechanisms. Space is concrete, physical, and tangible; its impacts, hence, are palpable, immediate and urgent.

The lack of space is distinctly perceived as such. There is, hence, a premium on space, both because it is so expensive and because there is a hunger for it. The loss of control over life becomes manifest, though not necessarily conscious or articulate. Disparities in the utilization of space are glaring. Deprivation and denial at the individual level parallels exclusion and banishment at the collective level. Both evoke strong, deep rooted and varied responses. Spatial constraints produce a sense of impermanence and insecurity in the minds of toilers and weaken the feeling of belonging to the city as a whole. They tend to strengthen traditional ties and identities, producing ethnic enclaves or sub-enclaves. A neighbourhood solidarity comes into existence which dominates, at times, over other solidarities. Solidarities also shape identities, particularly if they determine exclusion and inclusion and define conflict boundaries. There is a competition and rivalry over the available space, among groups of toilers themselves. Towards the elite occupiers and controllers of prime space there is envy as also a fear of their power. Occupation of public space, at least periodically, with the grudging consent of and legitimation by the entire urban society (e.g. religious festivals and processions) or by defiant coercion (demonstrations and riots) acts as a mechanism of assertion and cathartic release. Collective power is also realized in denial of space to the competitor or rival.

A particularly vivid illustration is provided by the invention in late December 1992, after the first outbreak of violence had abated, of the *maha-arti*. Whereas the overflow from Bombay's mosques during Friday noon prayers (*namaz*) had effectively blocked passage on adjoining streets for over a decade, the maha arti abruptly translated the offering of arti—normally a brief, indoor, devotional ritual—into a totally new large-scale outdoor gathering occupying public space—the road—for over an hour at a time when assembly had been prohibited. Again, during the second wave of violence in January 1993, gangs of men searching for apartments occupied by Muslim families, which they proposed to lay waste and loot, took over the streets in elite neighbourhoods, where under normal conditions no working-class person would venture. Similarly, during political demonstrations, there is often a concerted effort—which may succeed—to interrupt traffic of vehicles and pedestrians at strategic points in the city like Flora Fountain in the central business district.

Spatial deprivation and lack of control produce at one and the same time feelings of helplessness, powerlessness and dependence as well as resentment and anger—usually vague, nameless and unfocused. As noted earlier, there may result a defensive numbing of the senses—an acquired habit of ignoring unpleasant perceptions. This anaesthesia can apply to other aggressive impingements—economic, social, political and cultural —but it may be accompanied by outbursts of generalized hostile and destructive anger against other vulnerable groups. There are also extremely personal and individual (though common to many people) aspects of the forced changes in perception such as a continuous painful irritation and non-rest in day-to-day existence and a persistent sense of frustration. Personal relationships may be partial and to some extent non-fulfilling—whether or not the family is in the city with the toiler. Sexuality may be warped as a result of non-privacy and confinement. Gender relations are non-equal; the woman may serve as a domestic chattel, an additional source of revenue or a sex object. Traditional patriarchal relationships are, in effect, reconstituted in the city in a specifically urban form.

Time

Like space, time also is constructed and organized by the urban (commercial—industrial) agglomeration in a characteristic manner. In an age of generalized and universal commodity production (i.e., capitalism) labour power as a commodity is subjected to market operations of sale and purchase. It thereby acquires value and comes to have quantitative dimensions. Labour power and labour time come to require accurate and precise measurement. The informal, vague conception of time, dependent in pre-capitalist rural areas on natural occurrences (e.g. sunrise, crowing of the cock etc.) is replaced by a regulative, disciplinarian formal system.

Technological developments in production such as delicate or meticulous operations, automation, continuous process manufacture as well as in time measurement itself impart ever greater accuracy to time keeping in urban society. Work organization and discipline make observance of time schedules mandatory and time management crucial. Time becomes a tyrannical ruler in almost all spheres of human activity.

There is a constant effort to extend the time available as well as to intensify its use. Artificial lighting serves to prolong working hours. Recent experiments with the space mirror and literal obliteration of the night represent the most ambitious and extreme step in this direction. Time and work management techniques, and technology which converts the toiler into an automaton—a virtual extension of the machine, attempt to intensify the utilization of time by cramming an ever greater quantity of activity into each unit of expended time. The preoccupation which appears to be with time *per se* is in practice a quest for the most efficient utilization of labour-time, an endeavour to obtain the maximum returns from the purchased labour-power. Projects put forward in the guise of improvements in 'social welfare' and 'urban amenities' are often directed towards this very end. It is a characteristic of capitalist ideology that the effort directed at political-economic goals appears to have 'natural' and 'scientific' aims; the victory of one class over another appears to be an accomplishment of entire humankind over nature; extension and expansion of the realm of servitude appear as the deepening and broadening of freedom.

A measure of the capitalist-industrial-urban reconstruction of time is the departure from natural measurement of time to an artificial and mechanical one. The somewhat vagrant almanac based on natural events is replaced by a predictable, fixed, artificial calendar. Natural events like day and night, seasons, stellar effects are displaced from their regulatory role to suit the needs of productive activity which requires the greatest degree possible of accuracy in the measurement of time.

Loss of control over time and thereby over life activities not only at the work place during working hours but also during 'personal' hours at residential and recreational locations may produce disquiet if not distress. Domination by necessity (or unfreedom) becomes particularly intense in the case of time. Since time, however, is not concrete in the manner that space is, this loss of control is rarely felt as such by the toilers. The sense of deprivation may be all-pervading and abiding, as well as physically exhausting, but it is also vague and out of focus. Toilers do not perceive the englobing system as the cause of the discomfort; rather the malady seems to be existential and incurable. An obscure anger motivates a search for a vulnerable 'other' upon whom ills can be blamed. Contributing to the exclusion/inclusion mechanism this process works towards construction and reinforcement of separate identities.

A specific gender dimension applies to time in the city. Under capitalism domestic work which produces labour power on a generational as well as day-to-day basis is not considered 'productive'. Its dispersed, familial nature also contributes to its concealment. Time does not operate for the woman in the same manner as it does for the man. If she does not work outside the house, her labour power, that is, her time is not purchased in the formal labour market and is never paid for. Although it is not under direct and visible control as, for example, work in a factory, there is in fact no period of freedom for her. The institution of family and the internalized values ensure that she is on the job at all hours with no fixed routines and no statutory time off, except perhaps during serious illness. The woman's time, thus, because it is not to be compensated, remains without any accurate measure. As a corollary, most women have little access to time-measuring instruments. Because of the strict schedules of the revenue earning members of the family she is also subject to the tyranny of time management and schedule keeping, but there is no regularity to her own time and there is no recognition of its expenditure. The resultant ignorance becomes yet another reason for her relegation to 'subsidiary' spheres.

Rhythm

Changes in the pattern of economic activity, in the organization of space and in the management of time restructure the rhythms of life in the industrial city.

In the first instance, the relationship of life activity to nature, both internal and external, is torn asunder. The natural cycles of the day—physical and biological—are ignored and set aside. Light and darkness, heat and cold, sleep and wakefulness, energy and lethargy as time-bound occurrences cease to have any relevance. Periods of work and of respite are determined in an industrial urban environment basically by the necessities of production, specifically by work schedules. Round-the-clock economic activity leaves no space for any natural cycles; shift work obliterates the distinction between night and day. Human relationships to light and temperature change completely; sleep and wakefulness are reordered. The rotation of the same toiler among two or three shifts may preclude the establishment of any steady or permanent, even if 'unnatural', cycle to set in.

This reconstruction of the daily rhythm in work activity has an impact on the entire life of the individual, the family and the society. Although the compulsion is visible only with regard to the periods of work of the toiler directly employed in an industrial establishment, the chain reactions are multiple.

Obviously, a change in the timings of work will involve changes in timings of rest, eating and leisure for the entire family. If schedules of earning members of the same family clash, the whole household is affected by the strain. Alteration of daily rhythm impinges upon interpersonal communication as well as personal and social relationships. Participation in community activities may become virtually impossible. Isolation and atomization of the individual may result from urban work patterns.

The impact of changes in the daily rhythm is most visible in the case of those whose work involves attendance at work place in different shifts. It is not, however, confined to them. The non-shift worker, including the self-employed, has to extend his or her own activity to the limits of endurance in order to squeeze out the maximum from the working day or to squeeze in whatever leisure possible.

The rhythm of life is altered not only on a daily but also on an annual basis. Activity in an urban industrial centre does not relate to seasons or climatic changes. Natural events impose themselves on urban life only periodically, and then as obstacles. Urban activity remains, particul rly for the toiler, much the same throughout the year. Activity is essentially monotonous and repetitive. The exact effects of this disharmony with nature are yet to be adequately recognized and understood.

There need be no doubt, however, that this synthetic pattern of life with its artificial intensification of leisure as well as work has biological and social effects. Disregard for metabolism and for interdependence with nature cannot but impinge upon the physical and mental existence of the human being. However 'natural' the urban pattern of life may come to seem, imbalance in cycles of activity and recuperation, monotony and routinization of work, degradation of skill and individuality, automaton-like existence, obedience to mechanical rhythms must produce irritation and discontent. This 'conquest of nature' does not imply an extension of human freedom but rather an extension of the domain of necessity and unfreedom.

Toilers and 'Culture' in the City

'Culture' here is considered in a very broad sense to encompass the entire sphere of life outside the area of formally governed work. It is an attribute of collectivities and not of isolated individuals. An individual in this sense only represents the collectivity she or he belongs to. Culture includes a variety of beliefs and values, activities and practices, institutions and organizations that embrace the whole 'arena of freedom'. It thus shapes the life of an individual, a family, a community. It makes possible day-to-day functioning at the non-contractual, non-formal levels. It makes sense of life; imparts meaning and purpose to it; it defines, through permission and prohibition, beliefs and values; it provides a code of conduct and a reference mechanism as well as an internalized regulator. It crystallizes identities by defining affinities and distinctness. It spells out what is permissible and what is not. It creates precedents. It routinizes responses through codes and customs. It makes possible all collective activities. It shapes and regulates relationships and interactions. It provides the space and platform for fulfilment, flowering, and creative action.

Culture has necessarily economic, social and political dimensions and a material basis. Any collectivity or community is a complex entity that embraces many subsidiary groupings. It is also in a constant flux, being perpetually formed and dissolved through processes of construction and disintegration. The 'culture' of a collectivity is an agglomerate of many sub-cultures, depending upon the level at which it is delimited and considered. The community is not a haphazard, ecclectic lumping together of diverse sub-cultures. The existence of a collectivity depends upon its ability to resolve the contradictions between the component sub-cultures, to render them non-antagonistic if not complimentary, and to synthesize them into a new totality. To achieve this, commonalities are drawn out, emphasized and codified to create overarching beliefs and practices, but the sub-cultures themselves are not destroyed. Conceived in this fashion, collectivity is not a notional construct but an empirically existing social reality. Conscious efforts to create new collectivities and collective identities depend for their success upon the fulfilment of these tasks at the ideological and the practical levels. The bid by the Left to create a working-class consciousness in Bombay in the '30s, '40s and '50s succeeded during these years at the trade union level. It foundered subsequently because it failed to institute its own social and cultural beliefs and practices strong enough to override existing identities such as those of caste, language, place of origin.

The area of work is governed by formal, legal, contractual relationships and deals. These are imposed upon the toilers, leaving them no choice or alternatives. Toilers cannot, normally, modify these terms. For them the sphere of work is an area of servitude, of bondage, of no intrinsic interest. It is only an instrument, a means. Culture recognizably constitutes the other area of life, the 'sphere of freedom'. The two arenas or spheres, of necessity and freedom, are distinct and separate but constantly influence each other. Occurrences in one have an effect on the beliefs and practices in the other. The interpenetration is often so pervasive that the separation seems imaginary. Under capitalism the sphere of freedom is also shot through with commodity relationships. It becomes a mirror image, in many respects, of the economic sphere.

Cultural deprivation in such conditions is acute. The cultural arena is one in which an individual or a collectivity confronts its self-alienation, its sense of loss. Efforts are made here to overcome it, in a real or fantasized manner; to cope with existential anxieties.

The three factors discussed above, viz., space, time and rhythm are culturally crucial in many ways. These factors have a direct, dramatic, physical impact on life. There is no preparation for the impact nor any mechanism to deal with it. The forces themselves are technological and economic. The reconstitution of lives by them is an unanticipated, accidental byproduct that has turned out to be all-pervading. These forces affect all city dwellers but not in the same manner. The toilers are particularly vulnerable and defenceless. They cannot, barring exceptional transient situations, control any of the elements or mitigate their effects. They have no ways of subverting these forces, of turning them upon themselves for their own advantage. The toilers are completely dominated by these forces which do not even seem to them to be products of human creation. They appear as natural realities, as given immutable facts of life. They constitute, for the toilers, additional conditions of servitude, bondage and deprivation.

Reorganization of space, reconstruction of time and restructuring of rhythms are specifically urban factors. They are products of the conditions of industrial urbanization. They in turn shape the modern city. They affect the physical organization of the city, its attributes and services as well as life practices within it. They are in a way defining elements of the modern city.

Space, time and rhythm are also the elements that concretely shape the experience of self-alienation in the city. This is exacerbated by the penetration of the cultural sphere by commodity relations and formal capitalist institutions. These make collective activities and expressions more and more difficult. The industrialization of sport, entertainment and the like deny any effective participation in these activities to the toilers. High costs and organizational sophistication make such pastimes inaccessible. Participation is no longer direct and live but passive and vicarious. Opportunities for activity and expression outside the sphere of work become increasingly remote. Cinema, television and commercial proscenium theatre, music systems and orchestras replace neighbourhood and community-based artistic expressions; extravaganzas, expensive equipment, commercial formalization do the same for sport.

The toiler in Bombay is caught in multiple binds. In addition to economic and political deprivation there is low social status and lack of cultural opportunities. For these reasons, the toilers come to constitute a mass of people infused with deep discontent and a searing sense of loss, an army in search of an enemy, of a target to hit out at.

Cultural Identities in the City

Identities are operative self-perceptions of collectivities. They define similarities and distinctness. They therefore include and exclude. They represent real or imaginary communality of interests and provide the basis for common action. They are usually not amorphous and abstract but rather concrete and structured. Formation of an identity is a subjective phenomenon. Analytical categories do not necessarily correspond with or automatically yield collectivities with common identities. Construction of identities is a cultural activity. It is needless to add that this does not make them products of imaginary or voluntary exercises. They have a strong material basis. They are determined by (economic, social, political and cultural) life practices. The functions that they perform are also not merely psychological but strongly material. No identity without a function can exist.

Identities, as is well known, are multiple and simultaneous. Any individual or collectivity holds at one and the same time many different identities. Some of the identities may be subsidiary to others which dominate. The overarching identity may change over a period of time depending on numerous factors, which are themselves not cultural but material and social. Identities concretize collectivities. Membership of a collectivity or community concretizes non-commercial, non-contractual social relationships. It makes life possible.

The toilers, in the first instance, find in their collective identity a generalization of their deprivation. Banishment from certain areas of the city, servitude and loss of control over daily life appear not as individual misfortunes or, worse, results of mistakes or incompetence, but as a common condition of a large number of people. Collective identity creates a situation of relative fearlessness within the toilers' neighbourhoods. It provides the basis of harbouring simultaneously envy and ridicule for the middle classes and the elites. The collectivities also perform a large number of social security functions which the state and system do not.

Apart from day-to-day functions, the collectivities also provide a basis for defining the 'other', for the identification of an enemy, for crystallization of a target for anger. The collectivity provides for the toilers a justification of their own life and existence. It furnishes the opportunity for at least an episodic assertion of their own selves, for defiance of order and establishment.

New Economic Order and Changed Cultural Identities

Neighbourhood and local actions are not, however, enough to satisfy a mass which is deeply discontented and angry. They do not provide the satisfaction of strong defiance, of having suspended the conditions of servitude for any length of time. For this purpose collectivities going beyond the neighbourhood and embracing the city as a whole are necessary. Only city-wide actions bring about any significant change in power balances, force the enemies to negotiate or grab media recognition. Local actions can be petty; widespread actions become causes. Effective operation in the political arena requires a collective identity which is broad, and inclusive of various sub-cultures. In the period of anticolonial struggle, the toilers linked themselves with the national, anti-British identity. The general nature of the movement defined its ideology; every agitation had specific goals. The actions in the toilers' areas were characteristic, from the first political general strike of 1906 to the demonstration of solidarity with the Indian Navy ratings mutiny in 1946. During the period of industrial expansion in Bombay, the toilers saw themselves as part of the working class and joined in its revolts. The workers and their representatives in this period dominated. The larger and more generalized strikes and other manifestations were then not merely trade union actions but also community actions. They also, therefore, acquired political overtones. Up to the early '70s textile strikes are the best known examples of such collective actions. Other strikes evoked similar responses though on a geographically more restrained basis.

More recently economic stagnation as well as radical changes in technology have made industrial employment more and more scarce, even in engineering and the newer fields such as chemicals and electronics.

A chasm has developed between the organized workers and the others. The struggles of the workers have become restricted industrial actions with purely plant-level economic demands. Economism could not provide a basis for solidarity and unity at a collective level. Self identification as members, however removed, of the working class begins to recede.

The Shiv Sena in the late sixties and seventies furnished an ethnolinguistic identity for Marathi speakers. Mobilization on this basis led to dramatic but short-lived activity. Marathi identity could not be very effective in mixed neighbourhoods. Nor could it provide an encompassing solidarity. Targets proved elusive.

Changes in the economy create further complications. The working class is in numerical decline with the progress of informalization and expansion of non-industrial sectors. Its social and ideological weight exhibits a proportional decline. Informalization and expansion of self-employment also saps the basis of any occupational or class identity. It leads to a greater atomization and competition. The exploitative and oppressive nature of the system becomes increasingly invisible. Anger becomes ever more vague and unfocused. Dreams tend to be acquisitive and consumerist. Cultural activity becomes even more vicarious, standardized, repetitive and meaningless. The toilers are faced in this situation with an erosion of collective identity. Cultural deprivation, collapse of values and ideals, generalized corruption increase the sense of desperation. It is in this specific situation that *Hindutva* is put forward as the operative identity. It provides a spurious target by means of a misleading reinterpretation of history, a target which is frightening yet vulnerable. It provides a cause, however unrelated this may be to life situations. It provides rituals and collective assertive activities, opportunities for violence, rioting and shows of defiance. The limitations of this identity are obvious. Hinduism cannot provide an overarching identity that can resolve conflicts between the sub-cultures of toilers in the city of Bombay, nor can it provide in action a counter to the forces that shape their cultural servitude.

2

Bombay as a Business Centre in the Colonial Period: A Comparison with Calcutta

CLAUDE MARKOVITS

Comparisons between Bombay and Calcutta as cities are a fairly hackneyed topic. However, a systematic comparison between those two metropolises, focusing on their role as command centres, has, to my knowledge, never been done. This paper is a very preliminary attempt at such an exercise. It draws attention, firstly, to the existence of a pattern of dual dominance in the Indian colonial economy, which is generally taken for granted but actually calls for some explaining. Possible counterfactuals existed. By the middle of the 18th century, the emerging colonial economy of India had three major foci, Bombay, Calcutta and Madras, and a tripolar structure was a distinctly possible outcome. Why Madras, which was the oldest British colonial foundation in India, could not maintain its rank, in spite of the consolidation of its hinterland brought about by the annexation of the Carnatic in 1801, need not detain us here. But we should keep in mind the fate of Madras, for, had not certain chance factors intervened, it could very well have been Bombay's: to become a backwater of Empire. Leaving aside the question of possible counterfactuals, the paper will focus on an analysis of the dominant couple formed by Bombay and Calcutta and of the changes it underwent over time.

In the first part of this paper I shall therefore examine the unfolding of what I call 'dual dominance'. The story clearly falls into three periods: from 1830 to 1860 Bombay rose to parity with Calcutta; then, from 1860 to 1920 we have the heyday of dual dominance, with Calcutta as Number One, but Bombay as a close second; after 1920, as both cities went through the difficult interwar period, dual dominance, without being really challenged, found itself somehow eroded.

In the second part of the paper, I shall look for possible interpretations, focusing particularly on entrepreneurial responses. My hypothesis is that the better 'communal mix' of Bombay business, and in particular the lack of the kind of total European domination witnessed in Calcutta, was a major factor in Bombay's success, firstly at reaching parity with Calcutta, and then at maintaining it against heavy odds.

The Unfolding of 'Dual Dominance'

Even once it had securely displaced Surat as the main centre of colonial maritime trade on the western seaboard of India, by the middle of the 18th century, Bombay was nevertheless not in a position to compete on equal terms with Calcutta as a trading and financial centre. Its commercial fortune was largely linked, since the 1770s, to the China trade, with all the political and economic uncertainties this entailed, and it suffered from the absence of a rich and easily accessible agrarian hinterland, which was one of Calcutta's major assets. The successive annexations of Gujarat in 1800–03 and of the Maratha Empire in 1818 did not give it the boost which could have been expected, for they coincided with depressed conditions in the China trade and left unsolved the problem of better communications with the interior.

By 1820, even after the spate of annexations of the previous 20 years which had given it at last a proper hinterland, Bombay was still a fairly insignificant trading centre compared to Calcutta. In 1820/21 its merchandise export trade amounted in value to little more than a quarter of Calcutta's and its imports were valued at less than half Calcutta's.[1] The surplus of exports over imports was worth only a small fraction of Calcutta's surplus. Exports consisted mainly of cotton and opium[2] for the China market, which was then depressed. This depression persisted until the late 1820s. However, from 1830 onwards Bombay's trade

---

[1] The exact figures for Bengal were: exports, Rs 56,800,000; imports, Rs 22,500,000. See K. N. Chaudhuri, 'Foreign Trade and Balance of Payments (1757–1947)', in D. Kumar (ed.), *The Cambridge Economic History of India*, vol. 2, Cambridge, 1983, Table 10.4, p. 828. For Bombay, they were: exports, Rs 15,500,000; imports, Rs 11,000,000. See *The Gazetteer of Bombay City and Island*, vol. I, Bombay, 1909, Appendix IV, pp. 514–15, and V, pp. 518–19.

[2] Raw cotton exports were worth Rs 5,200,000 and exports of opium amounted to Rs 3,200,000. *Gazetteer*, ibid.

entered a period of rapid growth and, by the late 1850s, the commercial importance of the city was comparable to that of Calcutta.

Bombay's Rise to Parity with Calcutta—1830–1860

It is generally acknowledged that, prior to the railway age, there was no such thing as an 'Indian' economy; it was, rather, a congeries of regional economies loosely linked together, the major unifying factor being their growing subjection to British capital and to the needs of the metropolitan economy. In this context, 'dual dominance' is obviously not a relevant concept. We have to consider Western and Eastern India as two more or less separate economic entities within a nascent 'imperial world-system' of which the 'commanding heights' were situated in London, Liverpool, Manchester and Glasgow. Within this global system both Bombay and Calcutta can be seen as second-rank imperial cities, each having its own sphere of influence, with a limited amount of overlapping. Having very little industrial production prior to the mid-1850s, they functioned primarily as commercial emporia, draining the agricultural produce of their hinterlands and dispatching to the interior a growing but still limited quantity of imported manufactures in the fashion of the classical colonial port-cities. The only way to evaluate their respective importance is through a look at the statistics of the foreign seaborne trade.

It is therefore not surprising to find that a lasting upswing in the trade cycle was largely responsible for Bombay's surge of prosperity which allowed it to catch up with Calcutta and even, for a short while, to over-take it.

The upswing was mainly due to a rise in the Chinese demand for opium as well as to a growing tendency to ship the opium of Malwa through Bombay rather than through the ports of Portuguese India. The abolition of the Company monopoly of the China trade in 1833 stimulated that trade further. With the 'opening' of China by British guns in 1842, a huge market was securely offered to the enterprising Bombay merchants, the 'drug barons' of the 19th century. Before becoming the 'Manchester' of India, Bombay thus became its 'Medel-lin'. It also benefited from a renewed interest of the (original) Man-chester in Indian cotton as the textile industry of Lancashire went through a period of quick expansion and found American cotton prices too high.

Between 1830/31 and 1860/61, the value of merchandise exports from Bombay increased sixfold and the value of opium sales alone increased more than tenfold.[3] The share of opium in the export trade rose from 25 per cent in 1830/31 to 42 per cent in 1860/61, that of cotton from an already high 36 per cent to 44 per cent.[4] The growing dependence of the Bombay export trade on those two commodities is striking. Although Bombay's exports in 1860 were 40 per cent higher than Calcutta's, the latter offered a more varied range with, besides opium and cotton, indigo and sugar being also significant staples. Bombay's imports increased only fourfold during the same interval, the major increases being in cotton piecegoods (which accounted for 37 per cent of all imports in 1860/61) and metals, while a new item, railway plant, accounted for over 6 per cent of imports, signalling the beginning of the railway era.[5] Thus Bombay had a considerable surplus of exports over imports, the magnitude of which clearly surpassed Calcutta's. The western-Indian city seemed to be not only catching up with the capital of Bengal, but appeared on its way to displacing it as the 'Urbs Prima in Indis'. At some point in the 1840s, its population overtook that of its rival and the Census taken in 1864, at the height of the cotton boom, revealed a population of more than 800,000, a fourfold increase since 1818 (Kosambi, 1986, 36). Most of them were recent migrants from the Konkan area of Maharashtra; there was also a considerable influx of traders from Gujarat.

However, the foundations of this new-found prosperity were fragile. Both the opium and the cotton trade were very speculative in nature and closely dependent on the state of the Chinese and British markets, and Bombay's communications with its opium and cotton-growing hinterland were still, in spite of some improvements in the state of the roads, both costly and subject to seasonal interruptions when the monsoon rains raged over the Western Ghats. In the absence of good communications with the interior, Bombay could not fully exploit its advantages as the natural 'Gateway of India' for European commerce, although a regular shipping service with England via Suez and Alexandria had been established in 1858.

The most promising development in the 1850s was actually the establishment of the first modern cotton-textile mills, but in 1860 their future was still far from assured as they struggled to carve for themselves a

[3] In 1830/31, opium exports were worth Rs 6,300,000; in 1860/61 they reached Rs 66,000,000. Ibid.

[4] Calculated from figures in ibid.

[5] Total imports of metals were over Rs 12,000,000, some 13 per cent of the total value of imports. Calculated from ibid.

share of the Indian market in the face of fierce competition from Lancashire's mills. The beginning of the cotton textile industry in Bombay in 1854 preceded only by one year the starting of the first jute mill in Calcutta, and this synchronism in the use of modern machinery was eloquent testimony to the emergence of a structure of 'dual dominance' in the Indian colonial economy.

The Era of 'Dual Dominance'—1860–1920

In his compendium of the Indian Empire written in the early 1880s, W. W. Hunter remarked that, 'Calcutta and Bombay form the two central depôts for collection and distribution, to a degree without a parallel in other countries' (Hunter, 1886, 560), thus nicely articulating the thesis of 'dual dominance'. However, the reversal of the trend after 1865 must be noticed. While, from the mid-1850s, Bombay seemed on the way to displace Calcutta as the major centre, after 1865 it was never able again to clearly challenge the primacy of the capital of Bengal. The reasons for the re-establishment of Calcutta's supremacy have mainly to do with the political economy of colonial India, but conjunctural factors, such as the differential impact of famines and the financial collapse in Bombay consecutive to the sudden end of the cotton boom in 1865, have also to be taken into account.

But firstly it must be noticed that the last third of the 19th century saw some amount of real direct competition between the two cities. In the previous period, in the absence of an 'Indian' economy, there were very few opportunities for direct clashes of interests. With the advent of the railway age, it is generally acknowledged that the concept of an 'Indian' economy became more meaningful. Not that one should exaggerate the degree of unification of markets brought about by the construction of the railway network; in many ways both capital and labour markets remained segmented in colonial India; however, the railways eliminated the most glaring price differentials and stimulated the circulation of goods as well as men across the country (Hurd, in Kumar (ed.), 1983, 737–61). For three or four decades there was a certain amount of fluidity as the spheres of influence of the various centres underwent some redefinition at the margins. The birth of Indian nationalism during the same period also stimulated inter-city competition as the elites of both cities started to think in terms of the role of their own city in an all-India context and anxiously surveyed the progress of the rival city.

In the ongoing contest for supremacy between the two metropolitan cities of India, Calcutta's advantages were many. It was the seat of the colonial government till 1911, a not unimportant consideration since, in spite of its adherence to the Manchester school economics, the Government of India played a big role in allocating resources between regions, especially through the way it gave concessions to railway companies, and was particularly susceptible to pressures from Calcutta's overwhelmingly European business community. Calcutta had the largest concentration of European population and European capital in India; its European firms enjoyed particularly close links with the City of London, the financial hub of the world till at least 1914, and it drained Indian entrepreneurial talent and capital from as far afield as Marwar. It had easy communications with a vast agrarian hinterland extending from Eastern United Province to Assam, which produced most of the two major export crops grown in India, tea and jute, cotton having for its part never regained its shine of the boom years; and it had access to an abundant supply of labour attracted from this hinterland and even from as far as the Madras Presidency. It was close to the major energy source used in the 'modern' sector of the Indian economy, coal, which Bombay had to import from far afield. On the other hand, Bombay's area of labour recruitment was largely limited to Maharashtra (in particular the Konkan) and its indigenous entrepreneurial class came almost exclusively from Gujarat. As far as its European firms were concerned, they were less capitalized than their Calcutta counterparts, having more tenuous links to the City. The major advantages of Bombay over Calcutta were its better harbour and the shorter distance to Europe once the Suez route started being extensively used, which happened only in the 1880s.

A look at the statistics of the foreign seaborne trade reveals that over the 1871–1939 period Bombay on the whole trailed behind Calcutta but maintained a lead in the import trade. Table 1 gives five-yearly averages of exports and imports from Bombay and Bengal for 1871–1931 and 1934–1939.

On the basis of the data presented in Table 1, two major points need to be emphasized:

a) that, with the exception of the quinquennial period 1886–91, Calcutta's foreign merchandise trade was always larger than Bombay's, though not by a very big margin. The situation prevailing in the 1860s had clearly been exceptional.

b) that while, in the case of Bengal the curves of exports and imports were broadly similar, in the case of Bombay a certain disjunction is

Table 1. Five-yearly averages of merchandise exports and imports from Bengal and Bombay (Rupees, million)

Period	Bengal		Bombay	
	Exports	Imports	Exports	Imports
1871–76	242	168	221	119
1876–81	302	192	225	154
1881–86	341	222	320	210
1886–91	375	257	370	275
1891–96	433	277	385	282
1896–1901	484	318	326	348
1901–06	589	375	438	332
1906–11	771	498	510	428
1911–16	924	621	580	522
1916–21	1,291	1,015	880	839
1921–26	1,302	902	1,027	908
1926–31	1,305	802	705	805
1934–39	735	427	332	583

Sources: Annual Statements of the Trade and Navigation of British India, Annual Statements of the Seaborne Trade of British India, for relevant years.

noticeable at various points in time, particularly in the 1890s when imports surpassed exports during one quinquennial period and after 1926 when the fall in imports was much slower than the fall in exports.

It seems useful, for the purpose of more detailed analysis, to distinguish between the trends in the export and in the import trade. In the export trade Calcutta's supremacy over Bombay was never challenged after 1870, a trend which reflected the increasingly crucial role played in India's export trade by tea and jute (both raw and manufactured) which were largely or exclusively grown in Calcutta's hinterland. On the other hand, Bombay's export trade suffered from the gradual disappearance of opium as an export commodity, from a fall in foreign demand for the short-fibre cotton grown in the Deccan, and from an increasing diversion of the export trade of Sind and the Punjab to Karachi. The most successful new item in Bombay's export trade was cotton twist and yarn which started being shipped to China in 1873 and by 1900/01 accounted for 16 per cent of Bombay's exports in value, overtaking opium and equalling oilseeds (raw cotton accounted for 28 per cent).[6] However, after 1905 this export trade petered out and the relatively good

[6] Calculated from ibid.

performance of Bombay's exports in the 1916–26 decade is largely to be attributed to high prices for raw cotton and a good market for it in Japan. The value of wheat exports also increased in the late 19th century.

The trend in the import trade is more puzzling and therefore deserves careful analysis. What accounts for the fact that, at various points in time, and particularly in the 1886–1901 period and after 1921, Bombay's import trade surpassed Calcutta's in value? Moreover, how are we to explain that its overall share in India's import trade remained more or less constant during the period under study while that of Karachi increased mainly at its expense, without supposing that this loss, which could not have been compensated in its entirety by a gain at the expense of Madras, must have somewhat been made up for at the expense of Calcutta?

Very detailed mapping of the hinterlands of the various ports in India at different points in time has to my knowledge never been done (see however Banga, 1992, for a recent attempt), which is of course a limiting factor. Networks for the redistribution of imported goods are much more difficult to analyse than those through which agricultural produce is exported; the latter are, so to speak, visible 'on the ground' and have also attracted a lot of attention from colonial officials. The former, which distribute a great variety of goods often in limited quantities, operate in a less obvious manner. For reasons of space, I shall limit myself to general remarks which are in the nature of informed guesses.

At a somewhat theoretical level, Bombay's capacity to increase over time its share of the import trade of India to the detriment of Calcutta has to be explained by having recourse to one of the following hypotheses: either an increase in the size of its hinterland at the expense of Calcutta's, or, if hinterlands were relatively fixed, growing income disparities between Bombay's and Calcutta's respective hinterlands making for greater consumption of imported items in the area supplied by Bombay (supposing an equal propensity to import in all regions, a supposition we shall make for convenience' sake and which is in any case not entirely unsubstantiated by available evidence), or widely divergent investment patterns reflecting much more rapid industrial growth in Western than in Eastern India. Let us examine each of these hypotheses in turn.

Change in the size of hinterlands could be either the result of the spatial expansion of Bombay's sphere of influence at the expense of Calcutta's or of a quicker pace of demographic growth in its existing sphere of influence. The latter hypothesis can be immediately rejected. Evidence from the population Censuses between 1872 and 1941 tends to show that the rate of growth of the population living in the zone served by Calcutta was marginally higher than that of the population living in Bombay's sphere of influence.[7] There remains therefore the possibility that Bombay's sphere of influence increased spatially at the expense of Calcutta's. Actually there is some evidence that, during the first phase of the railway era, c. 1860–1900, there occurred a certain redefinition in the hinterlands of the various ports and Bombay managed, thanks to the railway, to capture trade flows which were previously channeled through Calcutta. Given the fact that Bombay was closer to British and European ports than Calcutta, it could have made sense for an importer operating in interior areas which were more or less equidistant from both ports to reroute some imports to the Western Indian port. One has also to take into consideration the fact that, in the 1880–1916 period, there was a sort of rate war between railway companies serving the three ports of Karachi, Bombay and Calcutta (Hurd, op. cit., 753–4). Although its outcome is not very clear, railway statistics indicate that Bombay increased its share of the trade of the United Provinces and Hyderabad State, two areas which in the pre-railway age were largely included in Calcutta's sphere.[8] So the pattern of railway development seems to have somehow favoured Bombay at the expense of Calcutta, and it had a greater impact on imports than on exports because the former were not subject to the kind of physical constraints which largely influenced the location of export crops. A change in the size of their respective hinterlands may therefore be the major explanation for Bombay's success in enlarging its share of India's import trade at the expense of Calcutta in the 1871–1901 period. Imports of cotton-textile machinery through Bombay also appear to have been always higher than imports of jute machinery through Calcutta, but the evidence of trade statistics is not enough to suggest

[7] During the 1871–1921 period, the east zone, which largely corresponded with Calcutta's hinterland had an average annual growth rate of 0.52 per cent, which was higher than the rates of the west zone (0.14 per cent) and of the central zone (0.47 per cent), which formed the bulk of Bombay's hinterland. [See L. and P. Visaria, 'Population (1757–1947)', in *Cambridge Economic History of India*, vol. 2, Table 5.8, p. 490.]

[8] In 1888/89, railborne exports from Bombay to the United Provinces represented 6.5 per cent of total railborne exports from Bombay and those destined for the Nizam's territory accounted for 5 per cent of the total. In 1907/08, the respective shares of the United Provinces and of the Nizam's territory in Bombay's railborne export trade were 8 and 6 per cent. (Calculated from figures in *Gazetteer*, op. cit., p. 448.)

widely divergent investment patterns in the areas respectively served by Bombay and by Calcutta.

During the following 20 years, while India's overall imports increased at a very quick pace, there was a reversal of trend as Calcutta regained some of the ground lost during the previous period and saw its import trade regularly surpass that of Bombay. It may be that this reversal was due to the changing fortunes in the rate war between railway companies, but I have not been able to test that hypothesis empirically. This was in any case a period of great commercial prosperity for India's two major cities, in spite of a certain amount of disruption created by the First World War.

However, since the middle of the 19th century, the economy of both cities had undergone some diversification as a sector of modern industry had developed and foreign trade can therefore no longer serve as the only gauge of their respective rankings. Bombay's cotton textile industry and Calcutta's jute mill industry were by 1914 largely comparable in terms of capital and output value while the labour force employed was much larger in the Calcutta jute mills than in the Bombay cotton mills (216,000 as against 110,000), reflecting the more labour-intensive character of the jute industry (Morris, in Kumar, 1983, 553–676). The two big cities then accounted for more than 50 per cent of total large-scale factory output in India.[9] In spite of the rapid development of the cotton-textile industry in a certain number of inland centres (Ahmedabad, Sholapur, Cawnpore) and of the location of the steel industry in Jamshedpur, the 'dual dominance' of Bombay and Calcutta over the large-scale factory sector remained basically unchallenged, especially if one takes into consideration that some of the largest factories situated outside Bombay and Calcutta had been set up and were controlled by Bombay or Calcutta-based firms (for example Tata Iron and Steel).

In the financial sector also, Bombay and Calcutta reigned supreme. They were the seats of the two major Presidency banks (the Bank of Madras operating on a much smaller scale) as well as of the exchange banks and most of the large Indian banks. By 1918, 83 per cent of the capital of all rupee joint-stock companies in India and 92 per cent of the

[9] Calculated from M. D. Morris, 'The Growth of Large-scale Industry to 1947', in *Cambridge Economic History*, vol. 2, Table 7.22, p. 641. Jute manufactures, entirely concentrated in Calcutta, represented 15 per cent of the net output of large-scale factory production, and cotton textiles 36 per cent, of which Bombay accounted for over 40 per cent. Assuming that the two cities accounted for approximately 50 per cent of the output of all other industries, i.e. around 25 per cent of total factory output, one reaches a total of 50–55 per cent.

capital of Sterling companies operating in India was controlled from Bombay and Calcutta (Goswami, in Chaudhuri, 1990, vol. II, 88). The respective shares of Bengal and Bombay were 43 and 40 per cent for rupee companies, 73 and 19 per cent for Sterling companies, the difference being largely due to tea companies which were almost all Sterling. Calcutta's largely European firms then controlled resources which were larger than those controlled by Bombay's mostly Indian firms, a fact which is not surprising, given the overall domination of British capital over the 'modern' sector of the Indian economy. But it does not invalidate the thesis of 'dual dominance'.

'Dual Dominance' under Fire—1920–1947

In the post-1920 period the dual dominance of Bombay and Calcutta over foreign trade, high finance and large-scale industry began to be somewhat eroded. At the political level, there was some shift in power and influence from coastal to interior areas, as exemplified by the rise of New Delhi as the effective capital of India in the 1920s and the emergence of the United Provinces as the main stronghold of the Indian nationalist movement. There were parallel trends in the economic domain: in a globally stagnant agricultural economy, the only region which continued to experience a significant growth in output was 'Greater Punjab' (Blyn, 1966). In large-scale industry, most of the growth of output occurred outside Bombay and Calcutta. After 1922, the Bombay cotton-textile industry ceased to grow and the 1920s and 1930s saw the rise of inland centres such as Ahmedabad and Coimbatore. Between 1920 and 1939 Bombay's share in India's cotton-textile industry fell from 43.9 to 28.3 per cent in spindles, and from 51 to 33.2 per cent for looms.[10] While Calcutta's jute industry continued to grow in the 1920s, although at a reduced rate, in the 1930s it actually contracted. The share of Bombay and Calcutta in global large-scale factory output had fallen to 30–35 per cent on the eve of World War II.[11] In the 1920s Calcutta did marginally better than Bombay but it was then more directly hit by the world depression which deeply affected the tea and jute sectors working almost exclusively for the export markets. In the late 1930s, however, Calcutta benefited from some investment in industry by large international firms, mainly British (Dunlop, Imperial Chemical

[10] See *Indian Textile Journal Jubilee Number*, 1940.

[11] Calculated from Morris, *passim*. The share of jute manufactures in total output had fallen to 8 per cent, that of cotton textiles to 29 per cent (of which Bombay accounted only for one third).

Industries, BAT, etc.) and its industrial base started diversifying away from jute, while no comparable move was noticeable in Bombay. Calcutta's mostly Marwari firms also played an important role in the development of two of the 'growth' industries in India, sugar and paper (Bagchi, 1973).

In foreign trade, the most striking development was, within a much reduced volume of business, the relative buoyancy of Bombay's import trade as contrasted to its collapse in Calcutta. If one agrees with Bagchi that, from 1914 onwards, there was 'relative stability of the outlines of the hinterlands of major ports' (Bagchi, 1976, 253), how to then account for post-1921 developments? In the 1921–26 period, while Calcutta's import trade contracted, Bombay's imports continued to increase, though at a rate which was much slower than during the previous 20 years. Part of the explanation seems to lie in the exceptional figures for imports of cotton-textile machinery during that quinquennial period: they accounted for 5.9 per cent of all imports (as against 2.2 per cent in 1916–21 and 2.4 per cent in 1926–31). During the same period imports of jute machinery accounted for 2 per cent of imports through Calcutta.[12] Most of the machinery imported through Bombay was destined for Ahmedabad and other inland centres. In the following period, the contrast between Bombay and Calcutta is partly explained in terms of the unequal pace of development of import substitution in cotton textiles: by 1930, Eastern India was by far the greatest consumer of imported British piecegoods, while in the rest of India the market had been largely captured by domestic producers. Between 1930 and 1939, Lancashire lost most of its remaining Indian market, mostly situated in the Eastern Region, and by 1939 piecegoods represented only 7 per cent of all Calcutta imports.[13]

In 1939, although inland cities such as Ahmedabad, Cawnpore and Coimbatore had emerged as important industrial centres and were the seat of some fairly large business groups (Kasturbhai and Sarabhai in Ahmedabad, J. K. Singhania in Cawnpore), while Karachi and Madras had somewhat enlarged their share of India's foreign seaborne trade (in 1938/39 the two ports accounted for one-quarter of total imports and one-third of total exports) the overall dominance of Bombay and Calcutta over industry, finance and long-distance trade remained, in a

---

[12] Calculated from figures of textile machinery imports in A. K. Bagchi, *Private Investment in India, 1930–1939*, Cambridge, 1973, Table 7.10, p. 258 and Table 8.1, p. 273.

[13] See *Annual Statement of the Seaborne Trade of British India, 1938–39*, Calcutta, 1940.

reduced degree. The two cities were then more or less evenly matched in terms of corporate power. A survey of the largest 57 business groups operating in India in 1939 (Markovits, 1985, 192–3) shows that 24 Calcutta-based groups controlled 645 joint-stock companies with a total paid-up capital of over Rs 100 crores, while 16 Bombay-based groups controlled 131 companies with a paid-up capital of almost 60 crores. In terms of actual economic power, the two cities were more evenly matched than the figures suggest, for many companies in Bombay were undercapitalized and had very large fixed assets.

The Second World War spelt doom for Calcutta's economy which suffered from the proximity of military operations and the impact of the Bengal famine. Partition was the decisive blow from which the city never really recovered. However it retained its slight lead over Bombay in terms of corporate power till some time in the 1950s. In that decade, the government's decision to equalize freight rates on coal took away its last advantage over Bombay. The political troubles of the late 1960s led to Calcutta's final demotion from its status as one of the two major centres of business activity in India. Bombay has clearly emerged as the winner in the two-century-long fight for supremacy. Calcutta is today struggling to maintain its second place in the face of the rapid rise of both Delhi and Bangalore.

In Search of an Explanation: Business Cycles and Entrepreneurial Response

The economic history of India between 1830 and 1950 has been characterized by large-scale fluctuations in the business cycle, some directly linked to international conditions, others more locally determined. Between 1830 and 1865, Bombay was the great beneficiary of the upswing in the opium and cotton markets, but in the next phase, lasting till the depression of 1930, Calcutta benefited by its proximity to the major producing zones of jute, tea and coal, which were the three major 'growth' commodities in the Indian economy. It would thus seem that Bombay's capacity to maintain global parity in the post-1865 phase was 'counter-cyclical' in nature. Why was Bombay over the long-term more successful than Calcutta at capitalizing on the upswings in the trade cycle? In the absence of a clearly interventionist policy by the colonial government aimed at redressing regional imbalances, the answer has to be found in differences in the behaviour of the business communities of the two cities.

Entrepreneurial Responses in Bombay and Calcutta:
A Global Comparison

Measured by most conventional standards (capitalization, profits, value of output), the performance of business enterprise in Bombay and Calcutta does not seem to reveal major differences before the end of the colonial era. Calcutta business would even appear to have done slightly better. However, on closer examination, the achievements of Bombay businessmen over more than a century appear more impressive than those of their Calcutta colleagues, if one recalls the many advantages enjoyed by the capital of Bengal within the political economy of colonial India.

Bombay's ability to maximize its few advantages and minimize its many handicaps has obviously to do with the specific way in which its business community responded to opportunities and challenges. A very general comparison between business behaviour in Bombay and Calcutta would bring out a greater flexibility and a greater capacity for innovation on the part of Bombay businessmen.

They seem to have been better at adapting to changing trade conditions. Thus, although opium had been the mainstay of the fortunes of so many businessmen, the decline of the opium trade in the 1860–1910 period does not seem to have had a very negative impact on Bombay business. Most firms which had been prominent in the opium trade managed a successful reconversion towards the cotton trade or the cotton-textile industry; the number of casualties does not appear to have been very high. By contrast, in Calcutta the collapse of the indigo market in 1833 led to the demise of the major Agency firms which never went back into business.

The story of the cotton textile industry shows the same kind of flexibility. At first the Bombay millowners tried to gain a share of the domestic market in yarn and cloth but, faced with fierce competition from Lancashire and, increasingly from other centres in India, from 1873 onwards they turned to the Chinese market in a big way. In the 1880s, 80 per cent of Bombay yarn production went to China (Buchanan, 1934). However, faced with growing competition from Chinese and Japanese mills, they turned gradually again to the domestic market and, taking advantage of the Swadeshi movement of 1904–07, they reoriented their mills towards the production of cloth for the Indian consumer (Mehta, 1954). On the other hand in Calcutta the jute industry did not manage to carve a secure market for its products before the 1890s and, after a period of exceptional prosperity up to the First World War, was faced with a diminishing market due to the progress of jute substitutes (Chakrabarty, 1989). While the Bombay industry constantly introduced changes in layout and organization to adapt itself to changes in market conditions, Calcutta's jute barons remained faithful to fixed methods and refused to see the writing on the wall.

More generally, Calcutta business was less successful than Bombay's at shifting its activities to the domestic market, once external trade went through a prolonged depression from 1926 onwards. Of the major industries working for the internal market and, from 1930 onwards, benefiting from a varying degree of customs protection, only two, sugar and paper, owed part of their development to Calcutta's entrepreneurs, while cotton, iron and steel and cement were all three dominated by Bombay firms.

Apart from greater flexibility, Bombay businessmen also showed greater capacities for innovation. Most of the 'firsts' in the history of Indian finance and large-scale industry originated in Bombay: the first successful modern factory was Cowasji Davar's Oriental Spinning floated in 1854. Modern methods of financial promotion were introduced by the extraordinary financial genius, Premchand Roychand, who towered over the Bombay financial scene for 15 years (Rungta, 1970, 81–3). The first Stock Exchange, however rudimentary, was started in Bombay in 1875, while in Calcutta the Stock Exchange was formally constituted only in 1908. Bombay entrepreneurs were responsible for most of the technological innovations in Indian industry: thus the ring spindle was first introduced and adapted to Indian conditions at Tata's Empress Mills in Nagpur, a Bombay-financed and controlled company; Portland cement production was started by the Bombay firm of Khatau; modern steel production started in 1913 in the works of Tisco at Jamshedpur, another Tata company; the first large-scale hydroelectric schemes were promoted by the Tatas in the Western Ghats; the automobile and aeronautics industries were started by the great Bombay-based pioneer, Walchand Hirachand. The contributions of Calcutta entrepreneurs were less numerous and less remarkable: George Acland started the first jute mill in 1855, using an extremely rudimentary technology; Sir P. C. Ray pioneered the chemical and pharmaceutical industries at the time of the Swadeshi movement.

Although one should beware of exaggerating the contrast between the two cities and of romanticizing Bombay entrepreneurs, among whom were included the usual contingent of crooks and failures, the fact remains that over a long period Bombay business showed more dynamism than Calcutta's.

Race, Community and Enterprise:
The Contrast between Bombay and Calcutta

Since Bagchi's pioneering study of 1970 (Bagchi, in Leach and Mukherjee, 1970, 223–56) drew attention to the contrast between the situation in Western India and in the rest of India, not much work has been done on the impact of race and community on business. However, I think it is in that direction that lies the most plausible explanation of the contrast between Bombay and Calcutta.

It has been often remarked that in Bombay relations between Indian and European businessmen were marked by less discrimination and less mutual antagonism than in Calcutta. To account for the difference, scholars have put forward two main explanations: firstly the fact that Western India was conquered by the British at a later stage than Eastern India, thus escaping the period of unabashed exploitation which cost so dearly to indigenous merchants in Bengal, and secondly the exceptional role played in Bombay by the Parsi community which was Indian but had a special relationship with the British. We need not go in detail into this problem here, but the situation in Bombay in the first quarter of the century is aptly characterized by Asiya Siddiqi who writes:

there was, on the whole, little conflict between Indian merchants on the one hand and, on the other, European merchants and the Bombay Government. The Indian merchants, along with the members of a small group of European agency houses, with whom they were often intimately connected as brokers and business partners, formed a remarkably close-knit oligarchy which governed both the island and its overseas trade (Siddiqi, 1982, 305).

The close relationship between the great Parsi entrepreneur, Jamsetji Jejeebhoy and the British China-merchant, William Jardine, exemplifies that situation. During the same period in Calcutta, the dominance of the European Agency Houses was well established and their Indian collaborators were never treated as equals. When the Agency Houses collapsed in 1833, it was precisely the group of Indian collaborators who paid the heaviest price (Bagchi, 1987, 147–9) and the story repeated itself at the time of the crisis of the Union Bank 'which shook whatever confidence wealthy Indians in Calcutta had in their ability to collaborate with Europeans on profitable terms' (ibid., 223). The contrasting fates of Dwarkanath Tagore and Jamsetji Jejeebhoy, who were near-contemporaries, highlight the different way in which partnerships between Indians and Europeans worked in Calcutta and in Bombay.

By the middle of the 19th century, the contrast between Bombay and Calcutta was clear: in Calcutta Indian businessmen were excluded from the upper ranks of the business hierarchy and operated only as brokers, not as partners, while in Bombay partnerships between Europeans and Indians, mostly but not exclusively Parsis, were a common feature of business life, in the opium as well as in the cotton trade. In the promotion of banks as well, between 1840 and 1860 Indians were as much involved as Europeans (Bagchi, op. cit., 357).

In the post-1865 period, indigenous business in Bombay suffered in its turn from the increasing European domination of international shipping and trading networks, but it nevertheless managed to retain strong positions in some fields of foreign trade (in particular, China, the Middle East and East Africa) as well as in the cotton-textile industry. In spite of losing ground to Europeans (and Japanese) in the cotton trade, Indian businessmen in Bombay maintained an overall position of equality with the Europeans. In no sector of the economy was European business in Bombay capable of establishing the kind of oligopolistic control that a few managing agencies exercised in Calcutta over jute, tea and coal. On the eve of World War II, the largest business firm in Bombay was an Indian firm, Tatas, with assets which were larger than those of the major European managing agencies such as Killick, Nixon & Co; Forbes, Forbes, Campbell; Wallace Bros.; and James Finlay & Co. Out of 16 business groups included in the above-mentioned survey, ten were exclusively under Indian control, four were British-controlled, but with Indian partners, one was Indian-controlled with a British partner (Associated Cement Companies) and one was controlled by a Baghdadi Jewish family (E. D. Sassoon & Co). By contrast, in Calcutta, out of 24 groups, 20 were under exclusive British control, one under American control (A. Yule), one under joint British and Indian control (Martin Burn), one British-managed but financially controlled by a big zamindar, the Maharajah of Darbhanga (O. Steel), and only one under exclusive Indian control (Birla).

Although most indigenous businessmen hailed from only one region, Gujarat, the ethnic and communal diversity of Bombay's business world was striking: it included merchants belonging to many communities of Gujarat, including the Parsis, the Hindu Vanis and Bhatias, the Muslim Bohras, Khojas and Memons, as well as businessmen from other provinces of India (Sind, Marwar), Baghdadi Jews (the different branches of the famous Sassoon family), non-British Europeans (the Swiss firm of Volkarts), Japanese (Toyo Menka Kaisha) and Britishers of various origins. The contrast was clear with the increasingly polarized and oligopolistic world of Calcutta where only two communities mattered: the Scots and the Marwaris. By 1914, merchants belonging to other communities (Bengalis, North Indian Muslims, Armenians, Jews) played only a minor role.

The polarization in Calcutta between the Scots and the Marwaris, the result of a symbiotic relationship which turned more and more antagonistic in the post-1914 period, had damaging effects on the fortunes of the city. The Calcutta Scots had become, in the second half of the 19th century, such an entrenched business community that they had taken complete control of trade in the three commodities which were the mainstay of Calcutta's prosperity: tea, jute and coal. During the same period, the Marwaris gradually replaced the Bengalis as brokers to the big European business houses in Calcutta (Timberg, 1978). The Scots behaved very arrogantly with their Marwari brokers who, in the jute trade, were an indispensable link to the rural areas, and did not form partnerships with them. The only way for the Marwaris to make a real breakthrough in the trade was therefore to resort to *fatka* (speculation) which they started doing around 1905 with a devastating effect on the spot prices of jute (Goswami, 1982, 143). As the Marwaris advanced from jute trading to jute baling, from there to shipping jute directly abroad and, after 1918, to setting up jute mills, the whole sector suffered from constant price wars which led to a very unhealthy situation. The racial arrogance of the Scots, signalled by their refusal to seek a compromise with the Marwaris, was partly responsible for the long-term decline of the industry in the post-1914 period. In the complex process of collaboration-cum-competition between those two business communities, they were both transformed. To fight European domination, the Marwaris were led to maximizing their existing assets, of which the major one was their skill at speculating. On the other hand, to prevent the growing inroads of the Marwaris into what they perceived as their preserve, the Scots increasingly relied on their political clout, which was however diminishing in a time of growing Indian nationalism. In the bargain they largely lost whatever entrepreneurial drive they ever had. Although the Marwaris emerged as the eventual winners, since by 1950 they controlled practically the whole of the jute sector and part of the tea sector, their victory was costly: they bought at highly inflated prices mills which were full of obsolete machinery, had a bad record of industrial relations and faced the problem of diminishing markets. They had wasted a lot of energy and money to control a declining business and in the process the whole of Calcutta's economy suffered since Mar,, wari capitalists, too busy buying jute mills (and tea gardens) invested little in the more promising fields. There are many causes to Calcutta's post-1940 economic decline but the racial polarization of its business world is not the least of them.

Of course Bombay's business world was not the picture of harmony either. There were conflicts galore, especially in the difficult decades of the 1920s and 1930s. Racial exclusiveness and arrogance on the part of British businessmen was not unknown either, but the racial conflict did not dominate everything as in Calcutta. The conflict between the 'industrialists' and the 'marketeers' on the Bombay cotton market (Gordon, 1978) was not primarily along racial lines. If the 'marketeers' were all Indians, the industrialists were also in their majority Indians.

Relations between Hindu and Muslim businessmen also appear to have been better in Bombay than in Calcutta. Bombay's active Gujarati Muslim business communities fully participated in the life of the various business associations, such as the Indian Merchants' Chamber, and a separate Muslim association was not created before the mid-1940s. In Calcutta, on the other hand, where Muslim participation in business was probably on the whole less important than in Bombay, but where there were a few powerful Muslim business groups (Adamji, Ispahani), a separate Muslim Chamber of Commerce was created as early as in 1932.

Less racial and communal strife in the business world meant a more rational use of capital resources. Businessmen belonging to various communities more easily formed partnerships in Bombay than elsewhere in India. Shareholding in joint-stock companies was more cross-communal in character there than in Calcutta.[14]

The conclusions I draw from this rapid study are mainly two: firstly that, within the common framework of a colonial economy, significantly different regional sub-systems can develop, depending on the specific curve of the trade cycle in different commodity markets and on the varying capacity of the local business communities to capitalize on the upswings; secondly, that over the long-term the particular ethos and 'communal mix' of the local business community can be more decisive than factor endowment in explaining the rise of a city. Thus, while Calcutta suffered a lot from being the sterile battleground of a racial war dividing its business community, Bombay benefited by a more dynamic

[14] As comes out of perusing shareholders' lists included in P. Lovett, *The Mirror of Investment*, Calcutta, 1927.

atmosphere of emulation and competition. This is not to say that the kind of capitalistic development that Bombay has come to exemplify is morally appealing; it is after all the city of the scam. But, in terms of efficiency, it clearly emerged as the winner.

Bibliography

Annual Statement of the Seaborne Trade of British India 1938–39, Calcutta, CISD, 1940.

Bagchi, A. K. (1970). 'European and Indian Entrepreneurship in India, 1900–30', in E. Leach and S. N. Mukherjee (eds) (1970). *Elites in South Asia*, Cambridge, Cambridge University Press, pp. 223–56.

—— (1973). *Private Investment in India, 1900–1939*, Cambridge, Cambridge University Press.

—— (1976). 'Reflections on Patterns of Regional Growth in India During the Period of British Rule', *Bengal Past and Present*, vol. XCV(I), no 180, pp. 247–89.

—— (1987). *The Evolution of the State Bank of India. The Roots, 1806–1876. Part I: The Early Years, 1806–1860*, Bombay, Oxford University Press.

Banga, I. (ed.) (1992). *Ports and their Hinterlands in India (1700–1950)*, Delhi, Manohar.

Blyn, G. (1966). *Agricultural Trends in India 1891–1947: Output, Availability and Productivity*, Philadelphia, University of Pennsylvania Press.

Buchanan, D. H. (1934). *The Development of Capitalistic Enterprise in India*, New York, Macmillan.

Chakrabarty, D. (1989). *Rethinking Working-Class History, Bengal 1890–1940*, Princeton, Princeton University Press.

Chaudhuri, K. N., 'Foreign Trade and Balance of Payments (1757–1947)', in D. Kumar (ed.), *The Cambridge Economic History of India*, vol. 2, 1983, pp. 804–77.

The Gazetteer of Bombay City and Island, (1909). vol. I, Bombay.

Gordon, A. D. D. (1978). *Businessmen and Politics; Rising Nationalism and a Modernising Economy in Bombay, 1918–1933*, Delhi, Manohar, 1978.

Goswami, O. (1982). 'Collaboration and Conflict: European and Indian Capitalists and the Jute Economy of Bengal, 1919–39', *Indian Economic and Social History Review*, vol. XXI, no 2, 1982, pp. 141–79.

—— 'Calcutta's Economy 1918–1970. The Fall from Grace', in S. Chaudhuri (ed.) (1990). *Calcutta, The Living City*, Vol. II, Calcutta, Oxford University Press, pp. 88–96.

Hunter, W. W. (1886). *The Indian Empire. Its People History and Products*, London, Trubner, (2nd ed.).

Hurd, J. M. (1983). 'Railways', in D. Kumar (ed.), *The Cambridge Economic History of India*, vol. 2, Cambridge, Cambridge University Press, 1983, pp. 737–61.

Kosambi, M. (1986). *Bombay in Transition: The Growth and Social Ecology of a Colonial City, 1880–1980*, Stockholm, Almqvist & Wiksell.

Lovett, P. (1927). *The Mirror of Investment*, Calcutta, Capital.

Markovits, C. (1985). *Indian Business and Nationalist Politics, 1931–39*, Cambridge, Cambridge University Press.

Mehta, S. D. (1954). *The Cotton Mills of India, 1854–1954*. Bombay, The Millowners' Association.

Morris, M. D. (1983). 'The Growth of Large-Scale Industry to 1947' in D. Kumar, (ed.) (1983). *The Cambridge Economic History of India*, vol. 2, Cambridge, Cambridge University Press, pp. 553–76.

Rungta, R. S. (1970). *Rise of Business Corporations in India, 1851–1900*, Cambridge, Cambridge University Press.

Siddiqi, A. (1982). 'The Business World of Jamsetjee Jejeebhoy', *Indian Economic and Social History Review*, Vol. XIX, nos 3 & 4, pp. 301–24.

Timberg, T. A. (1978). *The Marwaris: From Traders to Industrialists*, Delhi, Vikas, 1978.

Visaria. L. and P. Visaria (1983). 'Population (1757–1947)', in D. Kumar (ed.), *The Cambridge Economic History of India*, vol. 2, 1983, pp. 463–532.

3

Bombay in the Global Economy

NIGEL HARRIS

The paper assumes, but does not argue, that the present phase of capitalism is characterized by continuing integration such that one can begin to perceive a single global economy emerging from what have hitherto been constituent national parts. The process affects to different degrees capital, commodities and labour. However, most theorization about economies is still heavily dominated by assumptions about national economic autonomy, the characteristic feature of the preceding phase of the system, lasting for more than a century.

'Structural adjustment' as employed here is not primarily concerned with short-term adjustment (associated, for example, with the World Bank's Structural Adjustment lending programme to Sub-Saharan Africa), but rather with the continuing reshaping of national economic activity, of company structure and behaviour and the reaction of labour forces to increasing integration—or, the same thing, exposure to the predominant influences of external markets. That reshaping is essentially one in which local and changing comparative advantages in a world economy are developed and enhanced, while other features of the local economy are eliminated. Such processes are characteristic of all forms the economy, especially the more dynamic is the pattern of growth, so in principle the change need not cause particular alarm, although it is clearly important for economic managers to have timely warning of dangers to existing activity.

The type of global economy which is emerging is still only imperfectly apparent, but there is no reason to believe that poor countries or poor people within poor countries are peculiarly disadvantaged by integration.

On the contrary, it is national economic restrictions in the developed countries which inhibit the full development of the comparative advantage in cheap labour in developing countries. Integration can thus, for the first time, bring into world production the masses of underemployed workers of developing countries, a result clearly on the record impossible in the old order of nationally separate developing economies.

Nor is there evidence to suggest that external liberalization increases income inequalities. On the contrary, whatever evidence we have suggests the reverse—a semi-closed national economy can lead to the greatest income differentials, and can particularly distort the productive system in favour of upper income consumption.

In any case, the choices on integration seem to grow increasingly limited. Without joining the process, at best a country risks losing both capital and labour to the rest of the world; at worst, facing the sort of problems afflicting the old Soviet Union, culminating in the disintegration of the country and a forced programme of precipitate reform with very severe damage to popular livelihood and the basic economy.

Bombay

The degree of Bombay's internationalization is, by standards elsewhere, still quite modest, and the pace of change of the city's output relatively slow. However, it has changed and reduced its disproportionate dependence upon manufacturing (in 1962, manufacturing supplied 41 per cent of the city's jobs and generated 50 per cent of the income), permitting it to play the more important role of financial capital of India (including the headquarters of most major domestic and foreign banks and corporations, the nearest equivalent to a national stock exchange, the development banks, Reserve Bank of India etc.).

However, the character of the city's manufacturing also gives it a key role as supplier of consumer and other durables (television sets, two and four wheeled vehicles and parts, refrigerators, pumps and motors) to a growing market of middle-income buyers, a market on some estimates as large as 125 million. By contrast, Calcutta, so crucial for the macro-economic strategy of the Second Five Year Plan, has hardly recovered from the great shift away from public sector heavy industrial development.

In general, cities in developing countries have a lower degree of specialization than those in developed countries, a feature that arises from, among other things, the high costs of movement which inhibit the emergence of national interdependence. Large cities thus aggregate to themselves activities which, in a better developed transport system, might be spread among several cities. Certainly, modern economic activity frequently clusters closely around those concentrations of infrastructure and skilled workers which are the cities.

External liberalization will tend to enhance specialization. The process of developing external market-enforced specializations in some fields, however, is matched by losing them in others. Most obviously threatened are those sectors which have been important in the import-substitution strategy, whose survival depends most heavily on the continuation of protection.

The data to hand is very aggregated and the definition of a Bombay economy is arbitrary, but examining some of the main sectors may allow us to make some provisional observations about what structural adjustment might do in reshaping the city's output and employment.

Manufacturing Industry

Liberalization in Europe and North America produced, in the recessions of the 1970s and 1980s, a sharp decline in manufacturing in the older industrial cities (a decline, albeit less dramatic, also occurred in Tokyo). New York lost some 35 per cent of its manufacturing employment in the 1970s, and London some two-thirds over a longer period. In Bombay's case, despite the slow pace of change, there also already seems to have been some measure of deindustrialization. The city experienced stagnation in the seventies and decline in the eighties when total employment in the registered sector also fell; however, employment in the unregistered sector is estimated to have increased by 159 per cent between 1973 and 1987 (*Regional Economy of BMR*, n.d.). As the Deshpandes have shown (1991, p. 26), formal sector employment in industry declined absolutely in the 1980s (and manufacturing's share of the city's output had already declined in the 1970s from 41 to 37 per cent). The rate of growth of total output also declined quite sharply (from 4.2 per cent in the 1970s, to 1.9 per cent in the first half of the 1980s). Private manufacturing contracted by nearly 5 per cent per annum in the 1980s (falling in total from over 600,000 in 1980 to 450,000 in 1990).

While the bulk of this decline derived from the poor performance in cotton textiles and garments (employment here seems to have fallen from something over 200,000 to a remarkable 60–70,000 in the two decades to 1990), it also affected food, machinery and chemicals (negative rates by sector are listed in BMR, April 1991). Simultaneously, there was disproportionate expansion (150 per cent between 1975/77 and 1985/87) in rubber products, plastics, oil and oil products, and lesser expansion in wool, silk and synthetic fibres, and in transport equipment. Thus, it would seem from these figures (and they are somewhat out of date) that, like cities elsewhere, Bombay is beginning to decline as a manufacturing centre—or at least changing the scale of operation from registered to unregistered units—and its manufacturing output is now more narrowly specialized in the petrochemical field.

Bombay established its industrial pre-eminence through the textile industry, and it is surprising that the performance of the industry has been poor for so long. Although the composition of Bombay's industry has been changing—by the sixties, lower value production had moved out of the city, and the city's mills were more capital intensive and larger scale than the Indian average (and, as noted earlier, shifting from cotton to wool, silk and synthetic fibre)—protection for long inhibited the movement of the industry into the high-growth sector of world industry, ready-made garments (presumably the low cost of tailoring in the closed Indian market rendered ready-made garment manufacture unprofitable, whereas in the world at large, high-cost tailoring encouraged the reverse development). By contrast, it was the swift movement of the Hong Kong industry into this sector which created the basis for very rapid industrialization. Since the Indian industry, by contrast, has been focused on the slow growing domestic market, both its employment potential and its role in spreading industrialization have been frustrated. The 'sick' industry policy has only exaggerated the lack of dynamism. Nowhere is this more striking than in the, until recently, very disappointing export performance. Since the introduction of the reform programme in China in the late 1970s, textile and garment exports have soared to reach some 8.5 per cent of the world's trade in these goods by the 1990s; India's share has stagnated at around 2 to 3 per cent, barely more than fast-growing Pakistan.

Low profitability has led to low investment. It is said that half the machinery in Bombay's mill sector is 40 or more years old (operating at roughly double its rated lifetime). Poor profits meant that by 1987, it was said, the value of the land where many mills were located was greater than the value of the mills themselves. The owners pressed the government to be allowed to escape.

In an expanding city economy, this might have been a welcome opportunity for a major redevelopment of an important part of the city. In the past, the millowners have resolutely opposed any schemes for the relocation of their enterprises, keeping the city and a major part of its land trapped in activities which are inappropriate to the future of a large city like Bombay. The state and city's authorities have also equivocated as to whether they wanted the mills where they were or elsewhere in the Metropolitan Region. However, with a planned relocation, it might then have been possible to think seriously about the future economic role of the city and what would be the best use of the large land area suddenly made available. Part of that scheme would, of course, have had to include schemes for the retraining and redeployment of that part of the workforce which did not wish to relocate with the mills. However, in a stagnating economy, the desperate competition for work usually paralyses any such ambitions: the freeze on economic change then conceals a slow decay into depression, to the point where the industry is liable to become a write-off.

Most recently, however, it seems the more energetic parts of the Bombay industry have begun to respond to the loss of markets in the former Soviet Union and eastern Europe by searching out new markets in the rest of the world. In the first five months of 1992, exports grew by 17 per cent on the same period one year earlier, and by 33 per cent for garments. Has the combination of domestic reform, a depreciated currency and loss of market at long last produced an export boom? One year's results are hardly enough to support a firm opinion, but external markets are now, even if temporarily, stimulating significant increases in investment in parts of the industry. But India is still far behind its competitors in this field, and the reform programme still has a long way to go in terms of relaxing the restrictions on importing cheaper cotton and other raw materials, on the redeployment of labour and on exit terms for 'sick' mills.

Paradoxically, the finished output of—as opposed to the inputs to—the textile and garment industry has a relatively low level of protection, so that liberalization ought, on this restricted basis, in the short term, to stimulate expansion in India even if not in Bombay (where the industry may be redistributed to other localities). Other sectors of Bombay's manufacturing industry ought to have considerable potential in external trade, given the importance in the city and in world trade of engineering goods and chemicals. However, these are among the sectors most heavily protected, and therefore likely to be most negatively affected by any rapid external liberalization. A recent study of India's effective protection rates in the late 1980s (Aksoy and Ettori, 1992) enumerates the most protected sectors (in declining order) as follows: synthetic fibres/resins (162%); synthetic textiles (100%); electronic equipment and parts (92%); edible oils (85%); iron and steel products, and castings/forgings (72%); heavy chemicals (68%); non-electrical machinery (64%); cotton yarns (52%); electrical machinery (42%). Furthermore, upstream tax levels (particularly in steel and capital goods) exaggerate the uncompetitive character of the engineering and chemicals industries, often setting the prices of final output at 50 to 100 per cent above world market levels. It is not clear how, in policy terms, the government will tackle these severe difficulties; liberalizing the imports of inputs in order to make the engineering and chemicals industry competitive could in turn have strong negative effects in the steel and capital goods industries; on the other hand, without cheaper inputs, what ought to be Bombay's comparative advantage in manufacturing cannot be expressed.

The decline in the output of important manufacturing sectors in the 1980s may in fact be no more than a redistribution between different parts of the region. Medium and large scale industry has for long been relocating along the main highways beyond the boundaries of the city. The population has followed; the 1991 Census shows that while Greater Bombay's population increased by a fifth in the preceding decade (and the Island population declined absolutely, from 3.3 to 3.2 million, with much more rapid declines in the southern wards), some of the peripheral areas increased rapidly—e.g. Kalyan increasing by 645 per cent, Mira Road-Bhayandar by 584 per cent, and even Thane, by 157 per cent.

On an index where Greater Bombay's manufacturing employment equals 100, Thane increased its employment from 7 in 1961 to 25 in 1988, and Raigad, from 0.6 to 3.0 (calculated from BMR April 1991, Table 36, p. 73). Combining Greater Bombay and Thane's shares of industrial employment, on the State Government's 1986 figures [reproduced by the Deshpandes (1991)], 43 per cent of the jobs in chemicals and chemical products were located in Thane; 27 per cent of the engineering industry (basic metals, metal products, machinery, transport equipment)—but only 9 per cent of transport equipment; 43 per cent of non-metallic minerals; and a quarter of electrical machinery. Taking a larger territorial area would no doubt reveal other emerging patterns of territorial specialization which constitute the 'Bombay economy' even if this does not coincide with the boundaries either of Greater Bombay or the Metropolitan Region.

Indeed, the territorial extent of the Bombay economy may now be covering a still much larger area, with strong concentrations of linked manufacturing at the points, Pune and Nashik (Harris, 1991). Such a pattern would correspond to the emerging configuration in a number of countries—for example, Mexico City, with the fastest growing related manufacturing centres in a ring up to one hundred kilometres away. Thus, the loss of jobs in Bombay's manufacturing may be no more than a redistribution between the city and its periphery; Bombay's loss in this respect is less than the gain to other non-industrialized areas, particularly because relocation should remove the more labour-intensive and routine sectors of activity, leaving in the city those sectors which need to be there—the more skill-intensive, and the more innovatory (that is, the city should play an incubator role). Perhaps the much faster growth of the unregistered sector is an indication of the growth in this role.

In sum then, on this rather crude assessment, Bombay's emerging specialization in manufacturing—petrochemicals, vehicles and vehicle parts, electrical and electronic equipment—fit some of the high-growth sectors of world trade, particularly those where a number of Newly Industrializing Countries have experienced most success in exports (and where the comparative advantage of many of the developed countries is declining most swiftly). So far India has not benefited significantly from this change. Whereas Korea, Mexico and Brazil are building, on the basis of exports, world-class vehicle industries (with attendant effects in the growth of employment), with the aim of replacing Japan in the future, India has been very slow to become engaged. Car exports reached 23,000 units in 1991, with a modest target of 50–60,000 by 1995. However, the structure of protection poses severe problems in allowing the full exploitation of the strengths of the Indian economy— but without that, the successes could be so outweighed by the problems that the political will to persist is weakened.

Service

The future of Bombay in an open economy would seem to lie mainly in the field of high-value services, rather than manufacturing. There are severe difficulties here in discussing the issues because the data available are so limited, and its systematic disaggregation almost non-existent.

One of the core activities of Bombay's services sector is as the dominant financial centre for India, and presumably in an open economy, an important centre for Asia and the world, backed by a full array of supportive producer services. London is an extreme example of such a centre (and therefore not at all a model for Bombay), with some 620,000 employed in financial and business services, and a further 200,000 in supporting activities (accountancy, actuaries, lawyers, leasing and development agents, special printing services, information and computing services etc.). As noted earlier, manufacturing declined sharply in the recessions of the 1970s and 1980s, when financial and business services expanded rapidly (employment increased by 43 per cent in the 1980s). The most rapid growth, as we have seen, occurred in the 1980s, following the complete decontrol of 1979, major investments in telecommunications, in transport and other facilities (making possible 24-hour dealing and swift physical access), and the radical programme of market reforms in 1987, popularly known as the 'Big Bang'.

However, foreign centres of global finance suggest the preconditions for an international role—a favourable tax and regulatory regime (not biased against foreign participants), ease of access, adequate communications with the rest of the world, a physical development (of offices and buildings) which permits close personal and low-cost contacts, and a supportive quality of life (in terms of housing, culture, sport, education etc. [Kennedy, 1991]).

For the moment, the external sector plays a relatively small part in Bombay's activity (related, we presume, to external trade and capital inflows to India, with no third-country transactions). Bombay banks control 12 per cent of national deposits and a quarter of outstanding credits. There are presumably no forward markets, and the 1981 proposal by the Chairman of the State Bank of India to start an offshore banking facility was apparently vetoed by the Reserve Bank ('ISG', 1980). However, despite the relative underdevelopment of Bombay's financial markets, liberalization has already stimulated considerable expansion. As in China, it is the non-government sector which has benefited most from this decontrol, the private Indian and foreign banks.

The increase in financial activity is likely to stimulate greater 'distillation of land uses' (Dunning and Morgan, 1971)—that is, the increased profitability of some activities will drive out those with lower rates of return, producing an increased concentration of those with the higher yield. Presumably, the creation of Nariman Point offered an outlet to the old financial quarter for modern banking, brokerage firms, public issue promoters and other associated activities. With liberalization, a decontrolled land market and an increased tempo of activity, one would expect the more labour-intensive components of finance—for example, the mass of clerical occupations involved in the Life Insurance Corporation—to be forced out of the central area (as occurred in London in the 1950s). The creation of a new commercial centre at Bandra-Kurla in the northern suburbs of the city is already providing an alternative location for such activity. Thus, continued growth in activity (as measured by the value of transactions per worker) in the south of the city—including Backbay Reclamation—can, contrary to the fears of those opposed to continued growth in the south, be accompanied by a decline in employment and therefore in movement. Distillation of land uses, rather than increased intensity of employment, is of the essence of a dynamic central business district. However, at the moment, the privileged position of the public sector (for example, the LIC) as well as land and rent controls prevent this outcome and lead to 'overemployment' in the south.

The spread of services within the Metropolitan Region is, as in manufacturing, an important issue here, since it may indicate the development of a more elaborated pattern of territorial specialization. For example, in the decade up to 1987, Thane's banking employment increased by 360 per cent (compared to Greater Bombay's increase of 22 per cent, a growth below that for services as a whole).

What other services are, or might come to be, important in Bombay's economy? The city is already the most important transport junction in India, with associated passenger reception facilities and cargo terminals and warehousing. With the largest international airport, tourist arrivals are an important source of income for downtown activities (hotels, restaurants, entertainment, retail trade etc.), with multiplier effects in horticulture, manufacturing etc. The city is important in other activities which support tourism, both domestic and foreign—music, drama, dance, museums, historic monuments etc. Although international tourism in India is still small by world standards, it is almost certain to grow quickly and, provided Bombay can provide an adequate service, the city will be an important beneficiary.

The city is a major centre for the distribution of goods throughout India, with associated processing activity (for example, in vegetable oils). The wholesale markets, now relocated within the region, play an important role in this network and are major employers in the city (in the late 1970s, CIDCO [1980] estimated the daily employment at 88,000). The city is famous for its film-making (with associated activity in technical services and manufacture), for research and development (with the Atomic Energy Commission, research laboratories and centres, elements that relate to the role of the city as an incubator of innovations), for its complex of higher educational institutions. In the case of tertiary education, the system is overstretched relative to domestic demand, but in time, the provision of education could become an important export activity for south Asian and Sub-Saharan African countries where there is a great shortage of higher education facilities— and students add to the retail markets for food and accommodation, etc.

There are other activities which have been tried, some successfully. Thus, printing and publishing for foreign publishers provides an important source of income for some cities in developing countries (Bogota, for example; Hong Kong also earlier had a strong position in this field). Earlier efforts to develop this in Bombay foundered on problems of quality control and timing, but it is possible these have now been overcome.

Bombay is already a centre for software programming exports. There are other elements related to computer use of importance here. Data loading and processing is labour-intensive, so that a precondition for the exploitation of computer technology is the availability of low cost literate workers, a factor favouring developing countries. There are anecdotal illustrations of this—for example, British police records are currently being loaded in the Philippines (where specialized companies exist to tender for such work; perhaps they also exist in Bombay); the loading of Canadian medical records and some United States airlines' ticketing services have been relocated to the Caribbean; one of the largest Japanese real estate companies now processes its land records and transactions in Shenzhen in southern China. At the moment, Swiss Air is said to be transferring its accounts department to Bombay, and Singapore Airlines is said to be considering transferring to India its accountancy and computing departments.

Paradoxically—given the poor availability of medical services to an important part of the city's population—Bombay is potentially also strong in medical services, and, with market pricing for foreign patients, this might be an important export industry. The absolute size of the medical profession in India and, in certain centres, the quality of medical infrastructure, permits important economies of scale in an activity—including hospitals, clinics, convalescence homes, medically supervised retirement homes etc.—where labour costs are a high proportion of the total. An expanded market for Bombay's medical services could then allow a much better coverage of the Bombay population at lowered costs (because of economies of scale). For exports, the existence of the international airport is a key factor in providing access to medical services for the rest of south Asia and Sub-Saharan Africa. Furthermore, in the longer term, the demographic ageing of the population of North America, Europe and Japan will make for an increasing demand for labour-intensive medical and nursing services which cannot be met in the developed countries. Cities which build a comparative advantage in medical services—as Singapore has done in South East Asia—are likely to be able to exploit it well into the next century (whether the patients or the aged relocate themselves to India, or Bombay medical teams are despatched to other countries on short-term missions). The Mexican border with the United States shows some of the potential here; almost every township or city has an 'overdeveloped' medical services sector to meet the demand of aged north Americans wintering on the border and seeking to escape the notoriously high cost of United States alternatives.

Problems

This paper has in the main concentrated on some of the opportunities facing Bombay, precisely because everyone is painfully aware of the problems and their severity (D'Souza [1987], Sundaram [1989]). Yet the constraints on Bombay's capacity to exploit opportunities are considerable. For example, compared to the rest of India, the city is endowed with a good physical infrastructure (highways, railways, port, power etc.), but compared to its likely competitors abroad, it is poor. If the emerging global city is essentially a junction point in flows, Bombay is poorly equipped to manage those flows—with poor and unreliable telecommunications, congested transport junctions, slow-moving roads (with an average speed of 13 kilometres an hour in the late 1980s, and for many of the city's long-suffering inhabitants a commuting time of four hours or more per day in dreadfully overcrowded conditions). The suburban railways, in principle, an excellent means of access to the city, have for so long been unable to cover running costs (a managerial issue, not one of investment), they have been unable to invest to expand the service. The airports have been vastly improved, and are of vital significance for the city's financial and tourist roles; if just-in-time stock policies come to operate in Bombay's manufacturing as a result of increased international competitiveness, then air cargo will also become crucial for Bombay's manufacturing industry. But improving the movement through the terminals is of little value if the land access remains so congested—the gains in time saved in one mode are squandered in the other. In sum, the infrastructure of Bombay appears to impose such heavy costs on economic activity, one must presume the rates of return are unusually high to compensate for this. Only the apparently limitless patience of the citizens allows the city to operate at all.

The transport system is not the most striking example of the waste of resources implicit in the bad management of the city. The size and condition of the poor population is an even more vivid illustration of the waste of people, their energies and potential. Indeed, the economic costs of the waste of Bombay's citizens' time—for example, in ill health resulting from contaminated water supplies (only 60 per cent of city households are said to have access to safe drinking water), inadequate or nonexistent sewerage (a quarter of a million households have no access to lavatories), or the exhaustion of crowded commuting—if added to the costs of producing the city's output, might tilt the city's balance sheet to the negative.

The problems, as so often, reflect less a shortage of resources (Bombay is still the richest city in India), more a rooted incapacity in the public authorities to tap the resources which exist for low-cost service provision. At last, many non-governmental organizations in different parts of the world are demonstrating that there is no inevitability about the wretched provision of these services (for example, Hasan [1990]).

The key to a city's economic future are the skills, education and aptitudes of its inhabitants. India has not done well in the field of basic education—after nearly half a century since Independence, more than half the population is still classified as illiterate (and two-thirds of the female population), compared to 27 per cent in China (and 38 per cent of the females). Even if the national figures are poor, it ought to be the case that the figures for a city like Bombay should be close to full literacy, particularly if it is to perform its role as a centre of high productivity. However, a Bombay Labour Market Survey (cited by Deshpande [1991], p. 76) shows that a third of the casual and nearly a fifth of the factory labour forces are illiterate. The drop-out rate from slum schools is also notoriously high. In terms of public action to prepare for the future role of the city, basic education must assume a high priority.

Finally, in terms of problems, the quality of government, policy and institutions, is a major constraint on Bombay's capacity to change. National urban policy, marginal in its urban effects in comparison to the key components of macro-economic policy, has long been obsessed with irrelevant and unachievable objectives. Instead of being preoccupied with improving the efficiency of the operation of cities as a crucial contribution to national economic development, policy has been directed to preventing the growth, or reducing the size, of the city population. It is astonishing how long the pursuit of this will-o'-the-wisp of population dispersal has preoccupied policy makers. A national settlement system is not a random distribution of people, but more like the departments of a giant factory; it makes as little sense to seek to equalize the workforce in each department as it is to judge the performance of the factory on the basis of the physical distribution of the workers. It is the productivity of the enterprise which should be the criterion for judging how the workers are distributed. Despite all their painful disabilities, India's large cities are surprisingly productive, and their relative contribution to national output is growing. The National Commission on Urbanization (1988) reported that in 1950/51, the urban areas contributed 29 per cent of Net Domestic Product; in 1970/71, 37 per cent; and projected for the year 2001, 60 per cent. Those who feel policy should be directed at population dispersal should be required, in India's national interest, to demonstrate that this would enhance national productivity.

The national policy stance led to successive attempts to prevent the growth of employment in Bombay, culminating in 1975 in a ban on new large-scale industry or the expansion of existing industry in metropolitan areas (and a 1977 ban on new offices). There was little economic sense in these measures at the time, and it is unclear how effectively they have been implemented. Today, it is unlikely that large-scale manufacturing units would want to locate in Bombay's built-up area; indeed, if India attains the sorts of rates of growth which it should, it is to be expected that large-scale manufacturing in the city will want to relocate outside the urban area. That would be the outcome of a decontrolled land market for industrial land, and does not require government bans.

National urban policies are necessary where local authorities are very weak. Over the last one hundred years or more, centralization has been the tendency of government, in response to external competition, war and domestic threats. This has sapped the powers of local government and often demoralized its officers, reducing municipal government to inertia, unable to maintain and manage existing facilities, let alone extend them as populations grow. Rent seeking becomes the main source of vast systems of local regulation. However, over the past decade, there has been a growing recognition that national governments are incapable of substituting for local governments, so a preoccupation with decentralization (as well as privatization, the voluntary delivery of services etc.) has emerged. India's steps in this direction have been hesitant (Ray, 1992) but increased liberalization of external boundaries makes local decentralization urgent.

The Bombay Municipal Corporation has a unified administration with a buoyant local financial base, administering a relatively rich city. Yet this has not led to dramatic effects in overcoming some of the problems enumerated earlier. The municipal authorities rarely aspire to lead the process of structural adjustment which is implied by liberalization. Nor, so far as is known, do they form a pressure group to argue the city's interests at a national level. For example, the effects of the containerization of four Indian ports (one of which was Nava Sheva a nearly facility recently developed) were long nullified by the failure of the Indian Customs to change the classification of containers from 'transport equipment'; as transport equipment, containers could not leave the dockside without making a hard currency deposit of double the value of the container (Peters, 1989). Did the city leadership make it a matter of urgency to urge the Government of India to make the change so that the city could benefit from containerization? Is the city exploiting the opportunities provided by the export drive to improve the transport infrastructure of the city (as suggested by K. C. Sivaramakrishna; cf. Harris, 1992)?

However, criticizing the failure to argue the case for Bombay's economic future is perhaps unfair, since the issues have hitherto been outside the purview of local authorities (although, as the economic historians have shown, this was not true of the City Corporation in the nineteenth century (see Thorner, 1950). Liberalization and decentralization, however, change this old agenda so that the city needs to develop the capacity to monitor, to manage and to promote the city's economy. This suggests at least two levels of operation: first, developing a capacity for continuing research on the city's economy, involving the universities, research institutes and business associations, to cover the key sectors and subsectors of economic activity, infrastructure, education, poverty, the quality of life etc. Secondly, and closely related to the first, building the in-house capacity in the city administration, an Economic Advisory Unit, to give immediate advice to the city authorities on how they should respond to changes in the macro-economic framework (from world issues—for example, how will Bombay be affected by AFTA, the new free trade area covering the ASEAN countries, by the possible conclusion of the Uruguay GATT Round, Europe Project

1992, or the North American Free Trade Agreement?—to issues of changes in government policy, interest rates, oil prices etc.). Part of the work should be the production of a regular statistical year-book (with best estimates of the statistically unrecorded activity) as both a means of promoting the city and giving access to the data to the citizens at large. The Unit would have a primary responsibility to arm the city's managers with the data and arguments to advance the city's interests relative to national and state policy, and to key investments in the city.

* * * * * *

The programme is entirely utopian in present circumstances, but then so is the creation of an open economy in India. The speculation is about possible trends, not accomplished realities. Bombay's potential is enormous, but, as in India as a whole, most often the potential is frustrated. Sometimes that may be for sound reasons. India is in some respects a fragile society, and, as we noted earlier, liberalization may sap the sinews of national unity. It is assumed in this paper that, in the medium term, there is no serious alternative to liberalization and that, if managed effectively, this can lead to a radical change in India's domestic economy and a massive expansion in employment. But the process of management is precisely the area of greatest weakness, so that in the short term frustrating some of the opportunities of liberalization may be a reasonable response to the dangers. However, the drive to raise as swiftly as possible the employment, and enhance the productivity, of India's labour force sooner or later will oblige the country's incorporation in a global division of labour.

Bibliography

Aksoy, M. Ataman (1992). *The Indian Trade Regime*, Policy Research Working Paper 989, Washington, World Bank, Oct. 1992.

Aksoy, M. Ataman and Francois M. Ettori, (Oct. 1992). *Protection and Industrial Structure in India*, Country Operations Working Paper Series 990, Washington, World Bank.

BMR (April, 1991). *Employment Scene in BMR* (Revision of Regional Plan for Bombay Metropolitan Region), Working Paper No. 5, Bombay, Bombay Metropolitan Region.

——— (October 1991). *Industrial Growth Policy for Bombay Metropolitan*

Region. (Revision of the Regional Plan for Bombay Metropolitan Region), Working Paper No. 6, Bombay. Bombay Metropolitan Region.

———— (n.d). *Regional Economy of BMR*, Bombay, Bombay Metropolitan Region.

CIDCO (Nov. 1980). (For the Bombay Metropolitan Regional Development Authority). A Report on the Survey of the Vegetables, Fruits, Onion-Potato Markets in Bombay City, Bombay, Economics Section (Mimeo), City and Industrial Development Corporation, Nov. 1980.

D'Souza, J. B. (1987). 'The Management of Bombay' (a series of articles from *The Times of India*), DPU Working Paper 18, London, Development Planning Unit, July 1987.

———— (1991). 'Will Bombay Have a Plan: Irrelevance of Planners and Their Plans', *Economic and Political Weekly*, Bombay, 18 May 1991, pp. 1289–93.

Deshpande, Sudha, and Lalit Deshpande, (1991). *Problems of Urbanisation and Growth of Large Cities in Developing Countries: A Case Study of Bombay*, Geneva, Population and Labour Policies Programme, Working Paper No. 177, International Labour Organisation, Oct. 1991.

———— (1992). 'New Economic Policy and Female Employment', *Economic and Political Weekly*, Bombay, Vol. XXVII, No. 41, Oct. 10, 1992, pp. 2248–52.

Dunning, John H. and E. Victor Morgan, (eds.) (1971). *An Economic Study of the City of London*, Economists' Advisory Group, London, Allen and Unwin, 1971.

Harris, Nigel (1991). 'Some trends in the evolution of big cities: case studies of the USA and India', in Nigel Harris, *City, Class and Trade: Social and Economic Change in the Third World*, London, Development Planning Unit/IB Tauris.

———— (ed.) (1992). *Cities in the 1990s: The Challenge for Developing Countries*, London, Overseas Development Administration and Development Planning Unit, UCL Press.

Hasan, Arif (1990). 'The Orangi Project in Karachi', *Environment and Urbanisation*, London, International Institute for Environment and Development, Vol. 2, No. 1, Apr. 1990, p. 84.

'ISG' (1981). 'An offshore banking facility for Bombay?' *Economic and Political Weekly*, Bombay, 22 Aug. 1981.

Kennedy, Richard, et al. (1991). *London: World City Moving into the 21st Century*, London, London Planning Advisory Committee et al.

National Commission on Urbanization (1988). *Report*, New Delhi, Government of India.

Peters, Hans Jurgen (1989). *Sea Trade, Logistics and Transport* (Policy and Research Series 6), Washington, Infrastructure and Urban Development Division, World Bank.

Ray, Amal (1992). 'New economic policy and Indian federalism', *Economic and Political Weekly*, Bombay, Vol. XXVII, No. 4, 25 Jan. 1992., p. 14.

Sundaram, P. S. A. (1989). *Bombay: Can it House its Millions? A New Approach to Solving the Housing Problems of Third World Cities*, New Delhi, Clarion Books.

Thorner, Daniel (1950). *Investment in Empire: British Railway and Steam Shipping Enterprises in India, 1825–49*, Philadelphia.

4

Flying a Kite and Losing the String: Communication during the Bombay Textile Strike[1]

HUB VAN WERSCH

Background

On 18 January 1982, all workers in Bombay's textile mills started on a strike which was to become the biggest labour struggle India had ever witnessed. Probably, it was even the biggest strike anywhere in modern times. According to official statistics this strike lasted 18 and a half months and involved 240,000 workers. In the course of this gigantic struggle, triggered off by a bonus dispute, approximately 75,000 strikers finally lost their jobs.

Monetary gains were the main strike objectives of the workers but the struggle was also directed against the official 'representative union' in the textile industry, the Rashtriya Mill Mazdoor Sangh (RMMS). The workers were disillusioned with the performance of the RMMS and turned *en masse* for leadership to an outsider, Dr Datta Samant. Samant, at that time, had a reputation both for success and militancy and the workers wanted him to lead them in the struggle. For that purpose Samant founded a new union, the Maharashtra Girni Kamgar Union (MGKU), in October 1981.

Several aspects of this historic strike have been discussed in the literature (e.g. its presupposed violent character, the rejection by the workers of the legal apparatus for solving industrial conflicts, and the backwardness of the technology employed in the mills), but an aspect that has drawn little attention is the significance of the rural connections of

[1] I would like to thank Professor O. D. van den Muijzenberg and Dr D. Kooiman for their comments on an earlier draft of this paper.

the industrial workers. These connections may help a worker to tide over a strike period because they allow him to return to his village to await the outcome of the struggle. If workers avail of this possibility, there is at once another problem and that is the problem of communication. This problem affects both the strike leadership and the workers in the village, but it has so far not drawn serious attention, although the presence or absence of proper communication is ultimately bound to influence the continuation and outcome of a strike.

Communication Problems

This paper attempts to explore the most important aspects of the so-called urban–rural nexus during the Bombay textile strike.[2] The focus will be on the need of proper channels of communication when large numbers of workers try to survive a strike by staying in their villages of origin. The communication problem has a horizontal and a vertical aspect. On the horizontal plane there is the workers' need to stay in touch with other workers, the wish to know their views and movements. The vertical aspect refers to the relation between the workers and the strike leadership. Here too there is a need to know each other's views and strategies, although the mutuality of this wish may be questioned. Workers' committees may act as a hyphen between the strike leadership and the workers and in the best cases they do.

If workers avail themselves in large numbers of their rural connections, as was the case in this strike, and if the communication problems involved have not been anticipated, then the strike leadership is deprived of the views of these workers. Similarly, it may be very difficult to inform these workers about strike-related developments. The workers in the villages will find it increasingly hard to follow what is going on in the city. This breeds anxiety. If no precautionary measures are taken, the cohesion among the striking workers may rapidly crumble, their fighting spirit may be weakened and both these developments may affect the outcome of the struggle.

All this suggests that, although the rural hinterland serves as a safety net for workers at times of distress (particularly during a strike), this net should not be utilized without giving proper thought to the risks involved.

When tens of thousands of textile workers left the city at the beginning

[2] The basic material for this paper has been derived from a study which has meanwhile been published by Oxford University Press (van Wersch, 1992: 168–76).

of the strike, the exodus clearly illustrated the significance of the workers' rural connections. However, nothing much had been organized at that stage, no registration had taken place of those leaving the city. No serious thought was given to the question of how to stay in touch with these workers. In fact, when the strike leadership advised the workers to return to their villages of origin, this resembled the case of a man flying a kite and losing the string.

The economic importance of the rural–urban nexus is usually illustrated by pointing to the financial contribution of city-based workers to their dependants in the rural hinterland. Money commonly flows in one direction, i.e. from the city to the villages where it is used for several purposes. At times of distress, the picture may be reversed and it may be the village that helps the workers, who might otherwise be faced with starvation in the city.

Both aspects of this relation are to be found throughout the history of the Bombay textile workers, and they surfaced once again in the course of the textile strike in the eighties. It is possible that the significance of this urban–rural connection changed over the years but it is very hard to establish this point because of inadequate data pertaining to earlier struggles, and the corresponding impossibility to be accurate in the case of this one.

To be able to describe accurately the significance of the urban–rural nexus during the textile strike we need to know how many workers retreated to the villages and also to what extent they availed of the (employment) opportunities offered there. Unfortunately, such data were never systematically collected. In the absence of accurate figures we depend on estimates from those involved in the struggle, i.e. unions, government, millowners and critical observers. As may be expected there is no unanimity to be found here. A fairly moderate estimate puts the figure at 40 per cent, which means that 100,000 workers left the city in the early days of the strike. A figure twice as large has also been mentioned. But whether 100,000 or 200,000 workers decided to stay in the village to await the outcome of the struggle, there is no denying the possibility of the rural connection having had a strong bearing on the outcome of the strike.

The fact that the workers left the city in such numbers naturally raises many questions. For example, how did the workers survive in the village? What sort of problems did they have there? How were they informed about the strike? What possibilities did they have of influencing strike developments? How did their families react to the strike?

Although no large-scale research was done during the strike to find out what sort of work was available to the striking workers, allowing for a quantitative approach, some idea may be gained from a sample of 150 textile workers who were interviewed, in the period January 1987 to June 1987, about their views and strategies during the strike.[3] First, the characteristics of the sample workers in terms of their regional origin, economic status, level of education etc. will be described. Next, the way in which they coped with the strike will be discussed. Finally, the problems of communication will be dealt with.

Sample Characteristics

The workers sampled hailed predominantly from Maharashtra. Only 14 per cent came from outside Maharashtra, i.e. Uttar Pradesh and Andhra Pradesh. It is noteworthy that no more than 10 per cent originated from Bombay itself (see Table 1).

These facts, indicative of the strong and persistent migratory character of labour in the Bombay textile industry, are corroborated by other studies (cf. Vaidya, 1984: 12). From the Table it appears that most of the sample workers originate from Ratnagiri district but other districts too are strongly represented. It is likely that places of origin changed over the years as may be deduced from studies by Gokhale and Kooiman who found higher percentages of workers (hovering around 40 per cent) hailing from Ratnagiri (Patel, 1963; Kooiman, 1978). But Patel, comparing her findings with those of a study by Gokhale in 1957, noted that

[3] It must be pointed out that the basic idea of the sample was to throw light on the ways in which workers of two contrasting mills (one prosperous and one backward) coped with the strike. As hardly anything was known about those who lost their jobs in the wake of the strike, one-third of the sample was reserved for unemployed workers. The interviews covered many aspects of the workers' lives and the same material can be utilized to clarify differences in the position of workers who remained in the city and that of those who went to their villages. The division of the 150 sample workers is as follows:

	Mill A	*Mill B*	*Total*
Employed	35 permanent	35 permanent	70
	15 *badli* (substitute)	15 *badli*	30
Unemployed	25 permanent	18 permanent	43
	— *badli*	7 *badli*	7
Total	75	75	150

Table 1. Place of birth of sample workers

District or State	Total	Percentage
Ratnagiri	38	25.3
Satara	28	18.6
Sangli	17	11.3
Andhra Pradesh	16	10.7
Bombay	15	10.0
Pune	14	9.3
Kolhapur	11	7.3
Uttar Pradesh	5	3.3
Kulaba	3	2.0
Other	3	2.0
Total	150	99.8

the number of workers from Ratnagiri dropped to 23 per cent in the thir-ties as a result of the dismissal of jobbers from that district in the wake of the strike of 1929 (Patel, 1963: 6). It is possible that, when the number of workers from the Konkan shrank as a result of this, the number of workers from other districts in Maharashtra increased. Gokhale found that in the fifties large groups of workers from states like Karnataka and Uttar Pradesh were present in the Bombay work-force but they seem to have been gradually replaced by Maharashtrians.

Whether the workers predominantly come from the south or the south-east of Maharashtra, the distance between their village of origin and Bombay may be anywhere between 200 and 500 kilometres. These distances bespeak the need for proper channels of communication in case workers decide to leave the city in the course of a strike.

The importance of ties with the village may also derive from the possession of property there. Not less than 137 workers (91 per cent) stated that they owned a house or a hut in the village and 116 workers (77 per cent) appeared to possess land. This high percentage must be linked with their caste background (predominantly Marathas). The caste-wise division of the sample workers is as follows: Maratha 75 per cent, Padmashali 9 per cent, Backward Classes and Scheduled Castes 5 per cent, Vaishya 4 per cent, Other 5 per cent, non-Hindus 2 per cent.

One is tempted to believe that those without land had less capacity to continue the strike than their landowning colleagues. However, the average strike duration for landless workers was not different from that of workers who owned land. This means that ownership of land, although important for several obvious reasons, was much less important as far as the duration of the strike was concerned. Those who could cultivate their own plot had the advantage, of course, that they could derive an income from that. In practically all cases, the house and/or the land was/were owned by the family and, therefore, shared property. Although no details were collected about the type of land, its use or its fertility, the owners of some of the larger holdings volunteered to add that their land was rocky and infertile.

Deshpande found a much lower percentage of textile workers owning land in their villages, than we did. He reported that only 40 per cent of the textile workers in his survey possessed land and concluded that ownership of land cannot be considered an important source of alternative income for the striking workers (Deshpande, 1983: 10). There appears to be a gap between the 40 per cent mentioned by Deshpande and the 77 per cent found here. It is possible, however, that a caste difference between the workers in both samples can explain the gap. Deshpande does not mention the caste of his workers so this explanation cannot be tested.

The difference might also be explained by looking at the type of housing of the workers in Bombay and the concomitant length of stay. In Deshpande's survey less than 4 per cent of the workers were provided accommodation by a mill in a chawl whereas a much larger number of the workers in our sample were so housed. Yet, there is not much reason to believe that this last group of workers moved to the city recently. It appeared that 86 per cent had worked for five years or more in Bombay and 68 per cent had worked for more than nine years, usually in one and the same mill. The workers stayed in the rooms provided by the mill not because they had moved to the city recently but because chances for finding better accommodation were and are distressingly poor. It is hard even to find merely a hut in a slum. What happens is that workers ask their families to come over to Bombay if they are lucky enough to get a room in a chawl.

A study of the rural–urban economic ties of workers in the silk, textile processing and hosiery industries by S. Vaidya confirms that a high percentage of textile workers own land and other property in the village. She found that 60 per cent of the workers possessed land in the village whereas 85 per cent of them possessed a house (Vaidya, 1984: 15). On the strength of the available data alone no satisfactory explanation can be given for the differences between this study and the survey by Deshpande.

Maybe more revealing than the ownership of land itself is the acreage of the land possessed by the workers. The land-holdings of 63 workers are known and presented in Table 2. As may be expected, the large majority of the land-holdings is very small. But still there is a substantial minority possessing five to ten acres. This time the differences with Deshpande's study are less dramatic although not negligible. This author reported that of those who owned land in the village, 61 per cent possessed less than two acres whereas 25 per cent had three to five acres (Deshpande, 1983: 10). These figures suggest that the income derived from the smallest holdings, a substantial majority, will have been meagre. Even so, there remains a sizeable group with more than three acres and these workers might have greatly benefited from their possession of land. In fact, this is precisely what was reported by the workers in the course of the interviews.

The significance of the rural–urban nexus may also be derived from the number of dependants workers have. No less than 37 per cent of the sample workers bear responsibility for the welfare of seven or more dependants whereas 84 per cent have to look after at least four dependants. In the case of the workers with strong rural ties, these dependants lived in the village. Workers whose families lived in the village stated that family members contributed to the family income.

Given the number of dependants in the village, it is no surprise that the workers used to send money to them there. Prior to the strike 76 per cent of all sample workers sent money to their village of origin regularly. The rural ties of those who did not send any money were weak or nonexistent. Most workers in this last category naturally remained in Bombay. The amount of money sent by the sample workers is given in Table 3 (figures relating to the pre-strike situation).

It appears that the monthly transfer of money to the village is considerable. Although no large-scale data collection took place to find out for what purposes this money was utilized, practically all workers who were asked this question stated that it was used to meet the costs of living. Only one worker declared that part of the money was also utilized for land improvement and investment. This finding confirms the results of Vaidya's study of the use of money sent by workers to the village. From that study (based on repeated interviews with 500 workers) it appears that 71 per cent of the workers used to send money more or less regularly. From those who sent money, 84 per cent sent it to meet household expenses, 10 per cent intended it for special occasions (festivals, weddings) and only 3 per cent reported that the money was used for farming ends (Vaidya, 1984: 21–8).

Table 2. Size of land-holding of sample workers

Category	Total	Percentage (n=63)
1–4 acres	41	65.1
5–10 acres	14	22.2
11 or more acres	8	12.7
Total	63	100.0

Table 3. Pre-strike monthly remittance of money to village

Rupees	Total	Percentage (n=115)
50–150	49	42.6
151–250	27	23.5
251–350	15	13.0
351 or more	16	13.9
Irregularly	8	7.0
Total	115	100.0

It may be concluded that the money sent by the workers is badly needed in the village to cope with daily expenses. Any reduction in the earnings of the textile workers will therefore directly affect the standard of living of their families in the villages.

A further indication of the significance of the rural–urban nexus may be gained by taking a look at the occupation of the interviewee's father. It appeared that more than 45 per cent of the fathers of the interviewees were involved in agriculture. The textile industry turned out to be the second most important source of employment. More than a quarter of the fathers of the textile workers in the sample had been (in a few cases: still were) textile workers themselves. If we include handloom weavers, the percentage of those deriving an income from the textile industry rises to about 35 per cent. It may be concluded that agriculture and the textile industry together account for 80 per cent of the employment of the fathers of the sample workers. The remaining percentage includes occupations as diverse as postman, peon, policeman, soldier, vendor of fruit or vegetables, shop assistant, shopkeeper, cobbler, carpenter and medical practitioner.

Coping with the Strike

Having described the most relevant sample characteristics, we can now discuss the ways in which the workers coped with the strike. In this regard it is important to know where the workers stayed during the strike. It was found that a large majority spent time in the village as well as in Bombay and this threatened to blur the picture. But in most cases they stayed predominantly in one place. In order to be able to attach a label to them in terms of stay during the strike it was decided that a worker ought to be put in the category 'Bombay' in case he had spent 70 per cent or more of his time in the city. The reverse was true for the village. It appeared that 53.3 per cent of the sample workers remained in Bombay whereas 40.7 per cent stayed in the village. In the remaining cases (6 per cent) workers divided their time more or less evenly between the city and the village.

The average time workers remained on strike is important for the discussion of the significance of the rural connection. In calculating the strike period for each worker, one has to bear in mind that this can only be done for those who got their job back. Thousands of workers were simply dismissed without notice or not taken back. An additional problem is that this strike has never been called off and even years after the struggle collapsed some workers still claimed to be on strike. Therefore the average strike duration has only been calculated for those workers (100 in the sample) who, at greatly differing times, resumed duty. It appeared that the average strike duration for them was 12.9 months. For workers who remained in Bombay (49 workers) this average was 13.3 months, whereas the average for workers in the village (45 workers) proved to be 12.2 months. The remaining six workers were on an average 15.7 months on strike. The conclusion is that there is only a slight difference between the averages for workers in the city and those in the village. This implies that there is no remarkable difference between the city and the village in terms of possibilities of surviving a long strike. For those who believe the rural nexus to be the most important escape route for workers on strike, this finding may come as a surprise.

Although the average strike duration for workers in the city and those in the villages did not differ much, the alternative employment found by the workers was not the same. Table 4 shows what trades the 150 sample workers practised in the course of the struggle.

A large group of workers had to practise several trades which is why the total exceeds 150. It is clear that cultivation of land, be it as an agricultural labourer or as owner, was the most important source of alternative employment during the strike. Not less than 23 per cent of the sample workers were exclusively occupied with cultivating their own plots of land and/or herding their own cattle. In the case of 11 workers, this did not suffice and they combined cultivating their own land with agricultural wage labour. A group of 15 workers had to hire themselves out as agricultural labourers throughout the strike. They were employed in herding cattle, digging wells, constructing water tanks or as seasonal labour. A few were employed under the Employment Guarantee Scheme (EGS) in Maharashtra which provides work to the poor in rural areas. In a way, they were supported by the Government, although the income derived from work under the EGS is very poor (cf. Bagchee 1984). In all, 61 workers (40 per cent of the entire sample) were engaged in agriculture or related activities during the strike.

Village life offered many opportunities for workers to gain a moderate income and keep themselves occupied. But for a better understanding of its significance one needs to know how much time the workers really worked during the strike. Figures for the entire sample are given in Table 5 which shows that not more 16 per cent of the workers on strike worked less than 50 per cent of the time whereas two-thirds of the workers were employed for more than half the strike period. The finding is a clear indication of the importance of alternative employment during the strike, be it in the city or in the rural hinterland. The workers were apparently very resourceful and successful in finding such employment although the earnings were usually poor.

Workers had to face many problems during the strike and the hardship they went through has been described in numerous newspaper articles and in case studies (cf. van Wersch, 1992: 265–99). It was to be expected that financial problems would be mentioned most frequently. Another prominent category was boredom (see Table 6). As the excitement about the endlessly prolonged battle wore thin, other problems surfaced vigorously. Naturally, in most cases workers suffered from multiple problems at the same time, which is why the total is more than 150.

Going home at the beginning of the strike may at first have been a

Table 4. Alternative employment
during the strike

Category	Total
Farming	35
Agricultural labour	15
Combining farming and agricultural labour	11
Powerloom weaver	20
Textile worker*	6
Handloom weaver	2
Begari (unfree agricultural labour)	20
Mazdoor (labourers)	9
Factory work	7
Helper**	14
Selling on road	2
Vendor fruit/vegetables	14
Other***	17
Unemployed	16
Total	188

* Refers to workers who started working during the strike in mills other than their own.

** Helper in odd jobs, usually casual labour (e.g. watchman, hamal, bidi-making, painting).

*** Includes: shop assistant, shopkeeper, postman, peon, cobbler, carpenter.

Table 5. Time worked
during the strike

Category	Total
25% or less	7
26%–50%	17
51%–75%	28
76% or more	72
Unknown*	26
Total	150

* Workers who did various jobs but were unable to indicate for how much time.

Table 6. Major problems experienced during strike

Category	Total	Percentage (n=150)
Finance	131	87.3
Boredom	81	54.0
Tensions at home	60	40.0
Unfamiliar work	28	18.7
No problems	10	6.7
Other	11	7.3

pleasant surprise for the family, but very soon it was realized by everyone that hardship was to follow. Families who had till then regularly received money from Bombay were suddenly confronted with a substantial drop in income together with the necessity to feed one more person. Taking loans and thereby incurring debts was the most frequently mentioned way of making both ends meet. The sale of property (ornaments, livestock, land) was another important solution, one which is often self-defeating. It would have been worthwhile to interview families of workers in the villages but the available time for the research did not permit this.

Even without interviews with relatives of workers, no particular imagination is required to appreciate that the first three problem categories would have affected practically all workers who remained in the villages. Some 40 per cent said that marital tensions and friction with other relatives spoiled the atmosphere there.

Those who could not find any work were hit hardest in this respect, but even those who could had their share of problems. During the interviews many workers (28) stated that they hated the sort of work they had to do and that they longed to go back to the mills. They intensely disliked hard work under a burning sun and for long hours in the fields, and that for a (very) modest return. A much smaller group (12) said that they liked working in the open air but added that, in spite of their preference for cultivating the land, they had no option but to return to the mills because tilling the land did not pay. This finding is in line with work done much earlier by Patel who found that 64 per cent of the Bombay textile workers preferred industrial work to agricultural labour (Patel, 1963: 23). This author points out that what the workers disliked in agricultural work were the risks (uncertain yields, weather conditions, rent). What appealed to them in industrial labour were the higher returns (wages) and the steadiness of their income. If anything, this tendency seems to have increased over the years. The strong dislike of agricultural work found here may be indicative of a change in attitude in favour of city life and deserves further study.

Workers who had to cope with any or all of these problems needed support to boost their morale. A regular newsletter might have helped to raise their spirits and to combat their feelings of isolation. This, of course, presupposes literacy. The degree of literacy is very important if newsletters, newspapers or periodicals have to supply the worker with information regarding the strike. The educational level of the textile workers is such that this would not have been a great problem. It was found that the percentage of illiterate workers is limited (see Table 7). About 37 per cent of the sample workers claimed to have been educated above the 8th standard. This finding is corroborated by Deshpande's study in which it is stated that 36 per cent of the males reported education up to Secondary School Certificate (SSC) level.

There is a link between the views of the workers regarding the strike and the attitude taken by their families. If, for example, a worker's wife disagreed with her husband on the strike, this would certainly aggravate his problems. On the other hand, if a wife backed her husband in the stand he took, that would certainly have alleviated them and helped him stick to his guns. Just as the views of the workers developed in the course of the struggle, the same must have happened to the views of his wife and/or relatives.

According to the workers, the support for the strike from their families was much weaker than their own commitment. This is not surprising, particularly not for families living in the villages. They were ill-prepared for the strike as they had not been informed about it in timely and sufficient measure. Strike objectives, like the removal of the RMMS or the repeal of the Bombay Industrial Relations Act, did not appeal to them. They were suddenly confronted with a seemingly endless drop in their monthly income, something they had neither asked for nor foreseen. In many cases, even under normal circumstances, it was already difficult to make ends meet; the strike could only aggravate matters further.

According to the workers' statements, 28 per cent of their families were against the strike right from the beginning. They either opposed it actively (putting pressure on the workers to resume) or appeared to be in favour of the demands but not of the strike. Discussion with families

Table 7. Level of education

Category	Total	Percentage (n=150)
Illiterate	13	8.6
1st–4th	25	16.6
5–8th	57	38.0
9–11th	32	21.3
SSC	23	15.3

of the workers might have thrown light on the subtle ways in which they tried to influence the attitude of the workers but this aspect has not been investigated. Nearly 39 per cent of the sample workers stated that their families supported the strike in the first phase (till 1983) but that their enthusiasm gradually declined. A sizeable group of nearly 29 per cent of the families were in favour of the struggle for more than 12 months. Only two per cent of the families were indifferent towards the strike. The views of the remaining two per cent are unknown.

In order to strengthen the workers' determination to continue a strike one has to pay attention to his family, his immediate social environment. This is usually overlooked in the course of a struggle despite the fact that the outcome of an industrial conflict will, along with other factors, also be influenced by the pressures put on a worker by his family.

As discussed above, workers were subject to many pressures, such as lack of money, unemployment, boredom, family tensions, disturbing newspaper reports etc. Their freedom to decide on the continuation of the strike was curbed by these problems. One very important source of pressure emanated from the mills. Workers were cajoled into resuming work by the management of the mills and by the RMMS. The mills had the addresses of many workers at their disposal and the millowners and the recognized union could help each other in this regard. Letters were sent to workers on strike in which they were called upon to resume duty. The millowners also used newspaper advertisements for that purpose. When these efforts failed to produce sufficient results, pressure on the strikers was mounted further by sending them warning notices and by placing advertisements in newspapers with threats of dismissal.

Pressure to resume work by the mill managements and/or the RMMS was mentioned most frequently by the 150 sample workers (49 per cent), the second position (39 per cent) being taken by fear of violence from one side or the other. Workers were afraid of being beaten up (or even worse) by followers of Samant if they decided to resume duty, but they also feared the RMMS if they did not. Although violence and even murders did occur during the strike, the frequency of violent acts against workers has been grossly overstated for various reasons (van Wersch, 1992: 176–91).

Rightly or wrongly, the workers were strongly influenced by this fear and it mattered little in this regard whether they stayed in the city or in the village. It may be true that the city-based workers were in a better position to judge the scope of the violence (although one must not exaggerate this point in a metropolis like Bombay) but the workers in the villages filled in the gap in their knowledge with their imagination. They conjured up bloody pictures, based on newspaper reports and hearsay, and in many cases they decided to wait 'a little longer'. A quarter of all the workers interviewed admitted that they would have resumed earlier had they not feared violence. It cannot be denied that proper communication might have done a lot to spread a correct picture of the strike.

Communication: A Vital Weakness

It is here that one of the fundamental weaknesses in the organization of the strike is exposed. In a strike, labelled 'indefinite' by its leader at the outset, and in which the workers were advised to return to their village of origin, communication is of utmost importance. Without well-organized means to reach out to the workers in the rural areas, the leadership had great difficulty in conveying its views and (changes in) tactics to the striking workers, and the workers were left in the dark about developments in Bombay.

This, of course, created uncertainty and caused suspicion. For information, the striking workers now depended on scanty accounts in newspapers, news on the radio and reports from other workers in the neighbourhood. Newspapers proved to be the most frequently mentioned source of information but the reliability of their contents was questionable (van Wersch 1992: 135–44). Often these papers were biased against the strike and strike leader, Datta Samant, and, with rare exceptions, the papers did not report systematically on the various developments. The case of radio was worse.

Uncertainty creates fear; in the case of a strike, most of all fear of losing a badly needed job. It is not surprising then that many workers

went back to Bombay in the course of the strike to see for themselves
how the strike was getting on. A quarter of the sample workers who predominantly stayed in the villages mentioned visiting Bombay once in
the course of the strike. Another quarter went twice or more frequently.
Apart from getting acquainted with the latest developments, they often
used these visits for attempts to resume duty. Some 16 per cent of the
sample workers in the villages went more or less regularly to Bombay
with the double purpose of hearing the latest news and finding out
about possibilities for resuming duty.

Some people in the circle of the strike leader, notably the activists of
the Lal Nishan Party, were well aware of the importance and possibilities
of communication with the rural hinterland. They urged Samant, at an
early stage, to tour the regions where most of the workers came from.
Samant took the advice and, in February and March 1982, made a rural
tour in the course of which he visited the districts of Satara, Sangli, Pune
and Kolhapur.

The tour served several purposes: informing the workers, keeping
zeal for the strike alive, and raising funds for the continuation of the
struggle in the city. At the same time, an attempt was made to create a
lasting bond between industrial workers and agricultural labourers and
peasants but success in this direction was usually short-lived. The tour
generated a lot of immediate enthusiasm; thousands of workers and
peasants gathered to hear Samant speak, bringing bags of rice and other
grains or donating money. However, the money and food thus collected
were more in the nature of charitable donations than portents of a new
stage in the relation between industrial and agricultural labour.

Although food and money were collected, no coherent documentation
that would allow for an assessment of the scope of the support was done.
As a result, we are left with incidental reports of specific collections. In
sum, it appears that the total support from the rural areas was limited
both in duration (predominantly to the months immediately following
Samant's rural tour) and quantity. The money and food thus collected
(possibly Rs 3 crores—130 million—and several thousand quintals of
foodgrains like rice and *jowar*) cannot have been more than a drop in
the ocean.

This impression is confirmed by the interviews with the workers.
Many workers (40 per cent of the sample) appeared to be unaware of
the contributions and collections. Although this support (usually in the
form of food or money) coming from the rural hinterland or from the
city was limited, its psychological effect might have exceeded its physical

impact. The first condition for that would be, of course, that the striking workers would know of it. Unfortunately, far too few workers knew that it was given (see Table 8).

There is a notable difference between those who stayed in Bombay and those that lived in the villages. Nearly half of the workers in the village were unaware of support as against 35 per cent for the city-based workers. It is to be expected that the chances for being informed about support for the strike were much better in the city than in the rural areas. Even so it is remarkable to find that one-third of the city-based workers knew nothing of actions to support them. One is tempted to believe that both groups, i.e. village based and city based workers, would have benefited from such knowledge. A sagging morale might have been boosted with a regular supply of information.

In August and September 1982 jail *bharo* campaigns (courting arrest, literally filling up the jails) were launched in rural areas. The news regarding these campaigns was spread with the aid of pamphlets, posters and newspaper reports. It is very hard to obtain accurate data regarding the number of people arrested. An added problem is that the number of people taking part in these campaigns may not be deduced from the number of arrests because the police resorted to a strategy of dispersing mobs instead of arresting the workers, thereby robbing them of martyrdom and preventing an over-taxation of the jail system. It is likely that the total number of arrests in the course of the various jail *bharo andolans* in and outside Bombay hovers between 15,000 and 50,000.

It is likely that the success of the food drives, money collections and fill-the-jail campaigns would have been far greater if there had been a regular and reliable medium to communicate with the workers. In addition, such a medium would have stimulated the involvement of those who gave money, food and/or time to support the strike. Such people

Table 8. Views of support related to stay during strike

Category	Village	Bombay	Other	Total
There was no support	18	19	2	39
No knowledge of support	12	9	1	22
Support was insufficient	9	23	2	34
There was enough support	19	24	3	46
Other opinions	3	5	1	9
Total	61	80	9	150

might have felt encouraged and pleased on being informed about the appreciation of their efforts to support the strike.

Committees

The existence of mill committees has been cited often to explain the astonishing staying power of the workers during the strike. These committees are credited with having accomplished many tasks and are supposed to have been the hyphen between the strike leadership and the workers. To serve that purpose these committees should have been constantly in touch with the workers. This was even more important in a prolonged struggle in the course of which workers were scattered all over the rural hinterland. However, it was found that a large majority of the sample workers (63 per cent) was unaware of the existence of these committees, let alone the tasks that were assigned to them. This finding was so surprising that great care was taken to ensure that the workers properly understood the questions; various forms of explanation were tried, but the responses were unchanging. It is possible that ignorance of the activities of the workers' committees is tied up with the residence of the workers during the strike, but if we look at the place where the 94 workers who did not know of the existence of these committees resided, we find that there is not much difference between those staying in the village and those remaining in Bombay: of these 94 workers, 48 resided in Bombay, and 46 were in the village or other places. Thus, the larger number of workers who knew nothing of the existence or the work done by workers' committees resided in Bombay. The factor 'stay in the village' can therefore be safely ruled out. The finding is disturbing for all those who wish to believe that the committees represented the true feelings of the workers and were crucial in keeping the strike going.

Conclusion

Among the many tasks that had to be shouldered during the textile strike, Datta Samant omitted to give top priority to organizing communications. The strike, which started on a bonus issue in some mills was soon catapulted into the greatest industrial action of our time, paralysing the entire Bombay textile industry. The strike leadership knew well in advance that the struggle was going to be tough and would last at least six months. For that reason, Samant advised workers to return to their villages. He warned them again and again about the likely duration of

the 'indefinite' strike. Although there was sufficient time to set up
channels of communication, this aspect was neglected. In October
1981, Samant founded the MGKU, a valuable instrument which Samant
could have used to conduct the exodus in an orderly fashion. During
morchas (protest marches) and rallies leading up to 18 January 1982, the
day the strike began, Samant could have explained the importance of
reliable strike news and recommended that no worker should leave the
city without leaving his address with a member of a mill committee.
Although this would not have been easy, since it involved reviving or
even establishing such committees at short notice, it could have been
done. If it had been, Samant would have had a fairly reliable list of
workers in the villages, which could have become an instrument for
concerted action.

It would have been easy and not too costly to start a regular newsletter (e.g. every fortnight) with the help of which he could have informed
the workers on all strike-related matters: the need for fund raising and
food collection, the moves of the government and the millowners, the
jail *bharo andolan*, instructions as to what to do concerning threats of
dismissal etc. This would have ensured that the workers would receive
directly and in undistorted form Samant's statements on the position
and this would have greatly strengthened their motivation. A newsletter
could even have been used to assess the mood of the workers. With a
simple card attached to it, such a periodical might have been a useful
instrument in case a strike ballot was needed. A fortnightly might also
have been used to invite the workers to voice their grievances and their
worries in letters to the strike leader. In that way Samant would have
received useful information about the (changing) views of the workers.

Of course, this presupposes an awareness of the value of proper communication and a dedicated leadership devoting most, if not all, of its
time to the struggle at hand. The Bombay textile strike did not produce
a leadership matching these conditions. Datta Samant was an exceptionally busy man, handling the problems of hundreds or possibly even
thousands of unions (he was unable to tell). The strike and its leadership
were to some extent forced on him and all the energy and time he spent
on the textile strike kept him from devoting his attention to more re-
warding struggles in industries where success was less difficult to achieve.
As months passed by and negotiations proved fruitless Samant devoted
ever-lessening time to the strike. In the end, he never even bothered to
call it off.

In addition, his unyielding character and rude *modus operandi* stood in the way of his attaching any great value to the views of individual workers. As a seasoned trade union leader, he was convinced he 'knew' what was good for them and a periodical check at a mass meeting reinforced his conviction that he was still in tune with the workers' thinking. It is doubtful that he would have acknowledged the usefulness of even a simple newsletter had it been pointed out to him. The necessary funding would not have been a great problem and the fortnightly itself might have been used to raise money. In the absence of such a newsletter, the workers (particularly those in the villages) were poorly informed about the progress of the strike and Samant, in his turn, about the views of the workers. Given the fact that he believed that the vast majority of the workers stayed in the villages during the strike, one cannot but conclude that he was either unaware of the value of proper communication or purposely disregarded its significance. In doing so he ignored the fact that even a simple system of communication, a basic necessity in a struggle of long duration, would have greatly facilitated the leadership of the strike and would have immensely helped the workers.

Select Bibliography

Abraham, A. (1978). 'Conditions of Bombay's Textile Workerss', *Economic and Political Weekly*, Bombay, Vol. 13, No. 42, pp. 1761–2.

Anand, Javed (1983). 'The Tenth Month—A chronology of events', in *The 10th Month—Bombay's Historic Textile Strike*, Bombay, CED.

Bagchee, S. (1984). 'Employment Guarantee Scheme in Maharashtra', *Economic and Political Weekly*, Bombay, Vol. 17, No. 37, pp. 1633–8.

Bakshi, Rajni (1987). *The Long Haul*, Bombay, BUILD Documentation Centre.

Bhattacherjee, D. (1988). 'Unions, State, and Capital in Western India: Structural Determinants of the 1982 Bombay Textile Strike', in Roger Southall (Ed.), *Labour and Unions in Africa and Asia: Contemporary Issues*.

——— (1989). 'Evolution of Unionism and Labour Market Structure—Case of Bombay Textile Mills, 1947–1985', *Economic and Political Weekly*, Vol. 24, pp. M-67–76.

Chandrasekhar, C. P. (1984). 'Growth and Technical Change in Indian Cotton-Mill Industry', *Economic and Political Weekly*, Vol. 19, No. 4, pp. PE-22–39.

Deshpande, L. K. (1983). 'A Study of Textile Workers On Strike in Bombay', Paper, Bombay, Centre for the Study of Social Change.

Divekar, V. D. (1982). 'The Emergence of an Indigenous Business Class in Maharashtra in the Eighteenth Century', *Modern Asian Studies*, Vol. 16, No. 3, pp. 427–43.

Eapen, Mridul (1985). 'The New Textile Policy', Vol. 20, Nos. 25 & 26, pp. 1072–3.

Gokhale, R. G. (1957). *The Bombay Cotton Mill Worker*, Bombay, Millowners' Association.

Goswami, O. (1985). 'Indian Textile Industry, 1970–1984—An Analysis of Demand and Supply', *Economic and Political Weekly*, Bombay, Vol. 20, No. 38, pp. 1603–14.

Jain, L. C., (1983). 'Handlooms Face Liquidation', *Economic and Political Weekly*, Bombay, Vol. 18, No. 35, pp. 1517–26.

—— (1985). '1985 Textile Policy—End of Handloom Industry', *Economic and Political Weekly*, Vol. 20, No. 27, pp. 1121–3.

James, R. (1958). 'Trade-union Democracy: Indian Textiles', *The Western Political Quarterly*, No. 11, pp. 563–73.

Joshi, H. & V. Joshi (1976). *Surplus Labour and the City—A Study of Bombay*, Delhi, Oxford University Press.

Kadam, M. (1982). 'The Textile Strike and Datta Samant', *Frontier*, Vol. 15, No. 14.

Kooiman, D. (1977). 'Jobbers and the Emergence of Trade Unions in Bombay City', *International Review of Social History*, Vol. 22, No. 3, pp. 313–28.

—— (1978). *Koppelbazen, Kommunisten en ekonomische krisis; arbeidersorganisatie in de textielindustrie van Bombay 1917–1937*, Amsterdam, Rodopi.

—— (1980). 'Bombay Communists and the 1924 Textile Strike', *Economic and Political Weekly*, Bombay, Vol. 15, No. 29, pp. 1223–36.

Kumar, Radha (1983). 'Family and Factory: Women in the Bombay Cotton Textile Industry, 1919–1939', *Indian Economic and Social History Review*, Vol. 20, No. 1, pp. 80–110.

Kurian, P. & A. Chhachhi (1982). 'New Phase in Textile Unionism?', *Economic and Political Weekly*, Vol. 17, No. 8, pp. 267–72.

Lakha, Salim (1988). 'Organized Labor and Militant Unionism: The Bombay Textile Workers' Strike of 1982', *Bulletin of Concerned Asian Scholars*, Vol. 20, No. 2, pp. 42–53.

Lieten, G. K. (1982). 'Strikers and Strike-Breakers—Bombay Textile Mills Strike, 1929', *Economic and Political Weekly*, Vol. 17, Nos. 14, 15, 16, pp. 697–704.

Morris, Morris David (1955). 'Labor Discipline, Trade-unions, and the State in India', *The Journal of Political Economy*, Vol. 63, pp. 293–308.

—— (1965). *The Emergence of an Industrial Labour Force in India: A Study of the Bombay Cotton Mills, 1854–1947*, Berkeley, University of California Press.

Newman, R. (1981). *Workers and Unions in Bombay, 1918–1929—A Study of Organisation in the Cotton Mills*, Canberra, Australian National University.

Omvedt, G. (1983). 'Textile Strike Turns Political', *Economic and Political Weekly*, Vol. 18, No. 35, pp. 1509–11.

Patankar, B. (1981). 'Textile Workers and Datta Samant', *Economic and Political Weekly*, Vol. 16, No. 49.

———— (1983). 'Invincible Textile Workers', *Frontier*, Vol. 15, No. 46.

———— (1988). 'The Bombay Textile Workers' Strike of 1982: The Lessons of History', *Bulletin of Concerned Asian Scholars*, Vol. 20, No. 2, pp. 54–6.

Patel, Kunj (1963). *Rural Labour in Industrial Bombay*, Bombay, Popular Prakashan.

Pendse, S. (1981). 'Labour: The Datta Samant Phenomenon', *Economic and Political Weekly*, Vol. 16, No. 16, pp. 695–9; *Economic and Political Weekly*, Vol. 16, No. 17, 1981, pp. 745–9.

———— (1984). 'Politics and Organizations of Urban Workers', *Economic and Political Weekly*, Vol. 19, No. 8, 1984, pp. 340–56.

Ramaswamy, E. A. (1985). 'Trade Unions, Rule-making and Industrial Relations', *Economic and Political Weekly*, Vol. 20, No. 12, pp. 517–24.

———— (1986). Indian Trade Unionism: The Crisis of Leadership, Paper contributed to the Ninth European Conference on Modern South Asian Studies, Heidelberg.

Sheth, N. R. (1972). 'Management of Organizational Status: A Case Study of the Supervisor in a Textile Mill', *Indian Journal of Industrial Relations*, Vol. 8, July 1972, pp. 97–119.

Tulpule, B. (1982). 'Bombay Textile Workers' Strike—A Different View', *Economic and Political Weekly*, Vol. 17, Nos. 17 & 18, 1982, pp. 719–21.

Vaidya, S. A. (1978). *Industrial Worker in Bombay—A Socio-Economic Profile*, Bombay, Mill Mazdoor Sabha.

———— (1984). 'Rural–Urban Economic Ties—Flow of Industrial Workers' Earnings to Rural Areas', Paper, Bombay, Maniben Kara Institute.

van Wersch, Hub, (1992). *Bombay Textile Strike, 1982–83*, Bombay, Oxford University Press.

CLAIMS ON LAND, HOUSING
AND HEALTH

5

Signatures in Space:
Land Use in Colonial Bombay

MARIAM DOSSAL

By the 1870s Bombay counted among the colonial cities of significance within the British Empire. What had been a conglomeration of fishing villages and agricultural hamlets in the 17th century, had grown into a port-town in the 18th and a port-city of consequence in the 19th century. With the acquisition of the Peshwa's territories in the Deccan after the Third Anglo–Maratha war in 1819, Bombay became the seat of British power in western India. The needs of the colonial state, the entrepreneurial dynamism of its Indian merchants and financiers, the skill of its artisans and the development of a civic infrastructure all contributed to its urban transformation. Underlying the successive changes, the issue of control over territory remained constant.[1] Land was to rule and by

[1] While a substantial body of research bearing on Bombay focuses on the nature and extent of trading activities on the west coast of India in the 18th and 19th centuries, no comparable work exists on the question of land rights and land use in Bombay town and island. Yet, the very existence of Bombay as trading centre and political base of the English East India Company could be seriously undermined if its control over Bombay island was insecure. For accounts of trade on the west coast of India, see, Pamela Nightingale, *Trade and Empire in Western India, 1784–1806*, Cambridge, Cambridge University Press, 1970; K. N. Chaudhuri, *The Trading World of Asia and the English East India Company, 1660–1760*, Cambridge, Cambridge University Press, 1978; Asiya Siddiqi, 'Money and Prices in the Early Stages of Empire: India and Britain 1760–1840', *Indian Economic and Social History Review*, Vol XVIII, Nos. 3–4, 1981; Asiya Siddiqi, 'The Business World of Jamsetjee Jejeebhoy', in *Indian Economic and Social History Review*, Vol XIX, Nos. 3–4, 1982. For efforts made by the colonial state to assert its claim over all Bombay lands, see Mariam Dossal, 'Knowledge for Power: Thomas Dickinson and the Bombay Revenue Survey, 1811–1827', in Indu Banga (ed.), *Ports and their Hinterlands in India, 1700–1950*, Delhi, Manohar Publishers, 1991.

the middle years of the 19th century, major changes in land use and greater political domination were evident.

For Bombay town and island, two important and detailed land revenue surveys were undertaken during the course of the 19th century.[2] They contain vast amounts of information regarding Bombay's growth from a town into a city, reveal changing equations of power and afford useful comparisons. The first, known as Dickinson's survey, after Lieut. Thomas Dickinson the engineer who masterminded it, was conducted between 1811 and 1827. The second, known as Laughton's survey, after Lieut. G. A. Laughton who executed it, was undertaken between 1865 and 1872. We can use them as vantage points, from which to examine changes evident in both the urban morphology of Bombay and the nature of the colonial state. It is also possible, on close reading, to locate a wide spectrum of state–citizen relations which ranged from accomodation to protest.

The 40 years that separated the two surveys reveal two different Bombays.[3] One of the most striking differences between the two periods was in terms of the numbers of Bombay's inhabitants. In 1827, the population stood at approximately 230,000. By 1850 it had touched the half million mark, and in 1865, the year that Laughton began his revenue survey, the population peaked at 816,000. The dramatic demographic increase was understood as the result of the exceptional economic climate prevailing in Bombay city and western India. The unusually high demand abroad for Indian cotton and the expanding cotton trade had brought an influx of persons to the city. By the end of Laughton's survey in 1872, which coincided with the conducting of the first census on an all-India basis, the population of Bombay had levelled off to around 645,000.[4] The four decades had witnessed a three-fold increase.

[2] Geographer Mathew Edney in his work on the Great Trignometrical Survey stresses the political role of the surveys and maps. They were necessary to create 'an imperial space defined by European principles which enabled . . . [the British] to reduce India's immense diversity to a rational and ultimately controllable structure'. Mathew Edney, 'The Patronage of Science and the Creation of Imperial Space: The British Mapping of India, 1799–1843', *Cartographica*, 30, 1993.

[3] American urban historian, Sam Bass Warner Jr., pointed out in his study of Philadelphia that 'the Philadelphia of one generation barely resembled its predecessor. Since the eighteenth century . . . there have been many Philadelphias, one following the other in rapid succession'. Sam Bass Warner Jr., *The Private City: Philadelphia in Three Periods of its Growth*, Philadelphia, University of Pennsylvania Press, 1968, p. ix. This is true of Bombay and would hold true of most if not all cities.

[4] *The Census of Bombay Town and Island* by Capt. E. Baynes in 1849, *The Census of*

But it was more than numbers that had changed Bombay. The civic infrastructure had been improved and early attempts at urban planning were evident during these years. The introduction of the first municipal water supply system in British India, the beginnings of an underground drainage and sanitation system, land reclamation projects, railways and the expansion of the wharfing and docking facilities in Bombay harbour, all signalled a significant change in Bombay's urbanscape. This and the more heightened civic consciousness evident among sections of Bombay's society marked the shift from town to city.[5]

At the same time, and importantly, what had been a fractured system of control exercised over the subcontinent by the East India Company, gave way to a more confident state power. During the years 1800 to 1870, what had been a relatively weak and ineffective state emerged as a singular force. Its power never was and never would be comprehensive, its authority could be seriously undermined as the events of 1857–8 brought out clearly, but the shifts in the power equations were evident and the reach of the arm of the state longer than it had been before.

A Growing Concern

Though Bombay island measured no more than 18 square miles in the early 19th century, control over its space was crucial to the establishment of British hegemony in western India and the Indian Ocean.

The town of Bombay, located in the southern part of the island, had from its origin been divided into two quarters. The Fort or European quarter was separated from the Indian quarter (the old and new 'Native Town'), by an open *maidan* or esplanade. The central and northern parts of the island were used to grow coconut, date and brab (palmyra or *tadgola*) palms on *oarts* (farms), to cultivate rice and to lay out salt-pans. Important Indian communities living in this part of the island were the *kolis* (fishermen), *agris* (farmers), and *bhandaris* (toddy tappers). The old and new Indian town was settled by merchants and financiers from Gujarat, artisan groups and people in the informal trades from the Deccan, Konkan and Gujarat. In the mixed population

---

Bombay City and Island by Dr A. H. Leith in 1864 and *The Census of the Bombay Presidency (Bombay City and Island)*, part II, 1872, provide details of Bombay's population. Mariam Dossal, *Imperial Designs and Indian Realities: The Planning of Bombay City 1845–1875*, Bombay, Oxford University Press, 1991.

[5] Ibid.

of Bombay, the British numbered no more than one per cent of the total inhabitants.[6]

By the late 18th century, senior British administrators pointed to widespread encroachment on and sale of government lands. They feared that unless the matter was urgently rectified, the usurpation of the state's rights in the land would be complete, and British control over Bombay seriously undermined. The English East India Company, though itself a tenant of the English Crown, paying it an annual rent of £10, termed itself, in its dealings with Bombay's inhabitants, as 'Lords of the Land', and saw the Indians as but 'stewards of the soil', or 'tenants-at-will'.[7]

The Company's position, as legitimate owner of all Bombay lands, had been debated by the well-to-do Indian *fazendars* (landed proprietors) from the start. The *fazendars* had enjoyed substantial rights in the land during Portuguese rule and they resisted the move on the part of the Company to reduce them to the status of mere leaseholders, who possessed their land only by permission of the British.

For a century after obtaining Bombay island from the English Crown in 1668, the East India Company was compelled to adopt a conciliatory policy *vis-à-vis* Bombay's inhabitants. Its own position was much too insecure in relation to the other powers contending for control of the region's trade for it to wish to invite trouble at home. It was only by the 1780s, as Bombay became the base for territorial expansion into western India and revenue shortfalls became chronic, that a more aggressive stand was deemed to be imperative. The state had to construct its position anew. To do this, land rights had to be determined and new revenue rates fixed. Company officials turned to land documents and other records to shore up their claim. When the records did not testify to the Company's absolute rights in the land, they were nonetheless interpreted to its advantage.

In 1790 Collector John Richmond Smyth was assigned the task of making his way through the nine different land tenurial systems, complex land rights and customary practices that prevailed on Bombay island. He was ordered to 'discover every such alienation of the Company's property' that had taken place, examine all past transactions and cancel all sales which in his view were illegal, and ensure that no further alienation

[6] S. M. Edwardes, *Gazetteer of Bombay City and Island*, Vols. I–III, Bombay, Times of India Press, 1909–10.

[7] Government Notice issued by Maj.-Gen. William Meadowes, Governor of Bombay, Bombay Collectorate Records (hereafter BCR), Dickinson's Survey (hereafter DS), Vol. 10, 1816, p. 73.

took place. Indians who assisted in revenue collection, namely the *veriadores* and *mattaras*, were threatened with dismissal, and worse, if they were found to have abetted in illegal land transactions.[8]

Having searched 'every Book and Paper', and finding them inadequate, Smyth urged that a land revenue survey be undertaken which would equip the collector's office with vital information to enable it to carry out its new responsibilities.[9] At that time, however, neither the technical expertise nor the necessary funds were available in Bombay.

Matters came to a head with the outbreak of a great fire in the northern Fort on 17 February 1803. More than 450 buildings used for residential and commercial purposes burned down and the damage to business and trade was enormous. The Bombay government offered compensation to the landed proprietors paying the *Pension and Tax*,[10] many of them substantial Parsi and Bania merchants. To fix the amount payable as compensation and to distinguish the politically significant merchants from the rest of the claimants, required detailed information regarding the names of the landed proprietors, the amount of ground rent they paid to government, and the precise nature of the tenancy prevailing in that part of the Fort. Such information did not exist and this greatly hampered the work of the three-member Town Committee specially set up to examine compensation claims and to oversee new construction activity along planned lines.[11]

Thomas Dickinson and the Bombay Land Revenue Survey 1811–27

In this context of an insecure, alien state, equipped with limited information, the Bombay revenue survey conducted by Lieut. Thomas Dickinson assumes considerable political and economic significance. It coincided with the period when the Anglo–Maratha conflict came to a head in the second decade of the 19th century, continued through the period of acquisition of the Peshwa's territories and the reorganization of the new and enlarged Bombay Presidency under the governorship of Mountstuart

[8] Ibid., p. 74.

[9] Collector John Richmond Smyth to Robert Abercromby, President and Governor-in-Council, BCR, DS, Vol. 18, Appendix N, Bombay, 1790, p. 53.

[10] Special lands under this tenure were freehold and not liable to additional taxes. Persons who held land under this tenure were entitled to the highest rates of compensation when the land was appropriated by the State.

[11] S. M. Edwardes, *The Rise of Bombay: A Retrospect*, Bombay, Times of India Press, 1902.

Elphinstone. The introduction of the *raiyatwari* land revenue settlement in Madras Presidency and the importance given to land revenue
surveys since the time of Thomas Munro's surveys of the Baramahal
and Ceded districts in the 1790s, provide the wider colonial context of
Dickinson's efforts.[12]

When Dickinson began working on the survey in February 1812, it
had already been in existence for a year. The revenue survey initiated
by Lieut. John Hawkins had a relatively limited purpose: to survey the
coconut and brab tree *oarts* of the two revenue districts of Bombay
island, namely Bombay and Mahim districts. Its specific aim had been,
'to ascertain with every degree of exactness how many trees are yearly
drawn by the Bhandaris, that no evasions are practised, and that a full
number in a productive state, are assessed to the public revenue.'[13]

Frustrated by the resistance he met from the *bhandaris* and *fazendars*
alike, Hawkins was relieved to be taken off the survey. The result of his
year's work showed that Bombay district in 1811 contained 911 *oarts*
with a total of 59,494 trees. The urban settlement was still confined to
the southern part of the island and the agricultural land extended from
the north into the south-central parts of the district.[14]

From other sources we know that a suburban movement was then
already under way. By the late 18th century, the English had moved to
the outlying suburbs of Parel, Lal Baug, Byculla and Malabar Hill. Their
desire for larger dwellings in healthier surroundings was shared by
wealthy Indian merchants such as the Wadias, Camas, and Jejeebhoys.
The Fort area increasingly came to be used as a business district. In the
Indian quarter, residential and work spaces continued to be mixed,
with cluster patterns frequently following occupational and caste lines.[15]

Thomas Dickinson undertook the survey work in a very different
spirit than that of John Hawkins. For him, it was no mere job, but rather
'an important, laborious and scientific work of . . . magnitude'. He
believed it to be invaluable for revenue and statistical purposes. Early

[12] Burton Stein, *Thomas Munro. The Origins of the Colonial State and His Vision of
Empire*, Delhi, Oxford University Press, 1989; also, Burton Stein (ed.) *The Making of
Agrarian Policy in British India 1700–1900*, Delhi, Oxford University Press, 1992.

[13] Lieut. J. Hawkins to R. J. Goodwin, Secretary to the Committee of Buildings, BCR.
DS, vol 2, 19 December 1810, p. 17.

[14] Lieut. J. Hawkins to H. Munro, Collector of Bombay, BCR, DS, Vol. 2, 11 October
1811, pp. 32–3.

[15] James Forbes, *Oriental Memoirs: Selected and Abridged from a Series of Familiar
Letters written during Seventeen Years Residence in India*, Vol I, White, Cochrane and Co.
London, 1813, p. 22. See also, S. M. Edwardes, *Gazetteer*, Vol I, p. 37.

on in the survey, Dickinson made plain his views on political economy. His recommendations to the Bombay government, he said, were with 'a view of giving every encouragement to a spirit of agricultural specula- tion, tending so greatly to the prosperity of the Settlement, as well as to the increase of the Revenue . . . .' And his suggestion that *foras* lands (land reclaimed from the sea) be converted into freehold property was 'in strict conformity to those principles, which the Hon'ble Court of Directors have sanctioned for the administration of their Revenue at this as well as other Presidencies.'[16]

A substantial number of estates had been developed on what had earlier been rice fields and salt pans, as in Wadala. The value of these properties had increased substantially and Dickinson was keen to see that the share of the state increase proportionately. He also intended to convert the multiplicity of land taxes into a fixed money rent. Ground rent, believed Dickinson, had for long been forfeited by the state. Numerous shops and stalls had sprung up on Company lands in the town and yet paid nothing but a market fee. Equipped with information about the shop-owners and the sizes of their establishments, the authorities could collect ground rent regularly. Ground rent, he con- tended, was 'as much a component part of the Revenue as Pension from the Fazendar or Toka [tax mainly on salt pans and rice fields] from the Coorumbee [Kunbi]'.[17] Above all, he was determined to submit 'a plan sufficiently comprehensive for every purpose, that can hereafter be required'.[18]

Dickinson's commitment to the survey is evident in the effort that he put into it. His voluminous correspondence is available in the inward and outward registers. After completing the survey of a locality, he submitted an analysis of his findings in the form of a survey report. Each survey report was accompanied by maps drawn on the scale of 40′:1″, 80′:1″, or 100′:1″, depending on whether they were of built-up, semi- urban or agricultural land. The maps exhibited the boundaries of pro- perties, as well as every species of property. They were accompanied by a book of references detailing the nature of tenancy and the rents paid or outstanding, as well as, in some cases, a census enumeration. As work on the survey proceeded, Dickinson reported that many of

[16] Thomas Dickinson to Francis Warden, Chief Secretary to Bombay Government, BCR, DS, Vol. 18, 22 July 1814, p. 12.

[17] Thomas Dickinson to Francis Warden, BCR, DS, Vol 9, 6 May 1814, pp. 27–8.

[18] Thomas Dickinson to James Farish, Secretary to Bombay Government, BCR, DS, Vol 8, 29 May 1812, p. 3.

the properties were held under 'a precarious tenure'. The single most significant legal case which highlighted the conflicting views of the state and Bombay's inhabitants on the question of land rights was the Shamsett case. A large estate on Old Woman's Island had been procured at the Company's auction in 1764 by Pandurang and Balajee Shamsett's father for Rs 7,500. The land had been developed into a substantial coconut *oart* with water courses. Adjoining the Shamsett's *oart* was an artillery garrison. Men from this company frequently scaled the walls of the *oart*, drank toddy from its trees and used the *oart* for pleasure with women from the Colaba bazaar nearby. This was considered dangerous enough for an order to be issued by the Commander-in-Chief in 1804 that the *oart* be cleared. Overnight, the collector's men cut down the trees and laid the *oart* waste.

No matter how strongly the Shamsetts appealed to the authorities for adequate compensation and for an alternative site (such as had been provided to Ardaseer Dady, whose land had earlier been appropriated), the government proved intractable. Years later, with the dispute still hanging, the matter came before Dickinson for his opinion. Unbending, Dickinson pronounced in favour of the state. According to him, 'Government was merely exercising a Right vested in them by virtue of a specific contract, when, in compliance with the recommendations of the Commander-in-Chief, they conceived they were justified on grounds of state necessity, in giving directions to the Collector for clearing the spot of Ground in question, [and] that the amount also of the proferred indemnification was fair, and awarded upon the most equitable and liberal principle . . .'[19] Moreover, though government had allowed the Shamsett's to build a wall, Pandurang Shamsett seemed to have lost sight of 'the very precarious tenure by which he held that property: a Tenure certainly not of a nature to warrant any heavy expenditure on the part of the Landlord'.[20] The Shamsetts remained bitter at the manner in which their trees had been 'butchered' and no just compensation offered for the value of their land.

Such treatment was in marked contrast to that meeted out to Generals Hough and Waddington who possessed substantial properties in Colaba. When it was discovered by Dickinson in the course of his survey of the island of Colaba that their arrears of rent were substantial, he put on record that they ought not to be seen to be offenders, nor could 'a shadow of blame' be attached to them, as 'they had been led to

---

[19] Thomas Dickinson to Francis Warden, BCR, DS, Vol. 20, 24 January 1814, p. 10.
[20] Ibid., p. 11.

imagine' that they had paid the full amount for the ground which they occupied.[21]

The information provided by the revenue survey came in useful to the government on many counts. Numerous cases were identified of persons who had either encroached on Company land or who had defaulted in payments. The key issue hinged on the question of what was legal and authorized and what was seen as an 'encroachment'. The Bombay revenue survey came to an end in 1827; its provisions formalizing land transactions and the collection of land revenue on Bombay island were incorporated into Regulation XIX of 1827.

Bombay in the Mid-19th Century

As Bombay Presidency was enlarged with territorial conquests in 1818–19, the state's concern shifted to the surveying and mapping of the Deccan. Keith Pringle and George Wingate would extend Dickinson's work there, by recording area holdings, classifying qualities of soil, listing the nature of tenures and fixing the revenue demand. When cotton came to be cultivated in the Deccan on a widespread and commercial scale from the 1830s, information provided by the revenue surveys came in handy.[22]

The middle years of the 19th century saw efforts by Henry Conybeare, Superintendent of Repairs to the Board of Conservancy (Bombay's municipal body), to amend existing building legislation and enable government to supervise building activity more closely than it had been able to in the past. Conybeare also pressed for summary powers to taken action against all those found guilty of contravening building laws on Bombay island.[23] As Bombay grew in numbers and economic significance, it was not enough for the state to be equipped with updated information. It also required administrators determined to oversee and control urban activity in all fields.

In 1864, when the census of Bombay City and Island was conducted by Dr Andrew Leith, medical practitioner, statistician and sanitary reformer, the island covered 18.62 square miles and possessed a population of 816,562 persons. The urban concentration was dense in the

[21] Ibid., p. 15.

[22] Sumit Guha, *Economy and Society of the Bombay Deccan 1818–1941*, New Delhi, Oxford University Press, 1985.

[23] Henry Conybeare to Lord Elphinstone, Governor of Bombay, MSA, GD, Vol 3, 28 January 1850, p. 146.

southern part of the island. Habitation in the central and northern parts
of the island had increased, but much land there continued to be used as
salt pans and rice fields or lay vacant as hilly waste ground.[24]

Land reclamation in the course of the next decade added another
four square miles to south Bombay, where additional space was required
for commercial activities and docking space near the harbour to meet
the needs of Bombay's expanding trade. Wet docks, warehouses and
link roads were all included in the reclamation schemes. Reclamation
along the western foreshore was intended primarily for the construction
of the Bombay Baroda and Central Indian Railway.[25] Money for the
reclamation projects was expected from the high returns of the cotton
trade.

The cotton boom proved short-lived; many of the projects remained
incomplete, some were abandoned and others delayed. By the time that
Lieut.-Col. G. A. Laughton completed his revenue survey of Bombay
island in 1872, the island had been expanded and covered 22 square
miles of territory.

The many changes that had taken place in Bombay's urban topography during the mid-19th century made Dickinson's survey inadequate for the purpose which it was intended. The need for an updated
survey was expressed by senior government officials, especially during
the post-1858 period of administrative reorganization. In 1859 Collector
Richard Showell was asked to consider raising rents on Bombay island
in order to obtain additional revenues for the state. Showell pointed to
his inability to do so until he was in possession of information which
delineated the new property boundaries and detailed the various kinds
of landholdings on the island. Secretary to government, E. W. Ravenscroft supported Showell's position, writing that 'the very imperfect state
of land records' made it increasingly difficult to assess the 'great and
increasing value of landed property in the island.' In some parts of
Bombay, land prices were nearly as high as in London, but the rents
were considerably lower.[26]

Work on the survey was begun in November 1865 and continued
for seven years, till 1872. Unlike Dickinson's survey, Laughton's efforts
were part of a clearly coordinated programme of the state. A land revenue survey was programmed for the whole of Bombay Presidency. The

---

[24] *Census of Bombay City and Island* by Dr A. H. Leith, pp. 316–7.

[25] Mariam Dossal, *Imperial Designs and Indian Realities* . . ., op. cit.

[26] E. W. Ravenscroft, Secretary to Bombay Government, to E. C. Bayley, Secretary to
Government of India, MSA, RD. Vol 130, 18 October 1864, 1862–4, p. 19.

triangulation of Bombay island was carried out by Captain Nasmyth of the Great Trignometrical Survey, who (like Dickinson) surveyed open fields on the scale of 100′:1″, while urban built-up land, both in the Fort and in the Indian town was mapped on the scale of 40′:1″. Laughton meanwhile carried out the detailed work of surveying each separate piece of property on Bombay island.[27] Like Dickinson, Laughton was frequently asked for information which was urgently required by the Commissioner of Customs or the municipality to fix their rates. This compelled him to divert his attention from his ongoing work of surveying from the north of the island to the south, district by district, and caused the survey to take longer than expected.

Seventeen property registers of Bombay district and 22 for Mahim district were prepared by Laughton. Nine different land tenures still existed on Bombay island and the area under each was recorded in the survey. Boundaries of 21,575 properties listed on Bombay island were mapped. Laughton himself was satisfied with his work and termed it 'the most complete survey of the whole island in every detail'. The survey helped once again in raising land rents and in discovering encroachments. What was lacking was the analysis which Dickinson had provided in his survey reports.

The Census of 1872 relied heavily on Laughton's survey, with all land in Bombay island being classified as government land. Bombay was shown to have 31,477 houses on 8.6 square miles of ground, the rest of the 13.37 square miles of ground being occupied by roads, streets, tanks and wasteland.[28] The controversy over who owned land in Bombay was long over. Encroachments would continue, the government would constantly fear the hidden transfers and unknown transactions taking place without its consent or payment of its dues, but the revenue surveys by both Laughton and Dickinson had significantly empowered the state and put it on a firmer footing in its dealings with Bombay's inhabitants.

[27] S. M. Edwardes, *Gazetteer*, Vol II, pp. 322–3.
[28] *Census of the Bombay Presidency (Bombay City and Island)*, Part II, pp. 36–7.

6

Urban Development Process in Bombay: Planning for Whom?[1]

SWAPNA BANERJEE-GUHA

Each phase in Bombay's spectacular urban growth over the past century has given rise to new problems and new projects aimed at coping with these problems. The formulation of the successive development programmes and the administrative measures promulgated to implement them have inevitably reflected the balance of power of the existing political, economic and social forces. Our aim in this paper is to analyse the nature of post-independence urban planning in Bombay with special reference to three major projects. We shall examine in each case the adequacy and consistency of the plan proposals put forward by various agencies and the degree to which the interests of the inhabitants have been taken into account.

We shall look at (*i*) the Back Bay Reclamation Scheme—a proposal for the creation of new land in a vital location near the southern extremity of the city adjoining the major commercial centre; (*ii*) the New Bombay development—a project for building a twin city on the mainland as a counterpoise to the congestion of Bombay; and (*iii*) the Vasai-Virar Subregional Plan aimed at funnelling urban growth to a fringe area beyond the northwestern limit of the metropolis, and controlling the settlement pattern. (Figure 1).

[1] When an earlier draft of this paper was presented at the Workshop on the Evolving Cultural Identity of Bombay—held at S.N.D.T. University, in December 1992. Amiya Bagchi, A. R. Desai, Y. D. Phadke, Mrinal Gore and especially Gopal Guru provided valuable comments as did Nigel Harris with whom, it must be noted, there was a strong disagreement on the major propositions of the paper. I would also like to thank several other participants for suggestions and expressions of support which helped in the preparation of this final version.

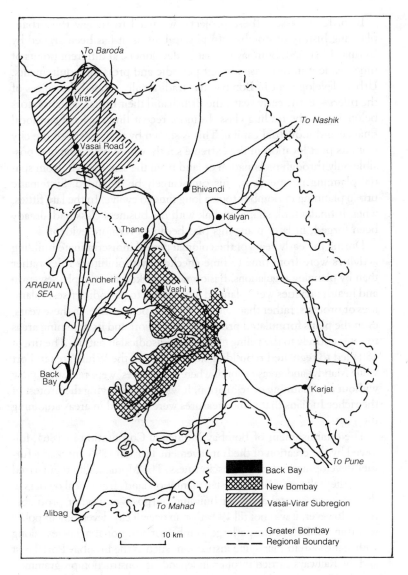

Figure 1. Location of Back Bay, New Bombay and Vasai-Virar Sub-region in Bombay Metropolition Region

In order to assess these projects, we need to review the urban-planning history of Bombay. In physical terms, it has been argued by Verma (1981: 29), Bombay is what its developers, at different points of time, made it in response to their periodic and pressing requirements. Urban development in Bombay has traditionally echoed the voices of the rulers—in the early years, the British and their Indian collaborators belonging to the trading class. In more recent times it has been local finance and industrial capital. This is shown by the growth of the city from its port location in the extreme south, where extension was possible only through reclamation of land from the sea; though, from spatial planning perspectives, this can scarcely be defended. Systematic urban planning in Bombay took a long time to evolve. In the late fifties, when it finally took shape, its link with the business class had already been forged; in later plans this bias became evermore evident.

During the early years of the colonial period indiscriminate building activities were from time to time checked by prohibitory rules rather than by planning regulations. Basic amenities like water supply, sewerage and health facilities were planned in response to periodic crises, calamities or protests, rather than with a long-term perspective. In these years, even the plans formulated primarily for the Fort and its adjoining areas to cater entirely to the ruling elite, were episodical in nature. The fire of 1803 led to regulated rebuilding activity only in the White area in Fort while Mandvi and areas beyond, where the 'natives' were relocated, grew without any planning or regulation. It was only following the protest of the richer Indians that some measures were adopted in areas adjoining the Fort.

The establishment of Bombay Municipal Corporation in 1865, followed by the creation of the Improvement Trust in 1896, marked a further development of civic consciousness. The Municipality regularized the earlier take-overs of extensive plantation lands from local owners in the southern coastal areas for building purposes and other profitable uses. However, it was not till 1909 that an overall city development policy was framed. Before this, a large number of additional agencies, along with some system-managing institutions such as the Bombay Port Trust and the Railways carried through independent construction programmes, not always integrated with the growth of the city as a whole. The government seldom exercised its power to intervene. No wonder, therefore, that the City Development Policy of 1909 had the unique idea of systematically segregating the residential areas of Bombay by income and class!

The conflicting requirements of the ruling British, the commercial and industrial interests, and the landowning middle-class led at times to contradictory decisions. In 1903, Tata's proposal to reclaim the Mahim woods was rejected by the Municipal Corporation; in 1914 the Mackinson Plan for the same purpose was accepted. By the early 20th century, extension through reclamation of land from the sea became a major feature of Bombay's growth.

The pattern of urban development that was fashioned during those years was, therefore, to deal with selective problems (Verma, 1981: 28–45). Although recommendations made in the 1909 policy and later in the 1913 review proposals were not implemented because of the First World War, the subsequent physical development of the city, the location of different components of the economy, differentials in housing and other services, all exhibited pronounced biases. The preferential locations offered to the ruling and 'native' elites on the western shoreline during those years served as an essential element of a west–east class divide in the social space of the metropolis in the following phases of growth. While it is, therefore, incorrect to say that *no* planning was involved in Bombay's growth, there was no holistic planning for the entire population or for the entire city. The mobilization of inputs was also haphazard. Exploitation of distant source areas for necessities such as water resulted in long and costly supply lines. On the other hand, many servicing and recreational institutions were located by the elite classes for their own use on public lands cornered by them at throwaway prices or on cheap lease.

The post-independence period has seen the articulation of demands for physical and social space by workers and a growing middle class. Politicians and urban managers officially responsible for responding to these demands, have, however, often allied themselves with business and commercial interests, especially in high-stake projects. In the name of representing community interests, they have in one way or another legitimized anti-people projects or blocked implementation of plans beneficial to the less privileged.

Planning Considerations in the Back Bay Reclamation Scheme

The Back Bay Reclamation (BBR) area is located in the extreme south of Greater Bombay, stretching from Chowpatty beach to Colaba Point. Land was originally dredged up from the sea in 1865 to extend the Bombay–Baroda and Central India Railway up to Colaba to serve the Cotton Green merchants in their auction and export activities. The second phase of the Back Bay Reclamation was initiated in 1913; the third phase was the really grandiose operation, taken up in 1922 after all the legal formalities had been completed by the government.

The area to be reclaimed was divided into eight blocks: 145 acres were reserved for parks and playgrounds, 100 acres for public buildings, 28 acres for recreational purposes, and 27 acres for educational use. The Development Directorate of the Improvement Trust was entrusted with the implementation of the scheme. Before the entire scheme could be completed, leakage developed in the sea wall that had been constructed to enclose the area to be reclaimed and, as a result, costs escalated to three times the amount originally estimated. Following serious public criticism, the Mears Committee was appointed to investigate the feasibility of completing the project. By then, Blocks 1 and 2 lying between Chowpatty and today's Sachivalaya; and Blocks 7 and 8, covering the present Navy Nagar and the Tata Institute of Fundamental Research had been partially reclaimed. The Committee recommended different methods of land-use for each remaining block and the laying of a uniform surface for all of them, except for Blocks 3–6, for which no further reclamation and development were proposed. Ultimately, the whole scheme was abandoned in 1930. The extremely uneconomic cost–benefit ratio of the project exposed its unrealistic nature.

The curtain rose again in the late fifties. In 1958, a one-man committee appointed by the Bombay State Government recommended the completion of the abandoned Back Bay Reclamation Scheme in order to create additional land resources close to the Central Business District (CBD) and Blocks 3 to 6 were taken up for development. Meanwhile, in 1957, the Bombay Town Planning Act (BTP Act), by dint of which the Bombay Municipal Corporation was made the legal Planning Authority for the Greater Bombay Metropolis, had come into force. In mid 1958 the Corporation initiated work on the draft development plan for south Bombay, including the BBR Area (for Blocks 3 to 6) and submitted it in 1964 for approval to the Government of Maharashtra which was and still is the final approving authority for all area development plans in the state. The state government approved the plan to be carried out in phases till 1968. By this time, the Maharashtra Town Planning Act of 1966 (MRTP Act), which entrusted the responsibility of preparing development plans to the legal Planning Authority, had come into force. It was made clear that the state government would take up the responsibility only if and when the legal Planning Authority failed to submit a plan within a stipulated period.

The draft plan was surprisingly vague about the BBR area. Although, to obtain the approval of the state government it was legally necessary to present a map showing all necessary details, the BBR area was merely marked black with no indication of specific land-use (residential, commercial, recreational etc.), no roads or other public utilities. All it did was to mention that a detailed plan for the BBR area was being prepared by the state government under the terms of the Bombay Town Planning Act, 1957. This Act had already been repealed in 1966 with the implementation of the MRTP Act! Since at the time of its sanction in 1967, the BBR plan carried no detailed proposals, Bombay's citizens and professional planners were deprived of their legal right to take cognisance of it and express their opinions. However, no sooner had the plan been put into execution than criticisms emphasizing its negative effects on people, environment and services began to be raised.

In 1958, a Study Group appointed by the state government under the chairmanship of S. G. Barve had already recommended reclamation of the Bandra-Kurla Complex located at the centre of the metropolis in preference to enlarging the BBR area and had also suggested shifting of office complexes to the suburbs.

In 1966, the Gadgil Planning Committee, to assist deconcentration, had recommended abandoning the BBR Scheme and stopping any further commercialization of south Bombay. The Committee strongly argued in favour of a multi-nuclear growth of the Bombay Metropolitan region to be achieved through building of new towns. For this purpose the committee recommended the creation of a Regional Metropolitan Board, which was constituted in 1967.

In the same year, the Metropolitan Transport Team appointed by the Planning Commission, Government of India, criticized the BBR Scheme on the ground that it would increase localization of commerce in southern Bombay, thereby exerting pressure on water and other supplies and services and straining the public transport system.

The Bombay Metropolitan Regional Planning Board (BMRPB), for its part had appointed two study groups. Both had recommended (a) creation of a new town on the mainland, across the Thane Creek; and (b) restructuring of Bombay by developing the suburbs. Both expressed strong reservations about pursuing the BBR Scheme in particular because of its bias towards commercial land-use.

In 1970, the BMRPB took the reports of the two groups under consideration and recommended the abandonment of the BBR scheme. The board also raised objections on the ground of legality as the draft plan did not show any details of the BBR scheme and was thus in violation of both the BTP and MRTP Acts.

Disregarding the board's recommendations, the state government deleted the specific paragraphs which recommended abandonment of the BBR scheme from the report and replaced them with a statement approving the scheme (Gandhi, 1975: 46–72). The only concession made to the criticisms was to earmark all reclaimed plots for residential use and to lower the proposed ratio of commercial to residential use to 20: 80. In actual fact, by 1992 the ratio stood at 80: 20 in favour of commercial buildings. The ratio originally suggested in the sanctioned plan of 40: 60 was subsequently reduced to 30: 70. However, large plots were sold in the sixties to commercial houses such as Air India, the Express Group of newspapers, the Mafatlals, the Shipping Corporation of India, and Mittal Associates. In 1978, the commercial/residential ratio in the whole of South Bombay was 60: 40; and in 1990, in the BBR area, it was 73: 27. Even this figure fails to give a full picture of the degree of commercial density achieved through the subdivision of each floor into innumerable small offices.

As predicted, this extremely concentrated commercial development in the southern tip of Bombay resulted in congestion, overcrowding and enormous pressure on road and suburban rail transport, water supply, sewerage and electricity. For workers jobs in the business district meant long hours and high cost of commuting. The abnormal rate of increase of real estate values resulted in a distorted land and housing market. A number of citizens' groups and concerned individuals moved the courts to stop the development in the BBR area but without any net result. The legal proceedings continued for years with the commercial interest winning most cases.

In 1983, the Bombay Metropolitan and Regional Development Authority (BMRDA) was made the Special Planning Authority of the BBR area for Blocks 3, 4, 5 and 6 with the responsibility to develop the area in a proper manner. In 1985 the BMRDA submitted a beautification plan by means of which 9.10 hectares of reclaimed land was reserved for a promenade open to the public. For the remaining 41 per cent of the BBR area, where no construction had yet been undertaken, and 100 per cent development had been advocated, the BMRDA drastically reduced the percentages. For Block 4 it suggested only 10 per cent development and 90 per cent as no development zones. This 10 per cent includes a sizeable fishermen's colony as well as land for two gardens. For Block 5, 60 per cent has been proposed as a no development zone. In the

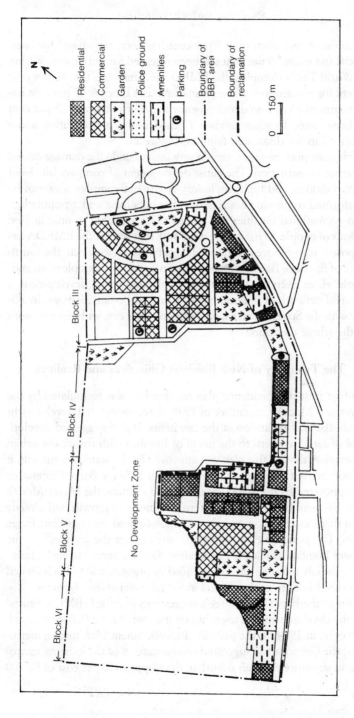

Figure 2. Development Plan of BBR area drafted by BMRDA, 1990.

remaining 40 per cent, only 5 per cent has been earmarked for commercial use while 35 per cent has been reserved for public use. Within the World Trade Complex, the BMRDA recommends that 30 per cent be kept for playgrounds and a gymnasium. For Block 6, 75 per cent has been earmarked as a no development zone. The remaining 25 per cent has been slated to accommodate a bus depot, a police station and a transit camp for dislocated families (Figure 2).

This draft plan, however, can do very little to undo the damage caused by earlier construction. The elitist development of compact blocks of office buildings and high-rise luxury-apartment complexes cannot be transformed to provide housing or other uses for a wider population. Even recreational facilities are bound to be available to only limited sections of people. What can be done and, that is what the BMRDA has proposed, is to reduce commercial density. In the long run, the fourth phase of the Back Bay Reclamation area presents an example of an anti-people, elitist exercise. In the name of planned urban development, a powerful network of finance, business and real estate interests, in alliance with the State, has reshaped a section of the city, with repercussions for the whole metropolis.

The Twin City of New Bombay: Objectives and Realities

The first post-independence plan for Bombay was formulated by the Mayer and Modak Committee in 1948. It recommended development of suburbs and expansion of the city limits. It also suggested development of satellite towns to the north of Bombay with the aim of urban dispersal. Although this plan was approved by the state government, it did not, in itself, have any legal sanction. In 1958 the Barve Committee was appointed by the State Government to examine the Mayer-Modak Plan. By then, however, the pattern of Bombay's growth had already taken shape essentially as an industrial spillover into the immediate fringe zones. The periodic extension of the area under the authority of the Greater Bombay Municipal Corporation (GBMC) served to annex formally to the city the areas already occupied by privately and publicly owned factories, builders or developers aided by government agencies.

One of the Barve Committee's suggestions that the GBMC accepted was the development of a township on the trans-Thane-Creek mainland. However, in 1964, in the published Development Plan for the metropolis, the Corporation suggested reorganization of the existing metropolitan structure through suburban development at the cost of Rs 700 crores and laid no stress on the proposal for a counter-magnet. Financing was envisaged by means of a development tax. Business and commercial interests opposed this plan as it did not grant them enough room for expansion. They also took exception to the prospect of any additional tax. Subsequently, the Gadgil Committee which was appointed under their pressure to review the development plan suggested a total halt to development in the metropolis. The 1964 Development Plan, by its simultaneous focus on development within Bombay and decentralization of its economic activities, thus proved to be self-contradictory. Since the plan concentrated mainly on the metropolis rather than on the region and since it lacked conceptual integration, the vested-interests group could brand it as a narrow, unrealistic and costly endeavour, thoroughly unsuitable for future regional development. As a follow-up to the Gadgil Committee report, the Modern Architects Research Group (MARG), headed by three well-known architects and backed by the business class, then projected through seminars, publications and media publicity the idea of developing a new city on the mainland. By 1968, the Municipal Corporation accepted the proposal for a New Bombay, to which official sanction was promptly granted by the state government. Members of the architects group later occupied crucial decision-making positions in the New Town Planning Body and paved the way for private interests to influence the policy of a public organization. As an alternative to reorganizing the vacant land of Greater Bombay and the open space owned by big business houses which even in the nineties remained untouched by any government mandate, the state government chose to develop a new city on the mainland. The earlier proposal by the Regional Board to develop a series of satellite towns was also dropped or at least postponed, to be reconsidered when New Bombay had become as large and crowded as Bombay. Till such time, it was assumed, satellite towns could wait (Verma, 1981: 28–45).

In fact, the state government simultaneously pursued the Back Bay Reclamation Scheme and New Bombay proposal when, from the planning point of view, one was the antithesis of the other. If New Bombay was to be promoted as a counter-magnet to Greater Bombay, encouragement to commercial expansion in south Bombay would achieve exactly the opposite result. This ambivalence was not, however, accidental. The two incompatible plans were backed by the same business interests who wanted both the projects to materialize because they saw possibilities of profit from both. Although the Estimates Committee appointed by the state government to look into the feasibility of the proposal strongly criticized the increase of power of the Back Bay 'commercial beehive' in curbing the attraction of the new city, both the projects proceeded simultaneously.

Objections raised by political groups, citizens' committees and individual concerned citizens against the New Bombay project were many. The critics argued that (*i*) the plan would aggravate the concentration of industries in the Bombay region; (*ii*) since its aim was limited to the decongestion of Greater Bombay, the new city would not address the larger issue of regional disparity in Maharashtra State; (*iii*) the cost of development of this colossal project would starve out development of many other centres and thereby increase disparity between the Bombay Metropolitan Region and other regions of the state; (*iv*) although the new city initially would be aided by the public sector with public funds, it would be taken over ultimately by the private sector with prices of basic amenities like housing, health and education rising to heights beyond the reach of the general population; (*v*) given the nature of its location, New Bombay would not be able to develop as an independent urban centre but would remain a satellite of Bombay; and (*vi*) the project would displace the local cultivators from their land.

The Estimates Committee and the state government, in reply to the above criticisms, claimed that (*a*) New Bombay was being conceived as a common-man-oriented city and would not become a preserve of the rich; (*b*) the project would ensure urban development in the entire region in a planned and balanced manner; (*c*) the city would develop on the basis of the sustainable economy of the already existing Thane-Belapur Industrial Belt and would create a new urban economic base as well, reducing the length of journeys to work and pressure on inter-city transport; (*d*) as far as possible, the new city would be made an air and water pollution free area with a balanced distribution of amenities and facilities for all sections of the society (Estimates Committee, 1973–74: 9–10). The casual nature of the treatment that these criticisms received is illustrated by the fact that in 1973, when New Bombay had already become a material entity with the opening of Thane Creek Bridge and the installation of residents in Sector 1 of Vashi, the Estimates Committee was still busy preparing its report on the feasibility of the project.

What are the locational and organizational characteristics of New Bombay today? Spread over an area of 343.70 sq. metres, it includes 95 villages, a big industrial area, as also huge areas of agricultural, marshy and barren land. It is a State project, promoted by the Government of

Maharashtra and implemented by the City and Industrial Development Corporation (CIDCO), a planning organization formed in 1970 for the purpose of developing the new town, wholly owned by the Government of Maharashtra. It was originally a subsidiary company of SICOM (State Industrial Investment Corporation of Maharashtra) Ltd, which itself was wholly owned and controlled by the state government. Later CIDCO was made the New Town Development Authority (NTDA), and later again the Special Planning Authority (SPA) of New Bombay and several other areas in Maharashtra under the provisions of the MRTP Act, 1966 (Verma, 1985: 50–4). CIDCO concentrates on those regions where the MIDC or SICOM has already chosen sites and puts in its complementary share of urban services. The BMRDA was designated the coordinating apex body to regulate and approve the development plans of both the GBMC and CIDCO Ltd.

In the development strategy of New Bombay (1971–91) the structural plan had envisaged a balanced urban development through a nodal pattern strung along a mass rapid transport line. Each of these nodes was expected, in the ultimate stage of development, to become independent and self-sufficient, with a strong economic base (Figure 3). In the course of 20 years, from 1973 to 1993, only seven of the originally planned 20 nodes were actually developed. The other major objectives of CIDCO in 1971 were, (*i*) to reduce concentration of population and economic activities in Greater Bombay; (*ii*) to furnish physical and social services to New Bombay residents, raise the standard of living and reduce disparities in the availability of amenities to different sections of the population; (*iii*) to provide a better environment to the residents of New Bombay; (*iv*) to rehabilitate the local population adequately and integrate them in the planned urban development by employing them in various organizations run by CIDCO; and (*v*) to support the state industrial dispersal policy (CIDCO, 1973: 5).

In the beginning the new city was meant to be a middle-class settlement. Land was treated as a resource which CIDCO developed and offered on lease to different sections of buyers. During the first 10 years CIDCO acted as developer, builder, civic authority and planner. The combined roles of CIDCO made a positive impact on public opinion and the gigantic project was seen not as a mere encroachment of urban land-use in rural areas but as a meaningful effort towards planned urban development in which all classes, including the local residents, would be integrated. What was achieved later was far from the planned objectives. But this was not an accident as the apprehensions expressed

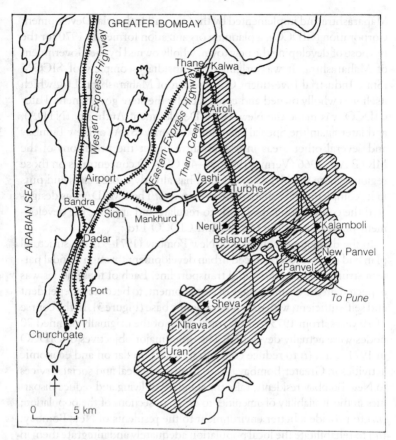

Figure 3. New Bombay (shaded area)

earlier proved to be well founded. A careful scrutiny of CIDCO's organizational set-up and use of land as a resource can help to explain the anomaly. CIDCO was a public limited company registered under the Companies Act. At the same time, it was a New Town Development Authority, wholly owned by the state government. Theoretically, it was thus a state agency to develop New Bombay in order to decongest Greater Bombay, for which goal it was provided the initial funds. Effectively, it became a public sector endeavour to promote market forces. CIDCO has always had private sector people in its executive body. The flexible planning strategy that it was authorized to adopt is significant in the above context. This allowed its executive body to

deviate from the original objectives. For example, the aim of rehabilita
tion of indigenous displaced population was simply dropped in 1981.

One of the chief arguments for the decision to create New Bombay
was that the price of land there was much lower than that of vacant land
areas in Bombay which were owned mostly by the private sector and
only partly by government. As a result of Back Bay development, the
cost of these lands had risen further and the owners were reluctant to
part with their assets. By contrast, the lands of the poor peasants of the
area beyond Thane Creek appeared to be more easily available. Over
the years, however, both the compensation amount and the development cost rose, since New Bombay was no longer a virgin location,
without any infrastructure. The argument of MARG that the cost of
reorganization of Bombay and that of the development of New Bombay
would be almost identical (Verma, 1981: 38) was actually baseless and
motivated.

The volume of private investment that has occurred in New Bombay
since the mid-eighties surpasses all plan projections. By contrast, public
facilities are few. With a population of nearly 200,000 in the early
nineties, the city does not have a single public hospital or health centre,
municipal or government school or even a properly maintained public
playground or recreational centre. The main playground of Vashi has
been divided up among different private schools while a large area has
been cornered at a cheap rate by a private club. A huge acreage in a
prime location of Vashi is again occupied by another private club
claiming to have the highest diving platform in Asia. History seems to
be repeating the earlier commandeering of substantial areas by Bombay Gymkhana, the Willingdon Club and the Chembur Golf Club in
Bombay on 99-year leases at a nominal rent of Re 1/- per year. Since the
early eighties, CIDCO has been advertising the sale of plots and houses
on a priority basis to non-resident Indians who can pay in foreign exchange (*India Today*, 1985: 17). The land-use policy also has undergone
considerable changes. Some northern areas located very close to the
NOCIL chemical plants, earlier declared as environmentally unsuited
for residential use, have been offered for sale to private co-operatives.
Similarly, certain vital facilities like sewage farming and parks or playgrounds were removed from the 1981 land-use plan. Instead of balanced
development among the nodes, Vashi—the location most favoured by
business interests because of its physical proximity to Bombay—has
emerged as the affluent core of New Bombay. This is evident from the
fact that 64 per cent of medical stores, 68 per cent of hospitals and

nursing homes (all private), 74 per cent of doctors, 60 per cent of hotels and restaurants, 63 per cent of banks, 60 per cent of commercial institutions and 55 per cent of schools in New Bombay are located in Vashi (Banerjee-Guha, 1989: 159–88). It has become the effective commercial centre of New Bombay, whereas the original plan called for creating the central business district in Belapur, the geographical centre of New Bombay. The major commercial area of Vashi has in fact been even renamed as a District Business Centre by CIDCO. As of the late eighties, Vashi offered 56 per cent of the total employment available in New Bombay while Belapur offered only 19 per cent. Of the private sector jobs in the city, 18 per cent were concentrated in Vashi while Belapur had only 2 per cent (CIDCO, 1987: 22). Even minimal housing in Vashi is beyond the reach of a middle-class family.

In early 1992, the New Bombay Municipal Corporation was set up with the hope of levying taxes from the nearby industrial area. However, its organizational and functional set-up are yet to be made operational.

New Bombay has been projected as an example of a planned urban development, the construction from scratch of an independent people-oriented city. As Bombay is saturated and virtually out of bounds to middle and lower income groups, the interior nodes of New Bombay were expected to offer them residential opportunities for years to come, but the nature of its development, the dominance of private capital in the prime nodes, the emerging nodal disparity and the total absence of a public sector in social infrastructure expose the hidden character of the plan. To a large degree, New Bombay has functioned as a satellite centre for the finance and industrial capital of Bombay and as a dormitory suburb. The indigenous population has been pushed to the periphery, both culturally—by displacement from their old settlement, and economically—by acquisition of their cultivable land. Many displaced families could not even find shelter in the sites aod services projects earmarked for them (Banerjee-Guha, 1991: 55–65). The gap between the stated planning objectives and the actual realities in this new metropolis continues to deepen.

The Vasai-Virar Sub-region: Forces behind Its Plan

Vasai-Virar is a small sub-region in the Bombay Metropolitan Region lying to the north-west of Greater Bombay. Except for the three towns of Vasai, Virar and Sopara, the entire area had remained primarily agricultural till the mid-seventies, when the land-use started changing, thanks to the enterprise of private builders. Up to the eighties the pace of change was slow. In 1981, the overall population of the area was 241,509. Excepting Agashe, no village had a population larger than 10,000 (Tinaikar, 1990). During 1971–81 the urban population rose by only 20 per cent. None of the towns, excepting Vasai with 34,940 population and Virar with 23,303 population crossed the limit of 20,000 in 1981. In some villages, as for example, Kaular B. K., and Rajavali, the population even decreased by 8 per cent and 17 per cent respectively. Only the town of Virar showed a steep rise of population of nearly 83 per cent during 1971–81. In Vasai, Sopara and Sandor, the three other towns of the area, population rose at rates of 14, 2 and 18 per cent respectively.

All these areas were dereserved and excluded from the green belt in 1988 and 1990; this freed them for urbanization. (Figure 4). The estimated 150 per cent population increase by 1991 which became the basis of the state government's decision concerning dereservation in fact represented an influx of households moving into huge residential colonies promoted by private builders and developers. The population of the four towns of Vasai, Virar, Sopara and Sandor rose by 44, 100, 1,000 and 18 per cent respectively and 290 per cent at an average during 1981–91. This sharp increase in residential population was not associated with the creation of any new economic base or any increase in non-agricultural occupations. Nor was it preceded by any infrastructural development. This type of runaway development was in flagrant violation of the Metropolitan Regional and Town Planning (MRTP) Act.

In 1975 builders were first allowed to invest in the sub-region when a sizable tract was excluded from the Urban Land Ceiling and Regulation Act. Permission to build a residential colony for 400,000 people was granted by the state government although, only a couple of years earlier, the BMRDA had formulated a comprehensive plan for the Bombay Metropolitan Region, including this area, according to which the towns of Vasai, Virar and Sopara were expected to house only about 60,000 people and to border a large green belt. With availability of cheap housing (as compared to what was available in Greater Bombay) and proximity to suburban rail stations, the settlements rapidly emerged as dormitory suburbs. A series of unauthorized constructions received the post facto sanction of the Town Planning Department of the state government, i.e., the District Collector of Thane. Till the BMRDA became the special Planning Authority for this area, authorization for building activity could be granted by the Town Planning Department.

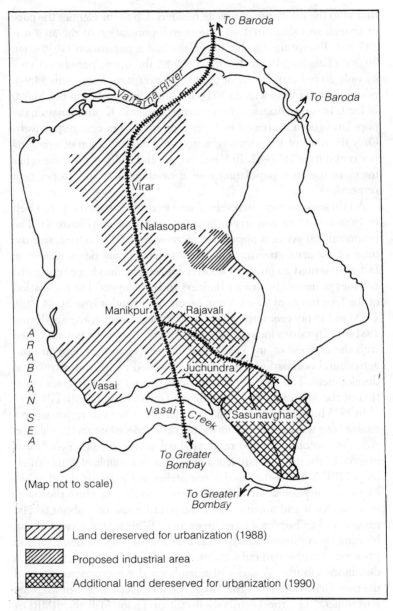

Figure 4. Vasai-Virar Sub-region.

On the basis of fictitious zonal plans, sanctions were granted with complete disregard to the availability of required physical infrastructure. When the BMRDA entered the scene, these violations were already *fait accompli*. Private developers and builders were able to operate through the government machinery, with total disregard for the BMRDA's plans. The main promoters of this development were big business houses such as Shaw Wallace, Mahindra and Mahindra, Larsen and Toubro and certain real estate magnates. The earlier practice of using urban planning as a facade that had been established by their predecessors in the city was repeated.

The existing social infrastructure of the sub-region had been insufficient for even the 1980 population. By 1991, the area received regular electric supply for only two days a week. There was no central drainage system. Supply of water from wells or tankers was severely short of demand. Two projects (Surya Valley and Ujgaon) nearing completion were expected to provide water to some 185,000 people. Another 415,000 would still remain without any regular supply. As of 1991, only 7 per cent of the area had proper motorable roads and the public transport network was archaic. At some locations people had to wait as long as three hours for buses to the nearest railway stations. Nonetheless, prices of flats reached Rs 300–400 per square foot in Virar and Rs 300 at Agashe, which is located 15 minutes by bus from Nala Sopara railway station.

It must be mentioned here that the MRTP Act requires a sub-regional plan to contain provisions for basic infrastructures of water and electricity supply, drainage, sewerage, transport, and social inputs like education, health care and recreation. The stepwise progression of the area for urbanizable use from 776 hectares in 1973 (as suggested by the BMRDA) to 2,353 hectares in 1983/84, to 9,140 hectares in 1988, and finally to 10,921 hectares in 1990 (i.e. 30 per cent of the entire Vasai-Virar sub-region) was not accompanied by any planning for the above-mentioned services. On the contrary, a tract of some 8,500 hectares of land earlier earmarked as greenbelt was also freed for urban use. The BMRDA's strictures against dereservation in 1987 were flatly rejected by the state government, while the Town Planning Department advocated further dereservation in 1990. By 1990, 600,000 people had come to live in the sub-region and the figure was expected to double by 2000 (Asabe, 1990: 6).

On the one hand, dereservation has been permitted by the state government; on the other, proposals for providing infrastructure have been rejected for want of finance. Local civic bodies have been asked to bear the cost of the supply of services leaving them with no alternative but to raise taxes. Thus the residents themselves are made to provide the required Rs 1,000 crores for infrastructure while the builders have already reaped their profit. With the prevailing land price of Rs 15 per sq. ft, construction in the entire 10,000 hectares could fetch Rs 1,695 crores. In the face of such high stakes for business and commercial interests, the goal of balanced development has been relinquished (Prasad, 1991: 5).

The entire process of subverting planning considerations reached its peak in 1990, when, by a drastic decision, the state government appointed CIDCO the Special Planning Authority of the sub-region, replacing the BMRDA. In its Interim Development Plan of 1992, CIDCO showed 55 per cent of the urbanizable area under residential use, without questioning the validity of such a high degree of residential activity with no supporting infrastructure. Actually, while CIDCO was carrying out surveys for preparing the Interim Plan, the region had already been developing in a haphazard manner.

Promoting residential use in an area suffering from acute lack of basic infrastructures goes against all norms of planning and development. Without the tacit approval of the state government, this abnormal growth would not have taken place. The earlier haphazard growth and the later facade of serious planning are equally hazardous for both the local residents and recent immigrants. In fact, planning in the Vasai-Virar sub-region has for long been totally subservient to business interests and callous towards the requirements of the population for proper regional development.

Conclusion

As happened in the case of the Backbay Reclamation Scheme and New Bombay, Vasai-Virar has of late become the subject of an ambitious urban plan. All three represent Bombay's distorted city planning traditions. Grandiose on paper, each of these plans has been shown to be fundamentally flawed when judged in terms of the housing, health and social needs of the vast majority of the residents. All three have proved to be hollow from the people's perspective. The Backbay Project, snatching additional land from the sea at the extreme southern end of the city, could lead only to the aggravation of the already severe geographical imbalance of the city at an enormous financial cost.

Proceeding with the reclamation at the same time as initiating the construction of a new town on the far side of the Thane Creek doomed, in advance, the hope of creating an independent counter-magnet to Greater Bombay. In the Vasai-Virar area, systematic planning came on the scene only after a decade of official disregard of a regional development policy had already created major ecological imbalances. In all three cases, a powerful coalition of commercial and financial interests, in alliance with State power, has managed to subvert the planning process. An intriguing comparison can be made with the interplay of federal, state and municipal levels of government with business, construction and real estate groups in the reshaping of New York City (Harvey, 1985: 144; 155). The state and municipal governments in Bombay which adopted one plan after another and the planning authorities they created to implement the programmes have been either unwilling or unable to enforce any people-oriented projects. All their plans have had distinctly uneven impacts on different classes; the net result has been not to integrate but to segregate the social space of the metropolis.

With the adoption at the national level of the ideology of economic liberalism, urban development practices in Bombay have become even more elitist. Privatization has been introduced in road and waterways construction, and in development and maintenance of railway stations and tourist spots. Official endorsement of the profit motive as the key to progress reinforces and perpetuates the logic that planning in Bombay has actually followed. Meanwhile, housing, transport, water supply, drainage and other infrastructural problems of the city accumulate while the prospect of solutions recedes.

Bibliography

Asabe, P. (1990) 'Vasait Abhadra Yuticha Dhamakul', in *Maharashtra Times*, Bombay, 29 July.

Banerjee-Guha, Swapna (1989). 'Growth of a Twin City: Planned Urban Dispersal in India', in F. J. Costa, et al. (eds.), *Urbanisation in India*, Honolulu, University of Hawaii Press.

——— (1991). 'Who are the Beneficiaries? Evaluation of a Public Housing Project for the Poor in New Bombay', in *Ekistics*, 58 (346/347), Athens, Greece.

Bombay Metropolitan and Regional Development Authority (1990). 'Report of the Draft Development Plan for BBRS Blocks III to VI', Bombay.

City and Industrial Development Corporation (1973). *Draft Development Plan of New Bombay*, Bombay, Nirmal Bhawan.

———— (1987). *Socio-Economic Survey of New Bombay*, Belapur, New Bombay, CIDCO Bhawan.

Estimate Committee (1973). *Fifth Report on New Bombay Project*, Bombay. General Administration Department, Maharashtra Legislative Secretariat.

Gandhi, J. (1975). Judgement on Back Bay Reclamation Scheme Case, Bombay, Bombay High Court, October, 1975.

Harvey, D. (1985). *The Urbanization of Capital*, London, Basil Blackwell Ltd.

India Today (1985). 'CIDCO', Bombay, 7 July.

Prasad, J. (1991). 'Urban Development Norms Violated', in *Indian Express*, Bombay, 1 October.

Tinaikar, S. S. (1990). 'Sub-Regional Plan a Sham', *The Times of India*, Bombay, 21 July.

Verma, H. S. (1981). 'Bombay for Businessmen: Vested Interests in Urban Development', in *State and Society*, 2(4), Kottayam, Kerala.

———— (1985). *Bombay, New Bombay and Metropolitan Region*, New Delhi, Concept Publishers.

7

Upgradation of Slums: A World Bank Programme

PRATIMA PANWALKAR

Bombay's current slum upgradation project, supported by the World Bank, can be placed in the context of the city's urban planning history. During the first half of the twentieth century there emerged a legal framework borrowed from the British town planning tradition. The first master plan for the city, the Modak–Mayer plan, was drawn up in 1948. The first statutory planning exercise was sanctioned in 1957. At this time the state government appointed the Gadgil Committee to look into aspects of planning for Pune as well as Bombay. On the basis of its recommendations, the existing legislation was revised to cover the entire region. Eventually a regional plan was prepared for the period 1971–91. The stated aim of this plan was to contain the population of Bombay City through local intervention and promotion of new urban centres. This approach evolved into the project for creating a counter-magnet town across the harbour, to be called New Bombay. For a number of reasons the new town failed to attract a substantial number of settlers. Meanwhile population in Bombay City continued to grow. The decade 1961–71 witnessed the highest rate since the years immediately after Independence, when Bombay received a massive influx of partition refugees.

At the launching of the 1967 Development Plan, the Municipal Corporation optimistically opined that it might be possible to clear the major part of the existing slum areas during the plan period. Principal reliance for fulfilment of this aim was placed on an ambitious programme of construction by public agencies together with efforts by the private and cooperative sectors. In the event, the slums persisted and proliferated.

Their location was largely determined by the longitudinal pattern of the city, stretching northward from a business centre concentrated in a small area of 65 square kilometres (25 square miles). The land available for squatting consisted of vacant plots within the city limits not protected or put to use by public agencies or private landlords as well as low lying marshy terrains in the suburbs.

The Maharashtra Slum Act of 1971 laid down criteria according to which the competent authority was to declare specific areas as unhealthy or otherwise unfit for human habitation. At that time the city's slum population was conservatively estimated at 1.3 million.

The first official enumeration of slum dwellers undertaken by the government was the census of 1976. This operation identified 2.8 million persons in 1,680 settlements. In 1983, at the instance of government, an effort was made to record the additional slum pockets that had established themselves since 1976. The total number of settlements had risen to 1,930. The population, including the natural increase in the 1976 pockets, was estimated at 4.3 million persons in 924,572 households. If we add to this figure 700,000 pavement dwellers, we arrive at an overall estimate of nearly 5 million persons living on the streets or in slums, approximately half the city's population.

Of 678,381 huts surveyed up to 1984, about 50 per cent were located on private land, 16 per cent on state government land, 6 per cent on central government land, 9 per cent on land belonging to the Maharashtra Housing Board and 18 per cent on Bombay Municipal Corporation lands.

In the early phase of industrial growth slums had tended to spring up around the mills and other workplaces. Today they come into existence wherever open spaces are available. Older slums in places like Byculla, Dharavi and Khar-Danda were originally villages supported by traditional industries such as tanning, fishing and agriculture. Evidence from recent studies shows that currently less than 10–15 per cent of slum residents work within the slum itself.

The rate of growth of slum population exceeds the overall urban growth rate. Protagonists of slum removal claim that Bombay is becoming 'Slumbay' and express fears that slums will overrun the entire city. These fears need to be checked against the available facts. Very little has been done by way of analysis as to how much of the surface of Bombay, slums actually occupy. Making use of the densities obtained from various slums studies, the High Power Steering Group computed in 1985 that, at the rate of 90 to 100 hutments per acre, a maximum of

7,000 to 8,000 acres of city land is covered by slums. If we allow for 700,000 huts and the surrounding open space, the gross slum area comes to about 436 square kilometres, not more than eight per cent of the land of Bombay.

Slum Improvement Schemes

From 1943 to 1956 the Government of the then-existing Bombay State disbursed scanty grants to various municipal bodies for improving unauthorized areas. Bombay was also one of the six pilot cities covered under the Central Government's Slum Clearance Plan of 1956. In 1963 the new state government passed its own law, the Maharashtra Slum Improvement Act, to coordinate and ensure speedier execution of this programme. The next step was the formulation in the early seventies of the state government's Slum Improvement Scheme and the Basic Amenities Programme of the Central Government. A Slum Improvement Board was created on 2 February 1974, but central financial assistance for this programme, however, was stopped with effect from 1 April 1974 and the state government had to carry on the improvement work within its own total plan allocation. In 1977 the Slum Improvement Board was merged with the Maharashtra Housing and Area Development Authority.

Most of the slums on state and municipal lands in Bombay City have been covered under the programme. In recent years the scheme has been largely limited to slums located on private and central government land. With some delays most central government departments have agreed to allow improvement on land in their possession.

In many areas that were declared eligible for slum improvement work, the budget allotments could not be fully utilized because of the sheer lack of the necessary physical space. Density is phenomenally high. In several instances, toilets and water taps intended to serve particular slum areas had to be located on pavements adjacent to or even a little away from the colony itself. Inadequacy of the amenities supplied, consequent overuse, and lack of provision for regular maintenance had the inevitable result that toilets and water taps fell into a state of disrepair and could not be used at all.

In certain areas slum improvement required ancillary work such as land filling, construction of retaining walls, and, for settlements located on hillocks, water supply schemes. Since expenditures on these works were disallowed, operations which had already been sanctioned could not be properly carried out. In the case of slums on private lands, legal action by landlords, who managed to obtain stay orders from the courts, made it difficult to put the schemes into execution.

Meanwhile a number of operators, locally described as 'anti-social elements', have engaged in large-scale trafficking at the expense of both slum dwellers and landowners. Their *modus operandi* is to construct huts on available open spaces and sell or rent them to families in need of housing. When the municipality or the state takes action against unauthorized encroachments, it is the occupants of the huts who are treated as having violated the law and may see their homes demolished. The builders are often able to get away scot free with their gains.

In 1977 the state government appointed a Controller of Slums with the rank of a Collector. His charge was to prevent proliferation of slums, to protect existing colonies from being encroached upon by new entrants, to protect vacant lands required for public purposes, and to coordinate the programmes of the various concerned authorities. He was provided with adequate staff for the management of slum colonies, for patrolling open areas, and for recovering compensation, services charges and other dues.

In a massive drive in 1981, the State Government evicted some 2,000 households from pavements and unauthorized slums without previous warning. Shocked by the human aspect of this operation, civil liberties groups swung into action and took their protest to the courts. The matter finally reached the Supreme Court, which issued a judgement in 1985. The court ruled that the government did not act correctly in vacating the slum dwellers since eviction entails a disturbance of the right to livelihood and thereby infringes on the right to life. However, the court accepted the state government's use of the 1976 and 1980 enumerations to identify slum dwellers whose resettlement was guaranteed if eviction was absolutely necessary for public purposes.

While the case was moving through the courts, the lower level bureaucracy of the Revenue Department, which was supposed to recover dues from slum dwellers and to prevent new encroachments, connived with the local leadership in the settlements to do very little of either. In the absence of clear-cut rules, a state of uncertainty and vulnerability persisted. Slum dwellers were left increasingly at the mercy of unscrupulous middlemen.

Bombay Urban Development Project

The sheer scale of Bombay's shelter problem, and the variety of the actions proposed or actually undertaken to deal with it by governmental agencies, served to make the city an ideal testing ground for interventions. A small but rather vocal number of non-governmental organizations began to show interest in housing. The Bombay Metropolitan Region Development Authority (BMRDA) formulated in 1977 a Sectoral Housing Policy. Many elements of this document paralleled the current thinking in the World Bank (WB) with regard to housing.

At this time the policy of the Bank with regard to the financing of shelter programmes had begun to shift from slum clearance to slum upgradation. Bank spokesmen paid tribute to the creativity and vitality of slum communities. A new approach, qualified as 'rationalist-humanist', placed emphasis on environmental improvement and security of tenure. A series of consultations between World Bank representatives and government officials took place between 1979 and 1982. Research sponsored by the Bank produced a 'Bombay City Study' in which the shelter sector was identified as deserving high priority.

A project of World Bank aid for Bombay emerged in final form in January 1985. An agreement between the International Development Agency of the World Bank (IDA) and the Government of Maharashtra and an accompanying Development Credit Agreement between IDA and the Government of India were signed in March. This launched the 282 crore Bombay Urban Development Programme (BUDP), with a Slum Upgradation Programme (SUP) component of 53 crores.

The stated objectives of the BUDP were:

i. to make a large increase in the public supply of affordable land, infrastructure and shelter, particular for low income families and small business;
ii. to substantially improve the local government's financial and administrative capacity to deliver and maintain services, particularly the infrastructure created under BUDP;
iii. to strengthen the government's institutional capacity to plan, coordinate, implement and evaluate BUDP projects, programmes and policies and to replicate the achievements;
iv. to aim through more efficient and equitable land-use planning and pricing policies and more appropriate performance-oriented design standards, development control and building regulations, at

improved public sector cost recovery and thus to a major reduction in the public and private costs of shelter investments; and

v. to direct a larger proportion of private investment into land servicing and shelter construction of low cost units for low income families.

Only those settlements which had been enumerated in 1976 or 1980 met the eligibility criteria for inclusion in the new Slum Upgradation Programme. At the time of SUP intervention, these settlements were already 30 to 35 years old. They were characterized by a fairly stable existence and well-defined political affiliations. Community-based organizations (CBO) and local action groups enjoyed a considerable degree of autonomy. The majority of the residents were gainfully employed or self-employed in the service and trade sectors. By means of collective action the slum residents had been able, from time to time, to exert pressure on political leaders who undertook to negotiate on their behalf for better amenities and facilities.

The individuals who took an active role in programme implementation were generally senior residents with experience of managing the local systems or second generation residents keen to collaborate with an intervention in which they saw a potential for rise in status. In the majority of cases these active members of CBOs managed to wrest the initiative from project staff and to embark upon a process of community involvement.

In keeping with the economic philosophy of the World Bank, the Slum Upgradation Project offered secure long-term, legal plot tenure to slum households on the basis of their transformation into investors in their own housing and payers of taxes for municipal services and facilities. Tenure was to be given in the form of 30-year renewable leaseholds. For each lease a ten per cent Environment Improvement Cess, standardized at Rs 200, was to be paid by the participating household. The balance of the purchase price was to be repaid at not less than 12 per cent per annum over the following 20 years. The total burden of land improvement and service charges was designed to be affordable, with maximum charges not to exceed 18 per cent of household income. Since insecurity of tenure was considered to be the main cause for non-payment of dues, security of tenure was expected to ensure cent per cent recovery of loans.

It was estimated that some 100,000 households occupying about 15 hectares of land would be covered. Although 65 per cent of slum households are considered to have incomes lower than the local poverty threshold, the expectation was that private individual investment would amount to Rs 7,000 per household. The total cost of the programme was originally set at Rs 36 crores and later raised to Rs 50 crores.

The households were to be drawn from 200 slum areas located in all the different wards of the Bombay Municipality. Almost 90 per cent of the operation was to take place on land belonging to the state government, where the basic policy decision to grant tenure had already been taken. Negotiations were undertaken in order that the remaining 10 per cent of the households covered would be located on privately owned land.

The selected slum areas were to be improved by provision of water, sanitation, roads, footpaths, drainage, street lighting and landscaping. Community facilities such as primary schools and health care facilities were not to be provided since these already existed in or near the chosen neighbourhoods. Space permitting, plots or additional shops and residences would be offered for sale so as to enhance revenues.

A Shaky Start

Two government orders issued in June and early July 1985 were integrated in a final Government Resolution dated 29 July 1985 which described elaborately the modalities of the Bombay Slum Upgradation Programme. The coverage envisaged in the World Bank assisted programme was limited; it targeted only some 10–12 per cent of the city's total slum population.

According to statements made at the time by the then Chief Minister of Maharashtra, it was his government's intention to grant land on lease to cooperative societies of slum-dwellers either free of cost or at nominal rates. To justify its progressive image, it was imperative for the state government to extend the benefits of the programme to as many eligible slums in the state as possible and it was, therefore, necessary to operate the programme in two sectors, one with WB assistance, and one without it. Hence the two orders issued at that time, both granting security of tenure, differed in regard to the mode of cost recovery from the participants. The SUP under BUDP (WB-sponsored) aimed at full recovery on the basis of an elaborate financial analysis. The amount payable by each member of the society would not be directly related to the actual expenditure on improvement but would be determined on the basis of the location of the slum, the area of the plot occupied and the use to which the plot/hut was put. The scheme outside the BUDP made no such demands on the participants and envisaged further scope for re-development by relaxation in Development Control rules, etc., whereas the SUP (BUDP) stopped short at *in situ* environmental upgradation.

Thus, at the initial stage, the programme was saddled with a startling discrepancy between the two orders, both targeted at identically situated groups of slum-dwellers. No attempt was made at that time to rectify the situation, even as the pronouncements of the then Chief Ministers complicated matters. The impact of the discrepancy between the two orders, on each other and on public opinion, did not take long to surface. The damage was more visible in the case of the World Bank aided SUP, since the release of instalments of WB grants to the Government of Maharashtra was subject to satisfactory periodic project appraisal and monthly update reports prepared by the BMRDA on fulfilment of time-bound financial and physical targets.

This confusing situation was ruthlessly exploited by critics of the programme. Active feedback from the Project team on the damaging effects of the discrepant orders, and constant persuasion by them, prompted the Government of Maharashtra to issue another set of orders, on 22 May 1987, which attempted to bring about some consistency in the implementation of Slum Improvement, Slum Upgrading and Prime Minister's Grant Project programmes. However, it was only in 1982 that the government agreed that all slum lands not required for any other public purposes and released to slum societies would be processed on the basis of the norms laid down by SUP, whether under BUDP, PMGB (Prime Minister's Grant Project) or SUB (State Upgrading Board) outside Bombay.

SUP–Communities Relations

The SUP necessarily involves granting of long-term leases on land to cooperative societies of slum-dwellers. The government could, of course, only part with such land as could be freed from development reservation for plan purposes. The other types of land on which slums had grown, namely central government and private lands, required special treatment. The issue of the extensive slums on private lands is complicated and programmes that do not address it cannot but be inadequate.

The BUDP policy-framers, alive to the difficulties involved in land acquisition, recommended that 10 per cent of slums covered under

SUP, could be those on private land. An attempt is currently being made to move in the matter of land acquisition under SUP, but progress has been so slow that one cannot yet claim with confidence that slums on private lands can be brought under SUP. The chances that slums on central government lands in the city can be covered under SUP are equally dismal. It is only recently that, after intense negotiation, the various central government authorities have allowed environmental improvement schemes in some slum pockets on their lands.

The Government of Maharashtra has taken the first step of constituting a Committee under the Chairmanship of its Joint Secretary, Urban Development, with representatives of concerned organizations as members, for examining Development Plan reservations on land encroached on by slums and the desirability of ending reservations. While, on the basis of identifying essential and non-essential reservations, the committee has cleared a number of slum pockets for implementation of the upgradation project, in most cases this clearance has been conditional. Continuous ongoing consultations on the latter issues have been taking place, and the project is struggling to net into the SUP more and more slum pockets as they become freed from reservation. In some cases, site inspection showed that not only had proposed road networks been encroached upon by slums, but even regularized and legalized structures had been erected on them. The question often asked by slum communities, for which there was no answer, was what would be the fate of regularized buildings on the site of such proposed roads, as and when the roads did become a reality.

It was accordingly decided that slum upgradation was to be taken up in the areas which were not affected by the essential reservations. During the execution of the programme, however, it was found that, though a slum may have been cleared for SUP by the study group, complications often presented themselves in the field. For example, there may be pockets of private land within or adjoining the slum and huts on such land cannot be regularized under the scheme; some slum huts might be situated right on the bank of a nullah while the BMC requires them to be 10–15 feet away from it; some part of a slum may be situated on a hill slope, on undulating land, or under high tension transmission cables—all considered to be dangerous locations and, therefore, precluding regularization.

Exclusions of this kind aroused considerable protest, which proved to be one of the most challenging of the problems faced by the community development teams, which spearheaded the projects. The qualitative and quantitative strength of the excluded groups *vis-à-vis* the rest of the community was a critical factor in determining whether a particular community would be allowed to participate in the scheme.

To overcome this problem, it was decided that technically disqualified huts would be allowed to remain in their present locations. However, when demarcating the cooperative society boundaries, it was to be ensured that these did not qualify for membership and would thus not be entitled to regularization of tenure on the land they occupied. Since the creation of societies would be followed by privatization of existing services within their boundaries, it was necessary to decide how services were to be provided to the irregular hutment dwellers. For them, it was proposed: (*a*) if space permitted, additional services should be provided; if not, (*b*) a mutual arrangement should be worked out between the excluded huts and the society whereby the dwellers in the former could avail of services provided to the society on payment of nominal charges, as agreed between the cooperative housing society and these hutment dwellers.

An equally complicated task was verification of the eligibility of an individual hutment dweller within the slums cleared for participation in the benefits of the SUP. It was essential to prepare a list of all the inhabitants of the slum being upgraded as this would be the basis for drawing up the list of members for the cooperative housing society.

This was no simple exercise. The list of slum pockets enumerated in 1976 and subsequently extended in 1980 covered the areas where SUP norms could be applied. In them, there was a range of residents of varying economic status. Depending on the availability of space and a family's ability to get the necessary clearances from the informal control networks, households had been settling in slum communities at different times. There was also a continuous process of sale and resale of structures, sub-letting of structures, and division of existing huts. The challenge for the project was to ensure that, at a particular moment, this ever-fluid stream of population could be stabilized.

With a view to bringing the maximum possible number of families into the scheme, a new cut-off date for eligibility was sought to be established. To make the scheme more attractive, a more liberal approach was suggested for SUP. It was initially agreed by government that the electoral roll of December 1984 would be used as a cut-off point. However, this also failed to resolve the issue. Further relaxations were incorporated in a series of orders, culminating in a directive by the project administration in November 1988 recommending that, except for huts coming in the way of environmental upgradation works, all other structures and residents of the area cleared for SUP would be eligible for membership in the society, once they complied with the requirement of the project, namely, payment of Rs 251 for the purpose of starting environmental improvement works. What needs to be highlighted is the severe strain that was to be placed on local community groups. Besides this financial contribution in this phase of transition from slum to cooperative society, the community would have to shoulder the tasks of checking of transfers, regulating of open spaces, etc.

An intractable dilemma facing the project relates to dealing with those families which are reluctant or ineligible to become members of a cooperative society when granted a lease on the land. There is constant pressure on government from community groups and activist members of the committees to strictly adhere to the rules and evict the uncooperative families. This is understandable as many of the cooperating families will have joined the scheme under great stress and, for them, considerable economic cost, because they want to improve their slum status. It is they who would be sharing the burden of management and maintenance of services, towards the cost of which the members of the society would be contributing appropriate service charges. If government did not take action against non-cooperators, they could happily continue in occupation of society land, and could enjoy all the benefits of the enhanced services without making any contribution to the cost of their maintenance. Obviously, this issue is fraught with tension between members and non-members; it also impinges on the crucial requirement that the programme must provide for full cost recovery. More and more communities coming into this scheme are facing these issues in varying degrees of intensity.

Even more challenging is the situation where, after having been cleared for SUP, the total community rejects the proposal. Such outright rejection is often the result of loss of community autonomy and decisions no longer being the reflection of an active process of consensus and consultation but, rather, that of external political interests. This opposition may arise either out of lack of conviction concerning the merits of the scheme or from a fear of loss of control over the community if the scheme comes into effect. Weak community structure or lack of organizational potential because of divisive forces and an excessive tradition of conflict within the community, are also factors that make it difficult to bring people together on a common platform. Even some professionals working in the field of shelter have been raising basic questions about the efficacy of SUP as a viable means of tackling the problems of unplanned settlements. Hostility is only to be expected when rosy promises have been made about easy finance being available and slum-dwellers have been led to believe they will very soon be able to walk into their own reconstructed houses.

Action against communities and individuals refusing to join the scheme, though theoretically conceivable, is practically impossible. Accordingly, the project team is relying heavily upon goodwill for the scheme among political leaders, local-level leadership and personnel of other governmental departments with which the project has to coordinate for smooth and timely implementation.

The concept of housing cooperatives was incorporated in the programme, (1) to sustain and develop the gains resulting from enhanced services and the potential gains from enhanced land values arising out of security of tenure; (2) to prevent misuse of these capital gains; and (3) to operationalize the concept of change of status of the community from one of slum dwellers to that of residents of 'Environmentally Acceptable Legal Shelter' (EALS).

Since most of Bombay's slum dwellers are by origin rural and the cooperative network in the rural Maharashtra is well established, dissemination of information on cooperation as a concept that must be institutionalized did not meet with any resistance; in fact there was an enthusiastic response. While residents of slums covered under the scheme were thus able to internalize the general concept, what needed more persuasion was to obtain acceptance of the specific nature of a housing cooperative within the context of the SUP. The programme was meant to enhance the quality of life of the participants, not just to allot land leases to cooperatives, leaving other conditions unchanged. It was expected that each society would be independent and have within its boundary its own private amenities, essentially toilet and water facilities. In practice, this was possible only in smaller slum pockets with 100 to 200 households, where services have been provided under SIP. In larger slums, the area was to be divided among a number of small and compact societies with enough space to provide the services. Failing that, SIP services would be so scattered as to make sub-division possible.

While forming societies, due consideration was given to local traditions and practices, so that, as far as possible, existing social contours could be maintained. Suggestions by local groups were actively sought and incorporated. By its very nature this process was very complex and delicate. The project officers had to achieve a mix and match of physical realities as represented by the services and their location in the slum and the peculiar social and political dynamics operating in the community, as exhibited by the settlement patterns. By and large, slums of 100–200 families opted to form single societies.

An intensive campaign was initiated to achieve maximum community participation in the programme through group discussions, the objective being to arrive at consensus on all issues relevant to it. Once the division of the area into small societies was confirmed, action was immediately taken by the programme administration for obtaining the necessary No Objection Certificates (NOCs) and even the execution of SUP works, without waiting for the formal establishment of the cooperatives. The idea was to encourage groups within the community which were eager to meet all requirements of the scheme so that they would serve as models for other groups. Services of a common nature, such as roads, drainage, water pipes and *balwadis* (children's centres) were to be handled by a federation of cooperatives covering the entire slum.

Since they would no longer be unauthorized squatters, entirely at the mercy of the local administration, but members of an independent cooperative society holding a valid lease to their landholdings, to represent and speak for them and willing to pay for services, the slum dwellers expected that the indifference to their needs exhibited earlier by the bureaucracy and local-level leadership would end, that they would now have easier access to community services. The representative structures that emerged with the formation of the cooperatives had, for their part, a unifying effect on the communities, which hitherto had displayed intense infighting. They now came together and strengthened themselves as collective entities in order to obtain the resources made available or, at least, promised by the project.

The slums were earlier large sprawling settlements, sometimes collectively mobilizing for common purposes, but often victims of manipulation by external leadership and/or local-level bureaucrats. Breaking them up into smaller areas of manageable size, perhaps done in an arbitrary fashion for SUP, but in consultation with local leadership and residents, has now given them a new, more precise identity. However, in the matter of services which are to be privatized and located within the boundaries of each society, some competitiveness and minor bickerings between various groups in the area are emerging. This competition is not so apparent at the physical level in terms where services are to be located but has surfaced with reference to influence over people. A small coterie of individuals, who formerly exercised control over larger geographical areas, must now function as members of committees including other persons capable of taking on effective leadership roles. These committee members, once in place and comfortable in their positions, may try to test their strength and bypass the central slum leadership which had earlier exercised influence over the whole community and managed all interactions of the slum with the larger municipal systems. That many more individuals are now drawn into the scheme is a desirable development, but it is looked upon with suspicion by those who formerly held sway over the entire area.

This is not to say that the introduction of cooperatives is a panacea for all the problems in a community. A cooperative, as is known, can serve as an instrument of exploitation if it falls into wrong hands and is monopolized by corrupt individuals or groups. Efforts are being made to intensify community education concerning the rights and powers of rank-and-file members of a cooperative society so that they can prevent misuse of the cooperative structure.

Encroachment Issues

Protection against encroachments on the area leased to a cooperative society was, until recently, the job of the tehsildar. Technically, today, under SUP, it is the responsibility of the cooperative society to deal with encroachments. However, not all society committees have yet reached the organizational level of strength to tackle them without the support of official power structures. The committees are also not confident that the project would support them if they took action. They therefore continue to rely on the concerned authorities to take steps to remove encroachments. Committee members are understandably reluctant to handle this very sensitive issue, action on which often leads to violent confrontations.

Another area of ambivalence is the sanction and supervision of repairs to existing structures. Previously, permissions for executing repairs used to be granted by the SUP authorities; this has now been taken over by the municipal ward office. However, it is the concerned cooperative that is charged with the responsibility of ensuring that 'repairs' do not trespass into total renovation, or transgress the rights of neighbouring huts, although it does not have any power to take punitive action against offenders. This is an area of uncertainty which if not handled properly could strengthen the peoples' scepticism concerning the project itself.

Thanks to the security of tenure that the project has provided, real estate values in SUP areas have been shooting upwards and the temptation to transfer *de facto* rights in plots in return for substantial monetary consideration will not always be resisted. Ingenious ways will be found to bypass the rules. Unless the project addresses this possibility seriously and consistently, the whole programme is likely to suffer grave damage.

Norms for environmental improvement under SUP are not very different from those that had been laid down in SIP. What is certainly very different is the process by which the community perceives these works. An intensive series of discussions precedes the finalization of engineering plans. Here too the emphasis is laid on full cost recovery. Throughout the discussions there is constant pressure from the local leaders for enhanced services and a greater variety of works. The slum-dwellers are no longer just mute beneficiaries of programmes. For most engineers as for most bureaucrats in public housing agencies, the militant postures and vociferous demands of slum leaders provide a new and not always welcome experience. Levels of expenditure in local areas being public knowledge, thanks to the process of calling for public tenders, etc., many communities have been in a position to calculate how much is being spent on their area and point out that this is less than what the community has paid to the project.

Reconstruction

An aspect of SUP which has aroused much debate and divided opinion amongst not only communities and political leadership but also among professionals and shelter activists is the choice between *in situ* upgradation and total reconstruction.

In areas where population density is very high and the location of huts is totally haphazard, there can be no space for additional service inputs, the possibility of *in situ* upgradation is vehemently challenged. This also amounts to a perpetuation of inequality because of the freezing of the area of hut occupancy with no possibility of modification. Communities and activists are challenging the justice and equity dimension of this phenomenon. At the same time, architects and planners would question the degree of relaxation and flouting of norms that should be allowed to render a slum area environmentally habitable. A reconstruction project envisaging self-contained units would take care of the public health hazards and substantially improve the quality of life of slum dwellers,

thus contributing to an enhanced self image. The fact that *in situ* upgradation does not address these issues has been considered the greatest
failure of the scheme by this lobby. For politicians and community
leaders, SUP emerges as a let-down after all the grandiose plans and
promises of 'houses' for all slum dwellers.

While the SUP programme was being promoted in various slum communities, there was a growing tendency on the part of slum-dwellers to
question the adequacy of *in situ* upgradation for their areas. In reply, the
project staff emphasized two arguments which had convinced many of
the communities that had entered the scheme earlier: first, the logic of
preserving inputs that households have already invested when constructing and improving their structures; second, the rationale of retaining
the present occupants in their existing sites, without the dislocation
which could arise out of total reorganization.

Today, differences of opinion continue but the scales are heavily
tilted, both politically and technically, towards reconstruction. Political
leaders are still making promises of putting slum dwellers in their own
houses with the help of loans at low interest and long-term repayment
schedules. If both political and administrative will are forthcoming, it
is possible to successfully to implement such a programme but equally
critical to its success would be the simultaneous provision of adequate
shelter units to other low- and middle-income households to ensure that
the better-off among them do not hijack the reconstructed slums.

Presently, redevelopment hinges on obtaining tenurial rights and
until recently the SUP under BUDP was the only available vehicle for
this. After resisting demands for this for some years, the Government
of Maharashtra, acceding to political pressure, announced yet another
policy of slum redevelopment in what is popularly called the '2.5 FSI
scheme' (April, 1992). The cornerstone of this scheme is the enhancement of FSI (floor space index: extent of floor space permitted to be
constructed as a ratio of plot size) to 2.5 for cooperative housing
societies (CHS) of slum dwellers on government, municipal and private
lands, with the corporation playing a major role in granting building
permission under the relaxed norms. Advantage can be taken of the
enhanced FSI either directly by CHS of slum dwellers, or by private
landowners and builders who, in active consultation with the slum
residents, can initiate reconstruction projects. Apart from a government
loan of Rs 10,000 and an initial contribution of Rs 50,000 per constructed
tenement of 180 sq. ft., costing minimally Rs 65,000 to Rs 70,000, what
is held out as a major incentive is the marketable value of the excess FSI

that will remain after the members have been rehoused. Under a very elaborate financial formula, the capital gains from this excess FSI will accrue to the CHS or the builders/developers who have invested in the projects. This approach has been justified on the ground that it attracts private capital investment in slum redevelopment. The ability of slum residents to withstand market forces if such a scheme is operationalized, has been questioned. It is claimed that prime locations of land will be released under the garb of slum redevelopment. Even in terms of technical soundness and practicality the scheme does not stand the test of scrutiny. In an elaborate analysis based on existing density in slums, the BMRDA document 'Shelter Needs and Strategies for BMR' (August 1992) has highlighted the fact that the scheme can be potentially useful for only 35 per cent of slums.

The political vulnerability of the scheme became evident when, very recently (August 1992), the Chief Minister of the state announced from a public platform an increase in area for huts from 180 to 250 square feet, in response to a pressing demand from political leadership in the slums.

Once again the government and the bureaucracy have managed to make the necessary expressions of concern for the plight of the slum dwellers, and renewed their commitment to rehousing them, without any concern for the practicality of their elaborate schemes. At the community level, these pronouncements come as appeasement and diversionary tactics. In the ensuing confusion, the vested interests and lobbies, this time local-level leaders and bureaucrats hand in glove with architects and developers, hope to profit. Many SUP societies have in recent months explored the possibilities of this option. It has been discovered that the proposal for collective tenurial rights with scope for realignment and shelter consolidation as promoted by SUP still holds out a greater promise in its practical application. This is now a time-tested approach which ensures a high degree of autonomy for the community-based organizations in the slums.

Bureaucratic Response to the Scheme

The slum, as a phenomenon, has always evoked mixed reactions from professionals and bureaucrats. Invariably, as individuals, the functionaries manning the programmes could not totally free themselves from the biases and prejudices of the class to which they belong. Often their preconceived perceptions inadvertently influence patterns of programme management and execution. Ostensibly, a high degree of objectivity was maintained, the standard defences against charges of bias being 'norms', 'rules' and 'regulations', but these in themselves reflect the bias of their origin.

In order to eliminate bureaucratic hurdles and accelerate the pace of implementation of timely decisions initiated by the project authorities, the government vested all powers of hut regularization in the project staff. The wisdom of this move has been indicated. The pace of implementation increased substantially and the advantages of the 'single-window' approach were demonstrated. By September 1993, about 15,475 households in some 140 societies had received collective tenurial rights.

At the initial stage of the project, most officials involved in programme implementation felt that it was too idealistic and would never get off the ground, because of the intractable nature of slum dwellers and what was perceived as their exploitative and parasitic relationship with the rest of the system. The unexpectedly positive response from the field and the support of most of the communities eligible under SUP created a piquant situation. The eligible communities are demanding the maximum gains available from the project while the project staff appear to be shying away from these demands, the major issue being that of land dereservation. Perhaps, it would not be too harsh a judgement to say that, at times, the reluctance of the project team to spend adequately on environmental improvement is a reflection of the grudging nature of the middle-class functionaries who are now duty bound to execute the scheme, despite their lack of necessary perceptions and commitment.

The programme in spite of high priority rating has not been able to free itself totally from bureaucratic and professional one-upmanship. The constant struggle between the generalist and the specialist is evident here also. Bureaucracy which gauges its strength from the power-base it can generate is not very keen on sharing power with the communities where the seeds of the scheme have been successfully planted. On one hand, the project offers greater freedom, self-reliance and status to slum communities; on the other, the process of implementation is beset with difficulties.

NGOs and Political Response

In the given administrative-political set-up the relations the bureaucracy develop with non-officials are crucial. Interests of political leaders in slum communities are well established. SUP officers who respond actively to local communities bypassing political leadership or infringing upon its prerogatives are bound to face the wrath of the politicians. Complexities in programme implementation are enhanced because of the various divisive elements within the communities themselves. Local groups may be divided along caste, language, regional and political lines.

Also present on the scene are the slum wings of most of the political parties. Their presence in the SUP has not so far been felt critically. A positive option could be their active utilization as programme partners. As of today, the SUP has not evoked any adverse reaction. Support in one community from an individual/group with a particular political loyalty may coexist with vehement opposition by workers of the same party in another area.

The response of the non-governmental organizations (NGOs) to the programme has been ambivalent, often bordering on indifference. Characterized by their ideological convictions and their propensity to mobilize international funding for their actions, NGOs have never exhibited much enthusiasm for getting involved in the nitty-gritty of programme execution under government auspices. Nonetheless, the role of the NGOs as active partners in programme implementation has been actively promoted by the project. In the field, there have been numerous instances of mutually beneficial collaboration. What becomes irksome for the NGOs is the slow procedural progress which punctuates each and every step in programme implementation. The aggressive reaching-out strategies adopted by the project may at times render the NGOs redundant. This situation can become explosive if fanned by mistrust and lack of confidence.

Conclusion

Over the last eight years, the SUP has been able to establish its presence in the field and is today the only programme of the state government under which the cooperative societies of slum dwellers can obtain tenurial leases on the lands they occupy. The Bombay Urban Development Project, which actively canvassed the concept and the projects, was officially wound up in March 1994, after having received an extension of six months from September 1993. In the meantime, however, a major development took place in 1992: the creation of three Boards in the MHADA the Maharashtra Housing and Area Development

Authority, (*i*) the Slum Board and Dharavi Re-development Project; (*ii*) the Repairs and Reconstruction Board, and (*iii*) the continuation of the existing Bombay Board. Under the Slum and Dharavi Re-development Board, it is now proposed to integrate three major activities related to slums in the city: (*a*) slum improvement, (*b*) slum upgradation, and (*c*) slum re-development. This ensures continuity of policies committed to the granting of tenurial rights to slum dwellers.

It is the experience of the project under BUDP that the existence of active local groups, with abilities to negotiate with the projects, has resulted in a definite, visible impact on the quality of the physical environment in the slums covered by the programme. The managing committees of cooperatives have played their role in the maintenance of services and the results of the shelter consolidation and upgradation process are evident. Out of the 141 societies to which leasehold rights were given, it can be asserted that the majority have vindicated the faith reposed in them by the scheme.

The declaration of the slum re-development policy under the relaxed, 2.5 FSI norms, has also set another process in motion. As of today (September 1993), there are about 80 such proposals pending with MHADA. The process of scrutiny and field negotiation is on. It is estimated that in the first phase about ten proposals will be cleared and, predictably, the majority of them are going to be from SUP societies—under both the BUDP and the Prime Minister's Grant Project in Dharavi. The process of community building and the skills that the committees develop in the SUP serve as a definite advantage in the clearing of cases for redevelopment, to the best advantage of the community. Slum redevelopment, with all its complexities, is yet to take off and needs to be promoted with greater caution to ensure that it can be freed from a possible negative impact on the present slum residents. Thus the field is still open for a stronger push towards the upgradation approach, which, amongst other things, validates the capacities of the slum residents to wrest into their own hands the responsibility for their own futures in an otherwise hostile environment.

References

Bhogilal D. and N. Seervai (1983). *The Shunned and the Shunted*: *The Slum and Pavement Dwellers of Bombay*, PUCL, Tata Press, Bombay. Regional Urban Housing Policy.

BMRDA (1977): Non-conventional and Alternative Approaches to Shelter the Urban Poor—Experience in Bombay.

BMRDA (1981): Affordable Low Income Shelter Programme in BMR.

BMRDA (1988): Shaping Bombay of the Nineties.

Gonsalves, C. and N. Panjwani (1982): *Bombay Housing Policy—Document and Critique in Urban Development Hand Book*. ISRE-Part, Yusuf Meherally Centre, Bombay.

Government of India (1983): Task Force on Housing and Urban Development.

———— (1987): *National Commission on Urbanization—Interim Report*.

———— (1988): National Housing Policy.

Government of Maharashtra (1976): *Tackling the Slum Problem—A New Deal for Urban Poor*.

———— (1981): *Report of the High Power Steering Group for Slums and Dilapidated Houses*.

Harris, N. (1978): *Economic Development of Cities and Planning: The Case of Bombay*, Oxford University Press, London.

Lall, V. D. (1985): *Economic Status of Households in Maharashtra and Policy for Specialised Housing Finance Institution*, Society for Development Studies, New Delhi.

Lindon, Jan Van (1986): *The Sites and Services Approach Reviewed: Solution or Stopgap to Third World Housing Shortage*, Grower Publication Co., Ltd., U.K.

Municipal Corporation of Greater Bombay (1985): *Redevelopment of Slums through Participation of Slum Dwellers*.

National Bldg., Organisation (1987): *Urban Housing Needs*, Government of India.

National Instt. of Urban Affairs (1988): *State of India's Urbanisation*, NIUA, New Delhi.

Phatak, V. K. and Vakil S. Gandhi, (1987): *Bombay Urban Development Project—Lessons of Experience*, BMRDA.

Planning Division, Bombay Metropolitan Region, Development Authority (1992): 'Shelter Needs and Strategies for BMR, Revision of Regional Plan for Bombay Metropolitan Region', Working Paper No. 7.

Richardson, H. W. (1980): *Bombay City Study*, World Bank, Washington.

Sharma, R. N.; Siva Raju and I. U. B. Reddy, (1988): 'A Feedback Study of Housing Schemes of MHADA' in *Main Towns of Maharashtra*, TISS, Bombay.

Skinner, R. J., J. L. Taylor, and C. A. Wegelen, (1987): *Shelter Upgrading for the Urban Poor: Evaluation of Third World Experience*, Island Publishing House.

Sukhtankar, D. M. and P. S. A. Sundaram, (1987): 'India' in *Urban Policy Issues*, Asian Development Bank, Manila.

United Nations (1987): 'India, Country—Paper' in *Report of the Tenth Session of the UN Commission on Human Settlements*, Nairobi.

World Bank (1985): *Staff Appraisal Report India*: BUDP, Washington.

Municipal Corporation of Greater Bombay (1992): *Redevelopment of Slums through Participation of Slum Dwellers*, Additional guidelines for the implementation of the Slum Redevelopment Scheme under Regulation No. 33 (10) of the Development Control Regulations for Greater Bombay.

8

Spatial Patterns of Health and Mortality

RADHIKA RAMASUBBAN and
NIGEL CROOK

Introduction

Before the widespread availability of effective curative medicine, the assumption regarding socio-economic differentials in mortality was that natural environment and nutrition were the main explanatory factors. There was of course a major debate as to which was the predominant factor, especially in the context of understanding declining mortality trends (McKeown, 1976; Curtin, 1989).[1] Once an appreciation of the possibility of prevention emerges, the role of the state's public health authorities becomes important (Mercer, 1990). With the increase in scientific knowledge regarding disease transmission, the role of the diffusion of knowledge, with or without the help of the state, becomes a further issue for debate (Ewbank and Preston, 1989: 116–49; Cleland and van Ginneken, 1988). With the progress of industrialization, the interests of different social classes also assume importance: the industrial employer is seen sometimes as an exploiter of the worker's health in his drive to maximize the extractable surplus, and sometimes as a champion of the workers' fitness, willing to invest in human capital (Navarro, 1986). Exploitation may be resisted by an organized working class (Cooper, 1983: 7–50). At the same time, once the state has learnt how to control the environment, the bourgeoisie seeks to protect itself from the deleterious effects of urbanization. Further, as Castells has pointed out, there may arise a conflict between the landed oligarchy and the industrial bourgeoisie, the former wishing to extract maximum rents

[1] This debate was carried over to their tropical colonies by imperial governments wrestling with the additional challenge of acclimatizing the European component of their armies and official populations to tropical conditions (Ramasubban, 1982).

and the latter seeking cheap land to house the industrial proletariat (Castells, 1983).

All these theories assume social differentiation in health status. Data for major cities like Bombay reveal spatial differentiation in mortality. Residential location theory would predict spatial differentiation by social class, as land rents fall from the central business district to the urban periphery (Henderson, 1977). Do spatial mortality differentials then simply reflect class homogeneity in the spatial domain?

This paper explores the dynamics of mortality decline in the city of Bombay, and their interaction with changing patterns of location as the city developed over the last 150 years.

The Late Nineteenth Century Expansion

The second half of the nineteenth century in Bombay is dominated by the rapid expansion of the textile industry. This shaped the residential pattern and the attendant spatial distribution of disease and mortality that we observe, with some variation, even today. Writers and researchers on the public health of the city are likely to be overwhelmingly impressed by the problems of water supply and sanitation that surfaced dramatically during this period, and the contemporary debate between the remarkable municipal officer of health at that time, T. S. Weir, and his opponents in the municipal corporation,[2] but the significance of the new industrialization, both in its requirements for space and in its requirements for labour, cannot be overlooked, since this was the driving force behind the sanitary compulsions and locational differentiation of the time.

Bombay's first textile mill was set up in 1857 at Tardeo (in D ward bordering on E ward).[3] Subsequent growth of the industry covered the area from Byculla to Parel (E to F ward south) with 82 mills employing 73,000 men by 1900, constituting 40 per cent of the city's workforce. The implications for residential location were important. Prior to this, middle class Indians had been settling the Girgaum area, while the Europeans and Parsis were colonizing Byculla. Further movement in this direction was now foreclosed, and, indeed, the Parsis began to shift

[2] See, for example, Health Officer's Report for Bombay Municipality, abstract in *Report on Sanitary Measures in India*, House of Commons, Accounts and Papers, 1889 and 1892.

[3] Ward identification used in the text refers to the approximate boundaries adopted by the mid-1980s. See Fig. 1.

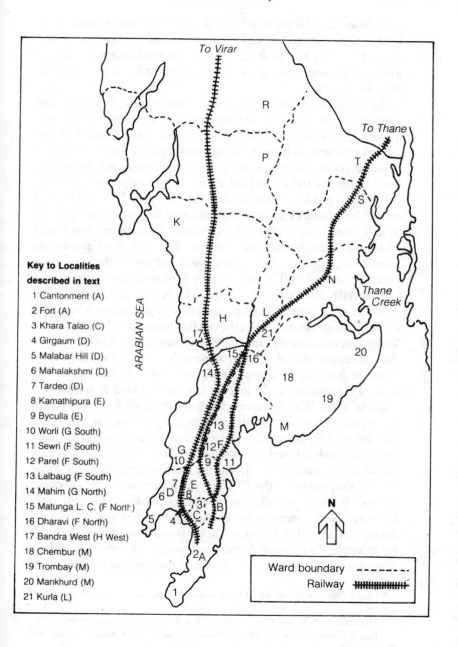

Key to Localities described in text

1 Cantonment (A)
2 Fort (A)
3 Khara Talao (C)
4 Girgaum (D)
5 Malabar Hill (D)
6 Mahalakshmi (D)
7 Tardeo (D)
8 Kamathipura (E)
9 Byculla (E)
10 Worli (G South)
11 Sewri (F South)
12 Parel (F South)
13 Lalbaug (F South)
14 Mahim (G North)
15 Matunga L. C. (F North)
16 Dharavi (F North)
17 Bandra West (H West)
18 Chembur (M)
19 Trombay (M)
20 Mankhurd (M)
21 Kurla (L)

Ward boundary — — — —
Railway ┼┼┼┼┼┼┼┼┼┼┼┼┼

Figure 1. Map of Bombay showing location of wards in the 1980s.

to Malabar Hill. For the time being the mills constituted the northern border of the city, and so long as they remained 'confined to the out-skirts of the city', T. S. Weir regarded them as a welcome development: a provider of employment in a zone where they would not be an environ-mental nuisance.[4]

But industrial expansion was not the only characteristic of the late nineteenth century that would impinge upon the health of Bombay. There were also years of famine which added to the steady drift into the city of destitutes from the countryside. In 1877 there was a major movement of people into the city to escape the famines that spread over much of western India. The localities to which these people came were Khara Talao and Kumbharwada (in today's C ward). The chief medical officer drew attention to caste differentiation in mortality in this local-ity at a time of crisis, when different classes found themselves forced into juxtaposition by the force of events.[5] The crude death rate among Hindus in general was 58.8 per thousand; but among the lower caste Hindus it reached 94.0. Somewhat later Weir again commented on the high mortality among destitute migrants in the city.[6] This is a theme that recurs in present-day discussions, and provides ground for debate even today: Do migrants arriving in the city for treatment or for subsistence 'bring their own mortality with them', so to speak; or is it rather the case that migrants are forced to live in overcrowded or marginalized localities where environmental conditions are at their worst? We can see the early signs of the creation of the modern C ward as a kind of ghetto.

In the 1880s Weir commented in some detail on Bombay's spatial mortality differentials. The highest mortality in the city as it then was (i.e. the modern Island City), were to be found in certain localities within the modern C and E wards. He noted that tuberculosis mortality was highest in these two wards also; it is still the highest in E ward today (though the presence of the TB hospital there may artificially inflate the figures). Water-related diseases do not necessarily peak in the same locations. Weir comments on the fact that cholera was widespread among dwellers in lodging houses, in Kurla and even in parts of D ward, for example. By contrast, A ward had lower mortality from cholera. Weir could not understand this, since the sanitary conditions he

---

[4] Health Officer's Report for 1874, abstract in House of Common Accounts and Papers.

[5] Health Officer's Report, 1877, abstract in House of Commons, Accounts and Papers.

[6] Health Officer's Report, 1889–90, abstract in House of Commons, Accounts and Papers.

observed there were appalling. We might comment that mortality has much to do with one's ability to withstand the worst onslaughts on the body from fearful environmental conditions: nutrition and (nowadays) access to health care are crucial in determining the mortality outcome. The social composition of the Fort area (which included the canton-ment) was on the whole more likely to represent a better nourished population than in the neighbouring C and E wards, whatever the envir-onment.

It may have been the case that the mill workers living in the Parel area also enjoyed lighter mortality as a result of fairly stable employment conditions at a time of economic boom. But by the 1890s Parel was also referred to as one of the high mortality localities, and Weir concluded that the very rapid residential expansion here during the previous decade was responsible. There were 30,000 mill workers in the 1880s, and 73,000 by the end of the century. He noted that the new residential areas had no sewerage connections.[8]

But parts of C and E wards continued to top the mortality list. Nagpada was regularly quoted as exceptionally bad.[9] Tuberculosis rates were twice as high there as in Byculla or Parel. These rates were not standardized for age composition, but that is likely to have been less important a problem than it would be today, when some of the inner-city areas have a significantly older age composition than those in the suburbs. It is likely that poverty explains these mortality differentials, reflected in both lower nutritional status and more densely packed liv-ing conditions, which aid the transmission of disease. Weir notes, and he may be wrong, that working conditions in the mills seem not to have given rise to high levels of respiratory mortality. If that is true, it can only remain true as long as the industry flourishes and income security is maintained.

By the end of the century the mills were no longer located on the fringes of the city. Weir recorded that areas such as Sion, Mahim and Worli had lower mortality rates than those further south (until you

[7] One is reminded here that even today it comes as a surprise to observe that mortality levels in slum areas infant mortality rates of around 75 per thousand (as in M ward in 1986 for example)—seem inconceivably low, even as an average, in an area of such appalling insanitary conditions, when, historically, rates of 250 per thousand were once common for the city as a whole.

[8] Health Officer's Report, 1889–90, abstract in House of Commons, Accounts and Papers.

[9] For example, Health Officer's Reports for 1884 and 1892, abstracts in House of Commons, Accounts and Papers.

reached south Fort or Malabar Hill). The death rates, about 20 to 25 per thousand, may have been under-recorded as these areas were then less developed. Similarly today, the new additions to the outer suburbs are not immediately well covered by registration systems. However, the low figures persisted over time. It is true that the elites were still resident in some of the new frontier regions (to the north of the mills), and were able to colonize the western seaboard, always noted for its fresh sea breezes (a location that 'filled up' much more rapidly before the advent of the luxury high-rise apartments). The middle classes could no longer move gradually northwards to less crowded areas as such a move by that time required leapfrogging the polluted area of the mills. Hence there was a considerable degree of juxtapositioning of poor and middle-income groups south of the mill area. In 1892 the south Fort locality returned a mortality rate of 8.6 per thousand, compared with 46.2 in Kamatipura. In nearby Mahalakshmi, the rate was only 15.3.[10]

The noted technical debate on the advisability of flooding the city with water from additional sources while the drainage system remained inadequate to take it away seemed to miss the important class and economic dimensions influencing the level of Bombay's mortality not only during the late nineteenth century, but for the whole of the twentieth century as well. However, at the same time, the debate did reflect the formation of class positions on public health, with property owners opposing the raising of taxes and the disruption that public works expenditures would entail, an opposition that culminated in hostility towards the establishment of the City Improvement Trust in 1898 (Aibara, n.d.).

The Plague Years

In 1896 plague struck the city. This truly awful event roused the municipal corporators to action as never before, and was sufficient to impel them into accepting the establishment of the City Improvement Trust. The elites might still be able to segregate themselves residentially to some extent, but they had to work in the city. It was clearly not possible to continue to preserve one's personal health in a drastically degraded environment. Plague had served to draw pointed attention to the city's predicament, but the heavy ongoing toll of mortality from other diseases could not be forgotten. In 1900 the death rate from TB

[10] Health Officer's Report for 1892, abstract in House of Commons, Accounts and Papers.

for low-caste groups was 12 per thousand, and from cholera 14 per thousand. Together they approximated the death rate from plague at 22 per thousand, while a further 22 per thousand died from 'fevers'. Although poverty and malnutrition undoubtedly played a major role, and Klein (1986: 725–54) rightly emphasizes the effect of a falling real wage during the early years of the 20th century, the deleterious effects of the poor sanitary environment and deteriorating housing, as correctly perceived by the local bourgeoisie, were also major factors. Undrained areas promoted malaria, high density dwellings furthered the transmission of TB, and the presence of waste matter ensured the reproduction of the rat population. No one was entirely safe from these everyday environmental risks.

The aggregate effect of plague can be gauged to some extent by the overall mortality figures: crude death rates of 30 per thousand from 1891–95 and 40 per thousand from 1906–10 bracket a sustained peak of close to 65 per thousand averaged over the intervening years (Klein, 1986 and Table 1). The class differentiation was particularly acute, with the European population suffering a rate of one per thousand, the Brahmins 13 per thousand, and the low-caste Hindus 22 per thousand (Klein, 1986: 724–54). In the case of this lethal disease, the cause of which was as yet unknown, the elites were well aware that their segregation within the city was insufficient, and sanitation and housing reforms, if ever they came, would be too late. Those who could, simply left the city. The population density in D ward fell between 1891 and 1901 from 75 persons per acre to 49, rising again to 70 by 1911. As we have already indicated, D ward was the home of the elites, both European and Indian, and this variation is clearly an indication of out-migration rather than increased mortality. Besides, the recovery is too dramatic for mortality to have been the cause (Table 2).

Not only the elites responded to plague by moving out of the city. The overall density of population fell in most wards. Historians who have documented the process tell us that the anti-plague activities of the health department (involving police searches, isolation of the sick, detention in camps of travellers and evacuation of residents in parts of the island city) were regarded as intrusive, offensive and almost as alarming as the rats themselves, besides being scientifically inaccurate (Ramasubban, 1982; Arnold, 1987). However, the working classes as a whole need employment to survive, and the terror of potential starvation is as terrifying as the risk of death from disease. Returning to one's village is not an option when secure employment is available only in the

Table 1. Crude Death Rates (per thousand),
Bombay, 1900–1970

Year	Rate	Year	Rate
1900	96.6	1940	25.0
1910	35.7	1950	14.7
1920	46.8	1960	13.5
1930	21.2	1970	9.8

Source: Annual Report of the Executive Health Officer for
1970, Bombay Municipal Corporation.

Table 2. Persons per acre, Bombay, 1881–1981

Ward	1881	1891	1901	1911	1921	1931	...	1961	1971	1981
A	52	49	40	49	52	36		76	71	65
B	276	251	214	215	203	179		288	290	244
C	447	432	325	384	431	373		769	714	568
D	63	75	49	70	90	95		216	234	232
E	61	77	92	109	114	113		272	290	283
F	7	9	13	18	31	34		105	127	156
G	13	18	24	39	44	43		150	187	223
Total	54	56	54	67	78	75		165	184	196

Source: Kosambi, 1986; Table 9.2.

city. The textile mills, supplying goods for consumers beyond the city,
continued to flourish, even while the rest of the local economy must
have faced a relative slump due to the disruption and outmigration
caused by plague. On the whole the mill workers stayed with their work.
The density in E ward actually increased during the plague years, as
against the overall trend.[11]

It is impossible to estimate what would have been the pattern of
mortality over time without the intervention of plague. The downward
trend in death rates is only observable after the disappearance of that
disease (see Table 1). Klein surmises that the decline in cholera, albeit at

[11] The famine which broke out in 1896/97 and which took a particularly acute form in
Bombay Presidency, with its worst period extending up to 1905, was also responsible for
the flow of migrants into Bombay from the surrounding countryside. In three months
alone—April, May and June of 1897—up to 300,000 migrants had come to Bombay in
search of work (Bombay Plague Committee Report, 1897–98, Bombay 1898).

a very slow pace, from the beginning of the century may be attributed to the major improvement in water availability following the opening of the Tansa supply in 1892. In doing so he is probably subscribing unwittingly to a water-washed theory of disease. Very substantial quantities of water were delivered to the city, but the ability to drain used and contaminated water away from the city was still insufficient, we would surmise, to ensure that water-borne bacteria and viruses were substantially reduced.

The Years of Depression

The economic depression of the 1920s affected Bombay severely. Wage rates declined, and in 1928 the cotton mills were closed for six months by a strike. Two years earlier the City Improvement Trust had been wound up owing to the financial crisis. The surplus needed to finance the infrastructural operations of a body of this kind has to come from local trade and industry, which in turn depends largely upon a supply of labour in a fit state to work. Indeed, the India Industrial Commission had argued in 1918 that local government should ensure adequate water supply, drainage, and housing before further industrial development was sanctioned. The labour shortages of the plague years (referred to in reports to the British parliament) had made their point: high mortality was expensive to industry. It should be remembered too that the natural increase in the population of India during the whole period from 1901 to 1921 was close to zero (not least due to the influenza epidemic (see also Table 3).

In contrast with the experience of the plague years, the working-class areas, particularly those associated with the textile mills, suffered a slight decline in population density. In E ward it went up from 109 persons per acre in 1911 to 114 in 1921 and then fell back to 113 in 1931 (Table 2). Elsewhere in the city, rising densities were still the trend. As we noted above, if the source of nutrition, namely employment, dries up, that is a more compelling reason for return to the villages than the plague (as was seen later during the long 1982 textile strike).

It is never easy to attribute changes in mortality rates to economic events, as problems with periodicity and confounding non-economic events always arise. There are available, however, meaningful data on infant mortality tabulated by a reasonable index of social class, namely number of rooms in the dwelling, and it is probably significant (and not an artefact of differential data improvement) that the infant mortality

Table 3. Population totals and percentage
decadal increase, Bombay, 1864–1981

Date	Population of Bombay City	Population of Greater Bombay
1864	816562	
	negative	
1872	644405	
	+20%	
1881	773196	
	+6%	
1891	821764	
	negative	
1901	776006	812912
	+26%	25%
1911	979445	1018388
	+20%	+22%
1921	1175914	1244934
	negative	+2%
1931	1161383	1268306
	+28%	+33%
1941	1489883	1686127
		+76%
1951		2966902
		+40%
1961		4152056
		+44%
1971		5970575
		+38%
1981		8227382

Note: Inter-censal percentage increase indicated between
the census dates.
Sources: Harris, 1976 (for the City); Bombay Metropolitan
and Regional Development Authority (for Greater
Bombay).

rate in families living in single rooms went up between 1922 and 1927.
For all other occupancy groups (two, three, and four rooms and above),
the infant mortality rate declined over the same period. The textile
industry remained the major industrial employer, with about 150,000
persons employed daily by 1920. Hence a depression in this industry is
readily reflected in data for the working class as a whole.[12]

---

[12] These data are quoted in Kumar, 1993.

By this period the mills had reached the height of their land colonization in the Island City. The spread had tended towards the north-west, so that Worli was almost entirely taken over as mill territory, while the eastern parts of the island (F ward) were less heavily colonized.

Kumar argues that the elites had earlier settled the eastern side more widely than the west, making land acquisition for industry there more difficult. It is also possible that the industry in question favoured the western coast as it had a guaranteed high humidity from the sea, a requirement of cotton spinning (much as the British textile industrialists favoured Lancashire over Yorkshire). The effect of this on the environment was, ironically, to steal land away from a potentially desirable residential area for the growing bourgeoisie. The location of the mills also served to blight the land lying eastwards with air pollution carried on the prevailing wind. Inhabitants of the remaining pockets of elite residence in F ward began to escape to healthier western locations north of the island.

Before the lowest point of the depression, the northern parts of F and G wards were being opened up for labourers' quarters, with the city's Development Department building chawls in Sewri and Worli, financed from the cotton cess. The focus of concern for health and environment seems to have shifted towards re-housing. But another note was also struck around 1915, which echoes the shift in political opinion observable in Britain at that time. In the face of a realization that sanitary expenditures and re-housing schemes would eat seriously into municipal budgets, at a time when the surplus from industry needed to finance them was faltering, the state decided to squeeze further resources from the labouring poor themselves. Literature and public rhetoric reminded the poor that their health was a matter of national concern, and that it was their duty to safeguard it (Kumar, 1993). Good hygienic and dietary awareness and behaviour were called for. No doubt, there are benefits to be gained from such information, and many well-meaning and genuinely useful initiatives were taken, some in the voluntary sector, at that time, but probably then, as now, the shift of focus was related to the pressure for cutting municipal and government budgets, a practice much favoured by the ideology of the time.

Renewed Growth—The 1930s and After

Economic growth revived in the 1930s, and this was reflected in the renewed growth in the population of Bombay (Table 3). After a decade of virtually no growth at all, the city population (defined to correspond to that within the current boundaries of Greater Bombay) increased by 33 per cent from 1931 to 1941. Since crude death rates were by then recorded as being around 20 per thousand (Table 1; compared with 40 per thousand a decade earlier), a combination of positive natural increase and net in-migration must have accounted for this growth. This itself (except at times of rural famine) is an indicator of the relative prosperity of the city. Densities went up everywhere in the city, even in C ward, which might have appeared to be close to the maximum possible without the technology of high rise apartments. By 1961 it registered 769 persons per acre (Table 2). But the weight of growth was shifting northwards. In the island city, F and G wards developed most rapidly. This was partly due to policy: in 1937 it was decided to open up areas north of the mills for working-class habitation, part of which was intended as resettlement to relieve congestion further south. The municipality constructed a series of lodgings—in this case tin sheds—which came to be known as the Matunga Labour Camp. Land here was relatively abundant, only the better parts of it being farmed, or colonized by the bungalows of the rich. The rest was marshy and probably malarious. A small amount of industry, mainly obnoxious, such as the tanneries at Dharavi, had been decentralized to these areas. The local fisherfolk also continued their trade there. Thus began the development of Dharavi, Worli, Mahim and Matunga as a residential area for the proletariat.

As mentioned above, during this period the crude death rate seems to have fallen, though only to a level that would be considered fairly high by the standards established after Independence. Similarly, infant mortality is recorded at about 200 per thousand by 1940 (Table 4). This is a high average, but it may have been a little lower than rural averages at that time. It is likely that the inter-war years witnessed a downward drift in death rates to somewhere below the rural average for the first time in the history of the city—at least as far back as the records go. This raises an intriguing question as to how this came about.

We would be tempted to argue that a combination of relatively healthy economic growth, sustaining the incomes of the industrial proletariat, and a gradual shift in the social composition with the formation of a burgeoning petty bourgeoisie, may be responsible. For it is unlikely that sufficient progress had been made in the wide availability of cheap curative drug therapy for this to have been the cause. Interestingly, the Labour Office Enquiry Board investigated the health of women workers in the 1930s, and the treatment they had received, and found that only

Table 4. Infant Mortality Rates (per thousand Births), Bombay, 1920–80

Year	Rate	Year	Rate
1920	552.2	1960	95.2
1930	296.2	1970	80.6
1940	201.4	1980	65.7
1950	151.6		

Notes: Rates refer to the City until 1950 and to Greater Bombay thereafter.

Source: Annual Report of the Executive Health Officer for the year 1981, Bombay Municipal Corporation.

20 per cent of mill workers reported seeking treatment when sick, and of those who did, only 40 per cent undertook allopathic drug therapy (Kumar, 1993). One of the present authors made a similar enquiry among men and women in slum settlements and pavement dwellings in Bombay in the late 1980s. By then, a little under 90 per cent of those reporting sickness claimed to have sought treatment, mainly from allopathic sources (see Crook, Ramasubban and Singh, 1991: 303–19). Hence, in a comparative perspective, we can say that the curative revolution had hardly begun before the Second World War. Furthermore, there can hardly have been any improvement in the sanitary environment. It is, however, possible that anti-malaria programmes were beginning to be effective.

The greatest demographic strain ever to be placed upon the city came with the economic stimulation of the war effort (1939–45) followed shortly by Partition. The combined effect was to increase the population of the region of Greater Bombay by 76 per cent between 1941 and 1951. It is likely that Muslims, fleeing the intolerance of small towns and the countryside, sought shelter among existing Muslim communities concentrated in the inner city (wards E and C) just south of the mills. Many also populated the new towns that had begun to develop outside —for example, Ulhasnagar and Bhiwandi.

A survey undertaken in 1956 described 76 per cent of buildings in C ward as 'old', which meant that they pre-dated the new building regulations of 1905, or else as makeshift dwellings (Bombay Municipal Corporation, 1956). By now this neighbourhood had become the most congested in the city. One hundred and twenty-five acres of E ward were designated as 'slum' by these criteria, i.e., consisting of buildings over

50 years old, built to obsolete standards and generally in insanitary condition. It should be remembered that by the end of the previous century
the chief medical officer had described the accommodation in parts of E
ward as intolerable. It was destined to remain a high mortality locality of
the poor, of refugees, of the badly housed. T. S. Weir had looked back
over twenty years of his experience in the city and asked what had been
done to improve the housing and sanitary conditions of these inner-city
localities. His exasperated reply: 'Nothing!'[13] How would he have felt a
century later?

Post-Independence: The New Industrial Expansion

Industrial diversification began during the Second World War, with the
setting up of a basic chemicals industry, electrical equipment manufacturing, and the processing of hydrogenated oils. The trend continued
during the First Five Year Plan (not a period of major industrialization
elsewhere in India), with the initiation of petroleum refining in Trombay.
This was accompanied and followed by the establishment of petrochemicals and plastics plants. In 1947, the Committee on Industrial
Development regarded the Trombay site as 'most suitable' in view of its
being in 'proximity to the deep water jetty and far removed from
residential populations' (Bombay Municipal Corporation, 1984).

The rapid industrial expansion during and just after the Second
World War had a huge impact on the demand for housing and its attendant infrastructure, which was left to be sorted out 'later'. The equally
rapid colonization of the suburbs and outer suburbs was reflected in the
successive decisions to merge these areas in the Bombay Municipality in
1952 and again in 1957. The residential sprawl followed the two main
railway systems and the branch to Mankhurd. This latter was the area
closest to the new industrial site, which could hardly remain long 'far
removed from residential population'. If the work-force had to grow to
man the new factories, where was it expected to live?

In 1954, legislation was passed to allow the Municipal Corporation
to clear slums. In 1956, the report on a survey of old and dilapidated
buildings in the Island city commented that, 'looking to the cost and
availability of open spaces in the City, it will not be possible to provide
all the [housing] units in the city proper, and fifty per cent of the new
units will have to be located in the suburbs where land is relatively

[13] Health Officer's Report, 1892, abstract in House of Commons, Accounts and
Papers.

cheap and easy to secure' (Bombay Municipal Corporation, 1956). There was apparently no appreciation of the productive role of the housing that had already sprung up in the suburbs. The same report referred to the haphazard juxtaposition of industry and residence in the course of the incremental growth which had occurred. That such a juxtaposition should solidify over time is explained in part by the need for the protection of the cotton textile industry from competition from south-east Asia and from Pakistan. The mills survived on land that could otherwise have been released for housing; the rent control act ensured that the poor tenements in E, F and G wards continued to house 'industrial workers and artisan classes belonging to the poorer groups of society' (Bombay Municipal Corporation, 1956).

The 1969 slum improvement board created by the Government of Maharashtra signalled a realization of the fact that mass re-housing from island to suburbs was not a practicable proposition. But it was a further two decades before demolitions ceased to be a major programme in the agenda of the dominant political parties. Real estate developers and landowners continued to see the advantage of mass rehousing, or at least mass dehousing, in order to release Island City land and inner suburban land for accomodating the bourgeoisie. On the other hand, industrialists continued to profit from the local supply of cheap labour; furthermore, this labour was increasingly being organized into vote banks.

Our discussion above has gone some way in explaining why in the mid-1960s the E, G north and F north wards still registered the highest mortality in the city, with infant mortality rates of 109, 109 and 103 respectively when the city average was 85.5 (25 per cent lower; see Table 5 for an index of wardwise variation in 1966–67).[14] The lowest mortality is recorded in the southern part of the City, wards A, B, C, and D. All these suffered less from increasing congestion during and after the Second World War. The outer suburbs also registered a relatively low mortality. This may reflect some under-registration (this certainly occurred in T ward even later on) simply because the rapid formation of populations on newly colonized land made immediate compilation of statistics impossible, especially for inter-censal years. However, it was also the case that the outer suburbs had pockets of relatively salubrious village-like settlements that had not at first outgrown the capacity of the local environment to absorb their wastes, and which were in relatively

[14] There is a major advantage in using infant mortality rates in that these are not affected by changing or different age compositions across the wards.

Table 5. Indices of infant mortality in Bombay by ward in relation to the ward average at three points in time

Ward	1966/67	1970/71	1985/86
Average =	100	100	100
A	81	92	83
B	85	93	85
C	82	88	122
D	84	86	79
E	128	120	120
FS	106	98	125
FN	120	118	129
GN	132	140	131
GS	99	105	99
H	102	92	87
K	91	90	94
L	—	—	118
M	—	—	123
L&M	102	98	121
N&S	111	106	90
P	72	77	82
R	—	76	76
T	103	94	84

Note: Actual rates averaged over two years are 88.8 (1966/67); 79.8 (1970/71); 60.8 (1985/86).
Source: Calculated from data given in the Annual Reports of Executive Officer of Health, Bombay Municipal Corporation, for appropriate years.

easy reach of the city's medical services. These latter factors may have worked towards a slightly lower mortality.

The response to the accelerating land shortage for new industrial development was partly organized policy and partly, as before, haphazard. In 1958 the Barve Committee recommended the development of the Bandra-Kurla region as a new industrial complex. It also suggested that a bridge be built across the Thana creek. The latter initiative, which eventually flowered into the New Bombay plan, was far too slow off the ground to provide alternative industrial and, above all, residential locations, despite the formation of a body, the City and Industrial Development Corporation (CIDCO), specifically charged with that task. The infrastructure arrived about two decades too late. Meanwhile, the

Bandra-Kurla belt developed apace, especially with small-scale industry, and the area around Trombay continued to attract large-scale public sector units in the fertilizer and oil industries. The extended suburbs provided the space needed for engineering, chemicals and pharmaceuticals, mainly on the eastern railway route, but also increasingly around Andheri in the west.

For residential purposes, the elites had begun to colonize the western half of H ward, with its amenity value of being by the sea, on the better of the two railway lines, and being unencumbered with earlier industry. Indeed, Bandra had been earlier an independent small town. The elites also continued to colonize D ward, a feat made possible without apparent congestion by means of high priced high-rise construction. Parts of A ward were reclaimed from the sea for a similar purpose. Note that all these localities are on the western seaboard, to the windward of city pollution. The bourgeoisie generally attempt to follow a similar location strategy, but opportunities are scarce. Much of the rest of the western seaboard of the Island City is already built over, e.g. with mills in G ward (Worli) or chawls housing the labour for these mills. Even in these areas, the elites have managed to squeeze into some small pockets. On the whole, middle-class residents have had to put up with localities that have started out as indifferent, e.g. Chembur, and then turned bad as new industrial development seized adjacent land. Chembur is particularly unfortunate in that the advantage of being to the windward of the Trombay industries is lost at night when the air reverses its flow. This misfortune afflicted both the bourgeoisie and the growing working class population in M ward. The latter had more to contend with since theirs was an unserviced environment that could no longer provide sufficient water and drainage. Actually, those households still locked in the central city, e.g. around Lalbaug, suffered the most from poor air quality, having the discomfort of pollution from the mills and gas works on the seaward side during the day, and the same pollution being blown back over them at night (with additional flavourings from Trombay). Cause of death statistics show that during the 1970s, respiratory mortality was not declining at the same pace as mortality from other diseases. Indeed, deaths from tuberculosis continued to grow at the same rate as the population (Ramasubban and Crook 1985: 999–1005).

The authors have made an earlier study of the mortality pattern by ward, and the social and environmental characteristics of these localities, for the years close to 1981 (Ramasubban and Crook, 1985; also see Tables 5 and 6). The mortality patterns described above for earlier years

Table 6. Infant mortality rates by ward, Bombay, 1980–1986

Ward	1980	1981	1982	1983	1984	1985	1986
A	58	62	54	58	56	53	47
B	65	49	54	56	65	55	48
C	94	77	84	77	73	83	65
D	47	45	49	48	48	50	45
E	68	76	70	70	68	74	71
FS	67	72	82	83	75	72	80
FN	91	83	87	88	82	82	74
GN	77	63	68	87	84	90	69
GS	58	75	61	68	60	65	55
HE	58	55	45	60	57	57	60
HW	52	52	48	43	46	47	39
KE	72	45	54	57	57	56	54
KW	71	59	76	61	62	63	56
L	72	63	85	66	73	72	71
M	91	72	104	89	78	74	75
N	66	58	72	65	62	62	55
PS	54	52	78	58	52	50	47
PN	48	58	56	54	50	55	47
R	52	52	48	55	50	44	48
S	61	51	55	60	46	50	53
T	27*	51	49	56	50	51	51
Average	66	61	64	66	62	63	59

* Almost certainly inaccurate.

Source: Annual Reports of the Executive Officer of Health, Bombay Municipal Corporation, for the relevant years.

have in the main been retained. However, there was increased segregation of H West and D wards from the rest, both having very much lighter mortality than the others, and more clearly so than before. Infant mortality in D ward was approximately 45 per thousand at this time, contrasting with neighbouring C and E wards where the rate was closer to 75 per thousand. In H ward the rate was between 50 and 55 (the lower figure referring to the west division). This contrasts sharply with M ward, where rates ranged around 90 per thousand. In other words, the ratio between worst and best is about two to one. These are substantial differentials when one considers that we are recording them by ward, not by social class, and that the wards house very large populations: from 300,000 in H West to 560,000 in M, for example.

It is clear which areas of the city continue to stand out, distinguishing themselves from the rest, both in terms of disease and mortality, and in terms of social and environmental composition. The statistical technique known as cluster analysis helps us to make the following observations: mortality and disease characteristics tend to separate out the group consisting of N, M, and L wards (on the eastern side; see Figure 2). The other groups that can be identified are: HW and D; A and E; GN, GS and B; and finally C. All the rest (10 wards) coalesce into a single group. It is interesting to compare these groupings with those which occur if the same technique is applied to the social and environmental analysis, using Census data on, e.g. literacy and scheduled caste/tribe, health department data on hospital beds, with other sources for data on slum population, and air quality (for further details, and alternative methods of analysis, see Crook, Ramasubban and Singh, 1991). For the latter, M and L wards are a separate group (Figure 3), GS and GN remain together, as do FS, E and B. D, HW and A form a group. The remaining eleven coalesce into a single group.

The groups that can be separated out by social and environmental criteria have many wards in common with those that can be distinguished in terms of health. It can also be seen from this exercise that there is today greater heterogeneity in the Island City than in the suburbs. The exceptions here are the trio L, M, and N, and also HW which tend to stand out as two distinct groups.

If we follow the data through to 1986, the latest data available, we can see that C ward has once again become a high-mortality district (Tables 5 and 6). It has also been subject to a long history of outmigration, and it is reasonable to suppose that it is the younger and better-off who are able to move out. M ward exhibits a mortality peak among the suburban wards that nearly equals the worst Island City peak. In both cases the index of mortality used is infant mortality as this, we noted above, is not biased by age distribution. By the mid 1980s the age pyramid is far from uniform across the wards, with localities subject to out-migration having a substantially older age composition than those subject to recent in-migration.

What is notable about the ward-level differentials in mortality, easily observed in terms of infant mortality, is that these are being maintained within a context of generally falling infant mortality rates for the aggregate city as a whole (See Tables 4 and 5). Whereas public health interventions against such diseases as malaria (and earlier, plague) may have once been responsible for some of the general decline, we have argued above that this can only be part of the story. As for the more recent period, it is difficult to pinpoint any major improvement to the

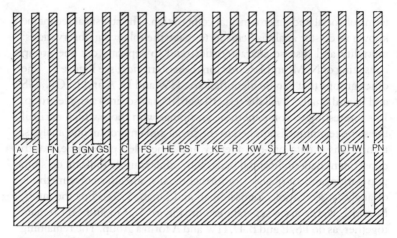

Figure 2. Cluster analysis of mortality characteristics by ward in Bombay

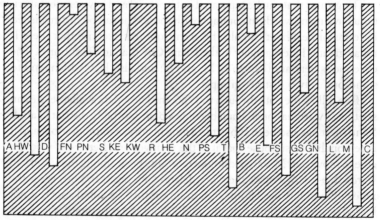

Figure 3. Illustration of cluster analysis of social and environmental characteristics by ward.

Note: The technique starts with each ward separately (at the top of the chart) and progressively combines them according to social and environmental similarity. Towards the bottom of the chart one can see which groups (or clusters) of wards still remain substantially different from each other.

Variables included are: In Figure 2: mortality from TB, diarrhoea and dysentry, bronchitis, ischaemic heart disease, accidents and infant mortality.

In Figure 3: Population density (by acre and per dwelling), air quality, water quality, industrial acreage, male literacy, scheduled caste/tribe composition, maternity beds and dispensaries. For technical explanation see, for instance, Statistical Package for the Social Sciences (SPSS), 1975.

environment that could account for a secular downward trend. Each new initiative with regard to water supply, for example, has simply served to offset some of the crowding effect of a city that has expanded in demographic terms at roughly 40 per cent per decade (Table 3). We have hazarded the guess that the increasing availability of curative drug therapy has made a large contribution to this trend in recent times. Nonetheless, the differentials have been maintained. Apparently the better-off population, which has the advantage of being able to live in certain areas of the city, has been able to make better use of the new therapy, especially where it is provided by the private sector. The point to stress is that, whatever the cause of mortality decline, the state has not brought about a levelling of the mortality differentials. Arguably, it could have done so. We have found in a simple regression that the most clearly distinguished determinant of infant mortality differentials was the availability of maternity beds (Crook, Ramasubban and Singh, 1991: 303–19). It is revealing to observe the change in provision of such life giving facilities over a twenty-year period from the mid-1960s to the mid-1980s (Table 7). For the city as a whole, the average provision has increased so that there are now about 26 births per bed per year compared with 33 in the mid-1960s, a fall of 20 per cent. The socially elite ward, D, had from the start enjoyed a more generous provision, with 10 births per bed. This has hardly changed over the twenty year period. In H ward the number of births began at 49 per bed at the start of the period, but fell to 26 by the end, in line with its increased social segregation as an elite ward (a fall of 47 per cent). Within H ward the contrasts are stark, with 13 births per bed in the West division and 80 in the East. Of course expectant mothers will cross ward boundaries to deliver in a better provided ward where possible, but this should not be necessary. Finally, L and M wards still suffer a low level of provision with 70 births per bed, a little better than the 84 births per bed in the mid 1960s (a fall of 17 per cent). It is clear that the state has not succeeded in narrowing the differential provision of health care between the wards. The differentials in infant mortality that remain must be attributed in a major way to this failure.

The 1980s and Beyond

The sanguine views of the 1950s on land availability are by now well and truly dead. Much contemporary political conflict is over land use and availability. This impinges directly on the health of the population, for it

Table 7. Births per maternity bed by ward in Bombay in 1966–67 and 1985–86, and an index of wardwise variation

Ward	Births per bed		Index (ward average=100)	
	1966–67	1985–86	1966–67	1985–86
A	12	9	37	34
B	23	23	68	89
C	46	41	137	154
D	11	9	33	36
E	51	27	153	102
FS	24	21	71	78
FN		26		100
GS	45	33	136	124
GN		38		144
HE	49	80	149	301
HW		13		48
KE	53	25	159	94
KW		18		69
L	84	88	254	334
M		60		228
N	54	27	162	103
PS	46	29	137	109
PN		28		108
R	24	26	72	97
S	—	43	—	164
T	31	26	94	99
Average	33	26		

Source: Annual Reports of the Executive Officer of Health, Bombay Municipal Corporation.

has been shown that even if all decent housing and sanitary requirements are to be met by upgrading of *existing* slums, it will still be necessary to acquire land since a proportion of slum dwellers are currently located on land that cannot be serviced, is unstable, or is dangerously close to railway or power lines (Sinha, 1989). The Urban Land Ceiling Act of

1979 has been shown in practice to be inoperable (Bapat, 1990). The demolitions of the early 1980s have given way to proposals to deal with slum dwellers *in situ*, though the fate of pavement dwellers is still under dispute, and demolitions continue. By 1985, both the ruling and the main opposition parties had declared themselves against demolitions. Only the Shiv Sena continued to support slum clearance as a policy, while at the same time itself building up vote banks in the slums (*Sunday Observer*, 26 October 1985). The politicization of the slum dwellers has been accompanied by the interest of international capital in helping to develop Bombay as a stable and lucrative base for market penetration. The international financing agencies see positive returns from investment in water and sewerage, and the former Prime Minister had similar hopes of profit from cleaning up Dharavi. Bombay is at the centre of India's industrialization and its commerce.

With no mass evictions envisaged, even though some 'gentrification' of slum settlements will result in displacement of the poorest, a continuing encrustation of the social mix on spatial lines is to be expected. An intriguing question is whether, as the middle class find themselves unable to move and the poor find themselves similarly locked into place, this juxtaposition will lead to a levelling in infrastructure provision, with only a few pockets of elite areas remaining socially segregated, and similarly a few working class zones.

If there were incipient evidences of such a development, their implications for mortality were abruptly offset by a major differentiating economic event of the early 1980s, a culmination of a process that had effectively started between the Wars. The textile strike of 1982, the longest in history, whatever it achieved, failed to save the textile mill industry from extensive closure, with a loss of some 100,000 jobs since Independence. Indeed, it hastened the final demise. The immediate result was, undoubtedly, social hardship, even though many migrant mill workers returned to their village homes. It is never possible to relate mortality data precisely to events of the period, as other factors, such as epidemics, may lead to fluctuations in demographic events. The municipal Health Department made the mistake of proudly announcing that morbidity from certain causes had fallen in 1982 because a new filtration plant had come on stream, without observing the cyclical nature of the diseases in question. On the other hand, the aggregate infant mortality data do plateau in the first few years of the decade at a level of about 65 per thousand, and especially so in the working-class localities of the Island City, and in L, M and N wards (Table 6). Losses in earnings are very likely to have combined with environmental or epidemiological conditions in those years to produce these results. Infant mortality in M ward was 62 per cent above the average in 1982 (but only 20 per cent higher in the previous year). Of course, infant mortality is an index of family hardship, whereas many of the textile workers in the city are single males. In this respect, we may note that tuberculosis-related deaths increased substantially in B, C and E wards during the first half of the 1980s, against a generally falling trend (Ramasubban and Crook, 1985).

The current obsession of the environmental health lobby is with air pollution. The issue commands political clout, especially since leaks from industrial units in Trombay alarmed the middle-class residents of Chembur, coming close as they did on the heels of the Bhopal disaster. It is to the advantage of the vast working-class population of M ward that objections to the emissions from new plants and environmental degradation from garbage dumping at Mankhurd have received support from middle-class voters, who may have greater influence in the municipality and state, and are certainly able to articulate their demands quickly through the press.

Conclusion

This paper has examined the social-spatial configurations of mortality consequent upon the evolution of residence patterns in the city of Bombay, from the late nineteenth century to the 1980s, against the background of the expansion of the textile industry, the years of plague, the economic depression, the renewed growth that started in the mid-1930s, the post-Independence industrial diversification, and the final run-down of the textile mills. The analysis has enabled us to reflect on theories of urban class conflict, urban land use theory and social-spatial differentiation, theories of mortality differentiation and explanations of mortality decline, and, above all, the interplay between these theories. Our aim was, in the process, to move a little closer to an understanding of the determinants of urban health.

An interpretation that emerges is, in our opinion, that the urban bourgeoisie will attempt to live in localities where natural environmental amenity is perceived to be high, while leaving other areas for working class residence. The outcome will be social segregation, reflected in social-spatial mortality differentials. This strategy, however, is limited by the industrial bourgeoisie's own industrial activity, which reduces the availability of land of high amenity value. In a city with geographically limited space like Bombay, the big bourgeoisie, including some of its allied professional classes, or what we may term collectively the elite, is the only section of society that retains its environmental advantages, through ultimately achieving a near total colonization of land with high amenity value. This homogenization of elite areas is in contrast to the strategy forced upon the small industrial and commercial bourgeoisie, which has to colonize less desirable locations, or locations that become less desirable, interspersed with working-class residences, and subsequently to attempt to upgrade their immediate environments, at least from a sanitary point of view. The emerging and ultimately persisting polarization within these areas, as the relative land shortage increases, is only partially reflected in the spatial differentials in mortality. For the latter, based as they are on ward boundaries, reflect the contrasts between the more heterogeneous areas and the enclaves of the big bourgeoisie, on the one hand, and the few relatively homogeneous working-class areas on the other. Given the constraints upon further progress toward homogenization of the first of these areas (those of mixed residence), public health activity by these resident sections of the bourgeoisie may lead eventually to a levelling in the provision of a healthy environment, with a consequent reduction in mortality differentials within those localities. Elsewhere in the city, however, the state still seems to be contributing to the persistence of social-spatial differentials, despite an overall trend of mortality decline.

Bibliography

Aibara, A. (nd). 'Municipal Politics and Urban Development in Bombay City, 1880s to 1907', paper presented at seminar held by Centre for South Asian Studies, School of Oriental and African Studies, London.

Arnold, David, 1987. 'Touching the Body: Perspectives on the Indian Plague 1896–1900' in Ranajit Guha (ed.), *Subaltern Studies* V: *Writings on South Asian History and Society*, Delhi, Oxford University Press.

Bapat, Meera, 1990. 'Allocation of Urban Space: rhetoric and reality—evidence from recent jurisprudence', *Economic and Political Weekly*, Vol. 25, No. 28, 1990.

Bombay Municipal Corporation, Annual Report of the Executive Officer of Health, various years.

Bombay Municipal Corporation, 1984. Report on the Draft Development Plan.

Bombay Municipal Corporation, 1956. Brief Report on the Survey of Old Buildings in the City.

Castells, Manuel, 1983. *The City and the Grassroots: A Cross Cultural Theory of Urban Social Movements*, London, Edward Arnold.

Cleland, John, and Jerome Van Ginneken, 1988. 'Maternal Education and Child Survival in Developing Countries: The Search for Pathways of Influence', *Social Science and Medicine*, Vol. 27, No. 12.

Cooper, Frederick, 1983. 'Urban Space, Industrial Time, and Wage Labour in Africa', in Frederick Cooper (ed.), *Struggle for the City: Migrant Labor, Capital and the State in Urban Africa*, Beverley Hills, Sage.

Crook, Nigel, Radhika Ramasubban and Bhanwar Singh, 1991. 'A Multidimensional Approach to the Social Analysis of the Health Transition in Bombay' in John Cleland and Allan Hill (eds), *The Health Transition: Methods and Measures*, Health Transition Series No. 3, Canberra, The Australian National University.

Curtin, Philip D., 1989. *Death by Migration: Europe's Encounter with the Tropical World in the Nineteenth Century*, Cambridge, Cambridge University Press.

Ewbank, Douglas, and Samuel Preston, 1989. 'Personal Health Behaviour and the Decline in Infant and Child Mortality: the United States, 1900–1930', in John Caldwell et al. (eds), *What We Know about Health Transition: The Cultural, Social and Behavioural Determinants of Health*, Health Transition Series No. 2 (Vol. I), Canberra, The Australian National University.

Harris, Nigel, 1976. *Economic Development, Cities and Planning: The Case of Bombay*, Delhi, Oxford University Press.

Henderson, J. V., 1977. *Economic Theory and the Cities*, New York, Academic Press.

House of Commons, Report on Sanitary Measures in India, Accounts and Papers, various years.

Klein, Ira, 1986. 'Urban Development and Death: Bombay City 1870–1914', *Modern Asian Studies*, Vol. 20, No. 4.

Kosambi, Meera, 1986. *Bombay in Transition: The Growth and Social Ecology of a Colonial City, 1880–1980*, Stockholm, Almqvist and Wiksell.

Kumar, Radha, 1993. 'City Lives: Women Workers in the Bombay Cotton Textile Industry 1911–47', New Delhi, Jawaharlal Nehru University Ph.D. thesis.

McKeown, Thomas, 1976. *The Modern Rise of Population*, London, Edward Arnold.

Mercer, Alex, 1990. *Disease Mortality and Population in Transition: Epidemiological-demographic Change in England since the Eighteenth Century as Part of a Global Phenomenon*, Leicester, Leicester University Press.

Navarro, Vincente, 1986. *Crisis, Health and Medicine: A Social Critique*, London, Tavistock.

Ramasubban, Radhika, 1982. *Public Health and Medical Research in India: Their Origins under the Impact of British Colonial Policy*, Stockholm, Sarec.

Ramasubban, Radhika and Nigel Crook, 1985. 'Mortality Toll of Cities: Emerging Patterns of Disease in Bombay', *Economic and Political Weekly*, Vol. 20, No. 23, June 8, 1985.

Report of the Plague Committee appointed by government Resolution No. 1204/720, on the Plague in Bombay, July 1897—April 1898, Bombay, 1898.

Sinha, A. P., 1989. 'Slum Development: Cafeteria Approach', *Urban India*, Vol. 9, No. 2, 1989.

9
Manifesto of a Housing Activist

P. K. DAS

'Concealed under millions of these roof-tops lies a city under siege. Bombay, a city of nearly ten million people where no less than eight million live on pavements, in slums and in dilapidated buildings known as chawls.' These are the opening lines of *Slum Bombay*, a film about housing for the poor,* which aptly introduces the city's social and housing environment. In spite of this dismal situation and the inhuman conditions in which the poor live, the various policies and programmes for slums and housing have never reflected the needs and aspirations of the slum dwellers and the working class in general. Instead they have furthered business interests in land and housing. In the recent past there have been several important announcements in the name of the poor, but our experience is that the more oppressive a policy, the more pretentions it has to helping the poor. The aim of this paper is to explore and expose the implications of some of the most important slum and housing policies of our time and to explain the need to combat them.

In July 1981, the former Chief Minister of Maharashtra, A. R. Antulay, initiated 'Operation Eviction' by rounding up thousands of slum dwellers and deporting them to far-away places in buses and trucks. In response, a couple of dozen democratic and revolutionary organizations came together to form a united front called the Nivara Hakk Suraksha Samiti to organize the slum dwellers for the defence of their homes. From this time onwards slums in Bombay came under sharp focus and the struggle for housing began to acquire new dimensions.

* Directed by Ralli Jacob and co-directed by Rafeeq Ellias and P. K. Das, produced by the Indian Institute of Architects in 1992.

In the Bombay High Court a stay order to 'Operation Eviction' was issued by Justice Lentin, but four years later, in June 1985, the Supreme Court of India pronounced judgements against the slum-dwellers. Ever since, demolitions have been carried out on a substantial scale. For their part, slum organizations have undertaken campaigns in the form of mammoth marches and demonstrations to fight against evictions.

As a sop, the Maharashtra Government announced that, in the event of demolitions, slum-dwellers who had been in residence before 1976 would be given alternative accommodation. The Nivara Hakk Suraksha Samiti attacked the policy of cut-off dates, and demanded that all slum and pavement dwellers be recognized as having rights and be offered alternative accommodation. As a result of popular struggles, the government eventually shifted the cut-off date for recognition of slum-dwellers from 1976 to 1985.

The situation has radically changed since the eighties, when the film *Hamara Sahar* ('Bombay, our city') was made by Anand Patwardhan. At that time upper and middle class people expressed directly and bluntly their hatred for slums and slum-dwellers, supporting and demanding demolitions and evictions. The brutal attacks on the poor by the State have been brilliantly captured in *Hamara Sahar*. The film also exposes the growing nexus among the executive, the judiciary, the police, the builders and developers, the 'lumpens' and other anti-socials. But today, the State and its various agents have become sophisticated. Though their actions and policies against the poor continue unabated, they are now not so crudely expressed. The single act of direct demolition has now been reinforced by several new policies and programmes with far greater consequences. As activists and also as concerned citizens, it is absolutely necessary for us to understand the undercurrents and the blatant lies that mark the various programmes and policies announced for the housing of the poor.

Privatization and the National Housing Policy

Privatization in housing is a part of the larger privatization thrust in the country. Both the World Bank and the International Monetary Fund are now actively involved in India. They support vigorously the policy of increasing the role of private enterprise. Simultaneously, they have directed the government to withdraw from all social welfare measures, including those for public housing. The overwhelming thrust of this policy is to shift the responsibilities for housing the poor completely onto the private sector. Housing is to be declared an industry, not in order that increased government funds may be available for housing the poor, but rather so that the private sector can obtain subsidies to build houses on a commercial basis for the middle and upper income groups. It is stated in the National Housing Policy that, 'greater emphasis will be laid on corporate development'. What the government is saying is that it does not own land in the city, that it has limited resources for housing and that it has not succeeded in improving the housing situation, whereas the private sector, i.e. the developers, builders and industrialists have both vacant land and capital to invest, so why not give them the opportunity to take over responsibility for building more houses. By doing this, the government is shirking its own responsibility for providing houses to the poor and is, further, encouraging and legitimizing the exploitation of the poor by the rich. This amounts to a formal surrender by the government to business interests.

Although the National Housing Policy professes to be in favour of housing the poor, its concrete programme formulations skillfully avoid practical proposals for achieving this. The draft National Housing Policy is so blatantly anti-working-class that it hardly ever bothers even to speak of housing the poor and, even when it does, it is in a token manner. Shockingly, there is no mention of either the Urban Land (Ceiling and Regulation) Act or of the Sites and Services schemes; it makes no mention of the existing slums or of the need to improve them; it does not talk of tenancy rights; it does not deal with services for the urban poor; it ignores questions of decentralization, population densities, transportation and environment; it does not comment on the failure of previous public housing schemes.

Urban Land (Ceiling & Regulation) Act

If, under the Urban Land (Ceiling & Regulation) Act, (ULC Act), the government had acquired the vacant and surplus land and given it to the poor at Re 1/- a sq. ft for housing, there would have been no shortage of land in the city. It must be understood at this juncture that the pattern of population growth in the city now is fairly stable and clear. In the past few years there has been a drop in the rate of migration to Bombay. At present, only about 40 families enter the city every day and not 300 as estimated earlier. In fact, census figures indicate that the population in certain wards is decreasing (for example, C Ward covering the

Bhuleshwar area). The natural growth in population can, however, be assessed easily and definite planning programmes can be framed to tackle the housing situation.

We consider the ULC Act to be a progressive measure and demand its strict implementation. Though it became law, and officially has been effective since 1976, the amount of land actually taken over has been very small. There are inherent weaknesses in the conceptual and legal framework of the Act which came in the way of acquiring land under its provisions. Besides, there are also administrative apathy, legal loopholes and, most important, lack of political will and commitment to the implementation of the Act. As a matter of fact, a capitalist government will always be opposed to the idea of nationalization of land and other such social measures. It will never allow rich landowners and industrialists to be adversely affected since it shares their beliefs and they mutually support each other. We also demand that land taken over under this Act be utilized for housing the economically weaker sections only. There should also be provision for housing new migrants and for accommodating the natural growth of the already existing population. This land could also be utilized for housing populations displaced by riots, natural calamities etc. and also to re-house people from slums where densities are too high and/or which are located on critical sites.

However, there has been mounting pressure on the government to scrap the ULC Act altogether. Developers and builders argue that the Act has been blocking the growth of housing stock and has, in fact, brought about a situation in which they have not been able to invest in and undertake housing projects which they are keen and willing to do. It must be realized that the idea of social welfare measures such as housing of the poor are contradictory to business interests and hence, under no condition will a private developer undertake projects for housing of the poor. As a matter of fact a few exercises in this direction have led to further displacements. Instead, if land is given to cooperatives of slum-dwellers, the people can decide on more appropriate housing and development programmes. This will allow for individual freedom and expression in housing, resulting in tremendous variety of form, structure and colour in the framework of an ever-evolving and living aesthetic. We could overcome the ugliness of apartment buildings and eliminate exploitation by developers and financiers who today control housing, who have turned it into a commodity where design is irrelevant and has no reference to the cultural and living pattern of our people. In a new situation, people would be able to establish control over their housing environment. We believe that, while land ownership must be nationalized, ownership of houses must be private.

Housing Finance

The government wishes to increase the investment in housing by involving the private sector. How does a private sector enterprise finance itself? In all its ventures, the private sector falls back on refinance from various government and semi-government institutions—banks, the Housing and Urban Development Corporation, the Housing Development Finance Corporation, etc. The newly created National Housing Bank (NHB), an offshoot of the National Housing Policy, has been set up to finance various developers and investors in housing. In other words, it is intended to support large corporate agencies to further their business interests. This will further institutionalize private profiteering from public funds. For the success of the National Housing Policy and the National Housing Bank, government proposes to offer income-tax concessions for fixed deposits and investments in the NHB, the idea being to tap individual and institutional savings for investment in housing. But all this effort by the public sector will ultimately benefit private developers and builders as it is they who will be refinanced by the NHB for promoting housing schemes. Instead of this, finance from the various government and semi-government agencies should be given directly to societies and co-operatives of the people. The societies can then appoint architects and project managers, who will in turn assist the society in the selection and appointment of contractors. The entire work can be undertaken and executed in such a way as to provide appropriate and effective housing.

Housing finance also includes the matter of housing loans. In these loans the World Bank and other foreign agencies actively participate. The government makes this out to be a big favour done to workers, but is this really so? By introducing the concept of commercial loans, what the government is actually doing is backing out from its own responsibilities. Almost half of the population lives below the poverty line. It is shameful to expect or demand that these people pay for their housing. Government is, therefore, duty-bound to provide housing to the poor either free or at highly subsidized rates. By introducing loans in housing programmes, the government has abandoned free and subsidized housing. It says to the poor, 'I will give you some money now, you can pay it back later', and thereafter proceeds to extract that amount from the poverty-stricken families together with interest. How many of the poor will get these loans in the first place? Very few, probably only the well-to-do. How many will be able to return the loans with interest? Only a fraction of the working class. We, therefore, reject the entire proposal for loans as basically against the interest of the working class as a whole. This loan system is essentially another way in which private developers and builders and also government seek to make profits at the cost of the poor and downtrodden. Those giving loans are doing so not because they want to help the poor but because it helps them to make further profits through interest payments. By adopting this policy the Government is ensuring profits to private businessmen. On one hand it is extending loans and other infra-structure support for undertaking and promoting housing schemes, while on the other hand under the guise of helping the poor it is offering loans for buying houses in the schemes promoted by the same businessmen.

Cross Subsidies: Instead of going to the root of the problem and so-cializing the housing sector, the government seeks ways and means of lessening its responsibilities and of shifting it on to the private sector. One such method is the cross subsidy scheme. For example, the government instead of taking over excess land under the Urban Land Ceiling Act, allows the landlord to retain the excess land on a mere assurance that the landlord will use a small part of the excess land for housing the poor. Thus, the government argues, the landlord is forced to use his land and his finance for housing of the economically weaker sections of society.

This approach never works for several reasons. First of all the apartments built are unsuitable for the poor and are also too expensive (priced at Rs 80,000/- or more). Accordingly, these accommodations are bought by the rich. Moreover, the buildings are designed in such a manner that a buyer can purchase a number of adjacent flats, break down walls and join them together. To add insult to injury, the government's cross subsidy schemes even provide that loans be made available to the poor to purchase such flats. We have already discussed the evils of the loan system.

We see housing as a right and as an essential need. Therein lies the crucial difference. In this context one more thing must be noted. In Europe and America and other developed countries, an average person spends a fairly high percentage of his income on housing and a relatively small percentage on food. In India the situation is completely reversed. The poor spend almost all their meagre income on food and only secondarily on health and the education of their children. Very little is left for housing. It is essential, therefore, that the government subsidize housing.

Floor Space Index

The government today has not only overlooked the irrelevances and failures of its various policies for land-use and finance for housing of the poor, but has also offered incentives to private developers. The most outstanding bonus for them has been the increase in Floor Space Index (FSI) from 1 to 2.5 for slums. Floor Space Index is a formula by which the area of construction allowed on a given plot of land is restricted. It is a ratio of the plot area to the built-up area. Under 2.5 FSI for slum lands, construction of a building with areas on different floors adding up to 2.5 times that of the plot area is permissible. The increase of FSI for slum lands to 2.5 will generate enormous profit for the developer. Take a plot of 2,000 square metres located in a slum. With an FSI of 2.5, 5,000 square metres of built-up area will be permitted. The normal FSI, which is 1, would be sufficient to accommodate all the existing slum-dwellers as they live mostly in ground floor structures. Therefore, the builder will have a surplus of 3,000 square metres of built-up area to sell in the open market. In addition, the land cost in this development is free to the builder. The price of built-up area in the suburbs of Bombay today may be taken as Rs 15,000/- per square metre and the cost of construction approximately Rs 3000/-. Hence, the builder makes a profit of Rs 12,000/- per square metre, which is about 400 per cent. Such a huge rate of profit will unjustifiably enrich certain influential sections of the society and will promote corruption in the administration. This process will also encourage forcible evictions and demolitions organized by real estate sharks who, as we already know, have a growing influence with the police and the local administration officials. Through a combination of force and persuasion, the slum-dwellers will be obliged to accept housing schemes promoted by developers.

In order to profit from the 2.5 FSI for slum lands, the developer will sell the surplus apartments to middle or high income purchasers, thereby adding to the number of housing units built for a small section of our population. We must remember that nearly 60 per cent of the city's population live in slums or in degraded housing conditions and a further nearly 10 per cent live on pavements. Any serious housing programme must cater primarily to this population. Simultaneously, we must remember that according to government sources there are nearly 100,000 surplus flats of the middle income and high income categories unoccupied, and owned by investors and speculators. Under the present policy, we will be only adding further to the already surplus housing stock for middle income and high income categories. The speculators and investors have been largely responsible for creating a highly inflated price structure for real estate and housing in Bombay. Developers and builders will under these circumstances aggressively advertise the new units for sale in other towns and cities of the country. If the advertisements are successful, more outsiders will come into Bombay, or they will keep large numbers of apartments locked up as speculative investments. The end result would be exactly opposite to that purported by government and the upper classes to be the limiting of migration to and population growth in the city of Bombay and increasing the housing supply so as to reduce the gap between demand and supply.

The enhancement of FSI in slum areas to 2.5 is thus altogether a dangerous proposition for mass housing and particularly for housing of the poor. Such an FSI can only lead to high-rise and high-cost construction. High-rise, to my mind, is irrelevant as a housing solution; it would only further displace and destabilize the settlements of the poor. High-rise builders require capital-intensive technology, not only for the initial construction but also for subsequent repairs and maintenance of the buildings. In Bombay particularly, because high rainfall and inferior soil conditions (as most of land is marshy and reclaimed), we face serious structural and maintenance problems in high-rise buildings. Often, major repairs including guniting have to be carried out, which are all very costly activities, requiring high capital expense. To perceive this as a part of a housing programme for the poor is ridiculous and an insult to those whom it is supposed to benefit. Another danger of high-rise development having units of 250 square feet (the area allowed for slum dwellers) will generate a very high density of population on the given land. The number of such units as compared to middle and high income category housing will be nearly three to four times on a given area of land. This population pressure on land would imperatively require infrastructure, such as roads, hospitals, fire stations and services such as water supply and sewerage. In the city today we are subsisting with dilapidated and archaic services. In order simply to keep going at the present level we are seeking World Bank assistance and foreign technical collaboration. Expansion of these services to support the increased population density which would result from construction permitted by a 2.5 FSI is not even envisaged as part of the programme.

Lastly, increase in FSI, resulting in high-rise construction and high density settlements would require large capital-intensive and corporate agencies to undertake the various projects. As a result, the control of the users over their own environment will altogether disappear. Even for further maintenance and management, the poor would be found to depend on various monopoly controls and financial institutions. It is often stated that space is most effectively utilized by high-rise buildings but architects have shown that this is not true. Well-designed low-rise and small buildings can accommodate large numbers of people, and achieve desirable density levels. This has also been established in the report of the Urbanization Commission, Government of India. Secondly, construction and maintenance of a house is an intensely, personal and creative experience. Individuals build, repair, maintain and develop their houses in unique ways, giving full expression to their cultural and religious heritage. Mass concrete jungles stifle the creativity of people and make them totally reliant on outside agencies for repair and maintenance. Where these agencies fail, the houses rapidly decline. As a result, the working class becomes more and more dependent and experiences a sense of helplessness and frustration.

FSI is not a game of numbers. Unfortunately, in this whole process, the various humane aspects have constantly been ignored. Any policy for limiting or restricting built-up area must be based primarily on population, which means norms for density must become the principal guiding policy.

Transfer of Development Rights (TDR): TDR separates the development potential of a plot of land from the land itself and makes it available to the owner of the land in the form of transferable rights. Such an award will entitle the owner of the land to FSI in the form of a Development Rights Certificate (DRC) which he may use himself or transfer to any other person. This concept of trading in development rights contradicts the very purpose of a development plan, which is meant to regulate and promote the orderly growth of a city, including its population distribution in relation to the services and infrastructure available. As a result of TDR, particular plots of land would suddenly achieve a higher FSI than surrounding plots, thereby not just creating aesthetic and environmental disorder but also imposing disproportionate pressures on the available services and infrastructure or upsetting the balance and distribution of services to other plots. This is particularly significant because no plan is made in such cases to simultaneously develop the services and supplies such as of water and electricity.

The Nivara Hakk Suraksha Samiti has strongly opposed the concept of trading in development rights because the imbalances it would generate would defeat the very purpose of town-planning norms. The Samiti also argues that this proposal has the ulterior motive of enabling contractor-builders and landowners to indulge in profiteering.

Alternative Technology and Low Cost Housing

At another level, architects, planners and other professionals who are concerned with the issues of housing for the poor are engaged in trying to cut costs in construction. They are constantly evolving alternative technologies and materials for use in low-cost housing for the poor. This exercise, without concern for larger social and political issues, becomes counterproductive and damaging to the interests of the poor. The protagonists of alternative technologies clearly distinguish between two different sets of materials for different classes, cement and concrete for the rich and mud for the poor. This distinction of material use on a class basis is unacceptable. The choice and use of material have to be based rather on geographical and climatic considerations. If concrete is the most suitable material in Bombay's conditions of climate and population density, then it should be used in the construction of houses for *all* classes of people in the city. If new and ingenious techniques in using cement and concrete are being developed, we welcome the idea as it expresses concern for careful and sensitive use of scarce national resources. In this case, these alternatives should become the material base for *all* construction.

Role of Voluntary Agencies: In the political game being played in the name of housing for the poor and low-cost housing, numerous voluntary agencies, often termed Non-Governmental Organizations (NGOs), some receiving foreign funds, are being used to divide and weaken the people and render them incapable of launching united people's struggles for equality and dignity. Their constant effort is to subvert, dis-inform and de-idealize people so as to keep them away from class struggles. They adopt and propagate the practice of begging favours on sympathetic and humane grounds rather than making the oppressed conscious of their rights. As a matter of fact these agencies and organizations systematically intervene to oppose the agitational path people take to win their demands. Their effort is constantly to divert people's attention from the larger political evils of imperialism to merely local issues and so confuse people in differentiating enemies from friends. Under the cover of a progressive mask, the NGOs preach about the failure of governmental systems, while propagating and advocating the need for a non-governmental or people-based development strategy.

Various NGOs receive funds from different foreign agencies with the full knowledge and sanction of the Indian government. This necessarily means that there are certain understandings between them and the government. In fact, these NGOs have always worked within parameters set by the government. For these reasons the Indian government has recently, in all its policies and programmes, entrusted a hefty responsibility to the NGOs. The ruling class considers the NGOs their partners in development. This policy is manifest in the National Housing Policy as well as in the various housing policies adopted for the city of Bombay. Further, to give this aspect of mutual cooperation due recognition, the Government of India, in its Eighth Plan, envisages an allocation of Rs 30,000 crores (Rs 300 billion) to the voluntary sector.

A large number of these NGOs or voluntary agencies are working amongst slum-dwellers. They are, on the one hand, actively engaged in providing services to the community, acting as a bridge between the particular programme of the government and the 'target group'; and, on the other, they are active in the areas of charity, relief, welfare etc. The latter activities were widely seen during and after the December 1992 and January 1993 riots in Bombay. Even providing direct financial assistance and other material support for housing and reconstruction of slums has been a part of their work.

The majority of the NGOs which we have observed are closely connected with various Christian missions and have also been receiving funds from them. Along with the Christian missions, several Muslim and Hindu philantrophic institutions and trusts have also been drawing immense funds from foreign sources and are, in a sense, media of imperialist penetration.

At times of ultimate crisis, or when a movement reaches an advanced state of confrontation with the authorities, and when demands are not met, these NGOs cleverly back out, leaving the people to face the wrath of the government. They even fail to evolve any alternate political and social programme which could sustain the movement. It is, therefore, necessary for all organizations of slum dwellers to understand the real intentions of the variously funded voluntary organizations and to oppose them and their intermediary role as agents.

Cotton Textile Mills' Lands: The new Development Control Regulations allow the cotton textile mills of Bombay to develop or redevelop their entire open land, including built-up area, for three categories of uses, viz., (1) recreation ground/garden/playground or any other use as specified by the commissioner, (2) development by the Maharashtra Housing and Area Development Board, and (3) residential or commercial use by the owner. The owner may keep about a third of the entire land for his own residential or commercial use. Most of the cotton textile mills are located in the F and G wards in the heart of the city. All starred category residential hotel buildings may be permitted to exceed the normal permissible FSI in the F and G wards by 50 per cent. This means that the cotton mill owners will get an FSI of 1.5, which will enhance their bonanza and their chance of profiteering. It is not coincidental that hotels have been permitted an additional FSI in F and G wards. Apart from the concentration of textile mills in these wards, there is no reasonable explanation why this has been done only in these wards. Granted that 1991 had been declared tourism year and an increased influx of tourists was expected that year, with increased demand for hotel accommodation, but, by the time the hotels could be constructed, tourism year would have been over, and also the rationale for the increase in FSI. As opposed to this, there are some 200,000 textile workers in Bombay who will be adversely affected by the permission granted to the millowners to shift their factories out of the city and to utilize the sites of the mills for residential and hotel purposes. The millowners have not framed a viable scheme to rehabilitate these workers in terms of employment and accommodation.

Communalism and Housing: The people's struggle for housing is faced today with the threat of communalism. Not only are the working class and the poor divided on religious and communal lines, but they actively oppose and attack each other. This has been clearly evident during the 1992–93 riots in Bombay. Apart from the slum dwellers, even the organized working class and their trade unions have failed to unite and oppose the communal forces. This phenomenon has greatly weakened the struggles and movements of the poor, including that for housing rights. Housing rights activists and organizations will have, therefore, to give priority to campaigns against communalism and to go far beyond the idea of communal amity, which to my mind is a typically upper- and middle-class slogan. The toiling masses will have to understand the weakness of this slogan and move ahead to opposing religion as the basis of division of society. During the recent communal riots in Bombay we saw an increasing trend of ghettoization. This too is a dangerous social and housing phenomenon which we have to strongly oppose.

The struggle for housing has therefore to be made part of a wider democratic movement. Housing must be seen not merely an issue of design, construction and technology, but as a social movement, fundamental to the growth and development of every individual and family. Housing in this context becomes a vital issue for organizing the millions of toiling urban poor against State oppression and increasing communal violence and criminalization of the masses.

Conclusion

Government has to recognize the needs of the slum-dwellers and legalize all slums. The State has to concede the right to housing as a fundamental right. It must cease all support, direct or indirect, to profiteering by anybody from housing. Denial of housing rights is equivalent to denial of the right to live and is a violation of basic human rights. The movement for housing will therefore have to become a major one; slum-dwellers have to wage an unrelenting struggle to win their due. The struggle for housing has to become a part of the larger movement for democratic rights.

References

Das, P. K. and Colin Gonsalves (1987). *Struggle for Housing—A People's Manifesto*, Bombay, Nivara Hakk Suraksha Samiti.

Development Control Regulation for Greater Bombay, 1991.

Government of India. National Housing Policy.

Gurbir Singh (1987). 'Nivara Hakk Suraksha Samiti' in *Struggle for Housing—A People's Manifesto*.

James, P. J. *Voluntary Agencies: The True Mission*.

Sebastian, P. A. (1991). Bombay High Court writ petition no. 963, 1991, filed for Nivara Hakk Suraksha Samiti.

POLITICS, POPULISM AND VIOLENCE

10

Saffronization of the Shiv Sena: The Political Economy of City, State and Nation[1]

JAYANT LELE

During the January 1993 riots in Bombay, the Shiv Sena once again displayed its muscle power. This time the mobilization of its troops had some distinctive features. It was far more systematic than ever before, in its organization, in the targeting of its enemy and in the total dehumanization and brutality of its methods. The rise and fall in the Shiv Sena's prominence in the political events of Bombay-Maharashtra has often been described in terms of waves of popularity and decline. The distinctive features of the events of 6–11 January 1993, however, require that it not be treated as 'just another communal riot'.

The blatant claim of responsibility for the orchestration of the riots without reprisal, and open threats of further violence if necessary, by the leader of the Sena, indicate the dramatic changes that have occurred in the climate of political legitimacy since the sixties. For the first time in Bombay's history, people were fleeing *en masse* from the city; over 200,000 are reported to have abandoned their possessions and their livelihoods to escape attacks of the Sainiks. That these included both Muslim and non-Muslim Maharashtrians, raises some questions about the authenticity and efficacy of the Shiv Sena's espousal of the 'Hindu' cause and about the concept of *hindutva* itself.

The open complicity of a substantial section of the police force and the involvement of white-collar neighbourhoods (e.g. 'middle class'

Insightful comments from Professors Y. D. Phadke, Sujata Patel, Alice Thorner and Aruna Pendse have helped me a great deal in revising this paper. Their contributions are gratefully acknowledged. Errors and omissions are a result of my obstinacy and the pressure of time.

women brutally attacking Muslim women and children) also demand some critical analysis and explanation. The purpose of this paper is to trace the transitions in the life history of the Shiv Sena over the last 25 years in such a way as to set an agenda for future research and practice, with the practical goal of finding ways to meet the Shiv Sena challenge.

Origins: the 1960s

When the Shiv Sena was launched in 1966 it had a simple programme and a limited constituency: the reservation of jobs and new economic opportunities for Maharashtrians, mainly in the lower echelons of white-collar employment. A wider programme, implicit in this demand, evolved over time. Since migration from other cultural regions was identified as the main culprit, demands were made to curtail it. Given the specific part of the job market the Shiv Sena wanted protected, the enemy was also specifically identified as 'South Indians', meaning mostly those from Tamil Nadu. The prominence of southerners had become noticeable in intellectual arenas such as journalism, culture and education, and had visibly increased since Independence. The noticeable presence of South Indians in clerical and lower management jobs in the burgeoning capitalist sector—industrial and commercial—was attributed to their command of the English language and to their willing subservience to authority. They became the prime target of Sena attacks. At the same time, Maharashtrians were asked to emulate those qualities.

Between 1960, when the state of Maharashtra came into existence and 1966, major changes in the structure of Bombay's economy occurred. The underside of state-sponsored private capitalist development, an 'underworld' of extortion, smuggling, drug trafficking and contraband peddling, had begun to emerge. The policy of prohibition produced a thriving class of bootleggers. For the residents of relatively homogeneous Maharashtrian white-collar neighbourhoods, these changes in the socio-cultural scene were peripheral and yet potentially threatening. When the Sena also promised to wipe out gangsterdom, it struck a sympathetic chord. By the end of the sixties, while publicly attacking the underworld, it managed to create within itself a strong and dedicated following that gave the organization its muscle power and in return gave those in the underworld the benefit of its organization and discipline.

The founder of the Sena, Bal Thackeray (BT), lived in Bombay's Shivaji Park area, surrounded mostly by Marathi-speaking professionals and administrative and clerical workers who responded readily to the attacks on the influx of 'South Indians'. It gathered momentum when he quite unexpectedly attracted a large and enthusiastic crowd at his first public meeting at Shivaji Park on 30 October 1966. Enthused by a speech that touched a nerve, many offered support. BT decided to follow a pattern borrowed from the Rashtriya Swayamsevak Sangh (RSS), a Hindu nationalist organization of long standing. *Shakas* (branches) were established in a number of neighbourhoods. Little thought was given as to how these were to be organized and what they were expected to do (Gupta, 1982).[2]

BT had worked as a cartoonist at *The Free Press Journal*, an English-language daily. He mastered the power of the caricature, of exaggeration, in capturing the anger arising out of distress and disappointment and releasing it as humour. He commanded a potent weapon for attacking those in power and exposing them in the eyes of subalterns. It is a weapon that can keep anger simmering, direct it into action under appropriate circumstances, or dissipate it. Perhaps because his position at an English-language newspaper offered no scope for the exercise of his acid tongue, he left his job and in 1960 and started his own Marathi weekly journal of cartoons, political comment and humour, and called it *Marmik* (that which grapples with the essence).

A popular movement, the Samyukta Maharashtra Movement (SMM), had preceded the creation of the linguistic state of Maharashtra with Bombay as its capital. The reluctance of the national Congress leadership to accede to the demand for the inclusion of Bombay city in Maharashtra made it possible for the leftists in the movement to interpret their struggle as aimed at alien (predominantly Gujarati) capital. While native speakers of Marathi comprised over 40 per cent of the population of Bombay, none of them occupied the commanding heights of its economy. The colonially defined boundaries of Bombay Province included regions of Gujarat and Karnataka and excluded the Marathi-speaking regions of Vidarbha and Marathwada. The struggle for the city of Bombay brought to the surface the contradiction between the dominant interests in agriculture (the rich and middle farmers of Maharashtra) and

---

[2] Neither BT's 'astute statesmanship' nor his 'charisma' were basic to the support received by the Shiv Sena. His talent as a cartoonist and as a writer of pungent prose made him popular. The issues he raised arose from an interpretation of his own personal experiences. That they struck a common chord among his fellow Maharashtrians in lower middle class neighbourhoods is a consequence of the shared impact of the structural changes that were occurring in Bombay.

those in industry (the non-Marathi commercial and industrial capital, concentrated in Bombay at this stage but with close links to local commercial capital in rural Western Maharashtra, Marathwada and Vidarbha). In the end, the demand for a Marathi state was granted only when the Maharashtra Congress Party persuaded the national leaders that it could guarantee that the interests of capital would be fully safeguarded while the dominant rural interest would be given its appropriate share of state resources.

With the creation of Maharashtra, the SMM lost its force as an all-party alliance. During the peak period it had successfully challenged the hold of the Congress Party over the electorate, even though most Maratha leaders, despite their strong support for the cause of United Maharashtra, had chosen to remain within the Congress Party. The Movement was therefore dominated by communists and socialists. Although all parties opposing the Congress Party had joined together to form the *samiti* (alliance), its real strength was in the left parties within it (Pendse, 1965: 574). A number of intellectuals and social activists who shunned party politics had also joined the SMM. They looked at the dominance of leftist leaders with suspicion. Staunch anti-communists were particularly distrustful and even opposed to the presence of the communists. BT's father, K. S. Thackeray, was one of them.

K. S. Thackeray was an eminent journalist whose 'art of writing was so pungent and biting that it could make the opponent under attack choke' (Phadke, 1982: 64). Both in terms of style and attitude towards communism, BT assumed his father's mantle when he started *Marmik*. Like his father, BT was disenchanted with the alliance because of the communists. At this stage, he treated all party politics as a self-serving activity of ambitious politicians.

Before the formation of the Shiv Sena, during its first five years, *Marmik* showed few signs of a clear ideological position, except for its strong anti-communism. That sentiment was further inflamed by the China–India war of 1962 and the reluctance of Indian communists to condemn China. A style of aggressive, 'below the belt' journalism was practised against everyone who disagreed with or criticized BT. Absence of commitment to a specific political party and its agenda made it easier to spread the venom evenly against all practising politicians and public figures who courted BT's disapproval. This struck a sympathetic note in the minds of most upper caste white-collar residents of Bombay who looked upon the takeover of state politics by Maratha 'peasants' as its degradation.

During this period BT clashed with Atre, the editor of a Marathi daily who also wrote with matching style and venom. BT denounced Atre with his ultimate insult, a 'communist with a dirty tongue'. During this prolonged battle of insults the sales of the two newspapers skyrocketed and BT's popularity among the lower-middle class and white-collar Maharashtrians grew rapidly.[3] A strong strain of Hindu nationalism was also visible in his writings. He objected, for example, to the fact that the President of India made a special trip to Bombay to meet the Pope.

These inarticulate tendencies (distrust of communists and a Brahmanic view of political propriety and social ethics) converged into a concrete programme with the launching of the Shiv Sena in 1966. The immediate and manifest provocation was a fear of the loss of jobs for Marathi workers in Bombay and a widespread belief that the continuing influx of migrants from the South was responsible for it. The real causes for the fear had matured over the years. Having won Bombay as the capital of the Marathi state against the resistance of Gujarati capital, there was an expectation among middle-class Maharashtrians that their job prospects in the city would substantially improve. During the first half of the decade, however, no dramatic changes had occurred in this direction.

Between 1960 and 1965 Bombay attracted a disproportionate share of industrial capital compared to the rest of India. Unlike most other major cities where state enterprises came to dominate the economic scene, the anarchic pattern of urbanization in Bombay involved subversion of many socially responsible development plans so as to allow relatively free rein for the growth of private industrial capital (see Verma, 1985).

Concerns about increasing congestion in the city prompted the Government of Maharashtra to set up a number of institutional mechanisms to encourage dispersal of medium and large-scale industry across the state and especially into the backward regions. While some progress was made in that direction during the sixties, industrial growth remained concentrated in and around Bombay (Greater Bombay and Thane together accounted for over 598,000 industrial workers, while Puné, the next largest district, had only 45,000 in 1967). In terms of population, Bombay had already grown to a point where, by 1965, the presence of over 3000 slums and a total population of slum and

---

[3] By 1966, *Marmik* had a circulation of about 60,000 and perhaps a readership of between 40 and 50 per cent of the literate Marathi-speaking adult (over 15 years) population. See Katzenstein (1979).

pavement dwellers of more than a million had become a cause for concern with respect to housing, water, sewerage, solid waste disposal, transport, pollution and law and order (Gogate, 1973).

The problems of Bombay did not grow in isolation from the wider and deeper malaise afflicting India's political economy in the mid-sixties. Despite 15 years of illusory calm and an aura of an assured socialist path to prosperity, the 'Nehruvian' industry–agriculture compromise remained inherently unstable. The tension became acute during the Third Plan period (1961–66) and was reflected in the slow growth of national income, dramatic price increases, shortages of raw materials and the growth of idle capacity in industry due to the low level of demand. By 1966, all these tendencies culminated in the stagnation of per capita growth, the decline in per capita availability of foodgrains and other essential commodities below 1956 levels, massive grain imports, rising unemployment, shrinking budgetary resources and a severe strain on the balance of payments. Between 1965 and 1970, the Indian economy experienced an acute recession.

Across India, the discontent over food shortages, rising prices, growing income disparities between classes and asset disparities between regions took a variety of forms. There were state workers' strikes, industrial labour strikes, student agitations, spontaneous popular protests and spurts of violent attacks on official state functionaries and institutions.

By focusing on South Indian managers and by accusing them of nativist preferences in employment for secretarial and clerical jobs, the Shiv Sena managed to deflect attention from the socio-cultural and economic consequences of unchecked capitalist development in industry and of the state-assisted distortions of land, housing, liquor, drug and job markets. These in turn fuelled the growth of a speculative, ruthless and crime-linked black (casino) capitalism. Some cautious warnings that such consequences would emerge from unchecked capitalist development had been voiced even during the Samyukta Maharashtra Movement (Pendse, 1965: 109). Conspiratorially or not, the Shiv Sena fought hard to divert popular attention away from the dominance of capital over Bombay. It in fact described some big capitalists as *annadatas* (food givers) of the Maharashtrians, while describing 'all the *lungiwalas*' (South Indians) as 'criminals, gamblers, illicit liquor distillers, pimps, goondas and Communists' (see Gangadharan, 1970: 19, 20).

During the 1967 elections much of the discontent was funnelled into electoral support for the older popular or new populist political parties and to temporary opposition party alliances. However, where skilful State leaders were able to contain and moderate elite rivalry within the Congress system, the impact of such discontent remained minimal. Rural Maharashtra was a prime example of the hegemony of the dominant caste landed elites.

In Bombay, where it faced serious competition from several other parties, the Congress 'had to be more selective both in its electoral appeals and in the interests to which it sought to accommodate itself' (Rosenthal, 1977: 125–6). There was also the rivalry between the Bombay (BPCC) and Maharashtra (MPCC) units of the party. The Bombay unit was dominated by the interests of capital. Given its non-party posture, the Shiv Sena was a potential ally and was courted by both. It gave its support to a Congress candidate who ran against V. K. Krishna Menon, and to several others from the Swatantra, Jan Sangh and Socialist parties. It also opposed others from the same parties, branding them 'communist fellow travellers'. The Shiv Sena thus made it clear that, under conditions of pluralist competition, it was as ready as the other parties to exploit electoral politics to secure its own support base. These and subsequent electoral alliances and successes at the polls gave legitimacy to the Sena when it transformed itself into a political party. It also gained access to substantial public resources for patronage.

The most important parliamentary contest was that of V. K. Krishna Menon, an old ally of Nehru. He was India's Defence Minister in 1962 when India suffered a humiliating defeat against the Chinese army. Menon's communist sympathies were blamed by many for the lack of preparedness of the Indian armed forces. He was then dropped from the cabinet and when denied nomination by the Congress party, decided to run as an independent from his Bombay constituency with the support of the remnant SMM. The Congress and its candidate were happy to receive the Sena's support. Menon, an outsider, a South Indian and a communist sympathizer, concretely symbolized the Sena's enemy. Whether the Sena played a decisive role in Menon's defeat is not clear. Its popularity no doubt soared as its 'anti-communist', 'anti-South Indian' and 'anti-traitor' cause received new legitimacy.

This flexible, purely instrumental relationship to other political parties persisted up to the seventies. For example, in September 1967 it allied with a number of independent candidates to capture control of municipal government in Thane, a large suburban Bombay town. It entered into an alliance with the Socialists to contest the 1968 municipal election in Bombay and won an impressive number of seats.

While the theme of anti-communism attracted groups and parties positively linked with the interest of capital to the Sena, its militant Maharashtrianism, aimed at South Indians, became a source of embar rassment to the parties claiming a pan-national constituency. Its avowed Maharashtrianism has always coexisted with a strong Hindu nationalist undercurrent. Apart from the various Hindu symbols, BT's RSS origins have showed through his beliefs, as, for example, in his opposition to family planning, based on the fear that it would work at the expense of Hindus and lead to another Pakistan (see Morkhandikar, 1967: 1906). The Shiv Sena's electoral strategy, the contents of *Marmik* and BT's utterances lend credence to the claim that the 'Shiv Sena opposed every variety of the left and supported all shades of the right making its allegiance quite clear' (Gupta, 1982: 160). What is not explained is the reason for its readiness to work during its first phase, with the 'left' (such as the Socialists), the 'centre' (the Congress Party) and the 'right' (the Jan Sangh, Swatantra) and to oppose them when convenient.

The roots of this apparent anomaly lie in the rapidly changing, un-stable political context, and the growing inability of the state to govern. The Shiv Sena was in that context 'a populist eruption'. It thrived paras-itically on diffuse and generalized discontent. It was both a consequence of and a contributor to the ideological confusion rampant among Indian intellectuals in the late sixties. Because of this confusion the Sena was able to strike many opportunistic alliances and to benefit from them. It also tried to broaden its appeal to workers in formal and informal sectors of the Bombay region, using its populist rhetoric and grassroots activity. However, the elite core of Sena leadership and much of its popular support remained concentrated within middle-class neighbourhoods for several years. In both the 1968 and 1973 municipal elections the major successes were confined to these constituencies.

The two spaces in which wealth and poverty as antithetical products of development polarize in a post-colonial city are 'the enclave-like sur-roundings of those who have tapped the avenues of power and owner-ship of resources' and 'the shanty towns made of rags, paper and tin' whose inhabitants 'eke out a living residing as it were on the periphery of both the spatial and the social world of the urbanites' (Chandoke, 1991: 2871). Squeezed in between is the spread of the actual or potential constituents of a populist organization like the Shiv Sena. Many have pretensions or dreams of belonging to the privileged few without being able to occupy the same space. They are Breman's (1980: 25) *petit bourgeois* or penny capitalists. The bottom layer of this class could easily merge into the opposite pole except for the precarious permanence of their jobs, steadily made more meaningless by the declining purchasing power of their incomes.

The most striking feature of this class now is its enormous diversity of occupations, age groups and residential locations. What its members have in common, however, is a sense of uncertainty about the future. With the nebulousness of the Shiv Sena's programme and it's disjointed understanding of causes of perceived injustices and immoralities, every grievance can find its reflection in the slogans, symbols and the identifiable enemy projected by the Sena.

In rural Maharashtra, the extended kinship framework of the dominant Maratha caste cluster, together with its traditional patron-like relation to the service castes, assured its social and political hegemony. (Lele, 1981). Where city dwellers had strong links to this powerful rich and middle-peasant network, it was often able to insulate them from populist or popular mobilization. One such example is the Maratha Mahasangh with its origins in the organization of the *mathadis* (porters) of Bombay.[4]

The textile workers of Bombay present another case in point. Omvedt (1976: 252, 263) shows how they have been subject to two types of unionism: one based on the social structure and the other on spontaneous worker radicalism and militant leadership. She cites 'an effective conservative, coopting response by non-Brahman leaders' as one of the important factors for the absence of radicalism in the earlier era, indicating that traditional rural links of the textile workers had been

---

[4] Organized in 1965 by Annasaheb Patil, as the Maharashtra State Mathadi, Transport and General Workers Union, the organization represented Maratha migrants from the core Maratha districts of Pune, Satara, Sangli, Kolhapur, Ahmednagar, Nashik and Solapur. It fought against arbitrary wage determination by the jobbers (*mukadams*). Y. B. Chavan, as the Chief Minister, supported Patil in the building of the organization and in subsequent years major Maratha Congress leaders (e.g. Rajarambapu and Vasant Dada Patil, Balasaheb Desai) became its patrons. In 1976 Patil also initiated the Maratha Mahasangh as an all-India federation of the Marathas. Declining Maratha hegemony was reflected in the internal leadership conflict of the Mahasangh. Its ability to constrain Shiv Sena initiatives was demonstrated, once again, when in November 1987 the Mahasangh both initiated and reined in the protest against Ambedkar's 'Riddles of Hinduism'. The Shiv Sena was forced to follow its lead (see Jadhav, 1988: 348–9). The Mahasangh's *Hinduism* resembles more the 'anti-Brahman brahmanism' of the NBM than the urban petty bourgeois ideology of the RSS. While the former emphasized the Maratha *Kshatriya* status and challenged Brahman domination, the latter asserts Brahman superiority. However, even the Mahasangh was forced to claim backward class status for the Marathas when the Mandal Commission Report was being implemented.

systematically exploited by elite Maratha elements to counter the emergence of trade union radicalism.

As the inheritor of that legacy, the Congress Party in Maharashtra continued to play the same role. During the Nehru era, the Congress-affiliated and officially recognized Rashtriya Mill Mazdur Sabha (RMMS) was dominated by those whose close links to the interests of capital were well known. A state-mediated capital–labour compromise was in effect (see Gupta, 1982: 59), equivalent to the Nehruvian rich farmer–capitalist compromise. This picture began to change as the anomalies of Nehruvian economic policies matured around 1966. An increasing discontent among workers led to the reassertion of the hold of the communist-led unions and was reflected in the election of three communist labour leaders to the Legislative Assembly in 1967. This became a cause of concern for both the Congress party and the Shiv Sena. Both had an opportunity to exploit the Maharashtrian identity of the workers with rural links. The Congress acted first. Recognizing that most of the communist trade union workers were from Satara and Sangli districts, it deployed the services of Vasant Dada Patil to take control of the RMMS. The Sena started its own Bharatiya Kamgar Sena (BKS).[5]

The failure of the BKS to capture the support of the textile workers at this stage is an example of the impotence of upstart populism in challenging the hegemony of the Maratha elites. The RMMS continued to control the lives of the textile workers almost until the historic strike of 1982.

With its Maratha labour constituency, the Congress was able to extend the cover of elite Maratha hegemony to other operations in Bombay. By contrast, for the 'upper caste' urban petty bourgeois supporters of the Sena, Brahmanic nationalism and opposition to the South Indians were equally appealing. Prejudice against the lower castes as impure, unclean and prone to immoral acts was extended to the somewhat visibly different and alien South Indians as criminals, gamblers, bootleggers, pimps, and communists. As inheritors of the non-Brahman movement, Maratha workers with close rural links found the Sena's upper caste leadership

---

[5] Set up with the explicit purpose of wiping out communism from the minds of the workers (Gupta 1982: 82), the BKS's interventions often included violent clashes with communist union workers. It was forced to soften its anti-South-Indian and anti-Muslim rhetoric in order to expand its labour constituency. Financed by the industrialists, it was able to spawn a large number of unions in diverse new industrial establishments. In the immediate post-Emergency period, the spontaneous radicalist dimension of textile worker militancy was captured by Datta Samant (for details see Pendse, 1981).

suspect. At this stage, the Brahmanic tenets of Hinduism were more of an anathema than communism.

In addition to the support of upper caste, white-collar workers and professionals, the Sena needed an army of activists to give credence to its name. The most obvious constituency, spanning the class and locational divide, was that of unemployed and underemployed youth. When *Marmik* began to publish lists of names of enterprises with South Indian managers and employees, it identified South Indians as controllers of the media, as the real perpetrators of an anti-nationalist ideology and of nativistic job preferences. These lists, published week after week, gave the new prejudice an aura of truth. At the same time, mutual supportive activities in many poor neighbourhoods gave the *sainiks* a sense of direction and control over an otherwise chaotic existence. Under the Shiv Sena banner these activities acquired the appearance of a historic struggle. Whether the task was that of burning and looting restaurants and hounding hawkers or that of paving roads and providing food, shelter, water or latrines (see Katzenstein, 1979; 105, 89), it could now be carried out under inspiration provided by and with the reflected glory of Shivaji and his latter day incarnation, the new commander of his army, (*senapati*) Bal Thackeray.

The desire to enter the ethnically diverse formal sector so as to wipe out the influence of communism in the labour unions, and the expansion of *shakhas* to incorporate the disenchanted youth (unemployed, underemployed and socially isolated from elite cultural and material styles of life), led to the weakening of the hostile agenda against the South Indians. With the adaptability and acquiescence of the weaker minority communities, the threat of attacks on property were easily transformed into a protection money racket and were made a source for financing many a *shakha* activity. The Sena could also be used to settle scores with rivals and competitors in business or in private life, regardless of their ethnic affiliations, or to extract quick results from recalcitrant bureaucrats. These emerging bases of the Shiv Sena's 'popular' support structured the future direction of its activism. Issues and occasions were often chosen and manipulated so as to retain this core of support. As an umbrella for all these activities, the theme of Marathi identity was retained as the main plank between 1966 and 1970. The hatred of and attacks on communists, South Indians and Muslims were interpreted as part of the historic struggle emanating from the proud and militant nationalist spirit of Maharashtrians.

The Beginnings of Saffronization: the 1970s

During the 1970s, the overt activism and the media profile of the Shiv Sena remained subdued. Its electoral support waned. By 1979, for example, it had no member in the state legislature or the national parliament and its strength in the Bombay Municipal Corporation declined from 42 in 1968 to 21 in 1978 (Katzenstein 1979: 191). The paradoxical contribution of these developments of the seventies for the Shiv Sena was that they strengthened the underside of its 'popular' support while throwing a major challenge to its electoral and 'legitimate' political aspirations.

The first significant event leading up to this period was the Congress split of 1969 and the emergence of Indira Gandhi's own populist-centrist strategy of governance and legitimation. She recognized that the Nehruvian compromise had provided only a small, selective and paternalistic trickle-down of benefits to the lower classes, in comparison to gains which had accrued to the rich and middle farmers, the big industrial and commercial capitalists, the upper echelons of white-collar workers, blue-collar workers in the organized sector and a few coopted members of the lowest castes. The marginalized sections, particularly those in urban areas, could be mobilized through waves of protests and agitations. Recruited mostly from upper and middle class families, students facing the prospect of rising unemployment had also become restive.

The populist strategy of the new Indira-led Congress focused on these prospective constituencies of the left parties. Internal divisions among the communists and between them and the socialists had made them ineffective. The vacuum was filled by regional parties and movements which mobilized opposition through religious, regional, tribal and language identities. They deflected popular anger over deteriorating material conditions onto scapegoats such as Muslims and *dalits*. As against these groups the new Congress Party claimed to speak for *all* 'poor people'. With its slogan of 'abolish poverty' and through a few token populist policy measures, it hoped to steal the thunder from the discrete regional/local mobilizations and to tighten its control of state power.

Despite the upheavals experienced by the traditional Congress elite elsewhere, the Maratha hegemony over the party and the government remained relatively intact in Maharashtra. The new 'Indira loyalists' were unable to take control of existing structures (cooperatives, village panchayats, educational institutions, for example) and had to scramble for other ways to establish their links to the electorate through patronage (see Lele, 1981).

Behind the apparent ideological paradoxes, there were some significant shifts in public policy and some real continuities. The asset-concentrating pattern of agricultural development of the Green Revolution was continued and actively fostered in the name of national self-sufficiency in foodgrains. While the American attempt to use food aid as a foreign policy weapon was denounced as blackmail, the new agricultural strategy, also forced on India by the Americans, was adopted in the belief that it could free India from foreign dependency and threats of starvation.

The root cause of economic stagnation was the fact that the project of industrial self-reliance was neither rule-based nor automatic enough in terms of clearly stated national priorities. It had been framed with serious ambiguities which ensured a determining role for bureaucratic discretion at all levels (Srinivasan, 1991). That pattern became even more entrenched. As a result, in the 1970s, a large parallel economy of 'black money' and super-profits emerged and became available to supplement financially the burgeoning parallel polity of 'Indira loyalists'. An example of the new arrangements was the ban on company contributions to political parties, 'followed soon thereafter by pressures from those in authority on business concerns to make even larger contributions than in the past, but in cash' (Paranjape, 1985: 1516).

In Bombay the 'abolish poverty populism' of the Indira Congress presented a serious challenge to the Shiv Sena by targeting essentially the same constituency for its support base. With its control over public resources (both material and coercive), it was better poised to succeed than the Shiv Sena, which had remained, even in its better days, a minority party in the Bombay Municipal Corporation. Even though it managed to exploit its legitimacy and the patronage potential to advantage, by winning mayorship and senior committee positions, its policy postures produced contradictory signals, and confused its diverse constituency consisting of the white-collar opponents of slums (and of the 'uglification' of the city that slums and pavement dwellers represented) on the one hand, and youth recruited from the pavements and slums on the other.

In State politics, both before and immediately after the 1969 split, the Sena had shown a distinct preference towards the MPCC over the BPCC, but was being courted by and received a great deal of covert support from both (Gupta 1982: 131). With the 'leftward' tilt of the

Indira Congress, immediately after the split, BT made common cause with the conservative Congress (O) and with the Swatantra Party.[6] At this point, the BPCC was trying to cultivate a radical pro-labour, pro-poor image. In the 1971 elections to the Lok Sabha, the Sena supported a number of right-wing candidates and put up some of its own. They were all defeated by the Indira Congress candidates. In the Assembly elections of 1972 the Sena won only one seat. In the Bombay Municipal Corporation elections of 1973 it formed an alliance with the Republican Party of India (RPI, a party of *dalit* leaders) and opposed the Congress candidates in 85 constituencies. It won 40 seats, still a minority. It subsequently sought and received support from the Muslim League in order to have its candidate elected the Mayor of Bombay.

It is clear that, at this stage, the *hindutva* aspect of the Sena ideology did not as yet have the same salience as its anti-communism. Both the populist Indira Congress and the traditionally labour-oriented leftist parties were seen as the main enemies, because they presented a direct threat to the Sena's own populist projects. It continued its efforts to penetrate the communist unions through violent clashes with union workers which culminated in June 1970 in the murder of Krishna Desai, a popular communist MLA from the Parel constituency. In the subsequent by-election, the Sena managed to defeat both Desai's wife and a Congress (I) candidate with the support of the Congress (O) and Swatantra parties, although by a very small margin. Its alliance with the RPI in the 1973 municipal elections was, for both, intended to counter the impact of the rise of a militant *dalit* movement, called Dalit Panthers. The Panthers were seen as closely linked to the communists and other leftist organizations of Bombay.[7]

The Shiv Sena's scramble for political alliances to keep its hold on its various urban constituencies seemed to offer a very weak antidote to all the new, radical and militant initiatives representing the upsurge of anger and disenchantment of the working classes. Instead of attempting to understand, guide or support these initiatives, the Sena chose to mute its attacks on Indira Gandhi. During the Emergency, it extended

[6] BT is reported to have opposed the Indira Congress 'because it is full of communists though Indira Gandhi herself is not one'. Cited from *The Times of India* in Gupta (1982: 182).

[7] Dalit Panthers were a radical reaction to the acquiescence of the Republican Party leaders to elite Maratha paternalism under the Congress regime. Many of the disenchanted *dalit* youth, not sharing the opportunistic anti-communist stance of these leaders, had joined leftist parties and were searching for an ideological basis for an independent, militant, and transformative *dalit* movement (see Kasbe, 1985: 73–81).

unquestioning support to the Congress government because of its agenda of enforcing a regime of law and order. It also participated in and profited from the parallel economy.

In the late sixties, the Shiv Sena had created for itself a significant support base in three somewhat disparate constituencies. A wave of sympathy and some activism had emerged among the salaried Marathi white-collar worker families through attacks on South Indians. Some inroads into the constituency of factory workers were made through the strategy of 'cooperation between the workers and the management' (for details, see Gupta 1982: 81–4). However, its greatest success, towards the end of the 1960s, was in mobilizing underemployed and unemployed youth, across class loyalty and ethnic boundaries. This was accomplished through a constructive strategy of assistance with the needs and diffi- culties of families in poor neighbourhoods.

Sainiks recruited from within these neighbourhoods, but supported by a larger network of Sena leaders, gained sympathy and support in slums and poor localities. At the same time, opportunities were opened for individual material gain through collective action of rioting, looting and extortion. Collaboration with and coercion of those benefiting from the underside of chaotic capitalist development (builders, importers, exporters, smugglers, drug pushers, bootleggers), as well as those in the forefront of 'cleaner' capitalist expansion (big and small industrial cap- italists and service and film industry magnates), were part of its second strategy. The Sena leader and the *sainiks* forged complex links between the two poles of the emerging capitalist nexus and profited from those links.

As the parallel economy and the parallel polity progressed, the Sena's hold on the third constituency of disenchanted youth also continued to grow, but with a clear twist. By the early eighties the most character- istic feature of the Sena was its image as nothing more than a network of gangs which thrived on extortion of protection money from hawkers, businessmen and shopkeepers. It also became known for extortion from and actual involvement in the various illegal deals in the larger construc- tion, contraband and drug-trafficking industries. This image led to some decline in its support from the white-collar and petty bourgeois elements whose sensibilities were injured by this criminalization. Some segments of the Marathi petty bourgeoisie were also disillusioned by BT's support of the Indira government during the Emergency.

As the face of the industrial map of Bombay changed in the seventies, the Sena also had to yield its foothold in the factory sector to the more

militant and far more professionalized activism of Datta Samant. Its
earlier opposition to the various workers' strikes had already led to a
substantial loss of support and sympathy from those in the formal sector.
In other words, while it may be an exaggeration to say that workers in
offices and factories abandoned the Shiv Sena or that its *shakhas* disappeared from middle-class neighbourhoods, it became clear that the
most abiding core of Shiv Sena activism was now located most firmly in
Bombay's lumpenized youth.

Expansion of Predatory Capitalism and Hindutva: the 1980s

When the Congress Party returned to power in January 1980, the most
significant force at work in India's political economy was the new asset-
and income-rich class of rich and middle-income urban and rural households. Nurtured by all regimes during the seventies, it permeated all
sectors of the economy, including agriculture, industry and services.
The economic policy of the new regime was largely driven by pent-up
demand for consumer durables and luxury goods from this class. This
new middle class was now perceived by the regime as the engine of
growth, as a category of efficient and avid consumers, savers and producers. In order to sustain their demand as a mechanism for stimulating
rapid industrial growth, the regime offered them a variety of fiscal and
financial incentives, including reduction in direct taxes (see BM, 1981:
1723–6).

Overt capitalist relations of production increasingly penetrated the
countryside. This had a gradual but decisive impact in eroding the
strength of the patriarchal-patrimonial ideology which had operated in
a 'religiously secular' environment of unchallenged hegemony. With the
decline of their hegemony, elites found it necessary to seek more militant
and overtly coercive ideological forms of assertion and implementation
of their dominance. This became the basis of the renewed alliance between the rich and middle farmers and the urban petty bourgeoisie. The
pan-national ideological cement for this alliance was provided by the
rising tide of *hindutva* and Hindu nationalism (Lele, 1993).

During the seventies, the Shiv Sena wandered through a variety of al-
liances and enmities in its pursuit of electoral success. It was supported,
used and maligned by the established political parties at different times.
It engaged in violent clashes against the Muslim League and the Dalit
Panthers but also accepted their support during mayoral contests.
Except for its persistent attacks on communists and communism, there

was little consistency in the level of commitment and vehemence with which it pursued the other elements of its ideology, such as Hinduism, nationalism and Maharashtrianism.

After having offered its support to the Janata combine in 1977, it switched to the Congress party in 1980, received its support in the municipal elections and managed to have two of its nominees sent to the state legislative council. It organized a procession to demand inclusion in Maharashtra of the Marathi towns in Karnataka. The *sainiks* turned it quickly into a violent riot and resorted to looting and destruction. Its battles with the established unions also continued as part of its attempt to replace their dominance. In the early months of 1981, leaders of the Congress-affiliated RMMS complained bitterly about the Shiv Sena's strong-arm tactics, and accused Chief Minister Antulay of covertly supporting the Shiv Sena (*Times of India*, 19 April 1981). Confined primarily to Bombay city and the surrounding industrialized regions, the Sena had not yet clued into the changing parameters of the political economy and the emerging ideological shifts in rural Maharashtra.

Attacks against *dalits*, tribals and Muslims had occurred, independently of each other, before and during the seventies, and they continued in the eighties. A highly publicized event in 1981 placed the fear of rising subaltern militancy in the larger context. With the conversion to Islam of a thousand *dalits* in the South Indian village of Meenakshipuram, the fear of loss of hegemony of *savarna* (upper and middle-ranking castes) elites came to be expressed as a danger lurking of Hindus being reduced to a minority in their own country. Discrete local acts of defiance by *dalits* and Muslims could now be explained as part of a nationwide conspiracy financed by foreign powers. The support received by the *janajagaran* movement of the Vishva Hindu Parishad (VHP) and the popularity of the slogan 'Say with pride, I am a Hindu' (*gauravse kaho hum Hindu hai*) bear testimony to the fact that changing conditions of material life were providing an easy breeding ground for an old ideology in a brand new manifestation.

Long-lasting and gruesome riots occurred across India between 1980 and 1984. In Maharashtra, starting with 1978, victims of such riots included not only Muslims but *dalits* and tribals as well. All these riots were part of an ideological movement aimed at creating a homogeneous Hindu consciousness (Vora and Palshikar 1990: 213–14).

The Shiv Sena's decisive turn to *hindutva* came in 1984 when it established its political alliance as a dominant partner with the BJP. At the time, signs of loss of its popularity in the Bombay region had become visible. Even among lumpenized youth it had to share its influence with a number of other competing forces. At the same time the declining hegemony of elite Marathas had led them to look upon militant Hindu-ism as a possible alternative ideology to help re-entrench their domin-ance over an increasingly differentiated and self-conscious group of subaltern castes. A strong sense of disenchantment with traditional forms of politics had permeated all sections of youth. Within Bombay, the appeal of anti-South-Indian Maharashtrianism had dramatically weakened. The relevance of the earlier posture of strong support to established industrial and commercial capitalists had declined with the shift towards the dominance of predatory capitalism.

With an efficient machine of cadres spread across Bombay's seg-mented underworld, with continued support from a core constituency in offices, factories and middle-class Marathi neighbourhoods, and with its history of anti-Muslim, anti-*dalit* and anti-communist rhetoric and practice, the Sena saw itself as well poised to capitalize on the spreading popularity of *hindutva*. In April 1984 BT tried to give his Sena national stature by initiating a confederation of Hindu organizations (Hindu Mahasangha). Because of its underclass image, most major Hindu organ-izations refused to cooperate with the Sena at this stage. BT's speeches became increasingly virulent in his attacks on Muslims as traitors and started fuelling anger and tension, especially in towns with substantial concentrations of Muslim population.

When news reports claimed that an angry group of Muslims in Parbhani, hundreds of miles away from Bombay, had retaliated with indignities to BT's photograph, the Sena demonstrated its strength by masterminding riots in Bhivandi, Kalyan and Thane (all on the outskirts of Bombay). Since then the Sena's initiation of and participation in anti-Muslim riots has followed a similar pattern. In each case it has tried to persuade its constituents that the tradition of tolerance and passivity of Hindus has made them vulnerable to the aggressive and conspiratorial actions of Muslims, that Muslims are the dominant element in the world of crime and that they have increasingly become a menace to national security because of their primary loyalty to Islam and thus to Islamic nations. It has thus managed to portray itself as a righteous vigilante organization, always on the alert to protect Hindu communities from this menace.

The opportunism of the mainstream political parties professing secu-larism is often blamed for the continuing strength of proponents of *hindutva*, such as the Shiv Sena. There is ample evidence to show how factionalism within the ruling Congress Party often gave the Sena a new lease on life. It would be inadequate, however, to rest one's analysis on these factors as the explanation of the Sena's viability. An encompassing explanation must focus on the shifts occurring in the material basis of its diverse constituency, its changing interests, and the different signals the ideology of *hindutva* transmits to various sectors of its support.

The most noteworthy aspect of that material base, most glaringly since the mid 1980s, has been the dominance of 'predatory capitalism' in India's political economy. This new form of enterprise works with super-mobile pools of money capital. It was nurtured by the 'license-permit raj' of the seventies. Having matured and with multiple links to the global political economy, it regards any constraints on investment and imports as shackles inhibiting its further progress. It has the new rich and vocal middle class clamouring for luxury products as its ally. With the connivance of international agencies such as the IMF and the World Bank whose hold over the Indian state has now become irreversible, it seeks avenues of exploitation that defy basic standards of social justice. It espouses a robber-baron culture of speculation, hostile take-overs and quick windfall profits. It is engaged in clever manipulation of the political environment that extends deep into criminality. It is also unrepentant about leaving behind a trail of environmental degradation and human suffering.

Prospects and Constraints: The 1990s

Like the drug trade, the arms trade is a prime example of predatory capitalism. It whets consumer appetites as it tries to satisfy them. It feeds on political instability, people's fears and leaders' ambitions. As the global armament industry expands, 'develops' and exploits new as well as old markets (private and public), Bombay has become its favourite playground. Many of the interests it serves are already dominating Bombay's political scene. Its fires are being fed through multilayered links that extend from criminal gangs to movie tycoons, from slum landlords and real-estate dons to respectable corporate and public sector executives. A range of 'service sector industries' are now thriving on the ideology of liberalization. From banking and stock market manipulation to gun-running and drug trafficking, there are chains of profit-sharing. These, it seems, extend from the peaks of administrative and political bureaucracy—local, state and national—to petty criminals. The latter can be routinely rounded up and scapegoated so as to protect the former. A promise of pushing India towards a miraculous leap into the 21st century, of making it a giant regional power, is bandied around in defence of the new capital-state-crime nexus.

While hard evidence is impossible to come by, there are clear enough indications that the Shiv Sena is involved in fostering and being fostered by this form of capitalism. It seems active at many levels and gains handsomely by protecting some and punishing others at will. The profitable paradox of its involvement is that it can also stand back and chastise the whole system for its immorality, its detrimental impact on national security and pride and its partiality towards traitors. When confronted with evidence of the Sena's complicity in the system, BT invariably points his finger at others in high office and argues that their crimes have graver consequences than those of his own followers.

Hindutva has become a convenient ideology in sustaining this posture in a number of ways. Since the 1970s the labour market in the Middle East has provided opportunities for work to some Indian Muslims. Bombay's commercial and financial links to the region have steadily expanded. Names of men who control Bombay's real estate, or handle drug traffic, labour migration and arms shipments to and from the city and who have found a haven, safe from Indian law, in places like Dubai, have surfaced from time to time. Such stories have helped create a false image of Muslims as the main perpetrators of criminal transactions in an otherwise fair market regime. The Shiv Sena has effectively used these images of individual Muslim dons of crime syndicates to convict the entire Muslim community as one of traitors, profiteers, criminals, ruthless and aggressive propagators of their faith and wanton producers of too many children. The fact that Sena leaders have selectively maintained contacts with some of the same entrepreneurs, and may even control some of them, has not been allowed to dilute the severity of the anti-Muslim rhetoric.

In essence, the project of *hindutva* is that of homogenization of a population with histories and practices constituted by diverse but intermeshed traditions. Despite flexible variations to accommodate changing material conditions, the common understanding of the word Hindu, shared by all Hinduist organizations, is based on convenient interpretations of Brahmanic texts. The need for enforcing homogeneity arises when oppression, embedded in hegemony, crosses the cultural threshold and leads to reassertion of suppressed diversity. Such a reassertion challenges those who control material and cultural production and use homogenized tradition to legitimize it. In order to emphasize commonality, to create an illusion of community, without abdicating dominance, the hegemonic project requires a clearly identifiable enemy.

During the 1980s, all political parties kept the issue of the distinctiveness of the Muslim presence in India at the centre of their political discourse. The Shah Bano case, Muslim Personal Law and the Babri mosque at Ayodhya became household words and middle-class support for the propagators of *hindutva* across India continued to grow. The Shiv Sena diligently used these issues and events to enter the rural scene. Its first major success, outside the Bombay region, came in the municipal elections in Aurangabad. It succeeded by bringing into focus local issues that could help confirm anti-Muslim prejudice. It started an agitation targeted at the presence of Jordanian students in the university as well as gambling (*matka*) and bootlegging enterprises of which Muslims were reportedly in control. These were combined with the issue of Muslim Personal Law. The agitation culminated in a full-scale riot (*India Today*, 15 June 1988). The Sena arrived in several other major towns also accompanied by anti-Muslim agitations and riots. In 1986 riots occurred in the towns of Panvel, Nasik, Nanded and Amaravati. As elsewhere, the Sena claimed that Muslims were the instigators.

In spite of the damage, disruption and instability they cause, the Shiv Sena's use of riots has managed to gain sympathy for its cause from bourgeois and petty-bourgeois elements in cities and towns. The reasons are understandable. Its targets are carefully chosen. Damage to public property and to the assets of non-Muslims is carefully avoided. In return, a sense of empowerment is created, not only among those who participate in the riots but even among middle-class onlookers. To quote Pannalal Surana:

The latent desires for revenge in the minds of the highly educated middle-class Maharashtrians came to be expressed through the acid tongue of the Shiv Sena. What they would have loved but could never do—to stop a non-Maharashtrian who has become a builder or a business tycoon overnight in the street and punch him in the face—Shiv Sena men were suddenly doing it. This gave them pleasure. They poured praise on the Sena through their newspapers ('*Don Shabda*', in Latpate, 1990, my translation).

For active participants, whose daily life is full of uncertainty, drudgery and subservience, riots give a sense of power, of taking control of the forbidden zones and territories in which the rich and the glamorous reside. They also bring material benefits from looting and prospects for ongoing extortion through threats of retaliatory actions in the future. The risks of injury or death have to be weighed against these benefits.

With increasing complicity of the *hindutva*-conscious police, risk of retaliation from those being attacked has been greatly reduced. The presence, in the midst of rioters, of the Sena's legislators, municipal corporators and community leaders—either before, during or after the riots—lends legitimacy to the claim that the riots were sparked not by the *sainiks* but by the militant Muslim instigators and 'antisocial elements'. Sainiks are painted as peacemakers and protectors. Brutal attacks on persons and property are described as spontaneous outbursts of moral anger.

The Sena's homogenization project has its own antinomies, revealed at times by the exigencies of electoral politics. The Sena must use *hindutva* to divide and conquer segments of subaltern classes from within the self-defined Hindu community. The easiest strategy here is one that divides working people along *savarna–dalit* lines. In 1986, the Sena initiated a programme of converting encroachments on public lands into projects of community benefit (such as social forestry) in rural Marathwada. What appeared to be a worthy project, on the surface, was clearly aimed at landless and landpoor *dalits* and tribals who had started cultivating sections of fallow public lands and community pastures in increasing numbers since 1982, in the hope that these possessions would be eventually legalized. Latent *savarna* anger at the quick transformation of yesterday's supplicants into landholders was thus kindled. *Dalits* and tribals were subjected to attacks in some 35 villages and the Sena gained new credentials with the *savarna* population as the protector of community property (see Latpate, 1990: 10–11).

Since neo-Buddhists (mostly ex-Mahars) are numerically larger and socially better off among the *dalits*, the Sena uses *hindutva* to split off the other castes within the community of *dalits*. It portrays itself as being opposed to caste hierarchy, with claims that it violates the true spirit of *hindutva*. It juxtaposes the minor gains made by segments of the ex-Mahar community, through education and militant action, against the continuing plight of other *dalits* such as Chamhars, Dhors and Bhangis. In 1988, the Sena mobilized these *dalits* as allies of *savarna* landed classes, and as the righteous *dalit* avengers who had courageously punished a bunch of Mahar *goondas*. It was actively involved, along with the Maratha Mahasangh, in the condemnation of Dr Ambedkar's remarks on Ram and Krishna, and of the Government of Maharashtra for publishing them.[8] The Sena also nominated a significant number from these castes to contest elections.

[8] While Ambedkar is 'Hinduized' at the theoretical level by claiming that his conversion

The Sena has also exploited the discontent of rich and poor peasants and rural workers from non-dominant *savarna* castes, against the concentration of political power, economic privilege and access to education and employment in the hands of the Marathas. Both in municipal and legislative elections in Marathwada, it nominated Mali and Vanjari candidates so as to broaden its base among these castes. BT subjected Maratha leaders to strong criticism for their 'political impotence' and as being 'responsible for the humiliation suffered by Maharashtra'. This criticism of political leaders also found resonance among younger Marathas who were frustrated by the stagnation in existing political opportunity structures and were experiencing the impact of declining opportunities for education and employment.

With the combined strategy (*a*) of riots to identify and punish Muslims (and in specific situations neo-Buddhist *dalits*) as the main perpetrators of the contemporary malaise affecting all sectors of the working population, and (*b*) of electoral enticements to divide that population through inter-caste, inter-religious competition, the Sena made substantial gains in rural Maharashtra during the 1990 elections. Of the total of 52 seats won, 32 were from rural Maharashtra. Its alliance with the Bharatiya Janata Party (BJP) gave both an opportunity to enhance their support base in rural constituencies.

That alliance remained uneasy during the 1990 elections. The BJP was aware of its inability to penetrate the lumpenized population in Bombay and other cities and towns and wanted to protect its urban petty bourgeois constituency. It was trying to project the image of a ruling party in waiting, as a more genteel parliamentary alternative to a Congress tainted by scandals and dominated by self-serving and corrupt politicians. The Shiv Sena's links to the underworld and BT's tendency to break out of the veneer of tolerance and to reveal the malignant side of the Hindu card often embarrassed the leaders of the BJP. The Sena leaders also often hinted at a break up of the alliance. However, after the substantial gains made by both parties in the 1990 elections, they have high stakes in staying together, despite mutual provocations. Nationally, a significant shift has occurred in the posturings of the BJP leaders. The very act of the demolition of the mosque in Ayodhya and its blatant defence as an act of spontaneous valour, places the BJP in the same

was consistent with the principles of *hindutva* and that he was basically anti-Muslim, the Hinduists (BJP, RSS, etc.) also try to coopt non-Buddhist *dalits* (Mangs, Chambhars, Dhors) in their opposition to separate *dalit* politics (see Guru: 1991).

camp as the Shiv Sena. Their continuing popularity and the inability of the Government to confront the arrogant defiance of law by both parties indicate a deeper change in the cultural fabric of the petty bourgeois constituency.

The inherent uncertainty of petty bourgeois life is now coupled with the accelerated pace of predatory capitalism in which the new rich seem to arise from the pavements overnight, while white-collar workers continue to crowd in front of their new television sets in the crammed and dilapidated, but inexpensive tenements of Bombay. An opportunity to be able to blame one's misfortunes on immoral and unpatriotic aliens, to be able to take vicarious revenge and to bask in the reflected glory of those who defy the corrupt and spineless occupants of state power, and to offer material, emotional and electoral support to the Rams and Shivajis of the 21st century, is what the BJP–Shiv Sena alliance now offers to white-collar workers and professionals.

The strategy of broadening its electoral support base through inclusion of non-dominant *dalit* and agricultural caste groups, while trying to capture as much of the Maratha vote as possible, has had some negative consequences for the Sena. In 1990, during the nomination process, major Maratha leaders in Marathwada became unhappy enough to leave the Sena, with a large number of their followers, due to lack of adequate representation for Marathas and Brahmans (*Maharashtra Times*, 26 January 1990).

The perils of party politics were graphically brought home when Chagan Bhujbal, a major contender for the legislative party leadership, a former mayor of Bombay and the only Sena legislator in 1985, defected to the Congress in March 1991. His defection, despite dire threats of retaliation from BT, was also a comment on the paternalistic control of the party by BT and his upper caste allies. Bhujbal had been held up by the party as its prime example of sensitivity to the importance of the 'Other Backward Castes' (OBCs).

In Bombay, the Sena has come to recognize the limits of the traditional mobilization strategies of its cadres. The small-time games of extortion and intimidation of hawkers and petty shopkeepers have yielded the place of honour to astute management of the new capital-politics-crime nexus. Both the December 1992 – January 1993 riots and the March 1993 explosions have shown decisively how the armaments market impinges on the daily life of the city. In that market, globe-trotting godmen, goons and 'Gandhians' have all become members of different, competing teams. The Shiv Sena's urban activities, following

the now well-established pattern of combining welfarism with protec-
tionism and extortion have been strengthened by this dramatic expansion of opportunities. BT's own status as the Commander-in-Chief of
Shivaji's army was no doubt greatly enhanced when the great Chandraswami is supposed to have asked for his help in legitimizing the decision of the Indian government to help the US government during the
Gulf War![9]

The Sena's electoral strategy will have to continue to contend with its
own contradictions. The malignant face of popular discontent, that is,
its nostalgic-instrumental appropriation and deflection into hostilities
against defenceless segments of society, is displayed by the activities of
the Shiv Sena. Its populist Hindu imagery offers a temporary nostalgic
reprieve but no permanent escape from the material and cultural degradation ushered in by the nurturing of predatory capitalism. The
image of Shivaji evokes the golden age of a regime that brought to the
masses a stable, just and prosperous life based on care and consideration. The myth of Shivaji captures for Maharashtrians a shared memory
and a cherished dream. Instrumental exploitation of such dreams and
memories is at the core of the current popularity of the Shiv Sena. BT
has combined media techniques that portray him as an incarnation of
Shivaji, as a deliverer of an unfulfilled promise with purely instrumental
alliances that have targeted Muslims, elite Marathas and Mahar *dalits* as
the enemy. A careful analysis of the legislative elections of 1990 shows
that elite Marathas have found it necessary and possible to infiltrate and
use the organization to their own advantage.

The only trump card the party has, at this stage, is BT's ability to control and release the muscle power of angry mobs. That power and the
anger that propels it are bound to grow as predatory capitalism expands
into more and more domains of our life.

Despite its own internal difficulties and counter-offensives from the
hegemonic castes, populist eruptions like the Shiv Sena will continue to

---

[9] Nemichand Jain, alias Chandraswami, is a friend and spiritual mentor of the Arab
armaments dealer, Khashogi. Both of them were to meet BT in Bombay on 7 February
1991. Khashogi could not make it. BT claimed, after a 30 minute meeting with Chandraswami, that both Khashogi and the swami were his old friends and 'we often meet'. BT is
claimed to have appealed to the swami that the Ram Temple issue should not be allowed
to split Hindu unity. Chandraswami is also a friend of the then Prime Minister Chandra-
shekhar who was being criticized for allowing landing rights to American planes on their
devastation mission to Iraq. It was rumoured that the swami was seeking Sena support for
the buffetted Prime Minister (*Maharashtra Times*, 8 February 1991; *Marathwada*, 15
February 1991).

exploit people's aspirations and dreams in the name of religion, region or language. Such oppositional exploitation of cherished identities cannot be countered through a crude class analysis that dismisses them as irrational or primordial. The homogenizing impulse behind today's Hindu nationalism dates back to the colonial era. As material conditions have changed, its manifestations have also changed. Its ability to capture the imagination of many, in a highly diverse and divided society, seems to be growing. It had maintained a subterranean existence during the Nehru era, both within and outside the Congress party and in the minds of many secularists. With the progress of predatory capitalism, its oppositional character and its need for forcible silencing of dissent have been revealed. To ignore these changing bases of the instrumental appropriation of people's dreams and aspirations, to treat it as a vindication of a threatened culture, is to become party to the homogenization project itself (see, for example, Jaffrelot, 1993). Searching for spaces that celebrate differences while enhancing the mutual strength of marginalized people is a task that a practice-oriented critical social science must perform.

Bibliography

Aslam, Mohammad. 'State Communalism and the Reassertion of Muslim Identity' in Zoya Hasan, S. N. Jha and R. Khan (ed.) *The State, Political Processes and Identity*. New Delhi, Sage.

AVS. Atyachar Virodh Samiti. 1979. 'The Marathwada Riots: A Report', *Economic and Political Weekly*, Vol. XIV, No. 19, 12 May.

BM. 1981. 'Internal New Economic Order', *Economic and Political Weekly*, Vol. XVI, No. 44–6. November.

Breman, Jan. 1980. 'The Informal Sector' in *Research: Theory and Practice*. Rotterdam, Comparative Asian Studies Programme.

Byres, T. J. 1974. 'Land Reforms, Industrialization and the Market Surplus in India: An Essay on the Power of Rural Classes' in David Lehmann (ed.), *Agrarian Reforms and Agrarian Reformism*. London, Blackwell.

Chandoke, Neera. 1991. 'The Post-Colonial City', *Economic and Political Weekly*, Vol. XXVI, No. 50. December.

Desai, P. B. 1979. *Planning in India: 1951–1978*. Delhi, Vikas Publishing House.

Deshpande, Lalit K. 1970. 'Competition and Labour Markets in India' in J. C. Sandesara and L. Deshpande (eds.), *Wage Policy and Wage Determination in India*. Bombay, University of Bombay.

Engineer, Asghar Ali. 1993. 'Bombay Shames India', *Economic and Political Weekly*, Vol. XXVIII, No. 3–4, 16–23 January.

Frankel, Francine R. 1978. *India's Political Economy, 1947–1977: The Gradual Revolution*. Princeton, N. J., Princeton University Press.

Gangadharan. 1970. 'Anti-social Movement', *Mainstream*, March 28 (17–24).

Gogate, Sudha. 1973. 'The Twin City: New Bombay' in V. M. Dandekar et al. *Economy of Maharashtra*. Poona, Samaj Prabodhan Sanstha.

Gupta, Dipankar. 1982. *Nativism in a Metropolis: The Shiv Sena in Bombay*. New Delhi, Manohar.

Guru, Gopal. 1991. 'Hinduisation of Ambedkar in Maharashtra', *Economic and Political Weekly*, Vol. XXVI, 7 February 1991.

Harris, Nigel. 1991. *City, Class and Trade: Social and Economic Change in the Third World*. London, I. B. Tauris and Co.

Holmstrom, Mark. 1985. *Industry and Inequality: The Social Anthropology of Indian Labour*. Bombay, Orient Longman.

Jadhav, M. H. 1988. 'Loyalty to Ambedkar Reaffirmed', *Economic and Political Weekly*, Vol. XXIII, No. 8, 20 February.

Jaffrelot, Christophe. 1993. 'Hindu Nationalism: Strategic Syncretism in Ideology Building' in *Economic and Political Weekly*, Vol. XXVIII, No. 12–13, 20–27 March.

Joshi, H. 1980. 'The Informal Urban Economy and Its Boundaries', *Economic and Political Weekly*, Vol. XV, No. 13.

Joshi, Heather and Vijay. 1976. *Surplus Labour and the City: A Study of Bombay*. Delhi, Oxford University Press.

Kakwani, N. and K. Subbarao. 1990. 'Rural Poverty and Its Alleviation in India', *Economic and Political Weekly*, Vol. XXV, No. 13, 31 March.

Kasbe, Raosaheb. 1985. *Ambedkar Ani Marx*. Pune, Sugawa Prakashan.

Katzenstein, Mary. 1973. 'Origins of Nativism: The Emergence of Shiv Sena in Bombay', *Asian Survey*, Vol. 13, No. 4.

Katzenstein, Mary. 1979. *Ethnicity and Equality: The Shiv Sena Party and Preferential Policies in Bombay*. Ithaca, N. Y.: Cornell University Press.

Latpate, Sunder. 1990. *Shiv Senecha Dhoka*. Pune, Sugawa Prakashan.

Lele, Jayant. 1981. *Elite Pluralism and Class Rule: Political Development in Maharashtra, India*. Toronto, University of Toronto Press.

———— 1982. 'Chavan and the Political Integration of Maharashtra' in R. M. Bapat (ed.), *Contemporary India*. Poona, Continental Prakashan.

———— 1990. 'Caste, Class and Dominance: Political Mobilization in Maharashtra' in Francine Frankel and M. S. A. Rao (ed.) *Dominance and State Power in Modern India*, Volume II. New Delhi: Oxford University Press.

———— 1993a. 'A Welfare State in Crisis?: Reflections on the Indira-Rajiv Era' in N. K. Choudhury and Salim Mansur (ed.) *Indian Economy and Polity, 1966–1991: The Indira-Rajiv Years*. Boulder, Colo.: Westview Press, forthcoming.

————— 1993b. 'Hindutva as Pedagogic Violence' in N. Crook, (ed.). *Transmission of Knowledge in South Asia: Perspectives on the Social Agenda.* London, School of Oriental and African Studies (forthcoming).

Morkhandikar, R. S. 1967. 'The Shiv Sena: An Eruption of Sub-Nationalism', *Economic and Political Weekly*, Vol. II, No. 42, October.

Offe, Claus. 1985. *Contradictions of the Welfare State.* Cambridge, Massachusetts, The MIT Press.

Omvedt, Gail. 1976. *Cultural Revolt in a Colonial Society: The Non Brahman Movement in Western India, 1873 to 1930.* Bombay, Scientific Socialist Education Trust.

Paranjape, H. K. 1980. 'The New Industrial Policy—A Rat Out of Mountain's Labour', *Economic and Political Weekly*, 20 September.

Paranjape, H. K. 1985. 'New Lamp for Old!: A Critique of the "New Economic Policy" ', *Economic and Political Weekly*, Vol. XX, No. 36, September 7.

Patnaik, Prabhat. 1992. 'A Perspective on the Recent Phase of India's Economic Development', in Berch Berberoglu (ed.), *Class, State and Development in India.* New Delhi, Sage Publications.

Pendse, Lalji. 1965. *Maharashtrache Mahamanthan.* Bombay, Sahitya Sahakar Sangh Prakashan.

Pendse, Sandeep. 1981. 'The Datta Samant Phenomenon', I and II. *Economic and Political Weekly*, Vol. XVI, Nos. 16 and 17, April 18 and 25.

Phadke, Y. D. 1982. *Keshaorao Jedhe.* Pune, Sri Vidya Prakashan.

Rosenthal, Donald B. 1977. *The Expansive Elite: District Politics and State Policy-Making in India.* Berkeley, University of California Press.

Rudolph, Lloyd I. and Susanne Hoeber Rudolph. 1987. *In Pursuit of Lakshmi: The Political Economy of the Indian State.* Chicago, The University of Chicago Press.

Sathyamurthy, T. V. 1991. State and Society in a Changing Political Perspective', *Economic and Political Weekly*, Vol. XXVI, No. 6, 9 February.

Sen, Probal. 1991. 'Growth Theories and Development Strategies: Lessons from Indian Experience', *Economic and Political Weekly*, Vol. XXVI, No. 30, 27 July.

Srinivasan, T. N. 1991. 'Reform of Industrial and Trade Policies', *Economic and Political Weekly*, Vol. XXVI, No. 37, (2143–5).

Thapar, Romila. 1984. *From Lineage to State.* Bombay, Oxford University Press.

Verma, H. S. 1985. *Bombay, New Bombay and Metropolitan Region Growth Processes and Planning Lessons.* New Delhi, Concept Publishing Company.

Vora, Rajendra and Suhas Palshikar. 1990. 'Neo-Hinduism: A Case of Distorted Consciousness' in Jayant Lele, and R. Vora (ed.) *State and Society in India.* Delhi, Chanakya Publications.

Weiner, Myron. 1978. *Sons of the Soil: Migration and Ethnic Conflict.* Princeton, N. J., Princeton University Press.

11

Cultural Populism:
The Appeal of the Shiv Sena

GÉRARD HEUZÉ

The Burning Puzzle

The first, and rather casual, approach that I made to the Shiv Sena dates back to 1982–83, at the time of the long textile strike. It was, for me, a discovery. This exceptional class movement did not prevent a large number of industrial workers and their families from displaying loyalties and exhibiting attitudes of a radically different nature: the urban and tough Shiv Sena culture. The organization and its social composition were already undergoing the evolution that culminated in the Bhivandi riots of 1984. Later, in 1986–1987, I conducted about 100 interviews of members and sympathizers in central and northern Bombay (in Hindi and English) and spent about two months with the *Shiv Sainiks*, the cadres, *shakha* activists and sympathizers. The Shiv Sena was deepening its pro-Hindu stance and the scene was becoming both more complicated and more polarized. Another set of approaches and interviews was undertaken after 1989 in the framework of a project to study unemployment and politico-religious movements. This study covered the Shiv Sena in Bombay and Maharashtra, as well as other, more recent brands of Shiv Sena that had developed during the eighties in Madhya Pradesh, Uttar Pradesh, Karnataka, Punjab, Gujarat, Delhi and Haryana. It is a somewhat difficult task for a sociologist to cope with the Shiv Sena. Shiv Sainiks are persons who like to explain their universe. They do not wish to be considered monsters or sinners. They nevertheless live so frequently among tensions and hate, that it is difficult to establish a long and effective relationship in their social milieu.

The Bombay Shiv Sena is the oldest and the best structured of the organizations which share the flag, the name and the themes of '*shiv sainism*' today. It organizes presently some 40,000 hard-core activists and perhaps 200,000 sympathizers through 210 *shakhas* (urban branches), about 1,000 sub-*shakhas* (*gata shakhas*) and several mass organizations, especially trade unions, the Women's Front (*Mahila Aghadi*) and the *Sthanya Lok Adhikar Samiti* that tries to procure jobs for the educated unemployed. Created in June 1966 in a park of Dadar (Bombay north), it was long a very specific contribution of the metropolis to the political and social scene. We will not try to explain here the specificities of a movement of which the first phase (1966–77) has been aptly described and analysed by earlier scholars (Katzenstein, 1979; Gupta, 1982). We only want to emphasize the multiplicity of references and the diversity of the strands that coalesced at the end of the sixties to invent, or perhaps only radicalize, a new brand of politics for the large Indian city under the name of *shiv sainism*. The assertion of a constitutional and problematic heterogeneity of the organization will be the basis for our first thesis. The Bombay Shiv Sena displayed for a long time a rare show of unity, related to the dictatorial pattern of a part of the organization and to the homogenizing nature of its dominant ideology. This façade hid, all along, very acute internal tensions. In our view, the Shiv Sena was, and remains a product of conflicting associations, related to the fragmented social world of a city in the making. It was led by 'dominated aspiring to the status of dominant' subalternized elites, and small-scale exploiters, supported by unemployed youth, industrial workers and office employees who had little to gain from the success of the venture, and had a variety of reasons for aligning themselves with the movement. It associated (under the uniting power of several brands of patriotism and parochialism) leading members of higher castes, a strong but not overwhelming Maratha support, a large following of the so-called Other Backward Castes, influenced for long by the Non-Brahman movement (Omvedt, 1976), and a motley mixture of 'others'. It encompassed in the same organizational framework office employees anxious about their social status, people afraid of violence in the metropolis, street roamers and petty gangsters. It promoted agitation in the name of order and spoke about 'total revolution' as well as military rule. It engaged in politics but pretended to hate and despise politicians. A perpetual suspicion has existed in the party against its own politicians (MPs, MLAs and Corporators—elected members of the national parliament, members of the state legislature, and members of the Bombay city

Corporation). This party is not reducible to the simplistic schema of a leader fascinating atomized masses that it itself promotes through its propaganda. There exist also a core of committed ideologues, inspired from the very beginning by the 'national-Hindu' ideology of V. D. Savarkar, a well-established coterie of the common type of power-greedy politician, along with representatives of more or less fragile social groups, who try to promote their interests through parochialism. The more or less organized groups, and the atomized masses are inclined to compensate their feeling of powerlessness through violence. The politicians and the ideologues use this violence for their ends. This could be a simplistic, but not false, presentation of the Shiv Sena.

These kinds of internal tensions are not unknown elsewhere in the Indian political system but the Shiv Sena was, and still is apparently, the place for an acute radicalization of the trend. The old network of paternalist patronage, associated with the relative passivity of the masses in the majority of large Indian political parties, is absent or highly unstable inside the organization. Rank and file Shiv Sainiks, and at least a part of the cadres, have to be young, perpetually new and assertive and involve themselves in a political work that is continuously considered as 'a struggle'. These internal tensions explain partially the continuities as well as the evolution of the Shiv Sena. The continuities are, for example, its activism, its habit of playing with violence and provocation, its use of emotional themes, its perpetual attempts at building the unity of its followers through any kind of tactics that might seem expedient. The evolution is seen in several important changes in political line, the (relative) shifting from parochial and local issue to *hindutva* and all-India nationalism, and the new importance given to the middle bourgeoisie and its desiderata (cleanliness in the city, security, etc). As is widely known, a part of the contradictions that agitate the organization have been overcome, though always provisionally, through violence. Yet, the organization has another face, that explains its political resilience and its ability to create and maintain bonds with an important part of the population of the metropolis. The casual 'social movement' of the beginning has lasted 27 years, and may well last longer, and this is because the Shiv Sena concerns itself with dimensions of the social fabric of the large city that the other parties and social organizations overlook or despise. Let's just call it 'popular culture', without trying to analyse it, and without questioning the theories dealing with it (see the Subalternists and Kumar, 1988). In this regard, our second thesis would be that the Shiv Sena has been able to take root and become an essential part of the city's life because it associated—with a mixture of calculated genius and rough spontaneity—this popular, syncretic, unpolarized, and complex 'popular' culture with a specific brand of violent mass politics—polarized, unified, elite-dominated and simplistic—a brand that belongs to the general, and very common type of populism. It is probably because the economic situation of many strata of the people (industrial workers, street vendors, students from the popular milieus, etc.) is getting worse, or remaining stagnant, that a cultural populist movement like the Shiv Sena could arise and remain for long in a prominent position. *Cultural populism arises, it seems, when culture is considered as the basis for the foundation of a nation, or of a sub-nation and when the 'people', defined as a unified entity, is considered as the main actor of history.* It seems integrable with the wide category of heterodox nationalism to which Hindu nationalism (of the VHP-RSS type) is also connected, but the large city adds a very specific touch to the scene. We will try to detail this aspect of the situation. We feel that the questioning of popular habits and lifestyles, the destruction of networks of relationships at the local levels, the gap between aspiration and reality are at least as important factors as the 'socio-economic' and measurable ones. These matters involve subjective appreciations. We will try to demonstrate that this is one of the reasons why they constitute the favourable and necessary ground for cultural populist politics. A particularly important factor is insecurity about the status, and position of many members of the popular strata in the city. Indeed, it is certainly not by chance that cultural-populism developed in the metropolis and devoted a large part of its energy to urban issues. The recent spreading of Shiv Sena organizations in the countryside does not seem to have been able to alter this trend.

Action

The Shiv Sena is clearly devoted to action, and, it could be argued at first sight, to action alone. The party had no programme at all during the sixties and seventies. It still does not have serious economic proposals. In some places, at the beginning of the organization, when a young man entered the Shiv Sena he received a knife and took an oath to be loyal and active. Presently, the aspirant only fills in a form in a *shakha*, but joining the Shiv Sena remains an important and emotional act, very different from other political commitments. With 'the people', the Shiv Sena builds another, and much more powerful entity: 'our people'. A very strong feeling of loyalty is related to the total availability of the activist. 'You go to the Sena because you want to do something'[1]; 'this situation was unbearable, you had to act'; 'I wanted to fight for justice'; 'we had to defend the people', are some of the ways *Shiv Sainiks* present themselves. People in the streets also recognize this image of exasperated activism rooted in strong cohesion as the main characteristic of the party. It is through action that the Shiv Sena wants to build a coherent, unified and reinterpreted popular image. Action is the catalysing factor of its work. A part of this action aims at building a positive image of the *Shiv Sainik* himself. It is very often directed against 'others'. In the Shiv Sena, you are always ready to react. The enemy builds you, in a sense. It does not matter much *who* the enemy is. Indeed, the enemies (non-Maharashtrians, communists, *bhaias* from Uttar Pradesh, Udipi shop keepers, *'lungi-wallas'*, pavement dwellers, Muslims and other non-Hindus . . .) have changed from time to time and may change again. In this ideological framework the 'people of Bombay' as constructed by the Shiv Sainiks appears as *the opposite* of these different kinds of 'outsiders', and it seems that the organization is really like an army. It builds a dualistic, and in this regard highly 'modern' framework.

Indeed, the daily reality is more ambiguous. During our 1986 study, we approached two types of *shakhas*, one set in Dharavi (where the Shiv Sena was implanted in a Koli settlement) and another set in Parel (with mainly Marathas and lower caste mill workers). In its day-to-day practice, the Shiv Sena did not function like an army. This remained true even during the highly tense days of December 1992–January 1993.

Among the youth of the popular milieus, the organization fulfils the functions of an alternative family, with a necessarily quiet and complicated daily life. At first, the organization depends largely on spontaneity. The cadres insist that they come on the scene only when the people have themselves undertaken some kind of action (Gupta, 1982). This action consists at the very least in buying and garlanding a Shivaji bust, but candidates to Shiv Sainism often also undertake some 'social service' and cultural activity before being integrated in the organization. They globally retain their previous habits, local and 'popular', inside the party. There were no records (Gupta, 1982), few files and comparatively little bureaucracy in the Shiv Sena at its beginnings. These features permitted it to penetrate the popular world. It also had a very loose and

Interview with C. Kanter and others, Parel, 1986.

weak organizational structure.[2] Today, the Shiv Sena has become 'fat', as many cadres and activists observe. It is now ritualized, bureaucratized and structured. It has a working machinery that does not depend upon the people's initiative. It is difficult to say what is more characteristic, this trend, or the fact that Shiv Sainiks regret it. It seems that many expressions of violence, tension and provocation are related to the fear that the party is becoming institutionalized, ceasing to be a social movement, and the most dreaded fate, beginning to 'look like the Congress Party'.

These features do not seem to be the result of a deliberate strategy. They derive from the history of the Shiv Sena, and from the nature of its relations with the popular milieus (we will use the term milieu instead of classes, it seems more adapted to the fluidity of the popular dimension of society). It is often described as operating recruitment through violence and coercion. This is usually a misunderstanding. There is no need to compel people, and especially the youth, to come to the Shiv Sena. It is very deeply rooted in young people of Maharashtrian origin, and it exerts a fascination upon several other strata also. During the seventies and eighties, the organization had three main sources of contacts among the popular milieus. These were not 'formalized' or bureaucratic. It was at first connected with the families. It is very common to observe a family collectively taking part in Sena activities, the case of Thackeray himself being only the most illustrious example. Within the *shakhas*, posts of responsibility are very often entrusted to a group of brothers, or brothers and uncle, sometimes sons and father. The *shakha* being considered as a new family, or as an extension of the family, is thus not just a simple metaphor. This is not unusual in Bombay politics. It is to be seen in every Indian political or cultural organization. The only, but important, difference is perhaps that here this is considered as perfectly natural and positive. The second source of integration of the Shiv Sena among the popular milieus is constituted by the informal networks of youth at the local level, especially the small brotherhoods built during college years. In Bombay, today, the majority of the youth go to school, and the majority of the males to secondary school. The fact that education does not bring great changes in the life of the youth is typical of the situation of the popular classes. The frustration associated with this phenomenon gives the Shiv Sena precisely the impetus it needs for growth Its popularity and strength would not be understandable without taking

[2] The feature is still predominant in the recent Chhattisgarh Shiv Sena. See Heuzé. 1992.

in account its ability to integrate very young people without disturbing their affinity groups. It does (or did) this by intervening directly on the pavements where the youth used to wander, using subordinately, but rather efficiently, student unionism.

The third root of the Shiv Sena force among the popular classes was, and apparently still is, a network of clubs, usually known as *mandals*, *samitis* or more specifically *mitra mandals* or 'friends clubs'. *Mitra mandals* are not necessarily connected with the Shiv Sena. Many of them are strictly committed to sports, leisure or community service. There are also *mandals* and *samitis* connected with the Congress, the Dalit movement, or more rarely the Left. Indeed, a lot of them are associated with the Shiv Sena. The explanation is cultural, and the processes take place at several levels. *Mitra mandals* are a prominent feature of popular life in Bombay. They are primarily a pillar of male culture and assertion. Shiv Sainism makes great use of this typical feature. Its assertion of virility seems normal and natural, and many young people go from the club to the *shakha* with a sense of continuity. Women scarcely enter the *mandal*. Female clubs exist, but they are scarce and often led by outsiders from the middle classes, prompted by a charitable spirit. The *mandals* are also the inheritors of a long tradition of popular organization. This cultural tradition was locally strongly influenced by three currents of historical experience: the non-Brahman movement, the spirit of brotherhood and assertiveness of the communist culture, and the Samyukta Maharashtra Movement that revived and brought to a point of explosive intensity the cult of Shivaji Bhonsle. The Shiv Sena is a strong and popular movement because it was able to gather and to use this cultural heritage as a whole. Communist and non-Brahman movements are certainly not part of Shiv Sainism as coherent ideologies, but Shiv Sainiks accept more or less openly their contribution to their movement and to the city. In the chawls of Chinchpokli and Lalbag where Shiv Sainiks had to physically fight against the Communists to impose themselves during the sixties and seventies, and where they presently exert a political hegemony, cadres of the Shiv Sena like to recall the 'red' past of the district. They appreciate the toughness and the dedication of communist leaders. Indeed, the Shiv Sena directly inherited a large part of the communist culture.

The *mandal* is a very important place for cultural interaction, and slow integration of the newcomers. When a club comprises non-Maharashtrians (a rather common occurrence) they are exposed to the influences of basic Maharashtrian cultural themes, and to Marathi songs and movies. The *mandals* often possess a few books on these subjects in their small libraries. The main channels for transmission of cultural themes and symbols are nevertheless chatting and group interaction, especially intense during particular festivals. Young people with the habit of spending very long hours in the clubs are inevitably exposed to the influence of particular cultural references, even when these references are unknown or rejected at home. Culture, in this context, assumes a peculiar evolution. It is *uniformized*, notably by way of competition between clubs during festivals. It becomes *more and more simplistic*. It is often a mere patchwork of references, creeds and symbols that are few and always the same. It displays more and more rarely the coherence and the complexity of true knowledge. This simplified culture, that does not exclude the presence of simple, but strict rituals, becomes also more and more an element of (any kind of) collective assertion. All events (like the riots of 1984) are interpreted through the local-minded, youth-oriented and male framework of the *mandal*. It is the place where the newspapers are read, and collectively discussed. The recruitment of the clubs is essentially local, the people, and especially the youth of a row, a chawl or a *mohalla* associating to constitute a *mandal*. Members often say that they created their club because there was another one not far away.[3] They wanted to prove that they were able to keep up with the neighbours. The clubs are perhaps primarily places where all the things that are perpetually at stake outside—status, employment, the daily struggle, etc.—are largely dedramatized. They play the role of privileged spaces of non-competition, non-exploitation and non-domination. There is a trend towards a formalization of the *mandal*,[4] internal elections being sometimes introduced, but the day-to-day functioning is largely unconcerned with (not opposed to) democracy. Barring sports, TV and sometimes 'parties' (for males only in the popular districts), the clubs are presently mainly polarized by preparations for the great Hindu festivals—Durga Puja, Ganesh Chaturti and Shivaji Jayanti essentially. They seem entirely unable and disinclined to develop a 'secular culture'.

Mitra mandals are not made for action. The *shakhas* are. Both are nevertheless associated, in varying patterns, in many places and at many times. The Sena has adopted a large part of the daily functioning of the *mandal*: a warm family-like atmosphere, informality, local rooting and masculinity. Nevertheless, the vigorous activity of the feminine branch

[3] Interviews with young members of clubs in Lalbag, Worli and Mahim, October 1992.
[4] Observations in Parel and Dharavi, September–October 1986.

of the organization may give rise to a certain intervention of women in the social sphere that was not seen in the 'popular', and non-politicized *mitra mandal* culture. The introduction of action as a central *raison d'être* is associated with a peculiar analysis of the present society, and with a rather special interpretation of history, but the references (social, historical, cultural . . .) are very often the same for the members of the clubs and for the *Shiv Sainiks*. Effort is certainly demanded of the youth entering the Sena, but this effort never, or very rarely, goes against the prejudices, references and affinities of the young people, as expressed through the *mitra mandal* culture, barring in periods of exceptional tension and mobilization, when 'war' is declared. The Shiv Sena allots, for example, a considerable place, in its day-to-day practice, to the 'discourse of self-depreciation'. This is a typical popular trend. Poor people (poverty remaining perhaps the main concrete specificity of the popular classes) used to, and still, at least in certain contexts, consider themselves as 'nonentities', or 'wretched human beings'[5]. This discourse is revived, and renewed with the extension of unemployment of the educated. It is partly a rationalization for inaction or non-participation in competition and partly a kind of philosophy, assigning to destiny (fate) a leading role in the events of life. The *mitra mandal* culture offers some relaxation of this process of self-depreciation, but nevertheless functions as a field for its development and diversification. The Shiv Sena also takes this feeling into account. It even provides new platforms for its expression.[6] The Sena's discourse adds nevertheless that, through perpetual conflict with convenient enemies, the 'wretched can become tigers', and the 'divided will unite'. It proposes in this regard a mixture of attitudes, according to which *fate*, as a framework for limited tactics of the popular kind, must not be opposed to the 'modern' (and also *Kshatriya*) ideology of a 'mastered' life.

According to our (very uncertain) estimates, 5,000 *mandals* among the popular districts of Bombay are influenced by, or at least are not opposed to the Shiv Sena ideology and practices. This is 25 times the total number of the *shakhas* (210). They constitute a permanent pool, where the organization can (or at least could) develop roots, find inspiration and remain in touch with the city people. Shiv Sainiks have evolved over time strategies regarding popular organizations. They

---

[5] Interviews of pavement dwellers in Byculla, September 1986. This trend is observed everywhere.

[6] The Shiv Sena certainly has psychoanalytic virtues at this level. See Heuzé, 1992.

support systematically all popular initiatives not directed against themselves. They give donations to puja committees and social service organizations, creating alternative structures when opposition arises to their support. They also devote specific attention to sports clubs, a direct and pervasive correlation existing between the male, competitive culture of sport and their own organizational culture. During the eighties, when the Shiv Sena leaders dreamed of regional or even national responsibilities, and when its cadres were mobilized by the Bombay Municipal Corporation, the relationship of the Shiv Sena with the popular classes through the network of cultural organizations seems nevertheless to have slightly faded. The development of clientele relationships in the framework of mass politics was not sufficient to counter this evolution. This could partly explain the receding popularity of the organization during the 1990–92 period. This recession of popularity nevertheless has other sources also, particularly the clashes of the leaders of the organization with backward-class feelings after the Mandal Commission episode, when the party was the only one in India to openly oppose the recommendations of the Commission, in the name of people's unity and the nation's integrity. It is only through the large-scale riots and tensions of the post-Ayodhya period that the organization was able to recover. Once more, a state of war permitted the rebuilding of the endangered 'unity'. After the crisis, the Shiv Sena has come back once more to its roots in the popular districts.

The intercourse of the Shiv Sena with the culture of the popular milieus is not unique. It was built in a somewhat contradictory atmosphere of people's assertiveness and growing disillusion. The social movement that took place around the figure of Datta Samant is perhaps the best example of *other relations in other fields* expressing the same type of tensions, and demonstrating the limited possibilities for change among the popular classes in Bombay today. Striking resemblances reside in the pattern of relationships of the organization with the people, concerning notably the free, or half-free hand given to certain popular habits and practices in a field (the union) that remained for long the monopoly of paternalist bureaucrats. Leaders were not of popular origin but the organization, and especially the leaders, relied a lot upon spontaneity. The style, if not the content, was considered as local, popular, and Marathi (Datta Samant is from the Konkan region). *Style is an ambiguous, but extremely important element of today's Bombay political scene.* These are the features where a comparison can be drawn with the Shiv Sena framework. Samant, unlike Sena leaders, had little 'cultural' connection with the workers. His language was economic. The leader never expressed any positive feeling towards Maharashtrian or Bombay chauvinism. He is among the rare trade unionists who do not exhibit Shivaji in their offices. This historical figure is to be found in the Chitnis office of the textile branch of the All India Trade Union Congress (CPI) in Parel as well as in the office of the RMMS (the large textile and semi-official Congress union) and even in the Sarva Shramik Sangh (Alternative Left) offices. The aim of the trade unionist was to better the wage-earners' position, and end the 'second class citizenship' of industrial workers. These are not the Shiv Sena's themes. Yet, many people refused to see an opposition between the two approaches. It was not uncommon, among the textile workers especially, simultaneously to support the Shiv Sena electorally and to follow the trade union leadership of Samant during the 1981–86 period. There were nevertheless, no *mitra mandals* backing the *Kamgar Agadhi*, the political wing of Datta Samant's movement (founded July 1983), but only a fragile network of committees created or revived during the textile strike. Devoid of cultural content, dependent upon the personal popularity of the leader, the Agadhi was unable to exert for long an influence upon the essential fields of aspiration, social representation, values and dreams of industrial workers and its popularity receded after 1986. This perhaps explains why tremendous popularity, backed by formidable experience, good political contacts and a capacity for analysis probably superior to that of the Shiv Sena cadres, failed to give birth to a stable movement, able to match the Shiv Sena in influence. W. Mahadik, a previous mayor of Bombay, was in third position behind D. Samant and a Congress-AICPI-supported candidate at the 1984 elections in Parel. He won, by an impressive margin, against Samant in 1989. Many people, currents and movements have tried to play with the passions of the Bombay popular classes; the Sena is the only one that has done this for so long, though in a very irregular manner: in a series of waves.

Between Paternalism and Populism

The Shiv Sena is not a totally new contribution to the political and social set-up of the large city. Indeed, it has borrowed many features from the global evolution of Indian politics, and especially from the Congress party, with which it maintains at different levels a specific love–hate relation. It has nevertheless been able to add a very special touch to the city scene, and, regarding some issues, it has developed an alternative model. This model is an essential part of the Shiv Sena relationship with the people. It is based upon a particular type of polarization—which helps explain why the organization is so often keen to indulge in confrontations.

The Shiv Sena introduces at first a trend towards masculinity. Symbols occupy a prominent place in this regard. Virile, and even 'heroic' clashes with the State, or other enemies described as the 'pets of the State' become an aim, the symbol of the assertion of another dimension, autonomous and self-assertive, of 'the people'. In the process, the political mediators, essential in the framework of the Gandhi-inspired system of relations, are frequently ousted. The political models of the Shiv Sena (the 'benevolent dictatorship', the *Chatrapati Raj*) also place 'the people' and the leader alone on the historical scene. They are also virile (*Kshatriya*) models, inherited from the Maratha upsurge dating from the end of the 19th century and the beginning of the 20th century. Combative reinterpretations of Hinduism initiated by Tilak, and modern-Christian influences from the top, combine with current popular themes and preoccupations to produce this 'virile' inflexion. *This happens when the town becomes, for the first time since the middle of the 19th century, a place for women*, and for women of popular origin. There were 192 males for 100 females in the city at the turn of the century, and the percentage of women was certainly lower among casual workers, millhands, streets pedlars and other constituents of the popular milieus. For generations, women had spent their youth in the villages and came only occasionally to Bombay. This virile turn does not seem to be the result of a plot undertaken by the Sena leaders (with the RSS background of some of them). In this regard, the organization seems to have passively followed the popular evolution, reflecting, without influencing much, present conceptions.

The promotion of the youth among the popular strata through the development of the Shiv Sena is also an important feature. This is not only done by the way of speeches and articles praising 'youth power' and the value of youth for 'regeneration' of a 'fallen nation or society'.[7] It is also demonstrated by the composition of the Shiv Sena itself, which was, and is still, an organization of young people. Besides, the name of Bal Thackeray itself refers to Energy and Youth. The leader, who is presently 66 years old, feels obliged to make up his face and dye his hair in order to appear as an eternally *young angry man*, the image which

---

[7] Interviews with Korade, Savant, Torsekar and others, Shiv Sena cadres, October 1986.

constitutes the most powerful mass symbol of identification of the Shiv Sena. The relationship of the party with youth clubs, individual students and educated unemployed guarantees the perenniality of this trend. The largely spontaneous way of functioning of the party offers a favourable field for the aspirations of young males. In the framework of the organization, but also in many *mohallas* far from any Shiv Sena intervention, the self-assertion of youths through violence *and* patronage has developed, and probably been legitimized, as what could be designated as a '*dada* culture': a culture of the goon, but also a virile and young power of the street, and further, at least symbolically, as the social assertion of the elder brother (also *dada*). This culture is not new on the pavements of Bombay (Chandavarkar, 1981). 'Dada culture' or 'dada power', what is termed *gunda raj* in Bihar, is not only political. It is a specific pattern of social functioning, outside and also inside the household, which originates, at least partially, in the popular culture and way of life, and is deeply connected with popular ways and habits. For example, if violence is a daily occurrence, negotiation of an informal type, using the existing channels (family and neighbourhood networks, etc.), is a more common occurence.

The prevalence of *dadagiri* (dada power) in several districts demonstrates the weakness of the popular milieu as a social entity, through the exacerbated strength of its wild elements. Its use, and somewhat ambiguous acceptance, does not constitute the only message and practice of the Shiv Sena regarding the question of violence and morality. On the contrary, the organization is at least as much polarized by social service, charity, and what is usually termed as 'positive action' as it is by expressions of crude violence. Enemies of the Shiv Sena, especially those who belong to the Left and to the educated milieus very often refuse to take into account the importance, and even the existence of the 'social service' of the Shiv Sena. They are definitely wrong, and they miss, in this way, the opportunity to understand the inner functioning of the Shiv Sena, and the nature of the internal tensions and contradictions that push it forward. Sports, cultural activities, schools for young children, help to the poor and the disabled, activism regarding concrete living conditions in the chawls and the blocks, social functions of multiple kinds, activation of networks for helping the unemployed to find jobs or revenue opportunities are not at all a secondary or fake aspect of the Shiv Sena programme. These activities exist; they occupy a considerable and highly valued place in the *shakhas* (which have nevertheless a very variable style), and they are appreciated by the concerned people. Some sectors of activities, noticeably medical help and cultural activities, are among the most efficient and appreciated that presently exist in the whole of Bombay.

Shiv Sena local cadres of the most common type (there are also deviances) are not continuously preoccupied with violence and confrontation. On the contrary, they are obsessed with charity, service, and the currently rather heavy bureaucratic management of these ventures. At this level, the Shiv Sena has striking resemblances with the Salvation Army, barring the fact that it is less paternalistic, and less focused upon the fate of the very poor. It is populist and preoccupied with the fate of 'the majority'. These ubiquitous facts have to be taken into account together with the visible and also fundamental presence of *dadagiri* and violence in the organization. There is a very specific ideology in the Shiv Sena about hooligans and violence. Many of the committed cadres consider that there exists a useful strength in the criminalized youth. This part of 'their people' must not be marginalized. The *dada* has to be nasty and dangerous for a while. His violence may be used for fighting the enemies of 'the people', and the opponents of the organization. It is also asserted that, among Shiv Sainiks, in an atmosphere of brotherhood, service and danger, the petty criminal will learn how to behave and become useful for the community. According to this pervasive ideology, which has practical consequences, *the Shiv Sena is the place where the bad can become good*. This implies a certain degree of sacralization of the organization, which is able to bring about the *redemption of the fallen young popular element*. Besides this, Shiv Sena leaders are among the most vociferous in condemning criminal activities, hooliganism, smuggling and so on. Usually, they say that it is not 'their people' who are involved, but only Muslims or other 'alien' (in their view) people. When things turn out badly, and when the organization is evidently implicated, as in January 1993, the guilt is always that of plotters of the underworld, supported by 'nasty politicians', infiltrated into the (pure and innocent) Shiv Sena. There exists at this level another, and very striking contradiction, arising from the fact that the 'redemption' work, the basis for somewhat regular and popular Shiv Sainism, seems to become less and less efficient. There are too many young people subsisting on underground and dehumanizing activities. Some of the 66 ambulances of the organization may be of use for smuggling or carrying weapons during riots, as it is commonly asserted. The organization might be soon engulfed totally by the *dada* lifestyle and practices, a trend that has already taken place in Thane. Cadres are aware of this. This is also why they insist upon the social service activities (every day in *Saamna*, the daily of the Shiv Sena, there are advertisements and reports about this) and they appreciate also the large-scale tensions that permit them to demand discipline from the troops and to strengthen loyalties. The Shiv Sena seems doomed to be more than ever the organization that sets fire to the city and then brings in its fleet of ambulances: a terrible but essential, constructive–destructive contradiction.

It is difficult to say whether a part of the popular milieus chose, in some distorted way, *dada*ism, as against a different kinds of paternalism and tutelage that long dominated the political scene. The evolution may rather be the result of an internal crisis of the agents of paternalism and tutelage at the top. They seem, everywhere in India, less and less motivated and inspired by their mission of protection and/or of 'uptlifting of the poor'. This is particularly clear in Bombay, where the rich protectors of the past want at present to get rid of the poor and clean the city. The development of *dadagiri* in the political sphere can be interpreted as a contribution of an assertive 'popular milieu' to the political life of the city. It is nevertheless probable that the Shiv Sena is only managing a situation that it did not create. It has only sharply aggravated the trend when it emerged. Shiv Sainiks are very conservative people who are in perpetual revolt. They do not want to endure any longer the tutelage of (real and symbolic) fathers, politicians and philanthropists, which is so ubiquitous in Bombay, in spite of the semi-anarchic atmosphere of the large city. On the shoulders of the popular milieus, there is a particularly high, even if unstable 'pile' of tutelage practices: the old philantropist networks, trade unionism with its outsiders and the bureaucracy of semi-official unions (textiles), the ideological yoke of Gandhism more or less imposed through the Congress influence, the local patronage of notabilities, which often uses the same channel, the very old, and comonly violent, tutelage of bureaucrats and police of the state administration, the more recent and particular moves of the welfare state: nobody among the popular strata escapes paternalism, and its diverse expressions of contempt. The more recent, modernistic tutelage of technocrats imbued with the sacred mission of building a clean city for the rich is certainly the most powerful and scornful of the present powers of the city. Shiv Sainiks have expressed their revolt against these practices at different levels. They have fought the Congress, trade union bosses, administrators and even technocrats. *They nevertheless lack any kind of clear conciousness of what they do and whom they fight.* They approve hierarchy and order. They replace bosses by petty dictators. The impossible break with paternalism, and its symbolic values in a world where social and uncontrolled evolutions lead to more and more frequent and radical clashes with it, is perhaps behind the most irrational and violent attitudes of the Shiv Sainiks. The assertion of 'the son' can take place only through violence and wickedness.

Through the development of Shiv Sena activism, 'the people' express the limits of their ability to change. They are rather narrow limits that they claim and from which they suffer in the framework of perpetually contradictory sets of attitudes. This is why the assertion of 'male power' and values and the development of a 'youth perspective' are not interpreted as motivations for clashes with established values, attitudes and people. Revolt does express itself in the Shiv Sena from time to time, but it is almost invariably ambivalent and reversible. This is why it remains 'popular' in nature within the Thackeray organization; the relative assertion of violent, and rather autonomous *dada* culture and practices seem to function as a kind of dynamic couple, conflictually associated with the dictatorial power of the supreme commander (*Sena Pramukh*). The existence of this central and specific nexus has not eliminated the old and pervasive paternalist attitudes within the organization. They characterize notably the relation between medium-range cadres and local activists. The ideology of 'social service', which is so important in the daily functioning of the organization, is largely borrowed from the ideological world of paternalism, without avoiding Gandhian influence. Though somewhat renewed by the spontaneous way of functioning of the party, the idea of an amorphous 'mass of poor people' waiting for enlightment or help often still persists, along with appeals to spontaneous action. These ideas and practices are partly imposed upon the popular milieus but they are also largely rooted in the popular classes' attitudes (enthusiasm, cynicism and distrust).[8] They sometimes get reinforced in the Shiv Sena.

Integration to the city

For the 100 and odd years between the middle of the nineteenth century and the Samyukta Maharashtra Movement, Bombay was a city with moving borders. It was continuously expanding and thus changing its geographical aspect. This fluidity was also reflected at the social level. Rural –urban connexions percolate the urban set-up and associated tiny but numerous parts of it to far-away villages and regions. Despite a preco-

---

[8] Interviews with Shiv Sainiks, Lalbag, October 1986.

cious process of stabilization of some of these relations, they were continuously evolving. During the 'first period' after migration, especially in the case of the popular classes, the solidarities were brought in from outside. The town framework was only able to disturb or to break them. There have been as many 'first periods' as groups migrating to and joining Bombay. A large part of the city's population was and is still perpetually moving. It is thus variably 'uncommitted' and, the Shiv Sena of today would say, 'disloyal' to the city. There were also, and there still are, a great variety of senses of belonging to the city, distinguished by their degree of rootedness in the place, as well as by the language, religion, type of social organization and work. Dominated for long by industry and casual labour, popular Bombay has not been able to give rise to well shared feelings of particularism of the kind of the 'Banarsipan' so aptly described by Nita Kumar (Kumar, 1988). For a very long time also, and this period is certainly not over, the city, and the sense of belonging to the city, were exclusive, or quasi-exclusive privileges of the elites. It concerned in fact only a small part of these elite merchant classes, for example, keeping alive very strong ties with Rajasthan, Gujarat or Punjab. There are distinct and hierarchically constituted districts in Bombay from the very beginning, a 'modern' character of social segregation that did not help to promote integration. Space, fresh air, hills are, as it is commonly observed, everywhere in India, reserved for the better off. The members of the elite display everywhere a tendency to consider the city as a whole, when the members of the popular classes are interested only in their *chawl*, and at best, in their *mohalla*. This trend, long dominant in Bombay, was nevertheless disturbed by the apprehensions of the elite with regard to the massive and unfrequentable character of the northern suburb (presently the mills districts).

In this framework, the cultural-populist movement appeared at the crossroads of fundamental evolutions, related to economic, demographic and social factors. Its particularity is to have been more or less able to translate into symbolical language (the human being is a 'symbolical animal'), with a mass appeal, and into political practice, the tensions arising from these evolutions. My feeling is that it represents, it interprets, it accentuates and it also, ultimately, mitigates and blocks the transformations, according to the moments, the fields and the situations, developing the mediating effects of culture into politics, and the reverse. It is *this mediating effect, in the frame of which symbolic aspects occupy a prominent place, that is considered as important* by its promoters. Concrete issues are subordinate elements. As a Bombay party and

movement perpetually preoccupied with building an image of the cohesiveness of the city, the Shiv Sena is a monster of ambivalence. It both
integrated and excluded. It invented limits, and scrapped them. It built
a town's image and destroyed its credit. It gave way to popular aspirations, and submitted before the 'little bourgeoisie's' fears and the big
bourgoisie's interests. The balance sheet is unclear, but the programme
was also equivocal. Uncomfortably situated between those who arrive
every day in the city, make it and 'live' it, and the dominant classes who
claim to possess it, cultural populism brings into light its own contradictions. It uses the city framework to generalize them. These contradictions again reflect, not too badly, the popular disarray in the face of the
new city scene.

Through several violent movements, but also in the course of day-to-
day activity, the Shiv Sena (and others) helped to open the town to 'the
people'. *Bandhs*, large demonstrations and riots are not new in Bombay.
George Fernandes, Datta Samant and innumerable unknown actors have
paved the way that Shiv Sainiks follow. The affluent and protected parts
of the city, from Victoria Terminus to the Mantralaya, have become accessible, from time to time, to popular masses, only because they were
'the masses': anonymous voters and degraded citizens, anxious to express through symbolic assertions the frustrations and the hopes of their
lives. Shiv Sainism gave a radical turn to this. Tigers have a divine right
to behave rudely in their city, that is also their territory, or fiefdom.
Demonstrations at Flora Fountain almost always give rise to violence
against shopkeepers or opponents. The great religious festivals, especially
Dassara and Shivaji Jayanti, help to attribute ritualistic and regular status
to these intrusions and symbolic appropriations. The issue of appropriation of the city is very alive in the popular districts. It is not a case for
theory, or even rhetoric. *It is a concrete and living aspiration* that may be
interpreted according to several patterns: as revenge, as the symbol of
democratic aspirations for citizenship, and as a collective pleasure. The
city has begun to often belong to its 'people', and especially to its young
people, through violent ways. This has taken place because the frustrated
egos of bruised people cannot imagine other possibilities, and also
because the control of the rich, and the grip of the State upon the city
has become more and more oppressive over the last three decades. So
'the popular' need a rape to belong to their city. Shiv Sena was thus
often the ideal structure (sufficiently unstructured) to lead, or to
accompany such a development. The process of appropriation is *highly
symbolic*. Symbolism plays an enormous role at every level of activity of

the Shiv Sena. *The pre-eminence of symbolical perceptions helps the Shiv Sena in this regard to get the support of very different kinds of people, who have opposed basic interests*: for example elements of the rich (the so-called 'middle class') looking for cleanliness, and slumdwellers craving for security. To the official and self-proclaimed owners-masters-citizens of the city, the Sena represents an unbearable violence. Its importance, regarding the relationships between the dominant and the dominated, must not be underestimated. Taking into account the geopolitical dimensions, the real balance of strength, the Sena's success is questionable. After decades of inferiority complexes among the popular classes, however, the Sena has sometimes scored tangible gains. It is nevertheless a highly volatile force and its achievements are often reversible, lacking the persistent dynamism essential for permanence. This is one of the reasons for the quest for conflict among the most popular and the least politicized Shiv Sainiks.

A specific ambivalence exists regarding the Maharashtrian character of the city. Bombay has not become a purely or predominantly Marathi-speaking place, which was for long a proclaimed aim of the Shiv Sena. According to the statistics, and despite the frantic efforts of cultural populist forces, it is even less the case today than before. Bombay itself has an estimated 45 per cent of primarily Marathi speakers, but the ratio seems even lower in the suburbs, with a very large, poorly reported, migration of people from the Gangetic plain. The aim was perhaps not attainable. The feeling of inferiority of the inhabitants of Maharashtrian and especially coastal origin has nevertheless receded. They are still often termed *ghatis* (a derogative nickname) by their employers and neighbours of Gujarati (notably Parsi) origin, but there are limits to scorn that did not exist before (the same process, with different actors, has occurred for the *dalits*). A demonstration of 'angry young men', or a shouting of slogans from the women of the Kamgar Aghadi are not infrequent occurrences, in case of aggression against the honour of 'the locals'. They can be very efficient constraints on the rich. The city image, and its concrete life, are nevertheless still structured by a kind of 'social geography of scorn', made of the interference of constantly moving collective entities. The scorn displayed by parts of the population is complemented, or countered, by more or less accepted feelings of inferiority. This geography delineates the borders, and the contents of citizenship and status. Its keys are both cultural and economic. It constitutes a field of reality in itself. Status, and representations of self at different collective levels, build imaginary, symbolic and 'phantasmatic'

fields of confrontation that have immediate and variable concretiza-
tions. They shape all the social milieus, but especially the popular ones
that have long received scorn but have had few occasions to give it
back.

The field of collective image-building, interpretation and comparison
is nevertheless open to everybody, not only to the rich and the powerful. Intervention on a large scale at this level necessitates new skills and
knowledge of specific rules. The expansion of cultural populism helps
one to understand what kind of skills are needed. This is not a new
phenomenon, but it is an evolving one. The change came from the intrusion of mass images related to a global representation of the city.
Mass democracy and consumerism offered new channels. The devalor-
ization of *ghatis*, to come back to our example, has been slowly replaced
by a new, or only accentuated attitude of scorn towards the country
people in general, and of those who *look* rural in particular. It becomes
more and more difficult to be respected (especially among the young
people) in Bombay, when using village references and wearing peas-
ant clothes.[9] *Once more, the Shiv Sena did not control this evolution. It
accompanied it. Its expansion proceeds nevertheless from its capacity to
produce, and to 'manage' new images of a city globally opposed to a 'backward' countryside.* It has used intensively the dualistic opposition of an
overpopulated, uneducated and useless countryside inclined to 'be-
siege' and 'spoil' the city. Innovation has varying senses. The organization remained at this level contradictorily influenced by its popular
base, with strong rural connections but a craving for recognition and
urban integration, and the pressures of a part of its cadres who develop
common views about the necessary ousting of 'unclean' elements from
the city.

The Shiv Sena is polarized by the idea of limits. It wants to delimit, to
fix the contents of the city. This was very clearly asserted in the video
cassette used by the party for the 1992 municipal corporation elections.
The speaker insisted at length on the idea that the Shiv Sena management of the BMC (eight years of municipal power) had given '*a shape*'
(*rup*) to the city. As if this city were, before the Shiv Sena intervention,
nothing but a kind of monster. There is correlatively also a very strong
insistence upon beauty. *Shapeless things cannot be beautiful.* Bombay
must become beautiful, and the Shiv Sena will bring beauty. Besides,
the importance of aesthetic preoccupations is noticeable at every level

[9] Interviews with young members of *mitra mandals*, Parel and Worli, September–
October 1986.

of the activity of the Shiv Sena, especially the universe of the cadres. The third theme is *modernity*. Bombay must be modern, hygienic and clean. In the minds of Shiv Sena ideologues, these themes are strongly correlated. The organization aims at including in the metropolis chosen people, with specific qualities, in order to get a purified and homogeneous entity. Origin and cultural characteristics are the criteria for the delimitation of who is and who is not a legitimate citizen of Bombay. Regarding the popular classes, the introduction of such a criteria has very unclear implications. It could perhaps put the so-called *ghati* working in a small-scale industry or the *hamal* with his load ahead of the *seth* or the large Marwari merchant. It helps in some situations to promote alternative appreciations of social status. It is nevertheless not clear if the ideological promoters of such appreciations would really like to use them as a yardstick to determine the access to rights of citizenship. This heterodox hierarchy is thus highly symbolic, and, it could be argued, phantasmatic. It has a very narrow field of relevance. Regarding the popular classes, it merely introduces new, or perhaps only, radicalized, lines of fraction. In correlation with ideological trends that value free enterprise and wealth, the right of the Gujarati *sheth* to be a citizen of Bombay has never been seriously questioned by the organization. It is a feature which differentiates the 'nativist' movement of Bombay from, for example, the Jharkhandi movement of tribals in eastern India (Weiner, 1988). It is the migrant, and especially the poor migrant, who is now more and more often threatened by expulsion.

These aspects of the Shiv Sena ideology are well known. Its integrative aspects are not so much publicized. This permanent but contradictory trend is a consequence of its modes of recruitment and functioning. Initially, the people of South Indian origin were described as 'enemies' of Maharashtrians and 'true Bombay citizens'. Their electoral support to the Shiv Sena was nevertheless noticeable even during the seventies (Katzenstein, 1979). It has grown since that period. The use of *hindutva* rhetoric, attributing to the organization a national role compatible with its initial 'Savarkarist' ideals, has been instrumental in this regard. The influence of the organization on the migrants through the youth clubs (see *infra*) has also been very important. It belongs indeed to a type of very widespread political entities of the present period. Young Sikhs, Tamils, and others found in it a very familiar pattern of thought and relationships, illustrated in Punjab, Tamil Eelam and elsewhere. Youth in general, and particularly the growing minority devoid of strong ethno-regionalist affiliations, esteem the urbanite and tough image of the Shiv Sena. The organization is *tej* (tough) as Bombay is. Joining it is considered as a way for learning the city codes and becoming integrated. The opposition of cultural populism to people of southern origin faded almost totally during the eighties. Since 1989, south Indians have been specifically targeted for recruitment, in places like Dharavi for example. Bal Thackeray himself recognized several times that the southern migration was no more a problem. The ambivalent character of the Sena regarding newcomers, even at the worst moments of parochial frenzy, must also be underlined. Exclusion is never absolute. The enemy changes from time to time, but it is also very often possible to change an enemy into an ally, if he offers allegiance. In this regard, and despite possible marginal trends, the Shiv Sena is not a racist organization. It displays more often a sectarian (according to Max Weber's categories) attitude. The only rule is, to continue action with the 'help' of a convenient enemy. Nothing prevents individuals of any origin from joining the *shakas*. People from Tamil Nadu, to a lesser degree Kerala, began early to vote for the Shiv Sena and sizeable groups of them entered the organization during the seventies. They have only to accept simple principles, especially the Maharashtrian nature of Bombay, and the importance of Shivaji. Many do it. Even some Muslims do it, despite the importance of the Aurangzeb–Shivaji symbolic opposition and of more concrete bones of contention. The case of a Muslim cadre of Kalyan who did not leave the party after the 1992–93 clashes is well known. His is not an isolated instance. There are several *gata pramukhs* (sub-branch organizers) of Bombay, and at least one *shakha pramukh* (branch organizer) of Pune who are Muslim. The organization thus puts before the in-migrants a choice. *The first term is a proposal for a complete integration.* It seems that the attitudes of many southerners towards Maharashtrian culture, values, and especially symbols, underwent very significant changes after integration of a part of their youth in the Sena, or the *mitra mandals* dominated by Sena culture.[10] The atmosphere of brotherhood centered on *action* gives the first place to emotional ties. This process is more fundamental, regarding the commitment of many young people of diverse origin to the Shiv Sena, than the image of Bombay promoted by the Shiv Sena ideologues. This image becomes nonetheless consistent through these ties. *The second term is complete exclusion.* It concerns theoretically the in-migrants, or Bombayites from non-Maharashtrian background who refuse the Shiv Sena influence, and the cultural-populist values, and especially powerful symbols like Shivaji. These people

[10] Interviews in two Dharavi *mandals*, October 1986.

are objects of hate. They must go out of the city. So much for theory. Cultural values and personal attitudes are indeed rather abstract criteria. Political opportunities, pressures from the top and legal problems lead to choosing specific types of recent and weak migrants as targets for exclusion (the exclusion that everybody fears to endure).

The choice, that is very often an abstraction, between complete integration or complete exclusion *contrasts* with the attitudes of the dominating powers in the epoch of Congress culture. In this framework of relations between the popular classes and those who 'possessed' the city, migrants were considered as necessary (as workers, servants and so on). They were invited, or authorized, to come to the city, the 'labour market iron laws', and, more concretely, plague or unemployment regulating their flow. Internal migration was never seriously controlled in India, perhaps as a legacy of British economic 'liberalism'. They *did not belong* to the city. The question of their integration did not arise. Very slowly, groups of migrants became parts of the city, as subaltern elements, but their integration was always, and almost necessarily, incomplete. There was a kind of hierarchy of citizenship. In the framework of this hierarchy, time of arrival to the city was only an element for appreciation. Every constituent of the social status had its importance. With the spreading of democratic, anti-hierarchic values, *of which the Shiv Sena is an illegitimate offspring*, and through the development of several mass movements, these old perceptions have been questioned during the sixties and the seventies. Since the Emergency, the pressure of the dominant classes and the elites, accentuated by the efforts of the white-collar workers who try to dissociate themselves from the popular classes, goes towards complete exclusion of the migrants, and generally of 'the people'. The ideal town, framed according to the pattern of New Delhi, would only need selected groups of servants and service workers, under strict police supervision, around the clean accommodations of the 'real citizens who pay taxes'. Industrial Bombay was and is still the target of planning, which takes these conceptions largely into account. By hesitating dramatically between integration and exclusion, the Shiv Sena asserts once more its ambivalent character. This ambivalence, the tension perpetually existing between the poles, seems more important, and more closely related to the social framework of the metropolis than the contents of its rather banal, chauvinistic ideology.

The tumultuous intercourse of cultural populism with the slumworld illustrates perfectly the dual character of the organization. There are about 4.8 million people living in the slums of Bombay, one half of the

10 million inhabitants (comprising people living outside of the Municipal Corporation borders), occupying about one per cent of the space. The 'invention' of a *Mumbai's essence*, along cultural lines, by the Shiv Sena had necessarily to deal with them. The *zopad pati* contains the totality (at least symbolically) of India, and sometimes elements of South Asia, while the Shiv Sena ideologues want to assert the 'difference' of its homogeneous contents. It constitutes almost a provocation for chauvinistic feelings. The participation of slum dwellers in Shiv Sena activities was nevertheless frequent and intense from the very beginning. Ideals of strength, male virtues and ability to fight were illustrated by the people of the slums where the youth has to endure difficult conditions for survival. Some ideologues found in the slum world a 'primitive' element able to 'regenerate' the city's 'decaying' world. The adhesion of the slum-world to the Shivaji cult, the *mandal* culture and mass *puja* was not total but it was massive in many cases. Slums gave the flesh (the *blood* in Shiv Sena ideology) for demonstrations, riots and electoral campaigning. It is not an exaggeration to say that the Shiv Sena was for two decades the party (but it is never only a party) which developed the most intensive and authentic relationships with the slum population, the largest part of the popular milieus of the city.

Strongly and early related to the slumworld, the Shiv Sena nevertheless did not recognize in it an ideal or superior status. It does not find virtues in poverty. This differs deeply from populist leftist ideologies that seek salvation of the society through the poor. According to the Shiv Sena's conceptions, the heart of Bombay, tenaciously proposed as an alternative centre, is not a slumworld, which has no centre, but the epicentre of the original industrial concentration, the Dadar-Parel area, dominated by chawls, and presently besieged by middle-class residences. Relationships of the Shiv Sena with industry are also rather unclear. The organization attributes great importance to industrialization, but it is nevertheless fascinated by 'traditional', and 'clean' middle class models, that aim at pushing industry, and especially industrial workers, to the fringe of society, or at least, out of the city. The relation with the slum depends on the political populism of the organization and *to the tactics of the slum dwellers themselves*. They 'use' the Sena as a tool for relative stabilization. They try to take advantage of its—very relative—protective capacity against bureaucrats and powerful interests (contractors). They act in this way with every political force. On the other hand, slum dwellers are receptive to the appeal of the cultural, simplified propaganda of the Shiv Sena, proposing integration *or* exclusion. This has not prevented the Shiv Sena from campaigning against the slums, in the name of '*Sundar* (beautiful) *Mumbai, Marathi Mumbai*'. It was subjected at this level to the pressures of middle-class voters and influenced by the interests of its own cadres, contractors and municipal corporators. Shiv Sena ideologues have problems with slums for other reasons also. The slum is a composite world, a mongrel-like city, a mixture. They dislike mixture. More generally, the slum displays a fuzzy and moving image of 'the people' that the organization rejects. It is a place where people change houses, cultures, dimensions, employment and even names (to escape moneylenders, for example, it is still common). One of the most concrete bases of Shiv Sena development is also its perpetual nightmare.

Initially, the Sena's action was not directed against the slum. The organization embarked almost casually upon a quest for coherence and status for the city, and for its inhabitants. Common origin, common fate, common loyalty, a single set of values, a homogenized way of life, have gradually become obsessions for the *Shiv Sainiks*. It was not conceptualized at the beginning. The movement realized slowly that it had to delineate proper, stable limits to the town and separate it from the countryside. Regarding the popular classes, the Sena wants both to infuse certain revised popular values in general public life, and to liquidate the mixed, moving, 'outside-related' nature of the popular milieus. These objectives cannot be reached if the burgeoning of slums changes every day the geography of the city, if the permanence of a universe of violence and paucity oblige the people to bring the countryside to the city, if slum people continue to change names, habits and even religion.[11] The agressiveness of cultural populism against slums is reinforced when their inhabitants, taking advantage of democracy, demand their integration with the city without abandoning their references and habits, and when they claim 'collective identities' that are often exacerbated or revived with the arrival in the city. The Shiv Sena could not have simple relations with the slumworld.

During the eighties the contradictions, within the Sena, and between it and the slumdwellers, were aggravated. Bal Thackeray promised to provide housing for four million slumdwellers (*a typically populist but also clearly integrative formula*), when Bhujbhal (the then Shiv Sena Mayor) was busy with cleaning pavements and other 'beautification schemes' brutally opposed to the slumdwellers' basic interests (1985–88). Far from working for the slumdwellers' general interest, the Shiv Sena

[11] Interviews with slumdwellers in Powai, Vikhroli and Sion, September 1986.

corporators promoted large-scale and expensive, often economically questionable, ventures such as the revamping of large avenues, a convenient way to get rid of pavement dwellers, making money with subcontracting, and satisfying the aspirations of the rich. Slums were nevertheless protected in specific areas, especially when they voted for the party. Shiv Sainiks are proud of their 'social work' in the slums. Today, the scheme for giving a decent shelter to four million poor people is being revived and used as a propaganda theme, the party having lost in the last civic elections. Indeed, it seems that another party would not have done very different things. There have been 'cleaning' operations in every large town of India during the eighties.[12] Everywhere, except perhaps in Delhi, these attempts were also mitigated by the pressure of populist politics. The miserable state of municipal powers and finance in India (Bombay enjoying in this respect a slightly better situation than many other Indian towns) is also not a creation of the Shiv Sena. Regarding the status of the city, the slums were also ruining the Shiv Sena dreams and pretentions. Opposed to the 'cosmopolitan' city model, it develops nevertheless the perspective of a capital city, a centre of power and strength. There lies behind this the ghost of a 'Maharashtrian model' of the Indian nation, with its partly *Brahman–Kshatriya* ideology, constructed during the 19th century around the Shivaji myth. The alternative model of culture, political organization and values, concretized in the city, would be efficient, male, industrial, organized, urban, violent and affluent. It is clearly opposed, at least in speech, to the 'emasculated' model of Gandhian (Gujarati) and northern origin. Contrasted with these ideal (and somewhat modern) images, the slum appears as the incarnation of opposite principles: a rural, passive, feminine, inefficient, poor and burgeoning world. If the slum world builds a great part of the present affluence, that is another story. It does not affect the dualistic frame of interpretation of the Shiv Sainiks.

Building and Interpretation of Popular Identity

Identification of 'the people' with the city is the only assertion of mass identity that has been located long and consistently under the influence of cultural populism. The Shiv Sena refers to a peculiar type of simple mass culture polarized around the idea of limits and strength and not to the popular culture as a whole. This may have constituted an answer

---

[12] See the *Unnayan* files. *Unnayan* is a social service and research institution focusing for years on the housing question.

to the frightening complexity of conflicting identifications. Yet, Shiv Sainiks have never been the sole promoters of polarization around symbols and simplification of the diverse elements that constitute the popular culture. It is a continuous process related to modernization, which also involved disaggregation of the complex social worlds of the past. It is especially active in the metropolis. At these levels, the intrusion of mass relations in the city and in the society, the development of mass media, the erratic course of education and the evolution of the labour market shape profoundly the 'building' of collective identifications centred on the city's image and practice. The promoters of cultural populism, and especially the first generation of Shiv Sena leaders, demonstrated a real sense of opportunity when they deserted the field of socio-economic relations, where the upper-classes dominate the scene, to give priority to cultural, and even 'aesthethic' struggles. This choice nevertheless did not permit these 'subaltern elites' to succeed in controlling the scene through the manipulation of culture. They only opened a field of mediation. This failure results probably from the fact that culture is not an all-powerful instrument for action. In the so-called 'modern' world, it is nothing without power. The problems of the Shiv Sena may also be related to specific aspects of popular culture in contemporary Bombay. It is indeed a rather inconvenient political tool. If several aspects of popular culture have been favourable to the birth and expansion of cultural populism, the stake being identification with the city, this development was always a fragile and reversible one.

There is no 'centre' of popular culture in Bombay. It is nonsense to try to describe it through an activity which could epitomize it. It exists nevertheless, and it existed already at the beginning of the present century in sets of attitudes, values and practices which could be described as representative of 'mainstreams'. The widespread features of popular culture underwent *significant but also very variable changes* during the past decades. Their meaning is not easy to synthetize, regarding culture itself. Concerning the evolution of the popular classes, their interpretation is perhaps more difficult. Let us take firstly the fundamental trilogy constituted by *akhadas* (gymnasiums), *tamashas* (folk entertainments) and gambling (R. Kumar, 1987). It was a prominent part of male popular mass culture outside the household for more than 30 years. It has not disappeared but it was gradually replaced during the fifties and sixties by another set of practices, mass sport succeeding to *akhadas*, cinema (then TV) replacing *tamasha* and *matka* (a highly organized numbers game) taking over from pavement and tea-shop gambling. This evolution

seems general, but its meaning is not one-sided. There is at first a process of 'massification'. Practices are standardized. There is also a noticeable trend towards *dispossession*, dispossession of the body when young
people become spectators of cricket matches after having been actors
(and valorized ones) in gymnasiums, dispossession of speech, the interaction of the public with *tamasha* actors and organizers, disappearing
during cinema and TV shows. These tendencies seem able to facilitate
processes of political polarization through social tension and frustration.
This has been perceived, and deliberately used by the Shiv Sainiks. The
trend towards 'massification' and dispossession has nonetheless been
counterbalanced by the development of small networks in clubs, the reorganization of marital relations to centre on the couple (under way for
two decades in the popular districts) and the privatization of habits, all
part of the same cultural evolution. Globally, the changes have not (or
not only) been imposed upon the popular masses, in spite of continuous
legal, moral and administrative interference of the higher spheres. The
earlier popular practices were considered old-fashioned. A part of the
popular culture underwent degradation of status, but the majority who
changed their habits felt the change as a positive evolution of status,
differentiating the 'urbanites', and the 'Bombayites' from 'Others',
sticking to old ways. Shiv Sainiks belong very often to the categories of
up-to-date young people who participate intensely in the evolution of
popular culture. There is nevertheless something in the process that
they cannot endure, the dispossessing trend of mass culture probably,
but they do not have possibilities (conceptual or political) for expressing what they feel at this level. Generally speaking impossible speech
and mute frustration are very powerful ferments of violence.

Let us now consider another aspect of popular culture. The introduction of motorcycles, scooters and mopeds in the popular milieus is a
great topic for discussion. Ways of transportation are not only (not
merely in this case) a constituent of the economic standard of living,
they are status symbols and, more generally, yardsticks used by popular observers to appreciate change and evolution. The motorcycle is a
modern incarnation of individual power. It is often a figuration of the
shakti of the *dada*. Its symbolical association with the horse (the horse
of Shivaji!) is also very clear. In the popular milieus, where it is often
impossible to assert oneself through housing, these machines often sym-
bolize the emergence of a tiny, but still popular, or even strongly popular, differentiated strata of people. This highly symbolic differentiation
of the popular milieus is the topic of innumerable controversies in the

mitra mandals or in the streets. It is sometimes considered as an honour for 'the people', it can also be interpreted as a division, as a threat, or as an insult to poverty. Shiv Sainiks, in the diversity of their expression, express very well this popular ambiguousness. The party is famous for its demonstrations of young men with saffron flags riding motorcycles. There are revealing pictures of this in the propaganda material of the organization.[13] The association of strength with modernity is perhaps one of the strongest ideological themes at the highest levels of the organization, enthusiastically supported by the youngest elements. Local cadres and older members of the organization, notably industrial workers, expressed nevertheless much more mixed feelings. There is an old and pervasive current in the Shiv Sena that dislikes the exhibition of riches. As we have remarked, the organization has inherited the core of communist culture in Bombay.

Concerning religious festivals, the evolution of popular culture was different. The intrusion of *pujas* (rituals) in the political field, and the promotion of mass *pujas* engulfing the whole of a city, were probably processes initiated through complicated historical evolutions, by the higher classes and castes. Tilak organized the first public *Ganapathi* festival in 1893, and the Shivaji festival in 1895. *Puja* associations emerged during the 1920s in the popular districts, when 'class identifications' and 'national identifications' were principally at stake. At the beginning they usually displayed a paternalist character. The *puja* committees were in the hands of notables who could belong to the popular elites (*akhada* patrons, 'jobbers', etc.) but who were also commonly members of the lower ranks of the 'central' elite. Mass *pujas* were nevertheless not imposed upon the people by the higher classes. Popular participation was immediately forthcoming, but popular religiosity was local and divided by many customs. Its mass expression was handicapped. It avoided the large avenues and the centre of the city. This is probably why the large ceremonies remained more or less under the control of notables before Independence. Mass *pujas* have now become a powerful but ambivalent medium for expressing popular feelings. Intervening at the very beginning in the construction of *mohalla* and small migrant group identifications, they can also serve to build a conciousness of the city. They constitute one of the strongest sources of melting-pot effects. In the whole of Maharashtra, the 'Bombay *pujas*' have a recognized

[13] Video cassettes edited by Raj Thackeray during the 1991 national elections campaign and the 1992 municipal corporation elections campaign.

reputation.[14] In the metropolis, the management of this popular religious culture in the public sphere is partially in the hands of the popular strata themselves, and particularly the youth. It is today partially controlled by rich notables and politicians, and partially in the hands of the Shiv Sena. *For 10 years, the latter has been the more dynamic agent of organization.* The largest mass *pujas* are organized by Shiv Sena dominated committees. Shiv Sainiks are very proud of their intervention at this level. It is a strategic field for them. They proclaim that 70 per cent of the Ganapathi pandals (temporary public shrines for worship of the elephant-headed god) are organized under their aegis. *Pujas* structure the party life (as it happens in the RSS). During Durga *pujas* 100,000 Shiv Sainiks ritually meet in Shivaji Park. The Shiv Sena management of mass *puja* borrows its style from the pavement youth, particularly the loud music and the aggressive pattern of competition for space, but it has also a connexion with the elite and a sense of management which is more related to their attitudes. The organization also adds a particular style. The mass *puja* is a very special moment, when (almost) everything is permitted, and when a different order of things emerges for a while. The Shiv Sena uses it at first as a field for demonstrating its ability to manage the city, and to appear as an alternative power. Then, it uses this privileged moment when the whole of space belong to its youth as a kind of symbolic battlefield. An army (*sena*) needs training. The *puja* becomes a 'euphemization of war' (as Mussolini said, but about mass sports), or perhaps only a preparation for riots.

Cinema also offers a rich field, but the industry is less amenable to the kind of direct influence that the Shiv Sena exerts upon the *puja* committees. The channels for intervention and interaction are different. The promoters of Shiv Sainism were interested in movies from the very beginning. They are in general very fond of arts, and especially of visual art (several of the main leaders are cartoonists). During the seventies, the Marathi cinema was promoted, and a specific organization created for artists. Personalities of 'Bollywood' are systematically invited to Bal Thackeray's house or to important functions of the organization and of its cultural fronts. The top male star, Amitabh Bacchan, has been a guest. Despite a certain animosity between the Shiv Sena and the industry, connected with the fact that Muslims are numerous in the studios, these tactics were not unsuccessful. The financial intervention of some prominent Shiv Sainiks also had an impact. The real root of the influence of the Shiv Sena upon the world of Indian (and not only Bombay) cinema

[14] Interviews with *mitra mandal* members in Pune, 1986–87.

may nevertheless reside elsewhere. There was a moment, during the eighties, when the evolution of commercial cinema met the Shiv Sena themes, its fundamental representations and the main drama that agitate its young and unemployed members. The mixture of realism and pathos that imbues Indian cinema was already a convenient field, but soon the hooligan and the violent avenger became the central heroes of numerous movies. *The theme of the downtrodden youth, passing through the worst degradations before meeting redemption or death was used in famous movies.* A large part of the urban pavement youth recognized itself in the drama. It is somewhat difficult to say if the Shiv Sena was modelled by this fantasy, or if it uses it to promotes its own views. Some film-makers, like N. Patekar, are known to be connected with the organiza-tion. His *Ankush* (1986) is an epitomization of the Shiv Sena culture. Films of this kind were and still are nevertheless also produced by people who do not belong to the cultural populist organization. Muslim or pro-Congress producers and actors make exactly the same kind of stuff, which seems an emanation of the metropolis itself. It is once more by taking into account the central trend, and slightly radicalizing it through its organized framework, that the cultural populist movement has been able to influence the scene.

In many other domains of popular culture, cultural populism is ob-liged to admit the relativization of its values and references. Shivaji has been *added* to the row of colour lithographs, already comprising Ganesh, Gandhi or Nehru, Bhavani, Sai Baba, Vithoba–Krishna and some recent 'secular' heroes that decorate the wall of the popular household. *He does not occupy the totality of space.* Shivaji Jayanti is revered but people do not want to forget May Day (a holiday, a day of freedom!), despite the admonitions of the cultural populists (and of the *seth log*). Popular culture seems able to display syncretic tendencies that mitigate the influence of the polarizations induced by the cultural populist violent or non-violent activities. The reversible, and often cyclical relationship of the popular milieus with the Shiv Sena can be interpreted in this light. *It seems thus totally impossible and irrelevant to find a single direction, and a sense, to the evolution of popular culture, and moreover to popular identification through culture, in contemporary Bombay.* This absence of a unique representative process, this global lack of relevance of unity at every level, is indeed one of the recurring characteristics of the popular culture and, it also may be argued, of the popular world at large. There is nevertheless continous evolution. Views about a traditional, immovable or a-temporal popular culture seem totally irrelevant. In this context, the intervention of cultural populism is as equivocal as in other fields. The Shiv Sena has been able to select themes and to promote changes in the popular contemporary urban culture because its own innovations are very limited in scope and influence. The efficiency of the Shiv Sena, the basis for the success of its cultural populist politics, are rooted in the deep knowledge that the cadres have of the present processes and evolution of forms of popular culture, their global acceptance of them, and their ability to use the field for inducing polarizations and tensions in other perspectives, especially the political one. For example, the tremendous potential of the TV cricket matches against Pakistan for building mass tensions, the creation of majority versus minority consciousness and the assertion of a city identification (the team being from Bombay) has very early been understood by the Shiv Sena. Generally, mass sport opens a formidable field for expression of parochialism and nationalism and, more widely, the creation of collective and limited identifications.

Cultural Populism, Concretized Fantasies and Dangers

With regard to the nature of cultural populism, there are many more questions than clear answers. It is nevertheless possible to ask if cultural populism is a normal vissicitude, a catastrophic and hazardous event, the result of a long historical process, or a simple inflexion of the dominant trends in the political sphere, especially in the Congress Party. It has indeed been all of these at different moments. It displays, certainly, very tangible concrete and political levels of assertion. The issue of space appropriation is for example a privileged domain of the cultural populists that does not distinguish them very much from dozens of other movements of diverse political colours in India. They have followed, but also intensified, the popular shift from rhythm to space preoccupations. Their strategy of conflict with some of the groups occupying the city's space is related to an attempt at globalizing the stake. Popular vision centred on space is usually both defensive and decentralized. The street, or a small part of the street, sometimes the slum or the *mohalla*, are the common notions of popular space. 'The people' defend their position at this level. The Shiv Sena deals with Bombay as a whole. This enlargement of perspectives aims at creating another level of mass identification, constituting the framework for ethnic purification and profound cultural change. By using simplified references, and playing with the different aspects of popular culture, the organization has been able to change the consciousness of segments of popular classes regarding space. It seems that this process of globalization, this emergence of an image of the city as the common space, also took place outside the influence of the Shiv Sena. *Cultural populism may thus benefit a general movement, filling the vacuum of still uncertain and new apprehensions of the city's space with its readymade, both sedative and exciting, conceptions.*

We would like to insist upon the variety of possible interpretations of action and inaction, the ambiguousness of channels for social intervention, the instability of ideological constructions which are so often presented as simple and evident, in the framwork of cultural populism. If we have deliberately avoided certain complicated and important aspects of Shiv Sainism (unemployment, political life, specific conception of history and 'communalism', for example) because they were less directly related to the question of culture and populism, it seems nevertheless possible to emphasize the importance of fantasy, aspirations and the dreams of the youth, as the basis and the medium for political intervention. Those who know how to manage these recent and ever-moving entities are those who win, in the short term, on the crazy scene of the tense metropolis. This is why we have insisted upon the importance of ambiguousness and reversability in the relationships of the Shiv Sena with the people, and the popular culture. It is present in all populist politics and to a high degree in this case. No important social process can be understood at this level without taking it into account. There is nevertheless a concrete organizational reality with precise political strategies and sharp ideologies accompanying this ambiguousness and this perpetual mobility. The Shiv Sena has always been an activist organization using phantasms as a substitute for action when action is incarnated into a conflict of the dominated with the dominant. When it deals with the dominated only, there is effective, and often violent action. These processes have permitted the assertion of a 'popular will' by making it more and more related to fancy. The Shiv Sena story is a mixture of dream and impotence, dream being active, and impotence a matter for dreaming. Impotence is a leitmotiv of Shiv Sainiks. Defeats of the working class movement, arrogance of the rich, evictions, brutal family-planning practices, social isolation, electoral corruption—everything feeds today the feeling of popular impotence. The Shiv Sena capitalizes on it. Malaise among the people in the metropolis made the Shiv Sena possible. The proper capacity of the organization for wild fabulation comes afterwards. The Shiv Sena

aggravates the popular malaise, and the process for perpetual radicalization goes on. Dreams turn into nightmares when the *masala* movie is
enacted on the streets.

Bibliography

Bakshi, R. (1987). *The Long Haul, The Bombay Textile Workers Strike*, Bombay:
BUILD Documentation Centre.

Chandavarkar, R. (1981). 'Workers' Politics and the Mills Districts of Bombay
between the Wars', *Modern Asian Studies*, vol. XV, no. 3.

———— (1992). 'La résistance ouvrière à la rationalisation du travail à Bombay
dans l'entre-deux guerres', in *Travailler en Inde* (edited by G. Heuzé),
Purusartha no. 14.

Facsheet collective (1982). *The Tenth Month*, Bombay Historic Textile Strike,
Bombay: Centre for Education and Documentation

Gupta, D. (1982). *Nativism in a Metropolis, Shiv Sena in Bombay*, New Delhi:
Ramesh Jain for Manohar.

Heuzé, G; (1989). *La greve du siècle*, Paris: L'Harmattan.

———— (1990). 'Workers' struggles and indigenous fordism in India', in *Work
for Wages in South Asia*, edited by M. Holmstrom, Delhi: Manohar.

———— (1992). 'Shiv Sena: From Unemployment Exchanges to National-
Hinduism', *Economic and Political Weekly*, vol. XXVII (October 3rd and
10th).

Jha, S. S. (1986). *Structure of Urban Poverty, The case of Bombay Slums*,
Bombay: Popular Prakashan

Joshi, C. (1985). 'Bonds of Community, Ties of Religion, Kanpur Textile
Workers in the Early Twentieth Century', *The Indian Economic and Social
History Review*, vol. 22, no. 3.

Joshi, H. and V. Joshi (1976). *Surplus Labour and the City: a Study of Bombay*,
Delhi: Oxford University Press.

Katzenstein, M. F. (1979). *Ethnicity and Equality. The Shiv Sena Party and
Preferential Policies in Bombay*, Ithaca: Cornell University Press.

Kumar, N. (1988). *The Artisans of Benares, Popular Culture and Identity
1880–1986*, Princeton: Princeton University Press.

———— (1991). 'Urban Culture in Modern India. World of the Lower Classes',
in *The City in Indian History*, Urban Demography, Society and Politics
(edited by Indu Banga), Delhi: Manohar.

Kumar, R. (1987). 'City Lives: Workers Housing and Rent in Bombay',
Economic and Political Weekly, vol. XXII, no. 30.

Masselos, J. (1978). 'Change and Custom in the Format of the Bombay
Muhurum during the 19th and the 20th century', *South Asia*, vol. V, no. 1.

Naipaul, V. S. (1990). *India. A million mutinies now*, London: Minerva.

Omvedt, G. (1976). *Cultural Revolt in a Colonial Society, the Non-Brahman Movement in Western India*, Bombay: Socialist Scientific Education Trust.

Pendse, S. (1984). 'Politics and Organisation of Urban Workers', *Economic and Political Weekly*, vol. XIX, no. 8.

Rajagopalan, C. (1962). *The Greater Bombay*, Bombay: Popular Book Depot.

Thorner, A. (1992) 'Le travail dans la vie des femmes des quartiers populaires de Bombay', in *Travailler en Inde* (edited by G. Heuzé), Purusartha no. 14.

van Wersch, H. (1989). *Bombay Textile Strike*, Doctoral dissertation: University of Amsterdam (published in 1992, *Bombay Textile Strike, 1982–83*, Bombay, Oxford University Press).

Weiner, M. (1988). *Sons of the Soil, Migration and Ethnic Conflict in India*, Delhi: Oxford University Press.

12

The Commissioner and the Corporators: Power Politics at Municipal Level

USHA THAKKAR

I

Civic leaders in Bombay unanimously deplore what they see as a drastic deterioration in the municipal administration and the political life of the city. Great expectations aroused by reverberations of the freedom struggle and the post-independence achievement of universal suffrage have often given way to pessimism. Local politics is perceived as reflecting sordid conflicts of interest rather than differing approaches to issues of public welfare. Expressions of dissatisfaction or dissent are frequent but fail to evoke the expected process of negotiation and reconciliation. Phrases such as 'lack of decorum', 'rampant corruption' and even 'criminalization' are used to categorize the officers and the elected councillors. This sad state of affairs is often attributed to a general fall in standards of honesty and propriety in the country as a whole. Specifically local factors are also mentioned.

To shed light on the complexities of the contemporary municipal scene, it is worthwhile to look back to the time when the foundations of local government were laid by the British rulers following a British model. The history of the century-old Bombay Municipal Corporation (BMC) can be divided into four phases.

Civic government during the first phase (1793 to 1845) was involved mainly with functions related to the police, administration of justice and collection of taxes. The creation in 1845 of a civic heptarchy representing diverse interests loosely blended into an executive body marked the beginning of the second phase (1845–72). An attempt to improve the administration was made in 1858 by providing for the appointment of three commissioners. All members of this triumvirate had equal powers, so, in the exercise of their divided responsibilities, they often obstructed each other's functioning. The need for a single, strong executive authority was increasingly felt and voiced. An Act of 1865 created the office of a single Municipal Commissioner, whose powers steadily increased with the passage of time. The Act of 1865 also created a body corporate of the Justices of Peace with powers to impose rates and taxes and to assume full control of the municipal funds. The people's voice was, however, not heard in this set-up. The demand for a responsible representative municipal body began to gain momentum under the leadership of Pherozeshah Mehta.

The introduction of an elective element in the municipal body in 1872 marked the beginning of the third phase (1872–88). The Act of 1872 granted franchise to certain classes of rate payers and created representative assemblies. Lord Ripon's pronouncement on local self government gave an impetus to the demand for extension of self-government to the municipal administration of Bombay.

The subsequent Act of 1888 can be taken as a landmark in the history of Bombay. It recognized the Corporation as the supreme governing body of the city, and the Municipal Commissioner as its chief executive authority, responsible for carrying out its will. It is this Act, with many subsequent amendments, that has provided the framework for city government during the fourth phase (1888 onwards) (Pinto: 1984: 14–44). As S. S. Tinaikar points out, the basic structure of municipal government in Bombay has remained unaltered over the last hundred years, even though the area of the Corporation has been expanded from 50 sq. km to 437 sq. km and the population has grown from 800,000 to 10,000,000. Over the century the number of councillors has increased from 72 (in 1922) to 221 and the nature and number of voters have changed from a few thousand ratepayers, some nominees of government and Justices of Peace, to an adult franchise electorate numbering 6,700,000 in the last election held in 1992.

The Act specifies seven statutory-collateral authorities, each charged with certain responsibilities: the Corporation, the Standing Committee, the Improvements Committee, the Bombay Electric Supply and Transport Committee, the Education Committee, the Municipal Commissioner and the General Manager of the Bombay Electric Supply and Transport Undertaking. The first five of these are deliberative bodies with powers to sanction funds; the last two are executives. The Act envisages a clear demarcation of functions between the executive wing (the Municipal Commissioner) and the deliberative wing (the Municipal Corporation). The Municipal Commissioner, drawn from the civil service cadre, is a government appointee for a renewable term of three years. He attends and participates in discussions at meetings of the Corporation and its committees, but does not have the right to vote. The exercise of some of his powers, such as awarding contracts and purchase and disposal of property, involving huge amounts of money, need the sanction of the corporation and some of its committees. He can be removed from office by the state government if at a meeting of the corporation not less than five-eighths of the total number of councillors vote for such a proposal, and also if it appears to the state government that he is incapable of performing his duties or has been guilty of misconduct or neglect.

The Corporation consists of representatives of the citizens elected for a term of five years on the basis of adult franchise. Since the 1952 general elections, the Corporation has become a purely elected body.

The Standing Committee is elected by the Corporation from among its members. The main functions of this committee are to sanction contracts, scrutinize estimates of income and expenditure framed by the Municipal Commissioner and frame the budget from those estimates, frame service regulations and sanction investment of funds (BMC Act: Sections 4–36, 42–49, 54, 64–66).

This paper focuses on the relation between the Municipal Commissioner and the elected members, that is the Corporation, in the second half of the 1980s, during the term of S. S. Tinaikar as Municipal Commissioner from mid-1986 to the beginning of 1990.

The idea of separation of functions can be traced back to Pherozeshah Mehta, one of the main architects of city government in Bombay, who believed that the main responsibilities of the Municipal Council were 'to watch and control the executive Government, to throw the light of publicity on all its acts, to compel a full exposition, and justification of all of them.' The vesting of executive authority in a Municipal Council would, in his opinion, 'have been to substitute in the place of the responsible executive office a heterogeneous body of men equally powerful, men incapable and difficult of being controlled and with their responsibility so attenuated by division and sub-division, as to render them practically and really entirely irresponsible' ('The Bombay Municipal Reform Question, 1871', pamphlet).

Interestingly, attention was drawn to the possibility of tension between the Commissioner and the Municipal Council in the Governor's Council when the Act of 1888 was on the anvil. Forbes Adams, who advised the Governor, Lord Reay, on important sections of the Bill said that, 'The idea of co-ordinate authority seems to be fraught with chances of friction and irritation. It is an attempt to reconcile what is irreconcilable.' (Wacha: 1913: 431)

The implementation of this dual control system has certainly not been easy. The Municipal Commissioner often complains that the elected members create obstructions in the path of administration by their intervention, and that they lack the expertise or technical knowledge required for certain matters. Added to this, there are pressures arising out of the necessity to capture and to retain seats in the Corporation. The elected representatives, on their part, often see the Municipal Commissioner as a rigid bureaucrat blocking the implementation of their decisions. The experience of a Municipal Commissioner indicates that this dichotomy between the place of authority and the place of responsibility makes the job of the Commissioner difficult, if not impossible (Chopra: 1985: 18).

Relations between the Municipal Commissioner and the Corporation during the second half of the eighties no longer remain merely exchanges between two branches of the municipal government but also reflect and are affected by the prevailing electoral politics, where winning is measured in terms of visible influence and tangible gains such as privileges, money and land.

II

The BMC Act of 1888 does not mention political parties, which at that time had not appeared on the civic scene, though eminent nationalist leaders like Pherozeshah Mehta, K. T. Telang, Ibrahim Rahimtulla, Badruddin Tyabji, Dinsha Wachcha, Homi Mody and Vithalbhai Patel played an important role in municipal affairs. The council was conceived as a body of civic-minded notables with no political affiliations. Following the introduction of universal adult franchise in 1948, political parties began to enter the municipal arena.

A quick look at the seats won by different parties in the last nine elections (see Appendix) shows that no single party dominated the scene. In the 1948, 1952 and 1961 elections the Congress emerged as a powerful party. The 1957 election brought in a multi-party alliance, the

Samyukta Maharashtra Samiti, which demanded and eventually obtained the creation of a unilingual State of Maharashtra. In 1968, the Shiv Sena emerged as a strong political force. In the 1973 election, the Congress suffered a setback but the Shiv Sena also could not retain its strength. By that time the Congress had split. In 1978, power was captured by the Janata Party, consisting of political elements opposed to the traditional post-independence ruling party—the Congress. The 1984 election once again installed the Shiv Sena but the 1992 election gave a thumping majority to the Congress. Particular interest groups and small parties have often emerged on the political scene and then disappeared either because of lack of popular support or merger with another party.

Both nationally and in Bombay municipal politics the game of electoral alliances has, on several occasions, brought about combinations of parties which would appear to represent opposing ideologies. This has particularly been the case of various attempts, some of them successful, to wrest power from the dominant party, usually the Congress. Examples of such alliances are the collaboration of the Congress and the Republican Party in the 1968 election, the alignment of the Praja Socialist Party and the Shiv Sena in the same year, the Bharatiya Janata Party associating with the Shiv Sena in 1985, and the coalition of the Congress and the Republican Party (Athavale Group) in 1992. By contrast, combinations of different parties in 1957 and 1978 had definite purposes, not altogether devoid of ideology.

Recent years have seen this dragging of partisan political considerations into discussions of matters of purely civic interest taken a step further downwards. Today the proceedings of the Corporation show that civic interests are now subordinated not only to party interests but also, and even more to personal ambition, and even personal greed. R. C. Ankleshwaria, who has spent more than two decades in city politics is of the view that 'Most of the working hours of the Corporation are wasted in political squabbles. Sometimes a rise in rates is necessary, but opposition parties oppose it just for the sake of opposition. Agreeing on some proposal/issue in the Mayor's chamber and changing their stand altogether afterwards is not uncommon among corporators. Vote-catching is the root of all evils.'

Dr Shanti Patel, an ex-councillor and member of Parliament, with long experience of public life from local to national level, is concerned about what is happening to the city. According to him, urban problems demand special attention and comprehension. Instead there is lack of foresight on part of the Corporation and the State government. Basic issues of interest to the city like industrial policy, structural policies, finances, transport, development control rules and development plans remain within the scope of the state governments while implementation at the civic level is the job of the Corporation. This may lead to friction between the state government and the Corporation and to neglect of civic problems.

Parties at local level cannot be different from those at State and national levels. The arithmetic of elections may work against workers at grassroots level and may push a candidate, who is not necessarily the choice of the majority of voters in the ward, to the winning position. According to a former Municipal Commissioner, J. B. D'Souza: 'For emerging victorious, the candidate has to merely win over a few *bastis* (slums), which he can do by holding a *Ganpati* festival. The number of goons entering BMC will increase and problems will centre around building one pipeline instead of improving the city's water works.' (IE, 28 Feb. 91) In addition to this, there is no necessary connection between the seats won and the total votes polled. For example, in the 1985 election the Shiv Sena captured 74 seats, though it had secured only 23.17 per cent of the total votes polled; the 17 independent candidates who were elected totalled 28.26 per cent; the Bharatiya Janata Party, with 13 elected members had obtained 10.53 per cent; the 10 members belonging to the Janata Party represented 8.52 per cent of the voters (TOI: 22 Feb. 86).

What is seen in the city politics of Bombay is only the tip of the iceberg. Over the years the process of fragmentation and division of all segments of political reality has steadily continued. Veterans talk with nostalgia about the times when elections did not involve such exorbitant expenses and when civic issues were given due importance (Interviews with Ankleshwaria, Gore, Dr Shanti Patel, Varde). They point out that, on the one hand, unplanned urbanization and growing economic deprivation generate insensitivity and brutalization, and, on the other, the emergence of new aspirations and political ambitions results in increasing reliance on slogans and rallies, and declining commitment to civic issues like health, housing and adequate water supply.

It is difficult to name the exact year when city politics started yielding to pressures from within and without, at the cost of civic concerns. Some relate it to the 1969 Congress split, some to Indira Gandhi's declaration of emergency in 1975, some to post-emergency developments and some to the time of the rise of the Shiv Sena. The fact, however, remains that, over a period of at least twenty years, city politics has been transformed. J. B. Mahajan, after serving the BMC for almost three decades stated, on the eve of his retirement, that in the earlier years of the Corporation, 'debates and discussions were serious and constructive. Corporators behaved with decorum in the house. These days there is only pandemonium. The issues are petty and the hassles personal' (*Bombay*: 22 July to 6 Aug. 89).

It was in 1977, when, most probably for the first time, a corporator was caught taking a bribe: Fakaruddin Qurban Hussain of the Muslim League was nabbed while accepting Rs 1500/- for assuring the necessary licence and connections for electricity and water for a fruit stall owner (JB: 14 Jan. 77).

Strange things now happen in the BMC and at its meetings: a corporator smashes a microphone in the house, calling the civic body a joke-house and a circus (IE: 6 July 83); important documents—correspondence between the World Bank and the BMC—are 'lost' (IE, 26 Sept. 84); one corporator waves his footwear at another (IE: 4 Aug. 85); pandemonium in the house over the allegation of corruption made by the leader of the house against the Additional Municipal Commissioner and the Municipal Commissioner's demand that the member substantiate the allegation (TOI: 21 Nov. 86); uproar caused by Mayor Ramesh Prabhu describing the Janata Party as antinational (IP: 9 Dec. 87); chaos over the claim by Rustom Tirandaz, an independent member, that he had a sound recording of Diwakar Raote, Standing Committee Chairman, trying to extort money from city traders and showing that the Shiv Sena had played a part in recent communal riots (TOI: 2 Sept. 88); disorder created by the allegation made by Chhagan Bhujbal, a Shiv Sena member, that Devchand Gala, a Congress corporator, had attempted to extort a huge amount of money from a builder and that Bhujbal had a tape-recording of the conversation (TOI: 9 Sept. 88); arguments among corporators going beyond words and leading to cross complaints at the police station (IP: 31 Dec. 89); throwing of shoes at a BMC meeting (IE: 24 June 92).

The tradition among the elected members and officers of the Corporation of working sincerely and honestly for the civic body is vanishing, says an insider. The increase in the size of the Corporation has not made any difference to its working say retired chief executives (*Bombay*: 22 Aug. 88; IE: 28 Feb. 91). The total budget of the BMC is huge; the budget for 1991/92 showed an income of Rs 1,730 crores. A criticism levelled by a responsible bureaucrat is that Bombay's municipal government is now little more than a giant welfare system for its 1,30,000-odd employees and its 170-odd corporators (J. B. D'Souza: Brihanmumbai Mahanagarpalika Patrika, 9 Jan. 92). The brazen way in which politics intrudes into civic affairs was illustrated when the late Ramdas Nayak, Shiv Sena-backed BJP chairperson of the Standing Committee, acknowledged that the ruling Shiv Sena was making money through the BMC. He told the Congress members that 'At least they [Sena] admit that; you don't even do that' (TOI: 3 June 89).

The tendency of criminalization of Indian politics in general has also crept into the civic body. Daljeet S. Bagga (*Onlooker*: 1–15 Oct. 1988) finds that at least a dozen corporators are facing charges ranging from murder and attempted murder to rioting and extortion. Jyoti Punwani as well gives information about some corporators who have criminal charges pending against them (IP: 20 Sept. 1988). Tracing the criminal links of some corporators, Ambarish Mishra (TOI: 21 Oct. 1990) writes: 'The political scenario at the BMC has undergone a drastic change, undeniably for the worse, in the last few years in view of gangland feuds, *supari* killings (contracted murders), extortion of protection money from traders and the proliferation of illegal structures.'

S. M. Y. Sastry, a responsible officer, now retired after decades of work in the BMC, summarizes the situation in city politics saying: 'There is so little available, and there are so many claimants; so the question is, who gets what. In reality, the question can be broadened to: who gets what and how. Soon it turns into who grabs what.'

III

The issues and tensions currently arising in relations between the Municipal Commissioner and the Corporation reflect some trends of this new politics. The relationship has sailed through some rough seas and stormy weather. Projects involving huge amounts of money and demanding technical expertise have often created areas of dispute. A World Bank aided integrated water supply and sewerage project involving a total outlay of $251 million was launched in 1976, in association with government both at central and state level. The multi-crore contracts under the project had to be approved by the Standing Committee which soon realized the power it could wield. This realization often led to delays in approvals, interference in matters of awarding contracts and even reopening of items which had earlier been approved. As S. S. Tinaikar points out, corruption was always there in some form or other, but, in the past decade it shot up tremendously, mainly because of the massive projects undertaken with World Bank loans and the high stakes involved in real estate transactions (TOI: 18 Nov. 86).

A major controversy arose in the beginning of the 80s, when there were differences of opinion between D. M. Sukhtankar, the Municipal Commissioner, and the Standing Committee over awarding a contract for the construction of a filtration plant. When his recommendation was rejected by the Committee, the Municipal Commissioner, concerned over the delay, invoked Section 69(C) of the BMC Act for the first time in the history of the Corporation. According to this section (inserted in 1971 to guard against escalation in costs resulting from possible delays), if a Commissioner's proposal is not passed by the Standing Committee within 15 days of its presentation, it could be deemed to have been approved by the Committee. The matter ultimately reached the High Court, which upheld the Commissioner's powers (Pinto: 1984, 151).

As the 80s advanced, many issues figured in the arena of city politics. One major event was the beautification of Hutatma Chowk (earlier called Flora Fountain), situated in the heart of the business section. The contract for this work, worth more than Rs 30 lakhs, was awarded without reference to the Standing Committee. A division bench of the Bombay High Court severely criticized the BMC for irregularities committed in the execution of the work. The judges observed that no previous sanction of the Standing Committee had been obtained, as required under the provisions of the BMC Act, and no tenders had been invited as required (TOI: 4 Oct. 1986).

In the years when the Shiv Sena dominated the Corporation, the Congress-I ruled the state. When a tough and upright person was appointed by the state government as Municipal Commissioner, tensions arose between him and the elected members of the Corporation mainly on issues of contracts and the Commissioner's attitude and behaviour towards members of the Corporation.

The Shiv Sena and the Municipal Commissioner repeatedly collided over the question of the powers of the Standing Committee in the matter of awarding contracts. In addition to two High Court judgements and the state government's backing, the Municipal Commissioner armed himself with the opinion of Y. V. Chandrachud, the former Chief Justice of India. The latter confirmed that if a proposal relating to a water supply and sewerage project was not approved or rejected by the Committee within 15 days, the Municipal Commissioner was duty-bound, under Section 69(c) of the BMC Act, to 'deem' it to have been passed and to award the contract. The ruling party in the Corporation, however, refused to act as the rubber stamp of the administration. Later because of pressure from both the World Bank team in the city and the state government, 22 pending contracts were approved at two marathon meetings of the Standing Committee in March 1987. When the Committee failed to approve the rest of items by 31 March, the Municipal Commissioner invoked Section 69(c) of the BMC Act and deemed the proposals to have been passed (TOI: 22 April 87).

Another impasse in the BMC was created over sewerage. The Chairman of the Standing Committee rejected a proposal put forward by the Municipal Commissioner seeking extension of the services of a United States firm as consultants for the World Bank-aided sewerage project. Not only the BMC but also the governments at the state and centre are involved in this project which covers sewerage systems in Colaba, Lovegrove, Bandra, Versova, Malad and Ghatkopar. The highly complicated nature of the project, underestimation of time and costs, poor management and disputes raised on contracts and consequent delays pushed the project cost, estimated in 1979 at Rs 147 crores and scheduled to be completed by 1984, to Rs 800 crores with a possibility of final completion by 1993 (*Business India*, 30 Oct. 88; *Bombay*: Dec. 90–Jan. 91). Pointing out that, out of the seven sewerage systems projected, only two have been so far completed, insiders suggest that the cost will eventually go even higher.

Another irritant was the difference of opinion between the Municipal Commissioner and the Standing Committee over the tender for site investigation for the marine out-fall project for construction of pipelines under the sea for a certain distance for discharge of sewage. Ultimately, the deadlock was broken by the intervention of the state government (TOI: 3 Feb. 89; IE: 7 Feb. 89). While tensions were rising, the Shiv Sena chief told journalists that his party would initiate a 'No Confidence' resolution against the Commissioner. Major opposition parties, however, decided to support the Commissioner (TOI: 11 Feb. 89).

With the Corporation and the Municipal Commissioner at loggerheads over contracts for basic civic amenities such as providing water, drainage, and clearing of debris from gutters, it is not surprising that many projects were delayed and civic work suffered. A survey by two journalists in September 1989 pointed out that a number of civic projects had been held in abeyance since 1986. Of 454 such projects, 202 were pending with the Standing Committee, 184 with the Improvement Committee, and 68 with the Education Committee (Glen D'Souza and Hemant Basu, IP: 17 Sept. 89). The state government had, for the first time ever, to act under Section 520(c) of the BMC Act, which empowers the state government to issue directions to the corporation requiring it to do or refrain from doing something, in the public interest. In the case of the Matunga–Mahalakshmi water tunnel project (a part of World Bank Project), the state directed the BMC to award the contract to a particular company (TOI: 5 July 89).

Unfinished projects are scattered across the city. Schemes for hospitals, schools, fire stations, cemeteries, swimming pools, welfare centres and dispensaries are started and then left half-way, resulting in waste of huge amounts of public money (V. Shankar, *Island*: 1 Jan. 88). Some vigilant corporators have voiced their concern over the situation but achieved little change. The 1989/90 audit report on the water supply and sewerage department of the BMC passed strictures against its methods of work (TOI: 23 Oct. 90). Brigadier Sethee was appointed by the Municipal Commissioner to look into the causes of the abnormal delay in sewerage works. The Sethee Report raised questions about the professional qualities of the city's engineers, the scope of the powers of councillors in awarding contracts, and the nexus that has developed between contractors, officers and councillors (Allwyn Fernandes, TOI: 15–16 July 90).

Unpleasant scenes over awarding of contracts during the 80s stand witness to the selfcentredness of the political system. Insiders whisper about 'the syndicate' which had allegedly been formed among members from different parties to secure illegal payments from contractors. Unsavoury hurling of accusations by the councillors at the Municipal Commissioner (especially during 1987–89) demonstrates the level of political communication which has come to prevail.

The BMC witnessed a stormy scene when the majority party in the House took objection to the Municipal Commissioner's remarks on the 105 martyrs of the Samyukta Maharashtra Movement and passed an adjournment motion to register their disapproval. He had maintained that the persons in question were victims of justifiable action taken by the then government of Bombay to maintain law and order at that time (TOI: 6 Feb. 87). Again, battle lines between the Municipal Commissioner and Indumati Patel, a Congress-I councillor, were sharply drawn over certain allegations made by her against G. R. Khairnar, a high-profile senior ward officer (ultimately the matter reached the law courts). Insisting on the presentation of proof for the charges, the Municipal Commissioner insisted that the character of officers could not be made the 'property of the House' and the councillors had no 'privileges', such as those enjoyed by members of the State Assembly and the national Parliament. The councillors, on the other hand, maintained that the Municipal Commissioner is a servant of the Corporation, having no right to insult the elected representatives (*Daily*: 27 Nov. 87; IE: 11 Dec. 87; Interview, I. Patel).

As the classical democratic norms of mutual respect and tolerance crumble, the new rulers, conscious of the powers they wield, crave for visibility. Their reluctance to secure this by constructive work pushes them to appeal to populist aspirations and to trot out formulas such as protecting 'honour'. This lends a certain coarseness to the behaviour and expression of the councillors as exemplified in their insistence on the exclusive use of Marathi in the Corporation, their constant demand for an increase in the corporator's discretionary fund (to be spent locally), their sharp reactions to cuts imposed by the Municipal Commissioner on grants to certain institutions, and their replies to the Municipal Commissioner's objections to their mixing official visits with pleasure trips. At one point, the Municipal Commissioner expressed his unwillingness to attend meetings of the standing committee. During his last month in service, Municipal Commissioner Tinaikar said about his tenure: 'Mentally it has been a war for an officer who has had to stand alone against all political parties. And certainly my experiences are like those of a warrior on the battlefield. One suffers wounds, but they only show that one has fought' (Tinaikar, *Independent*: 22 April 90).

No discussion on the BMC would be complete without reference to the issues of land and construction. Though it is the state government which has considerable power in this sphere, the BMC is also involved at many stages. Important Acts like The Bombay Tenancy and Agricultural Lands Act, 1948; The Maharashtra Region and Town Planning Act, 1966; The Maharashtra Land Revenue Code, 1966; The Bombay Metropolitan Region Development Authority Act, 1974; and the Urban Land Ceiling Act, 1976, directly impinge on the concerns of the Corporation. Bodies like the Maharashtra Housing and Area Development Authority, the Housing and Urban Development Corporation, and the City and Industrial Development Corporation, are deeply involved in the development of the city. In fact, such Acts and agencies have created a system which favours those with political and economic clout, and civic issues are very often lost in the labyrinth of power struggles.

The limited land of Bombay island is far from adequate to cope with the pace of development of the city and the constant influx of population, ranging from 200 to 500 persons per day (Gadkari, 1987, 428). One solution has been the creation of land by filling the sea. Awarding of contracts for these costly operations opened the floodgates for corruption and scandals. In the setting of rising land values and an accelerating demand for space and housing in the island city, particularly after the enforcement of the Urban Land Ceiling Act, the urban development portfolio acquired a place of importance at the state level. There are nearly 3,000 hectares of private vacant land in the city. Yet only 30 hectares of land were acquired in Greater Bombay under the Urban Land Ceiling Act. 80 per cent of the housing in Bombay has been provided by the private and cooperative sectors. The dividing line between these two is rather thin (Gadkari: 1987: 431–40). With a toothless Urban Land Ceiling Act, the state government has yielded to pressures from the construction and business lobbies (Gonsalves: 1981). Slowly there has emerged a nexus of builders, bureaucrats and politicians.

Red signals warning against the danger of allowing the proliferation of unplanned commercial and residential blocks were raised by N. V. Modak in 1949, the Sadashivrao Barve Committee in 1958, the Professor Dhananjay Gadgil Committee in 1966, and the Bombay Metropolitan Regional Development Authority in 1970. Ignoring these signals, the state government and the municipality moved ahead. Plans for reclamation of land from the sea were made and partially implemented. A special bill enabling the Corporation to prepare a Development Plan was passed in 1954. Development for Greater Bombay and new rules for construction have come to be implemented since 1966. The last report of the Development Plan of Bombay Island was sent to the state government for approval by the administrator when the BMC was dissolved, but the chapter is yet to be closed.

Meanwhile, the corporators elected in the 1985 polls appointed a small committee to prepare a development plan giving free concessions to landowners. The committee's recommendations were submitted to the Corporation for approval. Though not generally available to the public, the report was approved in a day and was sent to the state government in April 1986. When the scandal started becoming public, the matter was hushed up by declaring that some information should be kept secret in the public interest. Instances of irregular concessions in the matter of allotment of plots continue (Tinaikar: 1991, 48–52).

Ramesh Joshi, a vigilant city-level politician, expresses his concern at a scheme to get 285 plots dereserved (released from the requirement that they be kept for public uses such as schools, parks, fire stations)

Some other major land scandals concern cancellation of reservation of a plot by the State Government (IE: 9 March 83), granting of permission to certain textile mills in the city to dispose of their excess land for commercial or residential construction (Abhay Mokashi, IE 2 April 85), and changing of reservations in the revised development plans for the suburbs (TOI: 20 Jul. 86; IE: 12 Jul. 86).

The J. B. D'Souza Committee's scrutiny report on the city's Draft Development Plan is a scathing indictment of the Sena-ruled BMC. The Committee judged that builders' testimony had exerted undue influence in the drafting of the Development Plan (*Daily*: 22 Aug. 87).

The discussion on the report of the J. B. D'Souza Committee gave rise to ugly scenes. The leader of the opposition accused the ruling party of not taking the opposition into confidence and not conducting a healthy discussion on the subject before forwarding the development plan to the state government. The mayor's action in reserving his ruling and not permitting any discussion on the subject resulted in an opposition walk-out. Later, a virtual battle of words and blows followed between a Shiv Sena member and a Congress-I councillor. The House was adjourned and police complaints and counter-complaints filed (IE: 25 Aug. 87).

Irregularities in matters of land continue (IP: 5 Jan. 89). Big plots marked for recreation are dereserved (*Sunday Observer*: 5 Jul. 92), or allotted to a fictitious party (*Sunday Observer*: 22 Mar. 92), or are subjects of controversial sales (*Blitz*: 28 Mar. 92). A prominent part is played by politicians in all these deals (*Tele*: 5 May 87; R. Padmanabhan, *Frontline*: 28 Aug. 92).

With land being at a premium, the issue of construction assumes crucial importance, attracting fortune-hunters from every quarter. Connected with this are issues of relaxation of FSI (Floor Space Index) (i.e. the multiple of gross area of the plot that is allowed to be built as usable accomodation), unauthorized constructions, repair of old buildings, and slum-development. These involve various departments of the state government as well as the BMC. Their rules, regulations and policies weave such intricate networks that civic issues get entangled in them and are often lost.

The number of irregularities in the area of construction have been on the ascent since the beginning of the 80s. Scandals concerning buildings erected in violation of rules are common. At one point, when Chandrakant Tripathi, the Minister of State for Urban Development in the Maharashtra Government, talked about curtailment of the autonomy of the civic body in view of its 'irresponsible behaviour in civic life', the

Corporation assailed him for his alleged role in shielding anti-social elements involved in illegal construction (IE: 15 Jul. 83).

The state government decided to take over the powers of the BMC and to appoint an administrator in March 1984. The reason given was the BMC's inability to prepare revised ward lists and to hold elections before 31 March, 1984. As there was no provision in the Act for the supersession of the Corporation, the matter was placed before the Maharashtra Legislative Assembly. This step of the government was viewed by the opposition in the Legislative Assembly as an action aimed at serving the political ends of the ruling party at the state level. Chandrakant Tripathi, the state Minister for Urban Development, however, expressed the displeasure of the government at the functioning of the BMC, emphasizing that 'this goose that lays golden eggs' did not belong to any single person or party but belonged to the people of Bombay (Maharashtra Legislative Assembly Debates, 15 Mar. 84).

Though the mid-80s witnessed a crusade launched by Ward Officer G. R. Khairnar (later Deputy Municipal Commissioner) against unauthorized structures, building in violation of rules continued unabated. The Bombay Regional Congress Committee president criticized the rapid increase in unauthorized constructions (*Free Press Journal*: 11 Jan. 85). There were protests from some quarters, yet irregularities in granting FSI persisted (TOI: 18 Nov. 86). The nexus between councillors and bureaucrats can be illustrated by the fate of a proposal for the prosecution of two senior civic engineers who had allegedly conspired to commit a FSI fraud. The proposal was rejected in the Standing Committee by the Shiv Sena members with support from the Muslim League and the Civic Forum. Later, however, the ruling party changed its stand and permitted the Municipal Commissioner to proceed with criminal prosecution of the engineers (*Sunday Observer*, 16 Nov. 86; Teesta Setalvad, *IE*: 2 Oct. 86).

The three major opposition parties—the Congress, the Bharatiya Janata Party and the Janata Dal—alleged that the Shiv Sena had auctioned the city to builders and capitalists, though no party really could claim to have a clear record (*Evening News*, 30 Jan. 87). The issue of various political parties' offices housed in unauthorized places generated heat in the Legislative Assembly. Shripatrao Shinde, a Janata Party member, informed the house at a session that a list of 71 offices of the Shiv Sena and 20 of the Congress housed in illegal structures had been submitted by Ramesh Joshi, a Janata councillor, to the Municipal Commissioner, and the Commissioner had directed officials to take action in the matter. However, according to Dr V. Subramanian, the Urban Development Minister, the number of offices in illegal buildings was not available with the BMC (TOI: 24 Mar. 88). The issue continued to generate heated debate in the Corporation. At one meeting of the Corporation the entire opposition, barring the Bharatiya Janata Party, castigated the ruling party, the Shiv Sena, for its untenable stand that all illegal structures should be demolished before its own 'unauthorized' offices were pulled down. (TOI: 6 May 88). It was alleged that councillors from the ruling party possessed flats in illegal structures, one even enjoying a palatial house (Ambarish Mishra, *IP*: 11 July 88). Baburao Mane, a Shiv Sena councillor, had to be removed physically from the office of the Municipal Commissioner for his rude and intemperate behaviour over the matter of the demolition of Mane's illegal structure in the Dharavi slum. (IP: 4 Jan. 89).

The High Court's comments about the existence of unauthorized structures arising out of the relation between the wrongdoers and the authorities have not stopped this activity. According to 1991 BMC figures, there were 178 cases of FSI violation pending with them; unofficially, higher figures have been quoted (IE: 14 May 92). One ward alone is said to have 100 illegal structures. Unscrupulous construction flourishes mainly thanks to political patronage and involvement of antisocial elements (IE: 20 Aug. 92; TOI: 22 Sept. 92; Sambit Bal, *Independent*: 18 Oct. 92). A survey by the BMC in 1991 discovered that over 1,000 places of worship in Greater Bombay are housed in unauthorized constructions (Harini Swamy, TOI: 23 Feb. 92). Any attempt to demolish such places is bound to be explosive.

Despite the severe shortage of housing for Bombay's nearly ten million strong population, legislators bureaucrats and judges seek prime places for themselves and their kinfolk at the cost of violating the rules (Olga Tellis, *Sun. Obs.*: 2 Aug. 92; Geeta Sheshu, IE: 4 Aug. 92; Harini Swamy, TOI: 6 Sept. 92; Allwyn Fernandes, TOI: 18 Sept. 92). No one wants to own responsibility for this lawless situation. Javed Khan, housing minister of the state government, criticizes the BMC and the police department for not taking action on complaints by Housing Board staff about illegal construction in old and dilapidated buildings (TOI: 20 Aug. 92). On the other hand, Ramrao Adik, Finance Minister of the state government, blames outdated laws, politicians and inefficient housing agencies for turning Bombay into the most unplanned city in the world; and criticizes politicians for regularizing slums with the intention of creating vote banks (TOI: 24 Sept. 92).

The recent Development Control Rules have permitted a profit margin to builders from 15 to 25 per cent, with an increase in FSI from 1.33 to 2.5 justified as a measure to promote slum redevelopment. Sudhakarrao Naik, then Chief Minister, during his first visit to the BMC, made an important announcement: the hiking of the Councillors' fund to Rs. 10 lakh for each councillor and an increase of the plot area allotted for slum development from 180 to 225 square feet (IE: 7 Oct. 92). The ministers, the councillors and the Municipal Commissioner often discuss schemes for housing slum dwellers. But, according to Tinaikar, 'As builders and developers are promised a higher profit in the name of slogans of privatization and market economy, the naive ministers, ignorant bureaucrats and scheming politicians have pretensions to solving the problem of acute shortage of housing and proliferation of slums' (*Independent*, 16 May 92). Meanwhile, the campaign to demolish unauthorized structures has gained momentum under Sharad Kale, the present Municipal Commissioner, and G. B. Khairnar, the Deputy Municipal Commissioner, often referred to as a 'one-person demolition squad'.

IV

As the people of Bombay watch civic politics becoming embroiled in petty disputes and consumed by selfish interests, their responses tend to become confused if not paralysed. Daily life for many of them is an endless round of frustration and fatigue. Poverty, unemployment, unhealthful living conditions and divisions arising from factors such as language, region, class and caste, may serve to make people insensitive to what is happening around them. In effect, there are two Bombays, one a city of the privileged few and the other a slum of the deprived many, almost invisible to each other, living together in tense and distrustful hostility. Severe economic and social problems cannot be swept away by rhetoric about growth or slogans of beautification. Politics has become 'money, *maska* [sycophancy] and murder', says an insider. In addition to structural reform, and sincere efforts by both elected members and officers, what is needed is a sensitivity to the surrounding misery, a sense of identification with the city and a determination to rise above the 'we/they' attitude. The questions which cannot be escaped are: Can civic issues be separated from the prevailing power politics? Is it possible to visualize an urban government genuinely concerned with the real problems of the people of the city? What steps could be taken to make this actually happen?

Appendix
Seats Secured and Seats Contested in Bombay Municipal Council Elections, 1948–1992

Political Party	1948		1952		1957		1961		1968		1973		1978		1985		1992	
	a	b	a	b	a	b	a	b	a	b	a	b	a	b	a	b	a	b
Congress	47	94	56	105	54	110	??	120	65	104	45	139	—	—	—	—	—	—
Congress (I)	—	—	—	—	—	—	—	—	—	—	—	—	17	76	37	170	112	221
Congress (O)	—	—	—	—	—	—	—	—	—	—	4	68	8	64	—	—	—	—
Congress (S)	—	—	—	—	3	18	—	—	—	—	—	—	—	—	9	63	??	30
Congress Jan Parishad	—	—	—	—	—	—	—	—	—	—	—	—	—	—	—	—	—	—
Praja Samajwadi	26	48	36	42	27	32	14	47	11	31	—	—	—	—	—	—	—	—
Samyukta Samajwadi	—	—	—	—	0	5	3	13	2	36	8	54	—	—	—	—	—	—
Republican	7	9	5	11	12	14	6	41	2	15	0	12	—	—	0	18	—	—
Bharatiya Republican	—	—	—	—	—	—	—	—	—	—	—	—	—	—	1	49	—	—
Shiv Sena	—	—	—	—	—	—	—	—	42	95	39	99	21	117	74	139	70	211

a = seats secured b = seats contested

(continued on following page)

Seats Secured and Seats Contested in Bombay Municipal Council Elections, 1948–1992 (continued)

Political Party	1948		1952		1957		1961		1968		1973		1978		1985		1992	
	a	b	a	b	a	b	a	b	a	b	a	b	a	b	a	b	a	b
Communist	5	8	4	10	13	15	18	25	1	38	3	17	3	14	1	16	2	13
Communist (M)	—	—	—	—	—	—	—	—	2	9	1	5	1	7	0	14	0	5
Swatantra	—	—	—	—	—	—	—	—	1	44	0	7	—	—	—	—	—	—
Hindu Mahasabha	—	—	—	—	—	—	1	5	—	—	—	—	—	—	—	—	—	—
Jan Sangh	—	—	—	—	2	5	4	29	6	71	15	71	—	—	—	—	—	—
Janata	—	—	—	—	—	—	—	—	—	—	—	—	83	130	10	102	0	59
Bharatiya Janata	—	—	—	—	—	—	—	—	—	—	—	—	—	—	13	136	14	175
Janata Dal	—	—	—	—	—	—	—	—	—	—	—	—	—	—	—	—	8	144
Lok Dal	—	—	—	—	—	—	—	—	—	—	—	—	—	—	—	—	—	19
Independents*	21	81	23	104	13	129	18	151	8	257	25	285	7	569	25	796	15	1238

a = seats secured   b = seats contested

* Including Muslim League, Nagari Aghadi, Kamghar Agadi, Janata Aghadi, Lal Nishan, Revolutionary Communist

Bibliography

The Bombay Municipal Corporation (BMC) Act, 1988.

Chopra, R. N., 'Role of Municipal Commissioner', in Abhijit Datta ed., *Municipal Executive in India*, Indian Institute of Public Administration, New Delhi, 1985.

D'Souza, J. B., *Brihad Mumbai Mahanagar Palika Patrika*, BMC, Bombay, January 92.

Gadkari, S. S., 'Urban development administration in Maharashtra', Ph.D. dissertation, Department of Civics & Politics, University of Bombay, 1987.

Gonsalves, Colin, *Bombay: a city under siege*, Institute of Social Research and Education, Bombay, 1981.

Pinto, David Anthony, *The Mayor, the Commissioner and the Metropolitan Administration (Bombay)*, Vikas Publishing House, Delhi, 1984.

The Maharashtra Legislative Assembly Debates.

Tinaikar, S. S., Mahatma Phule lecture series (Marathi), Department of Marathi, University of Bombay, Bombay, 1991.

Wacha, Dinsha E., *Rise and growth of Bombay Municipal Government*, G. A. Natesan & Co., Madras, 1913.

Interviewees

(in September–November 1992)

Mr R. C. Ankleshwaria, Ms Mrinal Gore, Mr Ramesh Joshi, Mr J. Kanga, Ms Indumati Patel, Dr Shanti Patel, Mr S. M. Y. Sastry, Mr S. S. Tinaikar, Mr Sadanand Varde

Newspapers

Magazines

The Daily

Bombay

The Free Press Journal

Business India

The Evening News

Frontline

The Independent

Island

The Indian Express (IE)

Onlooker

The Indian Post (IP)

Janmabhoomi (Gujarati) (JB)

Midday

The Sunday Observer (Sun. Obs.)

The Times of India (TOI)

Acknowledgement

I thank Mr R. C. Ankleshwaria, Dr S. Gadkari, Ms Mrinal Gore, Mr P. A. Jani, Mr. Ramesh Joshi, Mr J. Kanga, Dr Y. D. Phadke, Ms Indumati Patel, Dr Shanti Patel, Dr Sujata Patel, Mr S. M. Y. Sastry, Mr S. S. Tinaikar and Mr Sadanand Varde for sharing their views/giving comments.

13

Chronicle of a Riot Foretold

KALPANA SHARMA*

On the morning of 9 January 1993, when the skyline over Bombay had darkened to near monsoon conditions as hundreds of fires across the city spewed black smoke into the atmosphere, one saw a graphic metaphor symbolizing one of the darkest periods in the city's contemporary history. The embers that lit those fires began glowing a long time ago; perhaps they were not visible to those who preferred to ignore their reality.

The genesis of the two sets of communal riots—in December 1992 and January 1993—that tore the metropolis asunder, could be traced to a series of developments— social, political and economic—going back at least three decades. With the benefit of hindsight, one can see today that these historical and sociological factors made the city ripe for a communal riot. But when the trouble first flared up, on the night of 6 December 1992, within hours of the demolition of the Babri Masjid in Ayodhya by hundreds of 'kar sewaks', the city authorities, including the police, were unprepared.

The strong reaction of Muslims in the city to the demolition of the Babri Masjid came as a surprise to some who had assumed that the Babri Masjid–Ayodhya controversy did not touch the lives of people in the city and was a remote 'north Indian phenomenon'. This was a gross

* In writing this article, the author has relied on personal experience in covering the riots for her newspaper, *The Hindu*, and on reports in other newspapers, particularly *The Times of India*, Bombay and *Indian Express*, Bombay. She has also referred to *The People's Verdict*, The Indian People's Human Rights Commission, August 1993, and *When Bombay Burned*, edited by Dileep Padgaonkar, (UBS Publishers Distributors Ltd, Delhi 1993).

misjudgement of the extent to which identities had become linked with community and religion. The communalization of politics had been taking place in Bombay through the 1980s, and particularly after the emergence of the Shiv Sena as a force in electoral politics. To assume that none of this would have any impact on people's perceptions was, to say the least, extremely naive.

A Changing Identity

The riots were considered a watershed in Bombay's contemporary history because they symbolized, in some way, the demise of the city's 'cosmopolitanism'. This had been viewed as a positive quality, reflecting an environment of tolerance. The reality, however, was somewhat different. For although some parts of Bombay, basically the island city, remained cosmopolitan with a mix of populations, it had already become evident in the last two decades that the new suburbs that were developing in the north were far more segregated.

It is noteworthy that some of the worst instances of rioting took place in these newly developed parts of the city and not the old city. The island city still has either Muslim majority areas or Hindu majority areas with some of the better off areas like Colaba or Malabar Hill fairly mixed in terms of communities. However, in the northern suburbs even the modicum of tolerance that existed in these older localities, by virtue of communities living cheek by jowl, sometimes separated by just one street, did not exist.

The main growth areas of Bombay lay to its north, around the industrial belt stretching from Thane almost up to Panvel, the next large urban centre. Another area of growth lay along the western coastline spreading northwards, where builders were reclaiming swamps and turning them into residential developments. These areas were like the Wild West. The writ of the civic authorities did not extend so far. There was no planning. Many of the buildings had failed to receive a no-objection certificates from the building authorities. They had no water connections or sewerage. Yet, the acute shortage of housing in Bombay forced thousands of families to move into these semi-complete structures.

In these new suburbs, the majority of middle-class cooperative housing societies enlisted people from the same community, or at least the same religion, with perhaps only one or two exceptions. For instance, Muslims who had been living in the crowded central Bombay localities of Dongri, Pydhonie or Nagpada, invested their savings into housing in areas like Mumbra, a north-eastern suburb where Muslim builders offered special concessions to such families. Similarly, Hindu families from central Bombay congregated in Ghatkopar and Bhayandar.

Apart from middle-class housing, the northern suburbs also accommodated some of the largest slum colonies as vacant land was available for the growth of such settlements. The pressures of urban living were felt most acutely in these new slum colonies where displaced families, either from central Bombay or from other parts of the state or city, set up home. There was no time to build a community. Many of these slums were not 'regularized', that is the government did not acknowledge their existence and thus felt under no obligation to provide them basic amenities. Thus, the struggle for basic amenities like water, for instance, often led to violent fights and was much more intense than in older colonies where some minimal facilities had been provided.

While the older slums in the island city had evolved something of a character and also had a longer experience in dealing with government and local politics (many political leaders had their bases in these slums), in the new slum areas there was no cohesiveness in the population. The local 'dada' or thug established control by using bully tactics to get basic amenities for the community. Such people, despite their obvious links with crime, became the favoured candidates for political parties to woo. Thus, a more open link between criminality and politics was evident in these slums than elsewhere.

Such communities are ideal for conflict. It does not take long for suspicions to grow to the point of open warfare. Even structurally and spatially they seem ideally designed for such low-intensity warfare. The rows of low-rise, semi-detached structures are ideal for young men to climb atop their sloping roofs, use improvised shields and target their 'enemies' with the home-made petrol bomb so beloved of social conflicts the world over.

Another focus for communal tension was what are termed 'transit camps'. These are barrack-like structures erected by the Maharashtra Housing Board in different parts of Bombay to temporarily house displaced families from central Bombay or the older parts of the city. These families had to leave their homes because their buildings were under repair. But the temporary period of stay in these camps usually extends up to many years.

The transit camps in which they are housed are single-room tenements with common toilets but individual water taps. Families do not know their immediate neighbours although they continue to fraternize with people from their original neighbourhoods who have also been relocated. The camps are mixed, with Hindu and Muslim families living side by side. After the riots, many people could not understand how people could not identify the family living in the very next room which had been vandalized even though both families had probably lived next door to each other for over a decade. The reasons were precisely this: they were all waiting to move back to their original localities and found no reason to invest in new friendships with accidental neighbours.

The growth in Bombay's slum population, a direct consequence of irrational and skewed land policies that benefit only the very rich, has also resulted in another schism—between people living in high-rise buildings and those in temporary shelters. It is most acute in areas where there are pavement dwellings. If the people living on the streets happen to be from a different community than those living in the buildings, then the feelings of hostility are exacerbated.

A Changing Economy

While the changing topography of Bombay imperceptibly altered the city's profile, the mutations in its economic map also had a lasting impact. Bombay was once known as the Manchester of the East with the chimney-stacks of scores of textile mills dominating its skyline. In the 1970s this began to change. The growing 'sickness' of the textile industry in the city, consequent to the unwillingness of millowners to invest in modernization, marked an important change in the economic profile of the city. Gradually, the organized sector began to disinvest and move production to the informal and unorganized sector. The textile mills, for instance, moved production out to the power looms of Bhiwandi and Surat. Even engineering units farmed out production to smaller units.

The reduction in the size of the manufacturing sector located in the city also affected the power of the trade unions in the city. The most powerful trade union for years had been that of the textile workers. The famous textile strike of 1982 finally rang the death knell for unionism in the city. The 18-month-long strike was broken when millowners refused to bend and preferred to close down their units. In the meantime, thousands of workers were reduced to penury. Many of them were forced to return to their villages as the city had few options left for them. The strike marked an important turning point.

Through the 1980s and early 1990s, most of the new investment went to the service sector. Manufacturing within the city limits was reduced to a minimum. Industry moved out to the new areas to the north and east of Bombay. These changes and deteriorating living conditions for the majority of Bombay's population—with roughly half the people living in slums—converted a once stable and efficient metropolis into a powder-keg ready to explode into sectarian violence.

A Changing Politics

Central to the changes affecting Bombay was the evolving politics of Maharashtra. The basic nature and politics of Bombay began to change once its political links with Gujarat were severed in 1960 and the city now danced to the tune of only one master, the newly-created state of Maharashtra. Up to then, and into the early 1970s, trade unions had played an important role in the city's politics. While the Congress trade union, the Indian National Trade Union Congress, dominated in the textile sector, other large groups of workers, such as those belonging to the railways, the transport system, the conservancy staff, owed allegiance to non-Congress unions, in particular socialist- and communist-led unions.

A reflection of the growing strength of unions was evident in the 1967 elections, barely seven years after the formation of the state of Maharashtra, when two trade union leaders beat strong Congress candidates at the polls. While George Fernandes of the Samyukta Socialist Party defeated S. K. Patil, the powerful chief of the Bombay Pradesh Congress Committee (BPCC), earning him the sobriquet of 'George, the giant killer', S. A. Dange of the Communist Party of India defeated the industrialist, Harish Mahindra.

But the evident growth and strength of the unions was indirectly responsible for the rise of the Shiv Sena which was born in 1966. With the defeat of two strong Congress candidates a year after, the Sena appeared to be the logical weapon for the Congress to use to contain the growing strength of Left unions. The then chief minister of Maharashtra, Vasantrao Naik, deliberately encouraged this newly formed political grouping—despite its narrow concern with Maharashtra for Maharashtrians—to break the sranglehold of the Left unions on the working class. Under the state's benign protection, Bal Thackeray's fledgling political group grew in strength.

However, its impact on the city's politics was not felt till much later. Anti-Congress feeling continued to grow after the 1967 elections and culminated in the 1977 elections, when the Congress Party lost all the six parliamentary seats in Bombay in the anti-Emergency wave that swept through the country. It saw no reversal of its fortunes even in the 1980 elections. However, it made a limited come-back in 1984, in the wake of Indira Gandhi's assassination.

The declining fortunes of the Congress Party in Bombay were also linked to the loss of power felt by the BPCC, which had earlier dominated the party's politics in the state because of its historical role in the freedom struggle. The defeat of S. K. Patil marked the end of the domination of the big chieftains in the party. The split in the Congress Party in 1969 further eroded the hold of the BPCC in state politics and the initiative was siezed by politicians who had their power-base not in Bombay but in the sugar-rich hinterland of Western Maharashtra.

The Rise of the Shiv Sena

The chronology of events in Bombay clearly reveals the link between the decline of the hold of the Left, through trade unions, with the rise of the Shiv Sena. The disinvestment in the formal sector led to growing unemployment amongst young qualified youth. Coincidentally, the majority of these were Maharashtrians as other communities had a longer tradition of self-employment. This was the base on which the Shiv Sena built.

Its efforts paid off politically when, for the first time, it was able to wrest from the Congress control of the powerful Bombay Municipal Corporation in the 1985 civic elections. Its victory suggested not just its own growing strength but also the division amongst the other parties and the apathy of voters who had taken it for granted that civic elections would inevitably return the Congress Party to power. The combination of these factors allowed the Shiv Sena to dominate the city's civic life. During this period, 1985–90, the Sena consolidated and extended its hold on the city. It rapidly increased the number of its *shakhas* (branches) and enrolled scores of young people. By the time the riots broke out in Bombay, the membership of the Shiv Sena exceeded the strength of the Bombay police force of 300,000 men.

In this five-year period the Shiv Sena also successfully extended its power base from just Bombay to the rest of the state. In the 1989 parliamentary and state elections, it formed an alliance with the Bharatiya Janata Party (BJP) and they emerged, as a block, as the largest opposition grouping in the state even though the Congress remained in power.

Bombay's changing politics and economy also had one more fallout —the increasing criminalization of the city's life. Smuggling of gold, silver and electronic equipment had been a traditional, and almost accepted, occupation amongst some communities in Bombay. Prominent smugglers like Haji Mastan and Yusuf Patel were household names. In a newspaper interview in 1993 (*The Times of India*, 11 April, 1993, 'The Reluctant Don' by Rajdeep Sardesai), Haji Mastan was quoted as saying, 'In a country with a coastline as long as India's, smuggling will always flourish'. He explained that, in the 1980s, drugs entered the smuggling network. 'Unfortunately', he said, 'the profits to be had in the drug trade are enormous. For 10 paise you can earn Rs 100.'

It was this period that saw comparisons being drawn between Bombay and Chicago with shootouts between the police and criminal gangs or gangland shootings being reported frequently in the newspapers. Along with drugs, the smuggling of arms was a logical extension. By the mid-1980s, the power of these gangs was openly acknowledged, even by political parties who did not hesitate to nominate known criminals to political office. In the municipal elections in 1985 in which the Shiv Sena won power in the BMC, it fielded a known underworld character, Kim Bahadur Thapa, even though he was in prison. The man won from his prison cell. A year later, in the Assembly elections, the Congress fielded two men with underworld connections, Hitendra Thakur from Vasai-Virar and 'Pappu' Kalani from Ulhasnagar. Both men won. In the 1990 municipal elections, when the Shiv Sena finally lost its hold on the BMC, over 40 men with criminal records were fielded as candidates by all parties.

Crime and Politics

In 1991, the first concerted effort to break the stranglehold of the underworld was made by the newly installed Chief Minister of Maharashtra, Sudhakarrao Naik, who had taken over from Sharad Pawar, the most powerful politician in the state. Pawar had moved to Delhi as the Defence Minister. Naik first arrested Bhai Thakur, the brother of Hitendra Thakur, and a few months later he arrested the politician brother and Kalani under the Terrorists and Disruptive Activities Act (TADA). Naik, a Pawar appointee and a man without an independent political base, was not expected to take such decisive action, particularly decisions that could displease the political bosses.

Until then neither the Shiv Sena nor the criminal–political nexus had been tackled by any chief minister. Naik's predecessor, Pawar, was known to have a fairly ambivalent position on the issue. He had been accused by his opponents of having close contacts with some of these groups and also of having made a deal with the Shiv Sena in order to maintain a semblance of peace in the city. If indeed such a compact existed, it was broken by Naik. To add insult to injury, Naik reshuffled his cabinet in November 1992 and dropped 11 members, all known to be supporters of Sharad Pawar. This open break with his mentor is significant in the light of the events that followed. It was the first indication of a schism in the party which would eventually be Naik's undoing.

The riots broke out in December 1992, just a month after the cabinet reshuffle. Initially, Naik displayed the same decisiveness he had in earlier months in dealing with the criminal-politicians. But this time, far from winning the admiration of Bombay's citizens, he became the focus of censure from all sides as it became evident that the majority of those killed in the riots were Muslims shot in police firing. By the time the second round of riots began, political pressure had begun to mount on Naik. Accentuating that pressure was the presence of Pawar, who flew down from Delhi and set up temporary camp in the city. This directly undermined the Chief Minister's authority as Pawar came to be viewed as a parallel centre of power to whom all those opposing Naik could turn. Pawar and his supporters were clearly unhappy with Naik's independent stance. The deteriorating situation in the city presented them with an opportunity to play up Naik's weakness and project Pawar's strength in contrast. Concerned groups of citizens, puzzled at Naik's sudden lack of decisiveness, readily turned to Pawar for leadership. Thus, at a time when Naik needed support and reassurance, factional politics within the ruling party were in full play.

It is possible that Naik could already see the way the wind was blowing and had decided to throw up his hands and give up in the face of determined opposition from within his party. Without a strong grassroots support, he could not confront the power of people like Pawar. This could partially explain the marked variance in the actions of the state government in the two sets of riots. It is also noteworthy that while Pawar held that the demolition of the Babri Masjid triggered off the riots, in Naik's view the first phase was fomented in implementation of a deliberate strategy by the underworld to undermine his government. Whatever the actual provocation for the riots, the fact that they continued for as long as they did, and the extent of animosity between

Hindus and Muslims that was on open display, can be traced back to the political, economic and social changes that had gradually altered Bombay's identity.

On 6 December, 1992, when scores of Hindu militants swarmed atop the three-domed Babri mosque and, with pickaxes and other implements, reduced it to a heap of rubble, the news travelled across India within minutes, thanks to the electronic media. In the Muslim-majority areas of Bombay, particularly around Mohammed Ali Road in South Bombay, an area where you can buy anything from a safety pin to a refrigerator, the news came as a shock. The reaction was almost instantaneous. Hundreds of angry people, mostly young men, streamed on to the road to express their anger. The police, partly caught unawares and partly over-reacting, shot into the crowd. Later the same night, a police constable was stabbed to death in an adjoining area.

The First Phase

Thus, began the first episode of blood-letting which was to last almost a week. The clashes were confined to a few areas and in the main consisted of attacks by the police on demonstrators and retaliation by the Muslims on police *chowkies* (outposts). However, in some areas the violence did assume the nature of a communal riot. For instance, on 6 December, in the vast slum agglomeration of Dharavi, members of the Shiv Sena and the Bharatiya Janata Party (BJP) took out a 'victory' procession to 'celebrate' the demolition of the Babri Masjid earlier that day. The march provoked a reaction and in the ensuing confrontation, which lasted for two days, 33 people died.

When 7 December dawned, after a night of rioting, the word had spread of the clashes between Muslims and the police. The next morning there were attacks on police outposts and some temples around the Mohammed Ali Road area. With police firing at crowds in the narrow and crowded bylanes around this commercial area, there were bound to be many casualties. There were numerous instances of innocent people, who happened to be standing near an open window or just passing by, being shot. Within a few hours, 43 people had been killed and 94 injured. The pressure on the J. J. Hospital, one of the largest public hospitals in Bombay which is located in this area, began to mount as a growing stream of the injured were brought in.

By the evening, the army had to be called out and curfew was declared in the jurisdiction of eight police stations in central and south Bombay.

At the same time, trouble had flared up in some of the northern suburbs. In one, a thousand-strong Muslim mob attacked a police outpost. In another two policemen guarding a temple were killed. This in turn triggered off retaliatory attacks which left 58 dead over the next three days.

While 7 December was the day the Muslim League chose to call a *bandh*, a general strike, to protest against the demolition of the Babri Masjid, the next day, 8 December, it was the turn of the Left parties and the Congress to do the same. But this did not stop the clashes which had by now spread further north to the suburbs of Jogeshwari and Kurla. By that evening, the official death toll had risen to 94—unofficial figures put it at 150 and above—and curfew was imposed in five more localities.

The day that will be remembered as one of the worst in this first phase of the riots was 9 December, when the Shiv Sena and the BJP called a *bandh* to protest against the arrest of some of their leaders after the incidents at Ayodhya. This was a signal for their followers to go on the rampage. They attacked mosques and Muslim establishments. In one locality, the Shiv Sena put up a notice announcing an award of Rs 50,000 to anyone pointing out a Muslim home.

The most horrifying incident of that day took place in Asalfa village in the north-eastern suburb of Ghatkopar. Hindu militants indulged in indiscriminate arson. Timber-yards and scrap-yards, of which the owners were mostly Muslims, were set ablaze. An estimated 300 huts located in the vicinity also went up in flames as people gathered their belongings and ran for their lives. By this time, the official figure of the dead had risen to 136. Of these the majority were Muslim and 90 per cent had died in police firing.

On 10 December, a battle-weary city tried to return to work. The suburban trains carried thousands of commuters to their offices. But by mid-afternoon the business district was deserted as people scurried home. The city was rife with rumours that the chief of the Shiv Sena, Bal Thackeray, had been arrested. Despite attempts by the police to quell the rumour, no one was willing to take a chance after the events of the previous three days.

Bombay's citizens held their collective breath on Friday, 11 December. The Muslims wanted to hold their prayers as usual. This would necessitate assemblies of more than five people, which was prohibited under the law. The police decided to lift curfew for the hours required for the Friday prayers. The *namaaz* went off peacefully in most areas except Dharavi, where the Hindus objected to the special concession being made to the Muslims. A minor flareup led to one death and several injuries.

But 11 December was important for another reason. For, on that day, the Shiv Sena discovered a pretext for launching an important component of its campaign which was to provide the spark for the second round of rioting. On Saturday, the Shiv Sena leadership demanded a relaxation of curfew so that a *maha-arti* could be held at Gol Deval. This temple is located in the heart of the city, close to the Muslim-majority areas and bordering the Hindu-dominated localities which are the strongholds of the Shiv Sena and the BJP.

A *maha-arti* is not an everyday Hindu ritual and even when one is held, it does not take place on the street outside a temple. Yet the Shiv Sena decided to make an issue of the fact that the Muslims have to spill out on the street during prayers on Fridays because their mosques are too small to accommodate the entire congregation. Their leadership was quoted as saying that this would help 'recapture the streets for Hindus and end the policy of appeasement of the Muslim minority'. Although this *maha-arti* passed off without incident, it set the stage for events that followed.

On 13 December, day curfew was finally lifted and the worst period seemed to have ended. The next four days saw a gradual reduction in tension as people tried to pick up the threads of their lives. By 16 December, the final death toll had been pegged at 227. On the surface peace seemed to have returned to Bombay. There were no major incidents of rioting between 17 December and 4 January. Yet the city simmered. There were isolated cases of stabbing and arson. On 2 January trouble broke out in Dharavi again. Yet, compared to the incidents in the early part of December, this appeared relatively minor and was not accorded much attention.

What also passed almost unnoticed was the Shiv Sena's campaign of holding *maha-artis* at all the important temples across the city. The campaign was launched on 26 December and by 6 January, when the second phase rioting had begun, a total of 33 such functions had been held. These *maha-artis* galvanized the Hindus, not just the followers of the Shiv Sena, and made a statement of militancy that was not lost on the Muslim minority.

The Second Phase

In the early hours of 5 January, two *mathadi* workers, men employed in loading and unloading ships in the docks, were stabbed to death in Dongri, a Muslim-majority locality in south Bombay. It has remained unclear whether the attack was due to union or other rivalry or whether it was communal. But given the charged atmosphere in the city, it was presumed that it was communal as the men were Hindus in a Muslim-majority area. By the next day, when the news of the stabbings had filtered through and the *mathadi* workers had come out in strength to protest, all hell broke loose. In Dharavi, groups of Hindus, wielding swords and crowbars, attacked Muslim areas. Scores of homes, shops and factories were set on fire and godowns were looted.

By the next morning, the attacks were beginning to follow a pattern. Taxi-drivers were the next targets. Anyone suspected of being a Muslim was forced to step out and his taxi was set on fire. Often the taxi-driver was stabbed. In retaliation, Hindu taxi-drivers were attacked in some of the Muslim-dominated areas. But once again, the majority of those hit were Muslims.

The turning-point in this second phase came in the early hours of 8 January, when the home of a Hindu family in the Gandhi Chawl of the Jogeshwari East slum in north-eastern Bombay was set on fire. Five people, including the couple who had lived in the house for 30 years, died. They included Rajaram and Sulochana Bane, Kamlabai Batlu and her 16-year-old daughter Laxmi, and Meenakshi Narkar, a handicapped 20-year-old. Vandana Kondalkar died later while her two children, who were also with her, escaped.

The Bane family had been one of the oldest residents of this part of the slum. Bane was a worker in a paint factory and a supporter of the Shiv Sena. However, he was not known as an active party worker. The family had been advised to move out of the Muslim-majority area after the first communal troubles broke out in the area in 1973. They refused. Subsequently, in 1990–91 there was another communal flare-up which was more serious. Even then the Banes did not see any reason to move although by this time the communities had become polarized to the point where there was little communication.

The scene for the 8 January incident had been set two nights earlier. On 6 January the Shiv Sena held a massive *maha-arti* at a nearby temple. After it ended the participants went on the rampage, burning down a Muslim-owned bakery and setting alight several Muslim homes. The next night, after 9.30 p.m., once again a crowd returning from a *maha-arti* threw stones at Muslim houses. Thus the anger and helplessness of the Muslims had already built up to explosion point.

The news about the attack on the Bane household had spread to the entire city by the afternoon of that day even though the morning newspapers did not report the event as it had occurred in the early hours, after the editions had closed. The Shiv Sena used its effective bush telegraph, a system of blackboards placed at strategic locations on which messages and news are written, to spread the news. Even before the attackers could be identified, the Shiv Sena had branded them as Muslims attacking a helpless Hindu family.

This triggered the worst phase in the rioting, beginning on 9 January and ending on 12 January, a day after Thackeray wrote in his party's mouthpiece, *Saamna*, that the attacks could now stop since 'the fanatics have been taught a lesson'. Muslim homes, offices, factories and shops were targeted. Gangs of youth went around areas where Muslims were in a minority and systematically attacked all such establishments. They would pull out everything from these shops, loot what they wanted and set the rest on fire in the middle of the street. Thereafter the shop or flat would also be ransacked, even the electrical fittings would be wrenched out and the place would be set on fire. One of the most heart-rending examples of such an attack was a building in the Muslim-dominated locality of Dongri, Dargah Chawl, occupied only by lower middle class Muslims. Every single room in that building was ransacked and destroyed.

The events of the previous two days had forced an inert state government to call in the state reserve police and the army. On 8 January a fire bomb had been hurled at the Police Commissioner, S. K. Bapat, narrowly missing him. Also on that day, Sharad Pawar, who was then the Union Defence Minister, flew down form Delhi to assess the state of affairs. As noted earlier, his arrival seemed to aggravate the paralysis afflicting the state government. The incumbent Chief Minister, Sudhakarrao Naik, was under attack not just from people in the city who thought his leadership ineffectual but also from people within his party. However, while the two men played out their political games, the city was literally up in flames.

On 9 January there were hundreds of incidents of arson. On the next day, the huge timber market on Reay Road near the docks was set on fire. As mobs went around with weapons and fire bombs, the police stood by and did nothing. And although the army made its presence felt by patrolling the streets, it had been ordered not to intervene directly without the express permission of the civilian authority. As a result, the city was literally handed over to marauding mobs while a 300,000-strong police force backed by additional paramilitary and army cadres could do nothing to bring this to a halt.

Although 12 January marked the end of the systematic attacks on and destruction of Muslim establishments and homes in many parts of the city, violence continued on a smaller scale for another three or four days. One of the worst incidents occurred in Pratiksha Nagar on Antop Hill, a barrack-like transit camp built by the Maharashtra Housing Board (MHB) for people whose buildings in the old part of the city were under repair. In a systematic orgy, gangs of youth went to each Muslim home, looting and burning everything belonging to the family. The houses and already been identified and marked by people pretending to be employees of the MHB.

The attacks began during the day, when most of the men were away at work. The women and children ran out of their homes, terrified, and waited outside the local police station begging for help. Even as they huddled together for two days and nights, no one came forward to help, or even offer them water or food. Help finally came two days later, in the form of an army convoy. But even as these traumatized women and their families were being evacuated, they were showered with soda water bottles thrown at them by Hindus living in the high-rise buildings that lined the narrow road leading out of the area. They were finally reunited with their men at the Musafirkhana, a hostel in south Bombay built by the Haj Committee for people going to Mecca for the annual pilgrimage. This was one of several relief camps that had come up overnight to accommodate thousands of displaced Muslim families.

Just when normalcy appeared to be returning—the city had survived a tense Republic Day on 26 January, when a threatened boycott of flag hoisting ceremonies did not take place—and the government responded to growing demands for a judicial inquiry by appointing Justice B. N. Srikrishna of the Bombay High Court to head a one-man commission of inquiry, the slum colony of Behrampada exploded in violence.

Behrampada is typical of many slums in Bombay. It grew incrementally as families occupied vacant land along a railway track. Although the land belongs to the railways, nothing was done to clear it until it was too late. Today, it is dense, crowded shanty town, dominated by Muslims, where people live in small, rickety, temporary shelters, mostly built with wood. A filthy sewer, which has never been cleaned, separates Behrampada from a middle-class locality of buildings constructed by the Maharashtra Housing Board. The majority of the families living in these buildings are Hindus.

For years the middle-class Hindus and the slum-dwellers of Behrampada have lived in an uneasy peace. Many women from Behrampada find work as domestics in the middle class homes across the road. But the tolerance on both sides was wafer thin even at the best of times. On 1 February, a row of huts closest to the Housing Board colony were set on fire. The people in these huts insisted that they actually saw people on the roofs of the buildings across the street from them hurling fire bombs into their slum. On the other side, the families in those buildings showed bullet holes in their windows and claimed that the trouble began when shots were fired from Behrampada. The incidents, however, laid the lines for a virtually irreconcilable division between the two communities.

The Behrampada explosion marked the end of the second phase, with only minor incidents occurring after that. But the price paid for this second phase was far heavier than the first. While the final toll in December was 227 deaths, in January it was more than double that number with 557 deaths. According to newspaper reports, 60–67 per cent of the people affected by the riots were Muslims who make up 15 per cent of Bombay's population.

The Impact

Apart from the major dislocation which marked the second phase of the riots, with large numbers of Muslims and Hindus moving out of their localities and seeking temporary shelter in schools, colleges, temples, mosques and even railway stations, the city also saw a massive exodus of its migrant population. And estimated 150,000 people left Bombay between January 10–15. The majority were men from north India taking their wives and children back to their villages which they thought would be safer.

In the first round of riots the trouble was restricted to some predict-able trouble spots, such as central and south Bombay where there is either an equally mixed population or a Muslim majority, or some of the slums which have witnessed communal violence earlier. Large parts of the city remained unaffected, specially the more wealthy western parts. In the second round, however, no one was spared. Muslims living even in the wealthier areas were targeted. Mobs would come by and ask whether any Muslims lived in the building and demand that their flats be identified. Terrified residents of buildings pulled down their name boards, set up special security and locked the gates leading into their building compounds. However, the very fact that all classes were touched by the second phase of riots, which brought bustling, business-like Bombay to a complete standstill, galvanized the elite of the city, who would normally never have stirred themselves, to form a citizens group. They undertook not just relief but also set up hot lines so that people facing problems could call and get the police or the army to intervene.

Role of the Shiv Sena

There were several aspects of the second phase of riots that need to be noted. While the first phase is largely seen as a reaction of the Muslims to the demolition of the Babri Masjid and the response by the State, the second phase was a more deliberate and planned affair. At the centre of that planning was undoubtedly the Shiv Sena. This has been established not just by what the party mouthpiece, *Saamna*, wrote in its daily editions but by evidence gathered through newspaper reports and non-governmental inquiries.

The second phase of rioting stood out not just for the planned manner in which Muslim homes and establishments were attacked but the participation and support of the Hindu middle class which, thus far, had distanced itself from some of the rougher tactics of the Shiv Sena. How did the Shiv Sena succeed in getting the support of this class? One strategy which paid dividends was the holding of *maha-artis*. This was a clever instrument to enlist the support of middle-class Hindus who would otherwise not have expressed their jaundiced view of the minority through any particular action. Using religion to bring such people out on the streets heightened their sense of religious identity. For the Hindu militants, these occasions fired them with such fervour that groups of them would follow the *artis* by launching attacks on Muslim neighbourhoods. A number of the attacks on such neighbourhoods in the January riots were traced back to *maha-artis*.

Although there were demands that the *maha-artis* be banned, this was a step an already beleaguered state government did not dare take. The Hindu majority could not be displeased even if the lives of lakhs of Muslims were in danger. Both the BJP and the Shiv Sena knew full well that the Congress Party, which was in power in the state and at the Centre, could not afford to hand them such an issue on a platter to be exploited at the next election. Thus, the state government looked the other way while the Shiv Sena and the BJP violated prohibitory orders by holding dozens of *maha-artis*.

At the same time, the Shiv Sena effectively exploited latent fears in the Hindu majority by spreading rumours about Muslim retaliation.

There was talk of shiploads of armaments landing along the coastline, of truckloads of attackers preparing to launch an all-out attack on all Hindu majority buildings. As a result many such areas set up vigilante squads of young men who remained awake all night waiting for attacks that never took place.

The irrational response of the middle-class Hindus revealed the extent to which the communalization of the polity had taken place. Deep-rooted prejudices and suspicions about Muslims were now openly discussed and used to justify such mindless behaviour. The fact that the Muslims were a small minority, that the majority of them lived in areas where they dominated, and that the small groups living elsewhere were not in a position to mount attacks on Hindu majority localities did nothing to dispel this belief.

A critical role was played in fanning the communal embers by the newspapers run by the Shiv Sena, the Marathi daily *Saamna* and the afternoon Hindi tabloid *Dopahar ka Saamna*. Day after day, both papers poured out open vitriol against the Muslims. Every Hindu death was announced in banner headlines. 'Muslim' and 'anti-national' were used synonymously. Editorials written in the early part of December 1993 stated, for instance, that 'all masjids have become storehouses of unauthorized arms' (8 December) or, 'streams of treason and poison have been flowing through the mohallas of this country . . . inhabited by fanatical Muslims . . . loyal to Pakistan . . . 25 crore Muslims loyal to Pakistan (constitute) one of Pakistan's seven atom bombs' (9 December). On 9 January, at the height of the second phase of rioting, the paper went even further in its provocativeness when it wrote, 'Muslims of Bhendi Bazar, Null Bazar, Dongri and Pydhonie, the areas we call Mini Pakistan that are determined to uproot Hindustan, took out their weapons. They must be shot on the spot.' Rumours about imminent attacks by Muslims were repeatedly printed in these newspapers as if they were the truth. The Maharashtrian middle class, including members of the police force, who formed the bulk of the readership of these newspapers (of an estimated 100,000), were bound to be influenced by this daily bombardment.

The Role of the Police

The second phase of the riots also exposed the extent to which the police force of the city, once considered one of the best in the country, had become communalized. According to the report of the two retired

Bombay High Court judges, Justice H. M. Daud and Justice S. Suresh, who held an inquiry into the riots on behalf of the Indian People's Human Rights Commission, 'These riots have revealed that a large number of police personnel identify themselves with the majority community, as opposed to the minority one. We have evidence to show that in certain police station, the police had insisted that the victims say "Jai Shree Ram" if they were expected to be shown any consideration, be it as simple as asking for and being given a glass of water.' Furthermore, intercepted radio messages revealed that policemen were using the foulest of language to describe the Muslims and deliberately delaying or stopping relief from reaching their areas.

The report of this inquiry, *The People's Verdict*, identifies over 80 policemen from 22 police stations who were named by victims in signed affidavits of having a communal bias. From these reports it appeared that policemen identified themselves with the Hindu youth who went on the rampage. Some eyewitness accounts held that, apart from standing by and allowing the looting to continue, on some occasions the policemen had also joined in. It was also suggested that the open sympathy shown by the police towards the militant Hindus was partly a reaction to the events during the first round of rioting, when they were the targets of the ire of Muslim youth.

Postscript

The two phases of riots cannot be examined apart from the serial bombings that shook Bombay on Friday, 12 March 1993. Within the space of a couple of hours, ten powerful explosions, shook different parts of the island city. The powerful explosive, RDX, had been loaded on a variety of vehicles which were parked at strategic points in the city, the RDX being sophisticatedly primed to blow up at an hour of peak activity. The targets included the Bombay Stock Exchange, located in the heart of the crowded business district, and the Air India building in what is known as the city's mini-Manhattan, Nariman Point.

As a result, an estimated 317 people were killed and for a moment it appeared as if the city would once again be thrown into chaos. The difference this time was that the strong man of Maharashtra, Sharad Pawar, had taken over the reins of power as Chief Minister. This was the first real test of his ability to manage the city better than his predecessor. In less than 24 hours, Pawar had the city back on its feet.

The reverberations from the bomb explosions, however, took a long time to die out. They left in their wake considerable resentment and deepened the division between Hindus and Muslims. While the alleged culprits of the blasts, the majority of them Muslims, were quickly rounded up and charged, those who had been seen instigating the riots, including prominent leaders of the Shiv Sena, remained free. Although the bomb blasts were seen as cathartic, as bringing the blood-letting that had gripped the city full circle, they did not solve anything. The divisions between Hindus and Muslims and between the Muslims and the police became more entrenched. The distrust did not disappear. Communities continued their business in the city of gold, but with much greater wariness than ever in the past.

The events of December 1992 and January and March 1993 left behind a permanently altered city and exposed its fragility. In the past, a shared history, the nature of the economy of the city from which many benefited, directly or indirectly, contributed to its stability. The riots revealed how the overt and covert changes in the city's economy and political life that had been taking place eventually contributed to the collapse that was witnessed in those weeks. On the surface, life appeared to return to normal shortly after the serial bombings. Yet, it became increasingly evident that Bombay has become a deeply divided city, not just between Hindus and Muslims, but also between those who are gaining from the changed economic environment in the city and those who are being left out. With the latter outnumbering the former, it could become the arena for more conflicts in the future.

Contributors to this Volume

Swapna BANERJEE GUHA, Social Geographer, Bombay
Nigel CROOK, Economist, Demographer, London
P. K. DAS, Architect, Housing Activist, Bombay
Mariam DOSSAL, Historian, Bombay
Nigel HARRIS, Development Economist, London
Gérard HEUZÉ, Labour Sociologist, Paris
Jayant LELE, Political Sociologist, Kingston, Canada
Claude MARKOVITS, Historian, Paris
Pratima PANWALKAR, Urbanist, Bombay
Sujata PATEL, Historical Sociologist, Bombay
Sandeep PENDSE, Writer, Political Activist, Bombay
Radhika RAMASUBBAN, Sociologist of Health, Bombay
Kalpana SHARMA, Journalist, Bombay
Usha THAKKAR, Political Scientist, Bombay
Hubert VAN WERSCH, Social Scientist, Amsterdam

Other Participants in the Workshop

Amiya Kumar BAGCHI, Political Economist, Calcutta
Vidyut BHAGWAT, Literary and Feminist Scholar, Writer, Pune
Raj CHANDAVARKAR, Historian, Cambridge, U.K.
Yashwant CHAUHAN, Trade Unionist, Bombay
Suma CHITNIS, Sociologist, Educator, Bombay
Suresh DALAL, Poet, Literary Scholar, Bombay
A. R. DESAI (1916–1994), Sociologist, Political Activist, Bombay
Neera DESAI, Sociologist, Feminist Scholar, Bombay
G. P. DESHPANDE, Playwright, Scholar, New Delhi
Lalit DESHPANDE, Economist, Bombay
Sudha DESHPANDE, Economist, Bombay
Namdeo DHASAL, Poet, Dalit Activist, Bombay
Norma EVENSON, Historian of Architecture, Washington, D. C.
Amrit GANGAR, Film Critic, Bombay
Shanta GOKHALE, Writer, Critic, Translator, Bombay
Mrinal GORE, Political Activist, Bombay
Sumit GUHA, Historian, New Delhi
Gopal GURU, Political Scientist, Pune
Adil JUSSAWALA, Poet, Journalist, Bombay
Amar JASANI, Public Health Activist, Bombay
Jamshed KANGA, Administrator, Bombay
Amit KHANNA, Television Producer, Bombay
Anthony KING, Scholar : Urban Studies, Binghamton, U.S.A.
Meera KOSAMBI, Urban Sociologist, Women Studies Scholar, Bombay
Shirin KUDCHEDKAR, Literary Scholar, Bombay
Krishna RAJ, Editor, Bombay
Maithreyi KRISHNARAJ, Economist, Feminist Scholar, Bombay
Françoise MALLISON, Scholar: Culture and Religion, Paris

Jim MASSELOS, Historian, Sydney, Australia
Rahul MEHROTRA, Architect, Bombay
Saeed MIRZA, Film Director, Bombay
Vivek MONTEIRO, Trade Unionist, Bombay
J. V. NAIK, Historian, Bombay
Nalini PANDIT, Economist, Political Activist, Bombay
Mitra PARIKH, Literary Scholar, Bombay
Gieve PATEL, Poet, Painter, Playwright, Bombay
Udayan PATEL, Psychoanalyst, Bombay
Anand PATWARDHAN, Documentary Filmmaker, Bombay
Y. D. PHADKE, Political Scientist, Bombay
Narendra PANJWANI, Journalist, Bombay
Ashish RAJADHYAKSHA, Film Scholar, Bombay
R. Raj RAO, Poet, Literary Scholar, Pune
Roshan SHAHANI, Literary Scholar, Bombay
Baburao SAMANT, Housing Activist, Bombay
Rajdeep SARDESAI, Journalist, New Delhi
Kunjulata SHAH, Historian, Bombay
Sonal SHUKLA, Journalist, Feminist and Literary Scholar, Bombay
V. SUBBRAMANIAM, Administrator, Bombay
Narayan SURVE, Poet, Political Activist, Bombay
Alice THORNER, Social historian, Paris
Jyoti TRIVEDI, Educator, Bombay
Raja VORA, Political Scientist, Pune
Rashid WADIA, Research Scholar, Bombay

Index